Idealism, Relativism, and Realism

Idealism, Relativism, and Realism

New Essays on Objectivity Beyond the Analytic-Continental Divide

Edited by Dominik Finkelde and Paul M. Livingston

DE GRUYTER

Printed with the generous support of the Fritz Thyssen Foundation.

ISBN 978-3-11-066720-2
e-ISBN (PDF) 978-3-11-067034-9
e-ISBN (EPUB) 978-3-11-066691-5

Library of Congress Control Number: 2020934489

Bibliografische Information der Deutschen Nationalbibliothek
The Deutsche Nationalbibliothek lists this publication in the Deutsche Nationalbibliografie; detailed bibliographic data are available on the Internet at http://dnb.dnb.de

© 2021 Walter de Gruyter GmbH, Berlin/Boston
This volume is text- and page-identical with the hardback published in 2020.
Cover: Peter Angermann: „Sonntagsphysik", Öl auf Leinwand 2005, © P. Angermann
Printing and binding: CPI books GmbH, Leck

www.degruyter.com

Table of Contents

Dominik Finkelde and Paul Livingston
Introduction —— 1

Part 1 Idealism

Sebastian Rödl
Metaphysics, Thinking, and Being —— 17

G. Anthony Bruno
Jacobi's Dare: McDowell, Meillassoux, and Consistent Idealism —— 35

Andrea Kern
How Not to Be a Naïve Realist: On Knowledge and Perception —— 57

Anton Friedrich Koch
Is Hermeneutic Realism a Dialectical Materialism?
    Thinking With and Beyond Heidegger and Adorno —— 81

Iain Hamilton Grant
Nature After Nature, or Naturephilosophical Futurism —— 97

Part 2 Relativism

Johannes Hübner
Metaontological Deflationism and Ontological Realism
    Eli Hirsch's Doctrine of Quantifier Variance —— 115

Martin Kusch
Stances, Voluntarism, Relativism —— 131

Dominik Finkelde
Subjectivity as a Feature of Reality:
    On Diffraction Laws of Consciousness and Reality Within Justified True
    Belief —— 155

Ray Brassier
Concrete-in-Thought, Concrete-in-Act:
   Marx, Materialism, and the Exchange Abstraction —— 175

Deborah Goldgaber
Matter and Indifference: Realism and Anti-realism in Feminist Accounts of the Body —— 193

Part 3 **Realism**

Markus Gabriel
Saying What is Not —— 217

Paul Livingston
Sense, Realism, and Ontological Difference —— 233

Graham Harman
Realism without Hobbes and Schmitt: Assessing the Latourian Option —— 257

Paul Redding
The Objectivity of the *Actual*: Hegelianism as a Metaphysics of Modal Actualism —— 275

Dieter Sturma
Nomological Realism —— 293

Jocelyn Benoist
Realism Without Entities —— 311

Notes on the contributors —— 325

Index of Names —— 329

Index of Subjects —— 333

Dominik Finkelde and Paul Livingston
Introduction

Ontology is the investigation into the most general aspects of reality, either by asking questions about "what there is" or by focusing on the basic categories of being and their relations. In recent decades, and into the present, these undertakings have been marked by the methodological and thematic divide between "analytic" and "continental" philosophy. However, the grounds for the divide have often been questioned in recent years, and one of the issues that has been much discussed is that of the role of empirical and formal science in serving as the ultimate measure of truth and reality. Even for those who challenge the claim that specific philosophical categories of ontology can easily be replaced with natural-scientific ones, it is significant that this does not imply that the guiding notions of truth and objectivity should similarly be rejected. The sixteen new contributions presented here combine theoretical investigation with reflection on the history of philosophy, representing diverse recent developments in the fields of contemporary ontology and epistemology, including those that have recently appeared under the headings of "New Realism," "New Materialism," and "Speculative Realism." Methodologically, two common goals that emerge are those of rethinking the Kantian opposition between the noumenal and the phenomenal, along with the metaphysical basis of the transcendental idealism it implies, and reconsidering the familiar philosophical battle-lines that divide positions of idealism and relativism on the one hand from varieties of realism on the other.

The refinement and articulation of the concept of *objectivity* poses both conceptual and methodological problems for contemporary philosophy. According to one influential conception, what is objective is supposed to be true outside the biases, interpretations, and opinions of a thinking subject. If this is correct, it is reasonable to think that objective claims and beliefs should instead have truth conditions that can be met by the way the world is. However, an important question that remains open is that of how such truth-conditions should themselves be defined. Is objectivity the relational and process-philosophical co-dependence of subject and object in time, as contemporary adaptations and developments of idealist philosophy sometimes hold? Is the structure of reality itself ontologically a book-like text that can be read by the human mind? Is objectivity a social property (like money or marriage) and, as such, primarily the possession of groups, rather than a property of mind-independent facts? Or is it, perhaps, dependent on economic conditions, rooted in an ideological 'world-picture'?

This volume focuses on these and related questions with the aim of clarifying the concept of objectivity as it functions within contemporary ontological and metaphysical debates.

1 Subject matter

Recent philosophical inquiries into ontology have been marked, and in some cases vitiated, by the widespread and pervasive divide between the analytic and continental traditions, and by the associated challenges and problems that have been raised by partisans of each of them for those of the other. For example, representatives of the so-called "continental" tradition have questioned the sovereign explanatory power of the methods of formalism, abstract argumentation and appeals to natural-scientific results characteristic of many currents of the "analytic" tradition, some of which have furthermore come under attack even by analytic philosophers themselves (P. Unger 2014). At the same time, contemporary philosophers have recognized classical phenomenology as having somewhat prejudicially enforced the strict distinction between philosophical and natural-scientific research and results by insisting upon the universal "bracketing" of the latter in the attitude of phenomenological reflection. But the same holds true in the opposite direction. For example, analytic philosophers have decried the apparent vagueness and lack of clarity of much "continental" writing and have bemoaned what they see as a relative lack of well-articulated argumentation for definite conclusions.

However, in recent years, authors working in texts and styles that are recognizably continuous with the "continental" traditions of phenomenology, German idealism, and structuralism have attempted decisive contributions to the traditionally "analytic" question of realism. Authors such as P. Boghossian (2006), R. Brassier (2007a; 2007b), M. Ferraris (2014), M. Gabriel (2014; 2016a; 2016b), I. H. Grant (2005; 2008), G. Harman (2010; 2011) and A. F. Koch (2014; 2015), among others, have all taken a stand on the topic – often in the name of a "New Realism" or "Speculative Realism". These authors frequently reject, on the one hand, the purely coherence-theoretical picture of truth often associated with certain currents of 20th century poststructuralist thought, but also, on the other, the reductionist picture of truth, via scientific positivism, which sees modern physics as contributing the ultimate criteria to define "what there is" (Quine). At the same time, positions such as those that have been called "new materialism" and "new vitalism" have opened up new ways of thinking of objectivity, realism, and truth, beyond coherence theory and scientific realism, in relation to feminist theory.[1] The innovation of contemporary discussions on idealism, realism, and relativism which this volume exhibits can be seen in the rejection of these two prevalent ideas about truth and reality along with the new focus on the concept of objectivity that this brings with it.

Many of the authors just mentioned oppose the idea that reality comes equipped from the outset with references to an "outside world" in which nature simply conforms to the framework developed by natural science as a homologous space of facts and states of affairs. However, they do not agree, either, that the critique of traditional realism means that the concepts of truth and objectivity must be dropped entirely or used only hermeneutically. For these authors, the assumption that science is not systematically the ultimate measure of truth does not mean that we should abandon the notions of truth or objectivity altogether. Here, the truth of propositions is not to be understood simply through the interpretation of the unitary existential quantifier, but is rather most typically understood in accordance with an ontological pluralism which opens up various truth-structures with respect to their corresponding logical forms.

The present volume reflects on these contemporary debates in their various differentiations and presents new answers and arguments with a special focus on what the indispensable concept of objectivity now stands for, in relation to and distinction from positions of idealism, relativism, and realism. The majority of the articles in the volume were presented in 2017 (Dec. 8th – 9th) at the international conference *Continental Realism: Ontology, Metaphysics and Politics Beyond the Analytic-Continental Divide* at the Munich School of Philosophy in Germany.

2 Background and context

Despite numerous shifts in the debate between analytic and continental philosophy, including the development of partly pragmatic theories of meaning in the second half of the 20th century (presented by L. Wittgenstein, D. Davidson, R. Rorty, H. Putnam, et al.), the idea of a significant divide has been supported, especially in the context of the philosophy of mind, by the persistence of strongly naturalist and eliminativist varieties of materialism. For adherents of this position (including A. Rosenberg, G. Rey, the Churchlands, and J. Ladyman), things are not in themselves as they seem to us every day. Rather, physics and biology show that reality consists, on a fundamental level, precisely of entities that hu-

---

[1] See, e.g., the positions treated in Kolozova and Joy (2016) and Behar (2016).

mans do not encounter, perceptually or conceptually, in everyday life. Wilfrid Sellars referred famously to this world picture as "the scientific image" of humans, contrasting it with the "manifest image" of our ordinary experience and practice (Sellars 1963).

In contrast to this (admittedly highly simplified) picture of contemporary materialism, representatives of continental or speculative realism have attempted to recapture the methods and ideas of authors of the classical continental tradition (such as Hegel, Schelling, Husserl, and Heidegger, among others) to show how the realm of phenomena can be comprehended by means of different logical forms which pertain to these phenomena themselves. These contemporary representatives are concerned, in particular, with showing that the differences between forms of truth cannot be reductively grounded simply in either a scientific or a postmodern conception of its overall character. As a result, the study of "what there is" is to be sharply distinguished from an unrestrained relativism, but is also just as sharply to be protected from reduction to a homogenous space of scientific facts. With regard to the natural sciences, one can even say that the cosmos, as an object of research, is only a partial, even tiny 'province' within the field human experience. Concepts, perspectives, or "fields of sense" (M. Gabriel 2015) are media of actual facts in the presentation of their logical and phenomenological forms. The question of "what there is," therefore, must be disconnected from simple reflection on the existential quantifier as an exclusive instrument of analysis for the truth-value of propositions.

In the English-speaking world, new concepts of realism have recently been presented by the philosophers R. Brassier (2007a; 2007b), I. H. Grant (2005), G. Harman (2010) and P. Livingston (2017). In the German-speaking world the philosopher M. Gabriel (2014) initiated the current debate. He introduced, together with the Italian philosopher M. Ferraris (2014), the concept of "New Realism" into the philosophical discussion, opening up a dialogue that has received much international attention and praise, and has been shaped – directly and indirectly – by numerous philosophers, including, among others, J. Hübner (2016), A. Kern (2014), A. F. Koch (2015), S. Rödl (2015), and John Searle (2014). It was also picked up by several philosophical journals (for example, the *Philosophisches Jahrbuch* and *The Monist*). Surprisingly, the discussion has also found a broad reception in public media, especially in Germany. It was introduced to a wider audience in regard to questions related to the nature of knowledge, particularly in popular discussions on "alternative facts" and "fake news". There have also been numerous conferences (Bonn 2012, Amsterdam 2017, Düsseldorf 2017, Sofia 2017, Munich 2017) dedicated to the topic.

A decisive impulse was marked by the re-orientation of a continental realism in 2006 by the philosopher Q. Meillassoux in his work, *After Finitude* (2008).

With his neologism "correlationism," Meillassoux described the circular structure by which, he argues, philosophers since Kant's Copernican turn have related subject and object, language and world, or, more broadly, thinking and being. According to this conception as Meillassoux understands it, it is not possible for us to have unmediated access to being in itself; all that is possible is for us to access it through its relationship with our thinking or representing. According to Meillassoux, contemporary philosophy should instead be based on both pre-Kantian and post-Heideggerian thought, embracing in place of correlationism a radical understanding of contingency as a neglected ground-structure of reality that overcomes both the formal, Kantian 'limits' of human understanding and the existential limits of Dasein (Heidegger). Similar to Meillassoux, Gabriel's investigations are concerned with overcoming the Kantian division between "things in themselves" and "phenomena" (Gabriel 2016a). He defends the claim that, beyond or before the (correlationist) construction of phenomena via *a priori* structures of the human mind, meaningful phenomena exist and have sense prior to their constructivist mind-dependent 'accounts'. For this reason, one cannot speak of "the" world in the singular, but only of a multiplicity of co-existing fields of sense where phenomena exist in different logical and mutually excluding forms even – and this is the caveat – somehow *before* their phenomenological instantiation, so to speak. Similar to the argument of Tim Crane (2013), Gabriel strives to characterize fictions, dreams, and hallucinations as fields of sense, where objects within them are real, having their own logical form, with the effect that the question of their 'true' existence dissolves. Through this re-employment of Frege's concept of "sense" different objects with different logical forms (moral maxims, neutrinos, qualia) can exist side-by-side without contradictions because there is no overall "world" that prescribes the sense of a unitary existential quantifier.

Both of these attempts to renew realism, to which other authors such as T. Garcia and G. Harman have contributed theories oriented to the description of the structure of objects as such (Garcia 2014; Harman 2011), aim to overcome what can thus be seen as a problematic point in much post-Kantian thinking. This is also dominant in P. Livingston's recent book (2017). He brings authors such as Frege, Davidson, Dummett, and Wittgenstein into dialogue with Heidegger's understanding of truth as "unconcealment", arguing that the theoretical and analytic understanding of linguistic truth also requires a parallel understanding of the prior availability of objects in their being, thereby providing a basis for new logically and phenomenologically based accounts of the overall structure of truth in relation to time. This might be compared with G. Harman's (2010; 2011) Heidegger-influenced view, according to which objects, thoughts, and fictions, as well as scientific theses, are essentially characterized by structures of obtrusiveness or 'withdrawal'. D. Finkelde pursues a similar line of thought in his book *Excessive Subjectivity* (2017), but from another direction: not from an object-oriented perspective, but rather a subject-oriented one. For him, subjectivity is a feature of reality, and not just a hallmark of the conscious mind. It is a formal and distorting factor within any account of how things really are. R. Brassier, on the other hand, argues in his already-mentioned book *Nihil Unbound* (2007) that reflection on the history and probable future development of scientific insight into reality and ourselves requires the eventual removal and disempowerment of the "manifest image" in favor of a thoroughgoing realist account.

The investigations mentioned above have been extended in articles and commentaries, especially by English and German-speaking epistemologists. Familiar topics from various realism-antirealism debates reappear here intertwined with the above-mentioned topics. Likewise, 'classical' questions of epistemology are addressed, such as the existence of certain entities, concrete or abstract (numbers, social facts, hallucinations, fictitious entities), questions about the existence of certain properties (redness, free will, morality), and the true sources of knowledge (Kern 2017).

3 The articles

First Section. Idealism: The articles in the first section present various interpretations of objectivity that are intrinsically linked to the respective research fields of the philosophers assembled here. German Idealism is generally, but not exclusively, in the background of the arguments, and several authors also consider the issue of objectivity with reference to contemporary analytic philosophy and its adaptation of idealistic thought. The authors develop an understanding of objectivity with reference to "self-consciousness" (Rödl), with a focus on knowledge as a "fundamental capacity of the human mind" (Kern), with reference to "principles of a general logic" (Bruno), or with an anti-David Lewisian understanding of "actuality" in the tradition of Robert Stalnaker (Redding).

Sebastian Rödl critically analyzes in his article "Metaphysics, Thinking, and Being" Barry Stroud's book *Metaphysical Dissatisfaction*. With reference to Aristotle's *Metaphysics*, Rödl challenges Stroud's claim of an inherent dialectic of knowledge and dissatisfaction internal to the project of metaphysics as a systematic knowledge of being *qua* being. According to Rödl, Stroud takes metaphysics to be the endeavor of comparing the ways in which we think with *what is*, in order to establish whether we, as we think in these ways, can actually grasp *what is* as well. But this construal of metaphysics makes it appear that there are two things, independently described and subsequently compared: i) how we think, and ii) how *what is is*, as we are thinking it. According to Rödl, Stroud is right to hold that metaphysics (i.e. the science of *what is*, insofar as it is) investigates being and thinking. But metaphysics does not investigate a relationship between the two. Rather, metaphysics arises from thought, from the kind of understanding of its object that thought itself is.

G. Anthony Bruno is concerned, in his article "Jacobi's Dare: McDowell, Meillassoux, and Consistent Idealism," with the nature of idealism in Kant. Does Kant's conception of knowledge sacrifice objectivity, as both historical and contemporary philosophers across "continental" and "analytic," divides have thought, starting with Jacobi, and including P. Strawson, J. McDowell, and (today), Q. Meillassoux? Or does this conception, rather, aim precisely to *describe* the logical structures of objectivity and the modal status of these structures? On the former opinion, presented most recently by Meillassoux, Kant's rejection of objectivity imposes a demand on contemporary philosophy to reject Kant's project in order to grasp instead the "in-itself". As such, Meillassoux demands that we renounce the project of defining the limits of the human faculty of reason. The consequence of the reading defended by Bruno, though, is that this is simply impossible. For Bruno, a proper account of objectivity, which idealism serves rather than disputes, requires us instead to subordinate the principles of general logic to what Kant calls the principle of synthetic judgment.

Andrea Kern offers, in her article "How Not to be a Naïve Realist: On Knowledge and Perception," a response to a dilemma that can be found in the debate between John McDowell and Berry Stroud. It is rooted in the assumption that perception can be treated independently of the question whether it does or does not figure in the self-consciousness of the perceiver. Kern argues that the obstacle that hinders us in understanding the idea of an intrinsically self-conscious capacity for perception is based on the false premise that perception and judgment are two entirely distinguishable capacities. By contrast with this "two-capacity" view, Kern argues that the capacity for perception must itself be understood as an intrinsically self-conscious capacity. Only as such can the conception of judging equip its bearer with genuine perceptual knowledge of the world. Knowledge is, on this view, a fundamental capacity of the human mind, since every act of perception is, potentially, already an act of understanding. Knowledge is, then, not a representational act of intellectual insight but enters already at the pre-theoretical level of the mind's sense-perceptual uptake, through intuitions, of how things are.

Anton Friedrich Koch unfolds, in his text "Is Hermeneutic Realism a Dialectical Materialism? Thinking With and Beyond Heidegger and Adorno," his understanding of hermeneutic realism. This position is based centrally on the philosophies of Kant and Heidegger and is spelled out in distinction to Irad Kimhi's theory of negation (2018) and the thinking-being relationship. Koch analyzes the basic structures of predication, which he partly interprets against Kimhi's claim for the primacy of the predicative statement of negation. He then comments, with reference to Aristotle's notions of "aisthesis" and "noesis," on Heidegger's theory of "unconcealment" and presents his own conception of a "hermeneutic realism," grounded in this theory, which combines the idea of an essentially interpretive or hermeneutic engagement with the world with an underlying realism about the world as thus engaged. Following Adorno, Koch here argues that thinking literally 'works' itself out of the raw materiality of nature through engaging hermeneutically in its constitutive confrontation with this same nature. It is in this sense that his understanding of hermeneutics is not only close to Hegel and Marx but is, as he argues, truly inscribed, as well, in the tradition of dialectical materialism.

Iain Hamilton Grant, in "Nature after Nature, or Naturephilosophical Futurism," interprets Schelling's understanding of "Weltgesetz," or the Law of World. He shows how nature is, for Schelling, a non-exclusive and open-ended system of multiplicity. Viewed as such, the quest for an objective ontology is not a quest for the objective furniture of the world. Schelling, instead, favors a first philosophy as ontogeny, or an account of the origin of the world. "World" for Schelling is thus not synonymous either with "planet" or with "the entire universe". Rather, the term means, in an important sense, that there is no whole – not even a paradoxical one including itself. As such, an objective ontology is, for Schelling, an account of the world turned inside out and with its center dispersed.

Second Section. Relativism: The second thematic grouping of the volume is dedicated to the contemporary understanding of objectivity in the context of epistemic and relativistic interpretations of it. Here, knowledge is, *inter alia*, understood as a social status that is essentially guaranteed by groups rather than primarily by individuals or by facts as they are 'in themselves'. This, though, also entails that subjectivity as a surplus feature of reality can have an impact on how things really are as well as socio-economic conditions and gender-related debates, which focus on the relation of biological bodies and their social-symbolical roles.

Johannes Hübner, in "Metaontological Deflationism and Ontological Realism" discusses Eli Hirsch's ontological deflationism as it is presented in Hirsch's doctrine of quantifier variance. On this view, ontological disputes about what there is can primarily be understood in terms of distinctions between different users' interpretations of the sense of existential quantification. Hübner shows how quantifier variance gets entangled with self-contradictions and as such cannot be maintained as a form of ontological realism, as Hirsch maintains. In other words, Hirsch proves to be an epistemic relativist and his talk of realism is, accordingly, misleading.

Martin Kusch, a leading proponent of a social theory of knowledge in the tradition of Bloor and Collins, explores in his text "Stances, Voluntarism, Relativism," several concepts and ideas presented in recent years by Bas van Fraassen. At center-stage of the analysis are two aspects of van Fraassen's work: (1) the latter's talk of "stances" as an adequate description of philosophical and scientific positions, including (by contrast with mere "doctrines") bundles of values, emotions, policies and beliefs and (2) van Fraassen's understanding of "epistemic voluntarism." This theory aims to reject both the view that principles of rationality can determine which scientific paradigms must be adopted and the view that epistemology is similar to a descriptive-explanatory theory of cognition. Kusch further relates both concepts (that of "stance" and that of "epistemic voluntarism") to contemporary debates on epistemic relativism.

Dominik Finkelde focuses, in his article "Subjectivity as a Feature of Reality," on how, in any account of how things really are, subjectivity can be both a formal and a distorting factor. He refers especially to Hegel and Lacan's adaptation of Hegelian dialectics. Lacan speaks of a pre-theoretical experience of being in the world where human beings are literally called by reality to be social agents and at the same time fill in gaps of this reality with their fantasies. As such, fantasies play an epistemic role often neglected in both epistemological and ontological debates. But since the status of reality is never total and complete, antagonisms within reality cannot be contained. Ontology, as our inquiry into 'what there is,' affects 'what there is' in that subjectivity, troubled by antagonism, always goes beyond established forms of facts, theoretically and practically. Finkelde argues, especially with reference to Kant and Hegel, that subjectivity, with its imaginary intertwinement of what Lacan calls the symbolic order, is a feature of reality as virtuality and not just a hallmark of the conscious mind.

Ray Brassier, in his article "Concrete-in-Thought, Concrete-in-Reality," shows how Marx's critical theory of economics can be epistemologically interpreted when read in the light of the works of Wilfrid Sellars. Taking into account the suggestion that reality is a social status and that basic structures of reality are, according to Marx, essentially ideological in nature (especially from the epoch of a capitalist economy onwards), the analysis of economics is – compared with epistemology – not of a different 'kind' but, rather, differs with the latter only in 'degree'.

Deborah Goldgaber describes in her article "Matter and Indifference" an ongoing conflict in contemporary feminist theory, which focuses on the question of whether gender should be understood as a constructivist or essentialist characteristic of the human body. Does the biological body itself produce "gendered" bodies through its discursive activity, as Karen Barad, among others, suggests against Judith Butler (et al.), from the point of view of a materialist feminism; or are "gendered" bodies the forceful and painful result of normative cultural practices? In the first case, the difference between nature and culture collapses insofar as nature is attributed a degree of primacy in the formation of biological bodies. In the second case, the nature-culture difference collapses again insofar as biology dissolves into power discourses. Goldgaber decodes this debate, with reference to some key authors, and shows how the arguments revolve around a constitutive irreconcilability of the two views which, time and again, nevertheless links them co-dependently.

Third Section. Realism: The third part of the book focuses on the notion of objectivity in the context of contemporary and "new" realism, especially as presented and defended by authors such as Markus Gabriel, Graham Harman and Jocelyn Benoist.

Markus Gabriel argues, in his article "Saying What is Not," that a major weakness of contemporary accounts of existence and non-existence alike arises from the tendency to believe that the answers to questions of existence can put us in touch with a distinctive "catalogue" of reality. Applying instead his ontology of "fields of sense," he questions both the idea of existence as dependent upon this "catalogue" conception of reality and, equally, the Meinongian and Neo-Meinongian positions recently defended by Graham Priest and others, according to which there are objects that do not exist, including even contradictory ones. While the first leads to a "furniture ontology," the latter produces semantic randomness, in that there is no longer any regular way to answer questions of existence. Gabriel's ontological descriptivism, by contrast, guarantees that the resolution to the question of objectivity depends on nothing but a coherent domain (a field of sense) and its objects.

Paul Livingston, in his paper "Sense, Realism, and Ontological Difference," brings Dummett's formulation of "realism" into dialogue with Heidegger's understanding of truth as "unconcealment." He argues, with references to Frege and Wittgenstein, that the phenomenon of truth can be understood theoretically and analytically as requiring a pre-theoretical appearing and constitution of objects, in experiential, practical, or explicitly linguistic modalities. This approach provides a basis for new logically and phenomenologically based accounts of the structure of objectivity within linguistic truth in relation to the appearance and being of objects. Within the context of a development of Heidegger's idea of ontological difference, this further implies that truth and objectivity must have a logically paradoxical structure. Even if Heidegger does not often say so explicitly, this paradoxical structure of objectivity and truth is centrally involved, as Livingston argues, in his understanding of the "clearing" and the interpretation it allows of beings "as such and as a whole."

Graham Harman, in "Realism Without Hobbes and Schmitt," contrasts "realism" in the usual sense of referring to the existence of a reality outside the human mind with his own Object-Oriented Ontology, which broadens the meaning of the term to refer to the existence of a reality outside any relation, including inanimate causal relations. The idea here is that the real is a surplus that is never quite reflected in any actual state of the world. In political theory, "realism" generally refers to a "hardcore" theory of politics, represented prominently by Thomas Hobbes and the later Carl Schmitt, that tries to get rid of hypocritical high-minded ideals, instead looking at political power in the way it actually works. Again in contrast to this, Harman defends a different sense of political realism, consistent with Object-Oriented Ontology and represented by recent works of Bruno Latour, according to which our understanding of politics must acknowledge both the inherent fallibility of our understanding of the world and the relevance of non-human actors and agencies to political problems and actions.

Paul Redding focuses, in "The Objectivity of the *Actual*: Hegelianism as a Metaphysics of Modal Actualism," on the relation between notions of objectivity and modality, including centrally the distinction of possibility and actuality. He maintains that a sufficiently robust sense of objectivity can be obtained by focusing on the notion of actuality in a way that recognizes the reality of possible alternatives to the actual, but also treats these as in some sense "internal" to the actual. This contrasts, for example, with David Lewis's conception of possible worlds, which locates the actual within a broader conception of reality in which it is not essentially privileged. Robert Stalnaker counts, for Redding, as a major representative of this kind of alternative to Lewis. He argues that the roots of such an approach to metaphysics are to be found in the idealist tradition and, in particular, in Hegel.

Dieter Sturma, in his article "Nomological Realism," considers several debates within practical and theoretical philosophy wherein certain forms of naturalism apparently conflict with anti-naturalistic interpretations, especially within the field of applied ethics. Sturma shows how Wilfrid Sellars already presented and addressed this apparent conflict by juxtaposing the "manifest image" and the "scientific image" of the place of human beings in the world. Sturma argues, following Sellars, that a position of "nomological realism," which combines realism about normative standards with the rejection of reification of these standards as if external to practice, can show how to de-escalate these tensions.

Jocelyn Benoist argues in "Realism Without Entities" that the true realist is not the philosopher who endorses, in the name (for example) of a Russellian project of analysis, the task of displaying the furniture of the world in some kind of idealized "list of entities." Instead, Benoist holds that, within realist projects, full weight should be given to reality in the way it is actually talked or thought about in the context of our actual concerns and practical lives. The claim here is not that our talk or thought determines reality, but rather that this thought and talk nevertheless essentially leaves its imprint, in some way, on any coherent conception of what this reality is like. To address reality, therefore, is not just to list entities, but, rather, to consider and focus on actual uses that come to grips with reality in diverse ways and connections. To attempt to keep our "hands clean" by placing reality beyond use and practice while trying, at the same time, to make sense of it as that which our thinking and knowing is *about*, is to pursue an ultimately contradictory project.

Bibliography:

Behar, Katherine, ed. (2016): *Object-Oriented Feminism*. Minneapolis: University of Minnesota Press.
Boghossian, Paul (2006): *Fear of Knowledge. Against Relativism and Constructivism*. Oxford: Oxford University Press.
Brassier, Ray, Iain Hamilton Grant, Graham Harman, and Quentin Meillassoux (2007): "Speculative Realism." In: *Collapse III: Unknown Deleuze*. London: Urbanomic.
Brassier, Ray (2007a): *Nihil Unbound: Enlightenment and Extinction*. London: Palgrave Macmillan.
Brassier, Ray (2007b): "The Enigma of Realism." In: *Collapse II: Speculative Realism*. London: Urbanomic.
Crane, Tim (2013): *The Objects of Thought*. Oxford: Oxford University Press.
Ferraris, Mauricio (2014). *Manifest des neuen Realismus*. Frankfurt/Main: Klostermann.
Finkelde, Dominik (2017): *Excessive Subjectivity. Kant, Hegel, Lacan, and the Foundations of Ethics*. New York: Columbia University Press.
Gabriel, Markus (2014): *Sinn und Existenz. Eine realistische Ontologie*. Berlin: Suhrkamp.
Gabriel, Markus (2015): *Fields of Sense. A New Realist Ontology*. Edinburgh: Edinburgh University Press.
Gabriel, Markus (2016a): "Facts, Social Facts, and Sociology." In: Werner Gephart/Jan Suntrup (Eds.): *The Normative Structure of Human Civilization. Readings in John Searle's Social Ontology*. Frankfurt/Main: Klostermann, pp. 49–68.
Gabriel, Markus (2016b): "Für einen nicht-naturalistischen Realismus." In: Magdalena Marszalek/Dieter Mersch (Eds.): *Seien wir realistisch. Neue Realismen und Dokumentarismen in Philosophie und Kunst*. Zürich, Berlin: Diaphanes, pp. 59–88.
Garcia, Tristan (2014): *Form and Object. A Treatise on Things*. Edinburgh: Edinburgh University Press.
Grant, Iain Hamilton (2005): "The Eternal and Necessary Bond Between Philosophy and Physics." In: *Angelaki* Vol. 10, No. 1, pp. 43–59.
Grant, Iain Hamilton (2008): *Philosophies of Nature After Schelling*. London: Continuum.

Harman, Graham (2010): *Towards Speculative Realism: Essays and Lectures*. Winchester, UK: Zero Books.
Harman, Graham (2011): *The Quadruple Object*. Winchester, UK: Zero Books.
Hübner, Johannes (2016): "Existenz und Ontologie. Anmerkungen zu Markus Gabriels ontologischen Thesen." In: Markus Gabriel (Ed.): *Jahrbuch-Kontroversen 2. Neutraler Realismus*. Freiburg, München: Karl Alber, pp. 150–164.
Kern, Andrea (2014): "Objektivität und Irrtum. Über die Möglichkeit und Wirklichkeit von Erkenntnis." In: Markus Gabriel (Ed.): *Der Neue Realismus*, Berlin: Suhrkamp, pp. 200–229.
Kern, Andrea (2017): *Sources of Knowledge: On the Concept of a Rational Capacity for Knowledge*. Cambridge, MA: Harvard University Press.
Kimhi, Irad (2018): *Thinking and Being*. Cambridge, MA: Harvard University Press.
Koch, Anton Friedrich (2014): "Wir sind kein Zufall. Die Subjektivittsthese als Grundlage eines hermeneutischen Realismus." In: Markus Gabriel (Ed.): *Der Neue Realismus*, Berlin: Suhrkamp, pp. 230–243.
Koch, Anton Friedrich (2015): "Neutraler oder hermeneutischer Realismus." In: Markus Gabriel (Ed.): *Jahrbuch-Kontroversen 2: Philosophisches Jahrbuch* 122, No. 1, pp. 163–172.
Kolozova, Katerina and Eileen A. Joy, ed. (2016): *After the 'Speculative Turn': Realism, Philosophy, and Feminism*. Goleta, CA: Punctum Books.
Livingston, Paul (2012): *The Politics of Logic: Badiou, Wittgenstein, and the Consequences of Formalism*. New York: Routledge.
Livingston, Paul (2017): *The Logic of Being: Realism, Truth, and Time*. Evanston, Illinois: Northwestern University Press.
Meillassoux, Quentin (2008): *After Finitude. An Essay on the Necessity of Contingency*. London: Continuum.
Meillassoux, Quentin (2007): "Subtraction and Contraction: Deleuze, Immanence and Matter and Memory." In: *Collapse III: Unknown Deleuze*. London: Urbanomic.
Meillassoux, Quentin (2007): "Potentiality and Virtuality." In: *Collapse II: Speculative Realism*. London: Urbanomic.
Nagel, Thomas (1986): *The View from Nowhere*. Oxford: Oxford University Press.
Nagel, Thomas (2012): *Mind and Cosmos. Why the Neo-Darwinian Concept of Nature is Almost Certainly False*. Oxford: Oxford University Press.
Rödl, Sebastian (2015): "Vernunft und Registratur. Zu Markus Gabriels Neutralem Realismus." In: Markus Gabriel (Ed.): *Jahrbuch-Kontroversen 2. Philosophisches Jahrbuch* 122, No. 1, pp. 173–176.
Sellars, Wilfrid (1963): "Philosophy and the Scientific Image of Man." In: *Science, Perception and Reality*. Atascadero, CA: Ridgeview, pp. 1–40.
Searle, John (2014): "Aussichten für einen neuen Realismus." In: Markus Gabriel (Ed.), *Der Neue Realismus*. Berlin: Suhrkamp, pp. 292–307.
Unger, Peter (2014): *Empty Ideas: A Critique of Analytic Philosophy*. Oxford: Oxford University Press.

Part 1 **Idealism**

Sebastian Rödl
Metaphysics, Thinking, and Being

Abstract: This essay critically analyzes Barry Stroud's book *Metaphysical Dissatisfaction*. With reference to Aristotle's *Metaphysics*, Rödl challenges Stroud's claim of an inherent dialectic of knowledge and dissatisfaction internal to the project of metaphysics as a systematic knowledge of what is insofar as it is. According to Rödl, Stroud takes metaphysics to be the endeavor of comparing the ways in which we think with what is in order to establish whether we, as we think in these ways, can actually grasp what is as well. But this construal of metaphysics makes it appear that there are two things, independently described and subsequently compared: i) how we think, and ii) how what is is, as we are thinking it. According to Rödl, Stroud is right to hold that metaphysics (i.e. the science of what is, insofar as it is) investigates being and thinking. But metaphysics does not investigate a relationship between the two. Rather, metaphysics arises from thought, from the kind of understanding of its object that thought itself is.

In his book *Engagement and Metaphysical Dissatisfaction*, Barry Stroud leads us into a disappointment. We are disappointed because we cannot obtain certainty that the world conforms to the ways in which we think it. Stroud calls the attempt to achieve this certainty "the metaphysical project"; the disappointment in which his book ends is that of the failure of this project.

Stroud misunderstands the metaphysical project because he misunderstands the object of metaphysics. His project does not exist and therefore neither does its disappointment. This does not mean that there is no metaphysical project. Nor does it imply that metaphysics has a different aim from that of comprehending the unity of thinking and being. On the contrary.

I will introduce metaphysics as Aristotle conceives it (in section 1), in order to show (in section 2) how Stroud's project emerges from an understanding of the object of metaphysics that differs from Aristotle's. I proceed (in sections 3 to 5) to recapitulate the considerations that lead Stroud into disappointment. In his train of thought we recognize the true idea of metaphysics in a distorted guise (Section 6).

1 Aristotle's determination of metaphysics; the character of the concept of its object

In the third book of the work entitled *Metaphysics*, Aristotle introduces a distinguished science: the science that treats of what is insofar as it is and what belongs to it as such. We shall conform to the traditional use of the word when we call this science "metaphysics". According to Aristotle, this science is unique in the way it determines its object. Other sciences, mathematics, for example, determine their object by delimiting an area within what is. The object of metaphysics cannot be determined in this way. It is illimitable.

> There is a science that investigates what is insofar as it is and what belongs to it as such. It is not the same as any of the other sciences; for none of these deals generally with what is insofar as it is. They cut off a part of what is and investigate determinations of this part – as do, for example, the mathematical sciences. (Aristotle 1984, 1003a21–26, p. 1584)

Aristotle appears to say that the object of metaphysics is more general than that of other sciences; it encompasses more. Other sciences investigate a part of what is, metaphysics, all of it. This would mean that metaphysics differs from other sciences by degree: were we to order all concepts in a series of ascending generality, so that along the series the extension of the concept increases while its content decreases, then the concept that designates the object of metaphysics would form the end of that series. But this is wrong. Any concept in this series distinguishes: it distinguishes what is determined by it from what is not determined by it; it distinguishes what can be thought under it from what cannot. The concept of what is does not do that. This concept does not distinguish what is determined by it from what is not. For, as Aristotle observes, that is a distinction within what is. The concepts in the series open up the opposition of 'is so' to 'is not so'; the concept designating the object of metaphysics does not do that. It is not a member and therefore not the last member of a series of concepts that distinguish. Rather, it designates what we understand when we understand that a concept distinguishes. For therein we understand wherein it distinguishes: something that is from something that is. (This explains why, according to Aristotle, metaphysics is the science that treats of the law of non-contradiction. Since its concept lies beyond the opposition of 'is so' and 'is not so,' it can comprehend this opposition.) The concept of the object of metaphysics is incomparable to all other concepts in that it does not determine one thing against another. It does not do this because it is the concept of what is understood in any act of determining. We can express this by saying: this concept is not more general than other concepts, but is their generality; it is not a concept, but *the* concept.

2 The understanding of metaphysics as a science of a limited object; Stroud's metaphysical project

We have introduced Aristotle's understanding of metaphysics in order to compare it to the way in which metaphysics and its object are determined today, in general and by Stroud. In contemporary philosophical prose, talk of what is has gone out of fashion. Other words are more popular. One speaks of the world, the objective world, or reality. These words seem so simple that there is no need to reflect upon them; one can dedicate oneself straightaway to the determination of what they designate. Thus one declares what truly exists and what principles govern what truly exists as such. Positively, one refers to physics or other sciences, which have discovered a great deal. On one's own authority, one makes primarily negative claims, explaining that such and such certainly is not to be found among what truly exists: colors, purposes, necessity, and other things.

When one proceeds in this way, it seems as though metaphysics delimited an object in the same way as the other sciences do. It is just a very encompassing one – indeed it is all reality. This, furthermore, gives rise to the notion that this object is distinguished from something else. Whereas other sciences isolate a part of what is, distinguishing it from other things that are, metaphysics will distinguish its object, namely, what is, from something that is not. What could that be? Well, it will be what seems to be real, but is not, what is made up, imagined, or fantasized. Thus, there is what is, and there is what we merely think, while in truth it is not. Thought opens up an area beside what is: the area of what is not, and yet is thought.

According to Aristotle, metaphysics is the science that investigates what is insofar as it is. There is no mention of thought here. However, shortly thereafter, he discusses the law of non-contradiction as the first principle of what is insofar as it is; among other formulations, he puts this principle by saying that is impossible for anyone to think that something both is and is not (Aristotle 1984, 1005b22–25). Thus, propounding the first principle of metaphysics, Aristotle speaks of thought. We will come back to this. For now we focus instead on how thought nowadays enters metaphysics, in general and in Stroud, namely as follows: metaphysics has a circumscribed object, namely what is, or what really is, as distinguished from what is merely thought, or made up. In order correctly to demarcate this object, metaphysics must assess whether what we think really is or whether it is merely thought. Thus emerges what Stroud calls the "metaphysical project". Stroud understands this to be the endeavor to compare the ways in which we think with what is in order to establish whether we, as we think in these ways, grasp what is.[1] This may be called the metaphysical project insofar as it seeks to distinguish the object of metaphysics from what is not its object: what is from what is merely thought, what really is from what is merely imagined.

The metaphysical project aims to reach a verdict about whether we, thinking the way we do, grasp what is, or whether we fail to do so. Now, in thinking, we always already understand what we think to be as we think it. The metaphysical project seeks to provide us with the certainty that we rightly so understand it. But not for the reasons for which we generally think what is to be as we think it. For these reasons themselves belong to what we think.[2] The desire for this certainty – we may call it the metaphysical desire, as it is the desire that calls forth the metaphysical project – satisfies itself in a positive judgement (Stroud calls it a "verdict") about our ways of thinking: the judgement that what is truly and really is as we think it. With this verdict, we can continue thinking as we do, in the awareness that, thinking this way, we know what really is as it really is.

Stroud finds that the metaphysical project fails: we are disappointed, our metaphysical desire is incapable of satisfaction. For a terrible dialectic unfolds: as we seek to reject a negative judgment about our ways of thinking, it emerges that precisely what makes it impossible for us to reach a negative verdict precludes a positive one. In the end, we are stuck with our ways of thinking, unable to attain the certainty that by their means we think what is and equally unable to find any flaw in them.

---

[1] "We … want to understand how we and our thoughts about the world stand in relation to a world that is not ourselves. The question is about the relation between the conception we have of the world and the world itself" (Stroud 2011, p. 6).

[2] The metaphysical project is therefore not just a reflection, but a "metareflection": "Metaphysical reflection seeks to subject that whole rich conception of the world to a certain kind of independent scrutiny and assessment. It is to that extent a meta-reflection. It comes after, and reflects critically upon, whatever we have already come to accept in our efforts to make sense of the world. […] Our questions are then directed toward our very conception of the way things are, not to our grounds for holding it" (Stroud 2011, p. 5).

3 A more precise account of the project in terms of the idea of a way of thinking

We have described the metaphysical project as the enterprise of seeking to vindicate that, thinking as we do, we grasp what is. Stroud initially does not talk about our thinking in general, but about specific ways of thinking. The expression "way of thinking" can have multiple meanings. What Stroud means becomes clear through the examples he gives: causality, necessity, the good. One way of thinking understands something as something that explains why something else is or happens. Another way understands something as something that must be as it is. A third way understands something as something that is simply good. The reason Stroud restricts his question to these three ways of thinking is that he feels the temptation to think that these determinations cannot be encountered in what really is.[3] They are to be found only in our thinking. They are thought, invented, fantasized, but not real.

The question whether a way of thinking agrees with what is arises within the thinking that accords with this way. For, thinking in a certain way, we understand that we do so. The generality indicated by "a way" is for us as we are thinking in this way. We do not simply think that what is is such that, for example, the water-tap leaks because the rubber seal has worn out. We also think that what is is such that something, which has happened, explains why something else is happening. We think that the concept of causation applies to what is. In this way, a way of thinking is not only a form of propositions, but is itself a proposition, which we may call a formal proposition, and a concept, which we may call a formal concept. Thus we can define the metaphysical project by the question whether certain formal propositions are true and whether certain formal concepts are knowledge.

The question of the metaphysical project – is what is the way we think it is? – may also be applied to ordinary propositions and concepts: Is what is the way we think it is, as we think it through the concept *mold*? Are things the way we think they are when we think that mold reproduces asexually? Stroud, however, wants to separate the metaphysical project from scientific inquiry. He thinks that metaphysics sets in after we have done everything to find out how things stand with mold and its reproduction. After this has happened and we have set down our purported knowledge of mold, the metaphysical proj-

---

3 "There is a metaphysical urge ... present, I believe, ... in our feeling the pull of a negative metaphysical verdict in those cases. I think most of us can feel that pull" (Stroud 2011, p. 159).

ect poses the question whether we therein apprehend what is. This question could appear to be void, since we have already answered it by saying what we do about mold. But it is not, since it is now directed towards the ways of thinking that determine our purported knowledge of mold. While, in our scientific inquiry, we examined everything that pertains to mold, we did not examine – so, at least, it seems – whether these ways of thinking are objectively valid; whether the formal propositions contained in them are true; and whether the formal concepts applied in them amount to knowledge. We investigated whether and how mold reproduces, but not whether the concept of causality contained in the idea of reproduction applies to what is.

Here we need to ask more precisely what it means that the metaphysical question does not refer to the concept of mold, but rather, for example, to that of causality. It may well be that the metaphysical project only emerges when we already know, or think we know, a few things about mold. Yet the scientific investigation, no less than the metaphysical investigation, inquires whether what is is as we think it is. Or should we say that biology leaves open whether what is is the way we think it is when we think that mold reproduces asexually?

The metaphysical investigation initially appears to be distinguished only by the greater generality of its propositions and concepts: the concept of causality is more general than that of asexual reproduction. But in what way? We can ascend to a higher species and expand our investigation from mold in particular to fungus in general without leaving the realm of scientific inquiry. Is the metaphysical inquiry perhaps even *more* general than that; is it perhaps the most general inquiry? Is there a species so general that, by attaining to its heights, we would elevate our investigation from natural science to metaphysics? Is this perhaps the highest species? For now we leave this question aside, noting that, until we have answered it, the metaphysical project remains undetermined, resting, on the one hand, upon the feeling that the concept of causality is more questionable than that of mold, and, on the other, upon the tradition in which philosophers have occupied themselves more with the concept of causality than with that of mold.

According to Stroud, the metaphysical project should discover whether certain of our ways our thinking are objectively valid. This seems to require that we first describe the way of thinking in question; we describe how we think. It is essential that we do this in such a way that we do not preemptively decide that what is is the way we think it, thinking it in this way. In describing the way of thinking under scrutiny, we assert something about ourselves, but nothing about that which we think in that way. Stroud also calls what we think "world". Hence, within the metaphysical investigation it is one thing to say how we are and how we think; it is another thing to say how the world is.

The metaphysical investigation concerns itself with us and with the world, and in such a way that we are distinguished from the world.

Stroud does not take this to mean that we are not part of the world; on the contrary. Rather, the world that is different from us is the world that remains when we and our thinking are subtracted.[4] Stroud is certain that something remains. For – this consideration is important in chapter five of his book – he himself will think no more at some time in the future, namely, when he will have died, and this will not bring down the world.[5] Moreover, we know that, at a certain time in the past, no beings capable of thought wandered the earth, and yet the world existed at this time. Thus we are a limited part of the world, which can be removed without the world's suffering any further harm. And for precisely this reason it is possible to investigate our condition – that is, how we think – without therein extending our query to the remaining world, the world that is different from us.

4 A more precise determination of the ways of thinking in question; *a priori* knowledge

With respect to each of the ways of thinking Stroud considers, he discusses the view that the way of thinking in question is a feature merely of us and does not comprehend the world that is different from us. And each time he comes to the conclusion that we cannot accept this negative verdict. We are unable to do this as we notice that, abstaining from the way of thinking in question, we do not think what is as it is in itself, but rather think nothing at all. The above-mentioned ways of thinking seem to be determinations of thought as such.

Stroud is not sure whether this can be shown, but he provisionally assumes it.[6] He provisionally assumes that certain ways of thinking are such that thinking anything at all is thinking in accordance with them. If thinking something is thinking in some specific way, then thinking anything at all is affirming the cor-

---

4 "The metaphysical project starts from this broadly speaking psychological part of our conception of the world – our believing the kinds of things we do – and asks how the things we thereby believe are related to the rest of what is really so" (Stroud 2011, p. 157).
5 "So the fact that Descartes thinks, or the fact that I think, or the fact that anyone thinks, are all things that can fail, or could have failed, to hold [...] In my case, it is true that I think, but ... in a few years it will be true no longer" (Stroud 2011, p. 127).
6 "The step involves showing, of certain specified propositions, that they must be accepted by anyone who thinks or experiences anything at all. And that looks very difficult to establish" (Stroud 2011, p. 138).

responding formal proposition and taking the corresponding formal concept to be knowledge. In the terminology of power and act we can say that such a way of thinking is a determination of the power to think and at the same time an act of this power: a proposition or concept. The proposition and concept in question are *a priori:* they are the act of the power to think that this power has always already performed through itself.

Stroud assumes that this is so and considers what would be the case if it were. We will follow his reasoning further in a moment. But before we do, we must take note of the strange position that the assumption in question occupies within the metaphysical project. For, first, the metaphysical project can be made intelligible only by means of this assumption. And secondly, within Stroud's project, it can be nothing more than an assumption.

We noted that Stroud's project is not so general as simply to ask whether what is is the way we think it is. Rather, the project restricts itself to certain ways of thinking. Later it becomes clear that, in truth, this restriction does not limit the question, since the ways of thinking under consideration are determinations of thought as such. This, however, is no surprise, since only this generality of the disputed ways of thinking explains why their investigation is not a scientific one.[7] Propositions and concepts that belong to the power of thinking as such cannot be validated by any empirical investigation. This explains the feeling that the ways of thinking discussed cannot be determinations of what is, but only of ourselves. For if one assumes that true propositions can only be verified by experience and that concepts only amount to knowledge when they can be referred to experience, then these propositions and concepts fail. So it is only in recognizing that the contemplated ways of thinking determine thought as such and that the corresponding propositions and concepts are a priori, that we understand what the metaphysical project is.

Only if Stroud's provisional assumption is true is it comprehensible what his project is. At the same time, within this project, it is impossible to see that it is true. This is so because we and our thinking appear in this project as a part of the world, distinguished from what remains when we and our thinking are subtracted. And, however it is further explained how we attain knowledge of this special part of the world and thus of how we think, it is clear that we do not thereby comprehend how thought is determined as such and thus necessarily. At best we will find that we cannot imagine how we would think if we did not think

---

[7] As Stroud notes: "In this way, metaphysics can present itself as just one among many more or less general kinds of investigation of what is really so. But that appearance will be misleading ... if the kinds of beliefs that are of metaphysical interest are fundamental to thinking of any world at all" (Stroud 2011, pp. 157–158).

in certain ways. And this is precisely what Stroud presents as the basis upon which he provisionally assumes that to think is to think in these ways.[8] Yet of course he knows that, from the fact that we do not understand how one could think otherwise than in the ways that we do, it does not follow that to think is to think in these ways.[9]

5 The disappointment, and its destruction

Stroud considers what would be the case if it were so: if the ways of thinking he discusses were determinations of thought as such. In that case, he explains, it would be impossible to judge that the formal propositions corresponding to such a way of thinking are false, the formal concepts corresponding to it not knowledge. For, in judging that, we think in accordance with the way of thinking in question, thereby affirming the proposition in doubt and taking the corresponding concepts to be knowledge. In passing a negative judgment about the way of thinking in question, we contradict this very judgment.

One might think that this brings the metaphysical project to a positive conclusion. For we have shown that the propositions and concepts in question are indubitable. However, Stroud thinks we see that this is not the case when we recall that the ways of thinking in question are *our* determinations and not those of the world, which is different from us. And therefore, it is also a determination of *ourselves* that we affirm the corresponding propositions and take the corresponding concepts to be knowledge. So it is with us. But our condition does not decide the condition of the world. That we necessarily judge that the world is a certain way, as we so judge in thinking anything at all, leaves open whether the world is that way.

It may seem to help our metaphysical project when we find that certain ways of thinking belong to thought as such. For this means that we cannot but affirm the corresponding propositions and thus we can neither deny nor doubt them. Yet when we consider that we thereby find only how things stand with us, who are different from the world, we notice that this not only does not further our metaphysical project, but conclusively establishes its failure. For the ways

---

8 "But if after careful examination we find we cannot understand how anyone could think at all without thinking in certain determinate ways, or without holding certain propositions to be true, we would be in as good a position as we could be in for declaring those ways of thinking to be indispensable to any thought or experience at all" (Stroud 2011, p. 138).
9 That our situation is as good as it can be does not mean that it is not catastrophic. See footnote 10.

of thinking in question are such that we cannot even interrogate them, a fortiori we cannot validate them, while at the same time we see that, as far as we know, the world may be otherwise than we think it is, thinking in these ways. So we are disappointed.

There are ways in which we think that are such that thinking anything at all is thinking in these ways. This is why it is impossible to negate the propositions belonging to them; indeed, it is impossible to doubt or even question them. To negate them would mean to assert something of the form: "it is so and it is not so." To doubt them would mean to say: "it is so, but as far as I know, it is not"; and to question them would mean "it is so, but is it really so?" Yet we are disappointed. For this only tells us that we necessarily think that what is is this way. It does not tell us that what is is this way.

Expressing our disappointment, we say: we think it is so and cannot think otherwise. And yet it may be otherwise. We think it is so and cannot think otherwise. And yet the question remains whether it really is so. So we speak, expressing our disappointment. The disappointment, however, arose when we realized that just this – what now is to express our disappointment – cannot be meaningfully stated. For it is equivalent to saying: "it is so, but as far as I know, it is not so" or: "it is so, but is it really so?" The assertion that expresses our disappointment is precisely the one we have seen to be meaningless, and just this insight is supposed to be the basis of our disappointment. The insight that we are to recognize as disappointing is thus not only that it is impossible to deny, to doubt, or to question the formal propositions and concepts in question. It is, as much and in one motion, the insight that it is impossible to find oneself disappointed in the desire for the metaphysical certainty that what is is how we think it is, thinking in these ways.

Have we now reached a positive conclusion? Have we recognized that our metaphysical desire cannot be disappointed because it cannot be significantly said that it is disappointed? No. For now we repeat what we said before: that we can neither say nor think, "we must think so, and cannot think otherwise, and yet we cannot be sure that what is in itself is the way we think it is" – that we can neither say nor think this tells us something about us and the ways in which we cannot but think. And this leaves the question untouched how what is is in itself.

The ways of thinking in question are a determination of ourselves and not of the world, which is different from us. And therefore it is also a determination of ourselves that we affirm the corresponding propositions and take the corresponding concepts to be knowledge. For this reason, it is, further, a determination of ourselves that we cannot be disappointed in the fact that we cannot obtain certainty that what is conforms to our ways of thinking. That is how things stand with us. But how we are does not decide how the world is. For the world that we want to think is different from us. That we cannot but judge that the world is so leaves open whether the world is so. That we cannot be disappointed in our desire to be certain that the world really is so leaves open whether the world really is so. We are disappointed.

We can now repeat and bring forward anew the same thought: is it possible to say and think that about which the renewed disappointment is disappointed? Do not the considerations that form the basis of this renewed disappointment show this to be impossible? Stroud's investigation does not end in metaphysical disappointment. It ends in such a way that the thought that brings about the disappointment destroys it, only to evoke it again in this very same thought.[10]

---

10 According to Stroud, Kant attempts to avoid this dissatisfaction in the following way. In a first step, Kant explains that certain ways of thinking are determinations of thinking as such. In a second step, he concludes that the world is as we think it is, when we think in these ways. Stroud believes that the second step requires Kant's transcendental idealism. In that he himself does not wish to take it, he finds the metaphysical project to be disappointed. The argument that Stroud ascribes to Kant is unconvincing, since it is impossible to know that certain ways of thinking are necessary if this does not mean that we, thinking in these ways, recognize what is insofar as it is. Stroud himself notices this. He imagines that we could convince ourselves that certain ways of thinking determine thinking as such: "If after careful examination we find we cannot understand how anyone could think at all without thinking in certain determinate ways, or without holding certain propositions to be true, we would be in as good a position as we could be in for declaring those ways of thinking to be indispensable to any thought or experience at all. Of course, what we state in such a judgment of necessity ... is not simply that we have found it impossible to understand how someone could think without being capable of the thoughts in question. But if we are right in what we say, and there is a necessary connection between thinking at all and thinking in those specified ways, that would explain our inability to make sense of the opposite" (Stroud 2011, p. 138). We find that we cannot understand how someone could think otherwise than in the way in question, and ask what it shows that we do not understand this. We answer that one possibility is that we cannot understand it because it is impossible. Now, that is one possibility. Another is that we simply do not understand it. It is ridiculous to say that the first possibility is more probable. We have nothing we could use to compare its probability with that of the second. Stroud says that this basis is the best one that we can have. That best basis is no basis at all. If, however, it were a good basis, it would be impossible to see what would prevent us from upholding the second thesis, namely in this way: "If we find we cannot understand how the world could be otherwise than in accord with our indispensable ways of thinking, we would be in as good a position as we could be in for declaring that the world necessarily conforms to those ways of thinking. Of course, what we state in such a judgment of necessity ... is not that we have found it impossible to understand how the world could be at all without being as we think it to be, thinking in those ways. But if we are right in what we say and there is a necessary connection between the way the world is and the way we think it to be, that would explain our inability to make sense of the opposite."

6 The underlying insight; thinking and being; the universality of metaphysics

This situation arises from the stipulation that underlies Stroud's project: we and our thinking are one thing; another is what is, the world we think. We wish to obtain certainty that the first agrees with the second and for that reason we have to go beyond ourselves and our thinking and compare it to what is. When this is laid down, it is therewith settled that nothing we may discover about ourselves and our thinking will satisfy the metaphysical desire.[11]

It is equally evident that there can be nothing in which we go beyond our thinking. This is obscured by Stroud for a moment by his refraining initially from posing the question of his project with the generality proper to it. In its proper generality, the question is: does what is agree with our thought? We cannot even begin to investigate this, since as soon as we undertake to specify how what is is in itself, we think it. Stroud obscures this by not talking about thought as such, but specific ways of thinking. Thus it seems at first as though we could consider what is without therein thinking in the specific way in question, as it is only a certain way of thinking. But the ways of thinking which Stroud chooses are just those that determine thought as such. And this is no coincidence. For only in this way can we understand why no empirical investigation can be relied upon to establish its objective validity. In order for the metaphysical investigation to get going, the investigated ways of thinking must be delimited. In order for what interrogates them to be a metaphysical investigation, these ways of thinking must determine our thought as such.

In pretending that Stroud's metaphysical investigation exists, we stipulate that it is one thing to describe how we think, and another to say how what is is in itself. Insofar as we hold to this, the disappointment is guaranteed. This does not mean that it is not helpful to follow the arduous path of Stroud's book. It does however mean that, once we have done so, we see that its point

---

[11] The cited passage, "The metaphysical project starts from this broadly speaking psychological part of our conception of the world – our believing the kinds of things we do – and asks how the things we thereby believe are related to the rest of what is really so," continues as follows: "But there is a question as to whether we can successfully separate that portion of our conception of the world in that way from all the rest of what we believe" (Stroud 2011, p. 157). This points to our incapacity, which is the root of the failure of the metaphysical project; it does not reveal either that this project does not exist or that it cannot exist. The mentioned stipulation is never put into question by Stroud. Of it he believes he must be quite certain, for reasons which will we discuss shortly.

of departure already implied its conclusion, without any of Stroud's discursive labors.

But how can we avoid stipulating that: that it is one thing to describe how we think, and another to say how what is is constituted? Is this not a matter of course? Is it not in general the case that it is one thing to say what someone thinks and another to say whether it is as she thinks it is? Do I not need to compare what someone thinks to what is in order to see whether what is is the way she thinks it is? And does this not apply to all of us? Do we not thus need to compare our thinking with what is in order to find out if the one agrees with the other? Stroud makes it clear that this consideration is the basis of his project. He realizes that, thinking that this or that is the case, I indeed think that what is is the way I think it is. But this leaves open whether it is this way.[12] The metaphysical disappointment is just this, expanded to a maximal degree of generality: from the particular judgment to thought in general. Insofar as I think, I indeed affirm the propositions that are contained in thought as such: I think that the world is as I think it is. But this leaves open whether it is so.

Therefore it is worthwhile to consider the elementary case. I judge that such-and-such is the case. In judging that, I neither doubt nor question whether it is the case. This does not, however, decide whether it is the case. In order for someone to decide this, she must compare what I think to what is. This seems easy. Someone thinks: "*Such and such is the case.*" I examine this and determine that, in fact, *such and such is the case.* I seem to compare her thought to the world, which is different from her thought and remains when I subtract her and her thoughts. What I know of her thought, however, the only thing I need to know of it in order to examine its truth, is what she thinks. Thus, the only thing I need from her thought in order to perform the comparison is what stands inside the quotation marks. This, however, is the same as that to which I compare it. I compare the same to the same. Of course, one term is contained within quotation marks. But these marks are irrelevant to the comparison; they are not a determination of what is being compared that I consider in the comparison.

Now, one will be ready with the requisite jargon to explain that there are indeed two things: the content of a judgement, a proposition, and the state of affairs, which makes the proposition true. We do not need to venture into the

---

[12] "It says only that no one could consistently deny propositions whose acceptance is indispensable for thought, not that such propositions could not possibly fail to be true if believed. The difference is brought out by a well-known observation of G. E. Moore. Someone who both asserts that he believes it is raining and denies that it is raining is inconsistent in asserting what he does. The two different propositions he asserts are not inconsistent with each other; it is possible for someone to believe that it is raining when it is not raining" (Stroud 2011, p. 137).

murky depths opening up here. It suffices to note that this jargon cannot elucidate the idea that we and our thinking are over here, and the world over there, because this jargon, on the contrary, assumes that we understand that idea.

"It is one thing to describe how we think; it is something else to say how what is is constituted." If we direct our considerations to thinking in a particular way, we see that this does not make sense. We describe a way of thinking, that is, we say how what is is thought being thought in this way. In doing this we place what we say in quotation marks. These marks indicate that the enclosed sentences do not describe the world, but a view of the world. We can give the quotation marks the form of a "we" to indicate that it is our view. Or we can apply a prefix such as: "Our view of the world is:" That is one thing. Then we describe how what is is configured. We do the same as before, now omitting the quotation marks. And then we compare. For the comparison, however, i.e. for the question whether the one agrees with the other, the quotation marks are irrelevant. We do not consider them in order to answer the question. And thus the metaphysical project can only consist in comparing one way of thinking with another; or else it compares one way of thinking with itself. If the way of thinking in question is a determination of thought as such, only the latter is possible.[13]

---

[13] Stroud expresses well how his metaphysical project blocks the entrance to metaphysics – the science Aristotle introduces. He notes that a positive judgment about a way of thinking only satisfies our requirement to understand it in its validity when this way of thinking is reduced to another one. "A reassuringly positive verdict would have been reached if it could have been shown that the very contents of the things we believe in the areas in question can be reduced without remainder to something that is uncontroversially so in the world as it is independently of us and our responses to it" (Stroud 2011, p. 125). And: "Accepting a positive verdict, along with the irreducibility of the beliefs, would seem to leave us with modal and evaluative facts as simply otherwise inexplicable aspects of reality" (Stroud 2011, p. 159). For if a way thinking is irreducible, then the positive metaphysical judgment about it exhibits this very way of thinking, and thus does not give any deeper insight into its validity than it does through itself. This explains how the metaphysical desire can take the guise of the feeling that a negative judgment of the relevant ways of thinking in question must be correct. "There is a metaphysical urge ... in our feeling the pull of a negative metaphysical verdict in those cases. I think most of us can feel that pull. ... There is a feeling that a negative verdict is ... obviously called for..." (Stroud 2011, p. 159). This may be disconcerting, for one will ask oneself how far one has estranged oneself from philosophy if one finds the feeling felt by "most of us" so utterly alien. One gathers courage as one notes that one really must feel drawn to a negative judgement. For if a positive judgment about irreducible ways of thinking destroys any hope that we could understand why we think the way we do and why what is is the way we think it is, thinking it this way, then this feeling is the only way left to the desire to understand – the philosophical impulse – to express itself.

Stroud notices exactly this and is disappointed. He is disappointed that he can only compare his way of thinking with itself. This disappoints him, for he thinks it shows that he cannot obtain certainty that his way of thinking agrees with the world, which is different from it. That is, however, not what it shows. It does not show that we are limited to saying how we think, and thus are unable to hold this thought against what is. Rather, it shows that describing how we think is the same as describing what belongs to what is as such. It does not show that we are imprisoned within one term of the metaphysical examination, our thought and its ways, closed off from what is, the unreachable Other. Rather, it shows that thinking and being are the same. The metaphysical project of obtaining certainty that our thought agrees with what is has already laid down, before it begins, that thought as such is not knowledge. It has laid down that our thought, and thus we ourselves, are something other than what is insofar as it is. It is Stroud's project that destroys the original certainty, which it then shows itself to be disappointed to be unable to provide.

One might think this means that we do not ever get beyond the scientific investigation in which we think in accordance with the relevant ways of thinking and think ourselves to know. One might think this means that there is no metaphysical project that goes beyond empirical inquiry. Then one could say, on Stroud's behalf, that it is in fact necessary to bereave us of the immediate certainty of the knowledge we obtain through empirical inquiry for the sake of something better. One could further claim that the human being will never allow herself to be talked out of this longing for something better. Stroud writes about the feeling that the metaphysical question must have an answer, whether affirmative or negative: "It shows that, for those parts of our conception of the world concerned with causal dependence, necessity, and evaluative matters, something more is thought to be required for a full understanding of the world and our relation to it than amply warranted acceptance or even knowledge of the truth of beliefs of those kinds" (Stroud 2011, p. 160).

However, what we have said above does not contradict this. It implies neither that there is no metaphysical project, nor that the latter longs for something else than comprehension of the unity of thinking and being. Rather, it shows that the desire for "full understanding" can only show itself, in Stroud's project, in a disfigured way.

As we noted above, the scientific investigation asks the same question as the metaphysical one, namely whether what is is the way we think it is. And scientific knowledge, insofar as it is knowledge, is the knowledge that what is is the way it is known to be in this knowledge. The metaphysical project thus does not distinguish itself from the empirical one by being reflective, but by its generality. And indeed, it is unrestrictedly general, as it concerns what is as such and, therefore, thought as such.[14] The considerations we employed to bring into view how Stroud's project collapses, in that he attempts to evaluate ways of thinking by measuring them against what is, exhibit throughout just this generality. Even when we spoke of a particular judgment, we spoke of a judgment as such; and so what we said belongs to the determination of what thought is as such. When we think this unlimited generality, that of thought as such, and thus that of what is as such, the first thing that we find is that thinking and being are the same. For we find that, comparing thinking to being, we compare thinking to itself.

Far, then, from it being the case that our consideration confines us to scientific inquiry – in which case we would need to thank Stroud for still being capable of the feeling of intellectual claustrophobia, extricating us from our intellectual confinement and waking in us a wish for something nobler, as problematic as it may be – it is rather this consideration in which the metaphysical project itself first originates, the very project whose distorted form confronts us in Stroud's book.

The metaphysical project appears distorted in Stroud because he does not perceive the form of its generality. Stroud wishes for there to be two things, independently described and subsequently compared: how we think, and how what is is configured. Yet there cannot be two things that manifest the generality of metaphysics. Where there are two things, standing in a relation one to the other, then both of them as well as their relationship belong to what is. The world, which is not us, is, and we are, too. The metaphysical project would then ask how one thing that is relates to another thing that is. And this is precisely how Stroud presents it. But then it is impossible to say why that should be a metaphysical project. If we understand it in this manner, the so-called metaphysical project has no right to call itself that. For metaphysics does not delimit an object and therefore does not concern itself with the relation of this object to another. It contemplates all that is, considering it with respect to that with respect to which it agrees with all that is: it contemplates what is insofar as it is.

This may seem to mean that the metaphysical project cannot treat of us and our thought in addition to what is insofar as it is. We and our thought are a part of what is. Thus, insofar as thought appears in metaphysics, it does not do so according to its particular determination as thought any more than mold appears

---

[14] Stroud seems to notice this himself. "In this way, metaphysics can present itself as just one among many more or less general kinds of investigation of what is really so. But that appearance will be misleading ... if the kinds of beliefs that are of metaphysical interest are fundamental to thinking of any world at all" (Stroud 2011, pp. 157–158). I understand Stroud as meaning to present the antecedent of the conditional as true.

in metaphysics in its particular determination as mold. Rather, both thought and mold are equally investigated in metaphysics according to their general character as things that are.

This conclusion must indeed be drawn if one understands the metaphysical project as Stroud does. But we see that it is false as soon as we consider anew the unlimited generality of metaphysics. For the concept that designates its object is not – as we have seen – a concept that distinguishes something that is from something else that equally is. Rather, that concept is already understood in every such concept as the concept of that within which a distinction is made. It is therefore the concept of that upon which thought is directed and thereby that which we understand in thought as that upon which thought is directed. This means that we use just this concept when we say what it is to think.

We have quoted Stroud's description of the metaphysical project: "We … want to understand how … our thoughts about the world stand in relation to a world that is not ourselves. The question is about the relation between the conception we have of the world and the world itself" (Stroud 2011, p. 6). If we consider this passage again, we notice that Stroud is concerned to investigate, not how our thought relates to the world, but rather how our thought *of the world* relates to the world. The object of our thinking – that which we think – is the world, what is or really is. It is not an enclosed part of the world, not a section of what is, distinguished from others. The object of thought is what is as such. And since we can only say what thought is by saying what its object is, thought exhibits the unlimited generality that is the mark of the object of metaphysics. We are not the world, Stroud believes. But we think the world. As we think the world, though, it is impossible to say what we are without deploying the concept that denotes the object of metaphysics: what is, the world, reality. The unboundedly general concept, generality *überhaupt*, is doubled within itself: as the concept of thought and as the concept of what is. This doubling is not, however, a contentful determination by which the two, thought and world, are set in opposition to each other. For generality *überhaupt* it has no contentful determination at all.

This doubling of the unlimited generality is not something that happens to it. No, this doubling of the unlimited generality in thought and being is what constitutes unlimited generality. We said above that, in that we think unlimitedly general, the first thing we think is that thinking and being are the same. Precisely therein the unlimited generality is doubled in thinking and being. And this is why Stroud is right to hold that metaphysics, i.e. the science of what is insofar as it is, investigates being and thinking. Not because it investigates a relationship between the two. But because metaphysics arises from thought, from the understanding of its object that thought itself is: the object of thought is what is as such.

If this seems dark, it is because we have not yet examined the generality that distinguishes metaphysics and differentiates it from other sciences. We noted above that it is customary to explain without further ado that one wants to know how our thought relates to reality, the world, the objective world, without accounting for what these words signify and how they signify. We have seen how this lack of reflection pulls Stroud into an oscillation in which he seeks to express a dissatisfaction whose cause is precisely that which makes it impossible to express it. We have negatively clarified that the metaphysical project described by Stroud does not exist (and therefore has never existed). And we have indicated what is needed in order to pursue a metaphysical project that comprehends a unity of thinking and being that, precisely as uniting them, holds them apart one from the other. To pursue this project goes far beyond the aims of the present essay.

(Translated by Dominik Finkelde, Stephen Henderson, and Paul Livingston)

Bibliography:

Aristotle (1984): *Metaphysics*. Translated by W. D. Ross in *The Complete Works of Aristotle, Revised Oxford Translation*, vol. 2. Princeton: Princeton University Press.
Stroud, Barry (2011): *Engagement and Metaphysical Dissatisfaction. Modality and Value*. Oxford: Oxford University Press.

G. Anthony Bruno
Jacobi's Dare: McDowell, Meillassoux, and Consistent Idealism

"Dwell in your own house, and you will know how simple your possessions are."
Kant (quoting Persius), Axx

Abstract: Does Kant's restriction of knowledge to phenomena undermine objectivity? Jacobi argues that it does, daring the transcendental idealist to abandon the thing in itself and embrace the "strongest idealism". According to Bruno, McDowell and Meillassoux adopt a similar critique of Kant's conception of objectivity and, more significantly, echo Jacobi's dare to profess the strongest idealism – what McDowell approvingly calls "consistent idealism" and Meillassoux disparagingly calls "extreme idealism". After exposing the Cartesian projection on which Jacobi's critique rests, Bruno shows that McDowell's and Meillassoux's critiques make the same projection. He argues that whereas McDowell offers an inconsistent alternative to Kant's idealism, Meillassoux begs the question against it. Finally, Bruno sketches the account of objectivity that follows from Kant's distinction between general and transcendental logic.

Transcendental idealism may seem, as it has since its first reception and to readers of various styles, to depict an insufficiently objective world. Kant's doctrine that objects have the "twofold meaning" (Kant, Bxxvii) of knowable appearances and unknowable things in themselves seems to contradict scientific and ordinary notions of objectivity. In a supplement to *David Hume on Faith, or Idealism and Realism, a Dialogue*, Jacobi issues a challenge to the transcendental idealist:

> according to the common use of language, we must mean by 'object' a thing that *would be present outside us in a transcendental sense* [...] But since the whole of transcendental idealism would collapse as a result, and would be left with no application or reason for being, whoever professes it must disavow that presupposition. For it must not even be *probable* to him that there be things present outside us in a transcendental sense, or that they have connections with us *which we would be in a position of perceiving in any way at all* [...] The transcendental idealist must have the courage, therefore, to assert the strongest idealism that was ever professed, and not be afraid of the objection of speculative egoism. (Jacobi 1994, p. 338)

It is apparently inconsistent of Kant to posit a transcendental object, for, given transcendental idealism, it cannot be present to us in possible experience.[1] He

---
1 See Kant, A46/B63, A109, A191/B236, A250.

https://doi.org/10.1515/9783110670349-003

must accordingly renounce his idealism or else reject the idea of a limitation on our experiential standpoint. But Jacobi aims to taunt, not to advise. The "courage" of denying objects "outside us in a transcendental sense" is, for him, the folly of abandoning objectivity altogether.

Jacobi's critique of transcendental idealism rests on a discernible Cartesian projection. As we will see, John McDowell's and Quentin Meillassoux's more recent critiques of Kant do as well. More significantly, they each echo Jacobi's dare to profess the "strongest idealism" – what McDowell approvingly calls *consistent idealism* and Meillassoux disparagingly calls *extreme idealism*.

In *Mind and World*, McDowell lauds Kant's insight that the world "must exert a rational constraint on our thinking," not a force incompatible with our "obligation to be responsibly alive to the dictates of reason" (McDowell 1996, p. 42). But he charges that Kant's "transcendental story" about the thing in itself yields a view on which "rational answerability lapses at some outermost point of the space of reasons, short of the world itself" (McDowell 1996, pp. 41–42). To posit an unknowable object beyond experience is

> to slight the independence of the reality to which our senses give us access. What is responsible for this is precisely the aspect of Kant's philosophy that struck some of his successors as a betrayal of idealism: namely, the fact that he recognizes a reality outside the sphere of the conceptual. Those successors urged that we must discard the supersensible in order to achieve a consistent idealism. In fact that move frees Kant's insight so that it can protect a commonsense respect for the independence of the ordinary world. (McDowell 1996, p. 44)

In order both to render idealism consistent and to respect the world's objectivity, we must take Jacobi's dare and deny any "reality outside the sphere of the conceptual". As McDowell notes, this is the German idealists' (Jacobi-inspired) strategy, which he invokes with the image of the unboundedness of the conceptual.[2]

---

[2] Cf. Fichte 2000: "It is contradictory to ask about a reality that supposedly remains after one has abstracted from all reason; for the questioner himself (we may presume) has reason, is driven by reason to question, and wants a rational answer; he, therefore, has not abstracted from reason. We cannot go outside the sphere of our reason; the case against the thing in itself has already been made, and philosophy aims only to inform us of it and keep us from believing that we have gone beyond the sphere of our reason, when in fact we are obviously still caught within it" (p. 39). Cf. Hegel 1991: "According to the Kantian philosophy, the things that we know about are only appearances for *us*, and what they are *in-themselves* remains for us an inaccessible beyond. The naive consciousness has rightly taken exception to this subjective idealism, according to which the content of our consciousness is something that is *only* ours, something posited only through *us*. In fact, the true situation is that the things of which we have immediate knowledge are mere appearances, not only *for us*, but also *in-themselves*, and that the proper determination of these things, which are in this sense 'finite', consists in having the ground

Meillassoux's *After Finitude* laments Kant's institution of a "correlation" between thought and being whereby absolute being is unknowable. Correlationism subverts the realist meaning of "ancestral" statements about the "arche-fossil" – scientific claims about the world prior to our species – by relativizing all truth-apt statements to the human standpoint. Rather than pretend to respect scientific realism, he says,

> the consistent correlationist should stop being modest and dare to assert openly that he is in a position to provide the scientist with an *a priori* demonstration that the latter's ancestral statements are *illusory* [...] But then it is as if the distinction between transcendental idealism – the idealism that is (so to speak) urbane, civilized, and reasonable – and speculative or even subjective idealism – the idealism that is wild, uncouth, and rather extravagant – it is as if this distinction which we had been taught to draw – and which separates Kant from Berkeley – became blurred and dissolved in light of the fossil-matter. Confronted with the arche-fossil, *every variety of idealism converges and becomes equally extraordinary* – every variety of correlationism is exposed as an extreme idealism. (Meillassoux 2008, pp. 17–18)

Idealism of any sort is allegedly incompatible with the scientific disclosure of an objective world and is called out to confess its "wild" essence. Unlike McDowell, Meillassoux issues the dare in Jacobi's spirit: he demands consistent idealism from Kant, but thinks it is unviable and instead pursues *"intellectual intuition* of the absolute" (Meillassoux 2008, p. 82).

To clarify the prospects of a transcendental idealist view of objectivity, it is worth assessing McDowell's and Meillassoux's critiques of Kant as well as their responses to the Jacobian dare. In 1., I articulate Jacobi's critique of Kant and expose its Cartesian projection. In 2., I detect Cartesian premises in McDowell's critique and show that his substitute for the transcendental story is inconsistently idealist. In 3., I show that the Cartesian premises of Meillassoux's critique beg the question against transcendental idealism. In 4., I briefly draw out the account of objectivity that follows from Kant's distinction between general and transcendental logic.

---

of their being not within themselves but in the universal divine Idea. This interpretation must also be called idealism, but, as distinct from the subjective idealism of the Critical Philosophy, it is *absolute idealism*" (pp. 88–89).

1

Jacobi's dare occurs in *David Hume*. But its appeal to the "common" meaning of 'object' invokes a form of realism he defends in *Concerning the Doctrine of Spinoza in Letters to Herr Moses Mendelssohn*. The *Letters* recount conversations in which Lessing declares there is "no other philosophy" than Spinoza's (Jacobi 1994, p. 187). "That might be true," Jacobi replies, but only because Spinoza is more committed than any philosopher to "the ancient *a nihilo nihil fit*," a negative formulation of the principle of sufficient reason according to which nothing exists without a ground (Jacobi 1994, p. 187). Casting grounds in terms of efficient causation, Jacobi says that committing to the principle entails determinism and that a "determinist, if he wants to be consistent, must become a fatalist" and renounce freedom as an "illusion" (Jacobi 1994, p. 187–188). Infinitely determined by other modes, we simply "accompany the mechanism" of nature (Jacobi 1994, p. 189). Yet Jacobi "love[s]" Spinoza:

> [H]e, more than any other philosopher, has led me to the perfect conviction that certain things admit of no explication: one must not therefore keep one's eyes shut to them, but must take them as one finds them. I have no concept more intimate than that of the final cause; no conviction more vital than that *I do what I think*, and not, *that I should think what I do*. Truly therefore, I must assume a source of thought and action that remains completely inexplicable to me. (Jacobi 1994, p. 193)

Since total explanation by efficient causes dulls our "intimate" sense of freedom, Jacobi must turn to conviction. Spinoza teaches him that where knowledge alienates us from our agency, faith is required: "to explain all things absolutely" is to "run into absurdities," like denying the "genuine human truth" of the reality of freedom. Faith dispels such unnatural doubt. With it, "we know that we have a body, and that there are other bodies and other thinking beings" (Jacobi 1994, p. 231). What sort of realism is this?

For Jacobi, faith is not an irrational leap,[3] but a "*salto mortale*," i.e., a humane reversal of alienation from our deepest convictions: "once one has fallen in love with certain explanations, one accepts blindly every consequence that can be drawn from an inference that one cannot invalidate – even if one must walk on one's head" (Jacobi 1994, pp. 189, 194). Reason wed to proof is numb to our lived context and even defies it, renouncing our will and our being unless they admit of demonstration. Hence Jacobi adopts Pascal's dictum: "nature confounds the Pyrrhonists, and reason the dogmatists" (Jacobi 1994, p. 237). Skep-

---

[3] See Crowe 2007.

ticism and dogmatism are equally insensitive to "*existence*," i.e., "the unanalyzable, the immediate", for which explanation, which is only "a proximate – never a final – goal," is mere "means" (Jacobi 1994, p. 194). As Jacobi tells Mendelssohn, conviction "by proofs is certainty at second hand," for true certainty consists in direct access to absolute, i.e., transcendentally real being. It is in this sense that rational conviction derives its force "from faith alone" (Jacobi 1994, p. 230). Jacobi's conception of faith thus supports a realism for which 'object' signifies transcendental reality.[4]

Transcendental realism frames Jacobi's dare to the idealist. In the *David Hume* supplement, he says that Kant gives an implausibly "alien meaning" to 'object', one that denies anything "*present outside us in a transcendental sense*" (Jacobi 1994, p. 338).[5] Kant seems, like Descartes, to restrict objective certainty to the contents of a mind, putting mind-independent reality into doubt. And with no divine intervention at our disposal on the Kantian view, "we cannot pass by inference" to anything beyond "determinations of our own self" (Jacobi 1994, p. 337). Jacobi cites passages in which Kant says space and time are forms "in us" and appearances are "nothing" outside them (Kant, A370–9) and says:

> what we realists call actual objects or things independent of our representations are for the transcendental idealist only internal beings *which exhibit nothing at all of a thing that may perhaps be there outside us, or to which the appearance may refer. Rather, these internal beings are merely subjective determinations of the mind, entirely void of anything truly objective.* (Jacobi 1994, pp. 332–334)

Even worse, Kant subverts "the spirit of his system" with the illegitimate idea of an unknowable source of sensory matter, since for him an empirical object "cannot exist outside us", whereas "we never know anything" of a "*transcendental object*" (Jacobi 1994, pp. 334–335).[6] Worse still, Kant's view that space and

---

[4] Jacobi 1994 clarifies his position in the second edition of *David Hume:* "My philosophy [...] claims but a single knowledge through sensation, and it restricts reason, considered by itself, to the mere faculty of perceiving relations clearly, i.e., to the power of *formulating the principle of identity and of judging in conformity to it*" (pp. 255–266).

[5] Cf. Strawson 1975, p. 235.

[6] Hence Jacobi famously states: "*without* that presupposition [of a transcendental object] I could not enter into [Kant's] system, but *with* it I could not stay within it" (336). Cf. Strawson 1975: "The doctrine that we are aware of things only as they appear and not as they are in themselves because their appearances to us are the result of our constitution being affected by the objects, is a doctrine that we can understand just so long as the 'affecting' is thought of as something that occurs in space and time; but when it is added that we are to understand by space and time themselves nothing but a capacity or liability of ours to be affected in a certain way by ob-

time constitute an "all-encompassing" whole of which objects are mere "limitations" is "entirely in the spirit of Spinoza," for whom modes are mere limitations of nature (Jacobi 1994, p. 218n30; cf. Kant, A25, A32). Transcendental idealism thus offers a determinism without even a pretense to objectivity, for it is the fatalism of a self-enclosed Cartesian mind – an egoism based on "*absolute and unqualified ignorance*" of absolute being (Jacobi 1994: p. 338), against which faith-based realism is the only defence.

But it is a Cartesian projection – and a false dichotomy – to hold that objects are mentally internal unless they are absolutely external, i.e., empirically ideal unless they are transcendentally real. First, we can distinguish senses of internality. Space and time "dwell in us," not as empirically acquired mental content, but *a priori* "as forms of our sensible intuition" in virtue of which the representation of content is possible (Kant, A373). Thus, whereas mental content is empirically internal to a subject, space and time are transcendentally internal to the standpoint of human experience. Second, as Kant argues in the Fourth Paralogism, we can distinguish senses of externality. Jacobi actually cites this argument, yet ignores these senses:

> since the expression *outside us* carries with it an unavoidable ambiguity, since it sometimes signifies something that, as a thing in itself, exists distinct from us and sometimes merely something that belongs to outer appearance, then in order to escape uncertainty and use this concept in the latter significance [...] we will distinguish empirically external objects from those that might be called 'external' in the transcendental sense, by directly calling them 'things that are to be encountered in space'. (Kant, A373; Jacobi 1994, p. 333)[7]

An appearance is empirically external in that it is spatially manifest in a possible experience whereas a thing in itself is transcendentally external in that it exceeds possible experience. Kant's conception of empirical externality thus captures the common sense view about objectivity, for it signifies the matter of what appears to us – rather than matter beyond sensibility, which "is nothing" for us (Kant, A370).[8] Ironically, it is the transcendental realist who alienates

---

jects not themselves in space and time, then we can no longer understand the doctrine, for we no longer know what 'affecting' means, or what we are to understand by 'ourselves'" (p. 41).
7 Cf. Kant: "it can very well be proven that there is something outside us of an empirical kind, and hence as appearance in space; for we are not concerned with objects other than those which belong to a possible experience, just because such objects cannot be given to us in any experience and therefore are nothing for us. Outside me empirically is that which is intuited in space [...T]he concept: *outside us*, signifies only something in space" (AA 4, pp. 336–337).
8 Cf. Kant: "there may very well be something outside us, which we call matter, corresponding to this appearance; but in the same quality as appearance it is not outside us, but is merely as a

us from the empirical meaning of objects as spatial and who thereby "plays the empirical idealist" (Kant, A369).

Since we cannot "think up" the matter of sensation, Kant says, it must be "really given." Although matter "cannot be actual" for us except through our forms of intuition, its source is a "transcendental object" (Kant, A373–6).[9] This object is "entirely unknown" as its concept cannot be theoretically schematized. Yet it is an "intelligible cause of appearances," for, even absent sensibility's "restricting condition" on its empirical significance, its concept still bears the "logical significance" of a unity of thought (Kant, A147/B186, A494/B522). As Kant says, we must be able to think things in themselves even if we cannot cognize them. Moreover, his argument in the *Critique of Practical Reason* that practical reason affords "cognitions of a supersensible order" – insofar as we can "cognize ourselves" as "intelligible beings determined by the moral law" (Kant AA 5, pp. 105–106; cf. pp. 5–6, 42–43, 49, 55–57, 97–98) – bears out his claim in the first *Critique* that the thought of noumenal causality can gain "objective validity" from practical sources of cognition (Kant Bxxvi-n; cf. Kant's notes at A542/B570, A571/B599), which, *contra* Jacobi, opposes the spirit of Spinoza's determinism. Just as no Cartesian gap divides us from empirical objects, so, too, the idea of a transcendental object is consistent with the spirit of transcendental idealism.

Jacobi helps to initiate a reading – resilient, as we will see – on which Kant implausibly and illegitimately posits an unknowable thing in itself. But Kant must posit it, on pain of thinking up the matter of sensation, and can posit it without schematizing its concept: it is simply the source of matter that is informed *a priori* by space as a form of sensibility. As he says in *Prolegomena to Any Future Metaphysics*, whereas "material or Cartesian idealism" is certain of the mind yet doubts the existence of spatial objects, "[f]ormal idealism" affirms the spatiality of matter given in outer sense (Kant AA 4, pp. 336–337; cf. B274). The one-dimensional character of a Cartesian conception of internality and externality obscures their transcendental and empirical senses, the grasping of

---

thought in us, even though this thought, through the sense just named, represents it as being found outside us" (A385).

9 Cf. Kant: "I call that in the appearance which corresponds to sensation its matter, but that which allows the manifold of appearance to be intuited as ordered in certain relations I call the form of appearance. Since that within which the sensations can alone be ordered and placed in a certain form cannot itself be in turn sensation, the matter of all appearance is only given to us *a posteriori*, but its form must all lie ready for it in the mind *a priori*, and can therefore be considered separately from all sensation" (A20/B34; cf. A143/B182). See Stang 2015 for an account of how sensation is not a hylomorphic compound, but rather "the 'prime matter' in Kant's hylomorphic theory of mind" (14).

which stops the oscillation between explaining objectivity in terms of either mental content or absolute being. Formal idealism thus initiates its own reversal of alienation, specifically, from self-delusion toward self-knowledge:

> understanding occupied merely with its empirical use, which does not reflect on the sources of its own cognition, may get along very well, but cannot accomplish one thing, namely, determining for itself the boundaries of its use and knowing what may lie within and what without its whole sphere [...] But if the understanding cannot distinguish whether certain questions lie within its horizon or not, then it is never sure of its claims and its possession, but must always reckon on many embarrassing corrections when it continually oversteps the boundaries of its territory (as is unavoidable) and loses itself in delusion and deceptions. (Kant, A238)

The reflective use of understanding affords self-knowledge because its empirical use is indifferent to, and thus liable to misidentify, its proper bounds. To correct alienation from our own cognitive faculties, we must distinguish the different senses of internality and externality.

Even if he misreads Kant as a Cartesian, Jacobi unwittingly inspires the German idealists' systematic refutation of nihilism.[10] In the second edition of *David Hume*, he describes the first edition's critique of Kant as a diagnosis of "nihilism" (Jacobi 1994, p. 544), a term he coins in an intervening open letter to Fichte to signify the denial of the immediacy of existence. For Kant, justificatory relations mediate our access to existence such that appearances lack any intrinsic nature, whereas things in themselves lack any manifest nature. This explains Jacobi's dare to the idealist to reject this core Kantian distinction and embrace nihilism in the guise of egoism, according to which nothing external is immediately present in perception (Jacobi 1994, p. 338). He chides Fichte for taking the bait and declaring the thing in itself "a piece of whimsy, a pipe dream, a non-thought," "the uttermost perversion of reason, and a concept perfectly absurd" (Fichte 1988, p. 71; 1994, p. 56). By eliminating the transcendental object or "*the true*," Fichte "ceases to feel its pressure" and so cannot "reach beyond" the I's "production" of objects in thought (Jacobi 1994, pp. 508, 511–512).[11] For Jacobi, by contrast, reason is "nothing but the *perception*" of the true. As he says: "I do *not* possess with this human reason of mine the perfection of life, not the full-

---

[10] See Franks 2005, pp. 162–174.
[11] Cf. Jacobi 1994: "The philosophizing of pure reason must therefore be a chemical process through which everything outside reason is changed into nothing [...It] *must* necessarily lay at its foundation that *will that wills nothing*, that *impersonal personality*, that naked *I-hood* of the I without any *self* – in a word, *pure and bare inessentialities*. For love of the secure progress of science you *must*, yea you cannot but, subject conscience (*spirit most certain*) to a living-death of *rationality*, make it *blindly* legalistic, deaf, dumb, and unfeeling" (pp. 507, 516–517).

ness of the good and the true [...] My solution [...] is not the *I*, but the 'More than I'!" (Jacobi 1994: pp. 514–515).[12] A philosophy that denies this "*higher* faculty of perception" must "lose itself" in a "void of cognition." With no friction from absolute being, Fichte's idealism is no more than "*Nihilism*" (Jacobi 1994, pp. 519, 544–545).[13]

Like Jacobi, McDowell rejects the twin perils of construing nature as a "lethal environment" that fatalistically excludes freedom and construing reason as "a frictionless spinning in a void" (McDowell 1996, pp. 11, 66, 98). Yet he dares to "discard the supersensible" in order to secure a "consistent idealism." I will show that his critique of Kant to this end shares Jacobi's Cartesian projection and then assess the consistency of the idealism to which he turns.

2

According to McDowell, an antinomy ensnares two powerful theses on the question of how thought is answerable to experience: experience either *must* or *cannot* stand as a tribunal over thought about the world. It must if thought is to be guided by sensibility about how things are, but cannot if thought is not simply guided by sensibility, but is itself a spontaneous ability to judge how things ought to be, i.e., a conceptual capacity (McDowell 1996, pp. xii, 67, 69). But, against the first thesis, if we are not rationally responsible for what is sensibly given, then what is given cannot figure in warranted judgment: any appeal to it is mythical. And, against the second thesis, if relations by which judgment is warranted are conceptual, then they are confined to the space of reasons, coherent yet unhinged from anything given in sensation (McDowell 1996, pp. 5–9, 14). The spoiling idea shared by both theses is that sensibility is not, in its use, a conceptual capacity. We can resolve the antinomy by rejecting this idea on the

---

12 Cf. Jacobi 1994: "[W]ithout the *Thou*, the *I* is impossible [...] God is, and is *outside me, a living, self-subsisting being*, or I am God. There is no third" (pp. 231, 524).

13 Cf. Jacobi 1994: "I summed up the result of Fichtean Idealism in a simile. I compared it to a knitted stocking [...] To this stocking of mine I give borders, flowers, moon and stars, all possible figures, and cognize how all this is nothing but a product of the productive imagination of the fingers hovering between the I of the thread and the not-I of the stitches [...] If this simile is so inappropriate as to betray a crude misunderstanding on the part of its author, then I do not know how [Fichte's] philosophy can pretend to be actually *new*, and not just a variant formulation of the old philosophy *based in one way or other on some dualism*; but then it would not be a truly and genuinely *immanent* philosophy, a philosophy *of one piece* [...] Should it turn out *only* to mean the same thing [as the old philosophy] *in any way at all*, empiricism ultimately remains still on top" (pp. 509–510).

basis of Kant's insight that "intuition without thought" is "nothing for us" (Kant, A111). As McDowell puts it, sensible receptivity "draws" conceptual spontaneity into operation insofar as empirical content is always implicitly conceptual, always a matter for judgment. In this sense, there is no space enclosing the space of reasons, no "boundary around the sphere of the conceptual" (McDowell 1996, pp. 13, 34). A world outside my thoughts neither entails nor requires a world outside what is thinkable. Echoing Kant's distinction between transcendental and empirical externality, McDowell notes that his distinction between what is thinkable and what one thinks avoids "ambiguity in phrases like 'outside the sphere of thought'" (McDowell 1996, pp. 28, 39).

However, McDowell claims that Kant's transcendental story is "incoherent" because the thing in itself exceeds our conceptual capacity. As it is simply given to us, the thing in itself places no rational constraint on judgment (McDowell 1996, p. 105). The threat, then, is that "the world itself" lies beyond the space of reasons to which rational constraint belongs. What sort of interpretation supports this critique of Kant?

Kant remarks that while mere intuitions are blind, mere concepts are empty (Kant, A51/B75). McDowell reads emptiness here as the absence of thought: "[Kant] is not, absurdly, calling our attention to a special kind of thoughts, the empty ones" (McDowell 1996, p. 4). But this conflicts with what follows Kant's remark, namely, that unifying the faculties of concepts and intuitions – understanding and sensibility – is necessary, not for thought, but for "cognition". We have "great cause" to separate these faculties in thought, for their rules are set by distinct sciences: logic and aesthetic, respectively. Logic is general when it sets the "absolutely necessary rules of thinking" and transcendental when it sets "the rules of the pure thinking of an object" (Kant, A51–7/B75–82). Hence, while concepts alone yield no cognition, they are not thereby thoughtless, for they are thinkable precisely for Kant's twofold science of logic.[14] Moreover, that we must think things in themselves follows general-logically or *analytically* from the fact that appearances are of what appears, yet follows transcendental-logically or *synthetically* from reason's demand for an "entirely heterogeneous" ground for the "homogeneous" series of appearances (Kant, Bxxvi; AA 4, pp. 354–355).[15]

McDowell's disregard for Kant's distinction between thought and cognition does not just happen to coincide with his claim that the transcendental story

---

[14] Cf. Bird 1996, pp. 228, 242; Moore 2006, p. 333.
[15] On Kant's analytic and synthetic commitments to the thing in itself, see Franks 2005, pp. 43–47.

is incoherent. Rather, it results from a Cartesian misreading of that story, one that echoes Jacobi's charge that positing the thing in itself is both implausible and illegitimate.

First, McDowell says that the thing in itself "present[s] itself as no more than the independence any genuine reality must have," which implausibly renders the empirical world's independence "fraudulent" by contrast (McDowell 1996, p. 42). Yet Kant presents the thing in itself as "more than" empirical reality to the extent that it analytically explains the matter of sensation and synthetically explains the unity of appearances. Analytically, "the concept of an appearance" entails "a relation to something the immediate representation of which is, to be sure, sensible, but which in itself, without this constitution of our sensibility (on which the form of our intuition is grounded), must be something, i.e., an object independent of sensibility" (Kant, A251–252). Appearance entails given matter, whose source is the transcendental object. But mere matter does not constitute "genuine reality," which belongs exclusively to the empirical world whose form is jointly supplied by the faculties of concepts and intuitions. Synthetically, theoretical reason's "highest end" is "a totality of cognition [...] without which unity our cognition is nothing but piecework." Since appearances raise empirical questions "to infinity," only a thing in itself can secure their "highest ground" and give reason "hope to see its desire for completeness in the progression from the conditioned to its conditions satisfied for once" (Kant AA 4, pp. 350, 354).[16] The idea of the thing in itself does not defraud, but unifies, the empirical world in a way that no aggregate of cognitions can. By misreading the thing in itself as "true objectivity" and opposing it to a "disingenuous[ly]" independent world (McDowell 1996, pp. 42, 96),[17] McDowell projects onto Kant a Cartesian sense of externality and internality, misplacing the transcendental and empirical senses that make available the very insight on which he draws.

Second, McDowell claims that affection by a transcendental object is illegitimate, since "by Kant's own lights we are supposed to understand causation as something that operates within the empirical world" (McDowell 1996, p. 42). This claim, which results from conflating thought and cognition, repeats Jacobi's charge that we cannot know a transcendental object, which, as we saw, neglects the logical significance of unschematized concepts. McDowell compounds this

---

[16] Cf. Kant: "[reason] sees around itself as it were a space for the cognition of things in themselves, although it can never have determinate concepts of those things and is limited to appearances alone [...Transcendental ideas have] led us, as it were, up to the contiguity of the filled space (of experience) with empty space (of which we can know nothing – the *noumena*)" (AA 4, pp. 352, 354).

[17] Cf. Strawson 1975, p. 38.

oversight by describing Kant's transcendental story as a third-personal or "sideways-on" view of something circumscribing the space of reasons (McDowell 1996, p. 42). Grasped synthetically, however, the concept of the thing in itself denotes, not a something, but a *task*. It is a concept "to which no congruent object can be given in the senses" and thus serves as an "idea." Kant views ideas first-personally in that they are "given as problems by the nature of reason itself" (Kant, A327/B383–384).[18] The idea of the thing in itself guides our pursuit of unified cognition, a goal set, not by "objects," but by "maxims of reason for the sake of its self-satisfaction" (Kant AA 4, p. 349).[19] Such an idea is legitimate precisely as a rule for "the pure thinking of an object."

Like Jacobi, McDowell misreads the transcendental story. Yet he dares to jettison it in order to avoid a form of Spinozism. As worrisome as the coherentist picture of reason as a frictionless capacity is the "disenchanted" picture in which natural law excludes reason as a spontaneous capacity. The worry is how we are free "to take charge of our active thinking" and how our bodily movements are intentional, not "mere happenings" (McDowell 1996, pp. 70, 85, 90). Kant does not allay the worry by restricting subjectivity to the formal referent of 'I' (McDowell 1996, pp. 43, 97, 102–103, 111).[20] McDowell's response is to argue that spontaneity "belong[s] to our way of actualizing ourselves as animals," developing through a formative process of initiation into the space of reasons (McDowell 1996, pp. xx, 77–78, 84, 88, 92).[21] Ensuring that this space is boundless (so as to dissolve the above antinomy) is the idea that social formation affords us the only capacity with which and the only context in which to reflect. McDowell infers that this, the ubiquity of social formation, "leaves no genuine questions about norms, apart from those that we address in reflective thinking about specific norms, an activity that is not particularly philosophical"

---

18 Cf. Kant's distinction between assuming something relatively (*suppositio relativa*) and assuming it absolutely (*suppositio absoluta*) (A676/B704).
19 Kant's view that maxims of reason are subjectively valid presuppositions (A671/B699, A680/B708) differs crucially from Jacobi's view that reason is "a faculty of presupposing the true, the good, and the beautiful," which presuppositions have "objective validity" owing to faith, construed as a faculty "*above* reason" (1994, p. 541).
20 See di Giovanni 1998: "The 'space of reasons' must be conceived [...] not as external to the realm of nature but, on the contrary, as the function of human activities such as are exercised in the first place by real individuals in the context of real life. This is where Jacobi had sought the object of his philosophy from the very beginning – a philosophy which, for Jacobi no less than for Strawson and McDowell, had therefore to be descriptive" (p. 78).
21 Cf. Jacobi 1994: "we are all born in the faith, and we must remain in the faith, just as we are all born in society, and must remain in society" (p. 230).

(McDowell 1996, pp. 80–81, 93, 95, 98–99). This suits his preference for a sort of quietism.

The idea of formation dislodges the picture of disenchanted nature by locating spontaneity in our "natural history" (McDowell 1996, p. 95).²² On its own, however, this idea does not face the justificatory challenge to which critique is a response. What is, for Kant, "particularly philosophical" is deducing our right to the "norms" or categories of experience. Facing the question of right is required for reason's maturation: if we do not ask it, reason stalls at its "childhood" (Kant, A761/B789).²³ Moreover, if McDowell is right that "the best we achieve is always to some extent provisional and inconclusive" (McDowell 1996, p. 82),²⁴ we foreclose the justificatory task of Hegelian dialectic, which negates ever-determinate categories in order to deduce "*a system of totality*" (Hegel 2010, p. 749).²⁵ Formation may initiate us into a space of reasons in ways that Kant overlooks, but it raises the issue of the principle that grounds this space and by what right we posit it. The principal thought for an idealist who is up to Jacobi's challenge is the thought of such a principle.²⁶

---

22 Contrast Pippin 2002: "Hegel has his own way of accounting for the 'place' of [anthropological] appeals, but that way does not require any second *nature*. The plot for his narrative concerns attempts by human spirit to free itself from a self-understanding tied to nature, and these anthropological elements are understood as initial, very limited successes" (pp. 68–69).
23 See Bruno 2018.
24 McDowell notes that formation involves "a standing obligation to engage in critical reflection" on tradition (1996, p. 126, cf. 99), but this is qualified by his prohibition on questioning norms in general.
25 The *Science of Logic* concludes: "The method, which thus coils in a circle, cannot however anticipate in a temporal development that the beginning is as such already something derived; sufficient for an immediate beginning is that it be simple universality. Inasmuch as this is what it is, it has its complete condition; and there is no need to deprecate the fact that it may be accepted only *provisionally* and *hypothetically* [...] The method of truth also knows that the beginning is incomplete, because it is a beginning; but at the same time it knows that this incompleteness is necessary, because truth is but the coming-to-oneself through the negativity of immediacy" (pp. 750–72). Cf. the Preface: "*Reason* is negative and *dialectical* [...I]t negates the simple, thereby posits the determinate difference of the understanding; but it equally dissolves this difference, and so it is dialectical. But spirit does not stay at the nothing of this result but is in it rather equally positive, and thereby restores the first simplicity, but as universal, such as it is concrete in itself [...] On this self-constructing path alone, I say, is philosophy capable of being objective, demonstrative science [...T]his culture and discipline of thought by which the latter acquires plasticity and overcomes the impatience of incidental reflection is procured solely by pressing onward, by study, and by carrying out to its conclusion the entire development" (pp. 10, 21).
26 See Bruno (forthcoming).

A Hegelian thought ostensibly sounds in McDowell's call to unify "reason and nature," but it is stifled by his claim that philosophical questions are unanswerable if their terms arise from antinomous theses. Dissolving such questions, he says, is the only "hard" or "constructive" work philosophy can do (McDowell 1996, pp. xxiii-iv, 108). But harder work is needed to realize Hegel's image of boundless conceptuality. Indeed, this image is more "threatening to commonsense" than McDowell suggests (McDowell 1996, p. 83). As Hegel says in the *Phenomenology of Spirit*:

> [T]he familiar, just because it is familiar, is not cognitively understood. The commonest way in which we deceive either ourselves or others about understanding is by assuming something as familiar, and accepting it on that account; with all its pros and cons, such knowing never gets anywhere, and it knows not why. Subject and object, God, nature, understanding, sensibility, and so on, are uncritically taken for granted as familiar, established as valid, and made into fixed points for starting and stopping. (Hegel 1977, p. 18)

On pain of deceiving "ourselves or others," there must, *contra* McDowell, be genuine questions about norms. In light of this, Hegel expands Kant's view of rational maturation, and in disquieting fashion: "[t]he onset of the new spirit is the product of a widespread upheaval in various forms of culture, the prize at the end of a complicated, tortuous path and of just as variegated and strenuous an effort" (Hegel 1977, p. 7). At the heart of German idealism is the justificatory work of deduction.[27] After all, beyond a mere tribunal of experience, there must be "a court of justice, by which reason may secure its rightful claims while dismissing all its groundless pretensions," which court is "none other than the critique of pure reason itself" (Kant, Axi-ii).

To be sure, in denying that we can restrict "the self-scrutiny of reason," McDowell echoes the German idealist aim of removing limits on reason's capacity to justify its claims, especially limits that Kant installs by denying cognitive access to a principle that grounds our forms of intuition and judgment (McDowell 1996, p. 52; Kant, B145–6, A680/B708).[28] Objecting that the transcendental story restricts our ability to "take charge of our lives" (McDowell 1996, p. 43) is, we saw, a misguided response to our inability to think up sensible matter. But when McDowell reprises his plea for "the unlimited freedom of reason" in "He-

---

[27] See Rödl 2007 on how the *Critique of Pure Reason* becomes the *Science of Logic* through a conversion of the Analytic of Concepts, the Analytic of Principles, and the Transcendental Dialectic into a single deduction of pure concepts, and why this conversion is more complex than the position defended in *Mind and World*. Cf. Gardner 2013, pp. 135–136.
[28] Cf. Strawson 1975, pp. 79–81. For an account of Fichte and Hegel's dissatisfaction with Kantian deduction, see Bruno 2018a.

gel's Idealism as Radicalization of Kant," he shifts to the objection that Kant posits forms of intuition as a "brute fact about us" that "remains outside" reason's deductive capacity (McDowell 2009, pp. 76, 79, 85).[29] We will see that his quietism skirts the hard work of deducing space and time.

The B-Deduction avoids the threat that space and time are conditions of experience that do not bear categorial unity, and that therefore render this unity a "subjective imposition" onto sensibility, by showing that combining a sensible manifold is unintelligible without intellectual activity. Intuition presents an object to thought only if it bears categorial unity (McDowell 2009, pp. 73–75).[30] The deduction avoids the threat of subjective imposition, McDowell says, but remains saddled with the "brute-fact externality" of space and time, for Kant argues that they are forms of intuition yet sees no reason why they are *ours:* they are imposed by our peculiarly human sensibility and so we cannot be said to have any right to them. By conceding brute facts, Kant's deduction limits reason's freedom (McDowell 2009, pp. 76–77, 86).

McDowell's response to Kant is to replace transcendental idealism with Hegel's consistent – what he now calls "authentic" – idealism, according to which space and time derive from "the sphere of free intellectual activity." He adds that only this can ensure "commonsense realism about objective reality" (McDowell 2009, pp. 75, 80–81). But McDowell remains at odds with Hegel, for while he says that we must "eliminate the externality that vitiates Kant's Deduction," he prefers a "simple" path to the position to which Hegel's own path is "more complex" (McDowell 2009, p. 89). Complexity, of course, is the necessary positive work of dialectic, which quietism shuns. And, as we saw, commonsense is one of the external, i.e., self-alienated aspects of thought that Hegel sublates. Thus, by foregoing Hegel's deductive argument for the unboundedness of the conceptual, McDowell stalls on his path to consistent idealism.

Perhaps "successful critical idealism would have to be speculative in a Hegelian sense" (McDowell 2009, p. 79). But if we forgo the "tortuous path" to this end, we pass over Jacobi's dare in silence. In that case, a transcendental idealist is free to prove that categorial unity is not a subjective imposition and, furthermore, to make a case for acceptable – because insuperable – brute facts of experience.

---

29 McDowell's new objection hints at the old by charging that transcendental idealism, by making the form of objectivity "a mere reflection of a fact about us," "degenerates into subjective idealism" (2009, pp. 78, 83). Cf. Strawson 1975, pp. 22, 35, 91.
30 Cf. Rödl 2007.

To be sure, although Jacobi's critique of idealism prefigures a McDowellian attack on frictionless belief,[31] he indulges mythical givenness in denying that sensibility is conceptual in its use: "as a realist I am forced to say that all knowledge derives exclusively from faith, for *things* must be *given* to me before I am in a position to enquire about relations" (Jacobi 1994, p. 256). But if McDowell has any advantage over faith, it is diminished by his quietistic response to Jacobi's dare.

3

The fate of reason after Kant involves, for many post-Kantians, the exclusion of absolute being, i.e., of a world outside possible experience. Meillassoux traces this fate to the turn from the pre-Kantian commitment to the "real necessity" of the existence of an entity such as God (Meillassoux 2008, p. 32) to the Kantian rejection of this commitment as dogmatic. Kant replaces this necessity with an account of what we may call the anthropic necessity of the conditions of possible experience. Critique secures these conditions against the "groundless pretensions" that render metaphysics "complete anarchy" (Kant, Aix). In this, it serves the task of "self-knowledge", i.e., knowledge of the nature and bounds of our understanding (Kant, Axi). For Meillassoux, by substituting anthropic for real necessity, we overcome metaphysical anarchy at the cost of subjectivizing ontology. In particular, by restricting necessity to conditions of experience, Kant neglects the alternative, which Meillassoux defends, that contingency itself is necessary, i.e., that everything is *"capable of actually becoming otherwise without reason"* (Meillassoux 2008, p. 53). If contingency is "an absolute ontological property, and not the mark of the finitude of our knowledge" (Meillassoux 2008, p. 53), then we can speak of necessity while avoiding both metaphysical anarchy and subjective ontology. Only then can we pursue *"intellectual intuition of the absolute"* (Meillassoux 2008, p. 82).

According to Meillassoux, we neglect the necessity of contingency if we confine understanding to the correlation between thought and being. Correlationism posits an insuperable bond between thought and being that renders absolute being unknowable. This, for Meillassoux, is the "exacerbated consequence" of the "Kantian catastrophe" of interpreting "scientific objectivity" in terms of "*intersubjectivity*," according to which an objective judgment is of an experience that is possible for any judger and is therefore valid for any judger (Meillassoux

---

[31] See Bowie 1996.

2008, pp. 4, 124). By proscribing knowledge of "the uncorrelated" object, correlationism violates the scientific spirit (Meillassoux 2008, pp. 4, 8, 13, 16, 28, 124). According to Meillassoux, scientific statements about events prior to our species purport to refer to "ancestral" reality, which is *"anterior to every form of human relation"* (Meillassoux 2008, pp. 10, 15, 20). In other words, they purport to refer to transcendental reality. Thus, when we hear that ancestral statements have "a realist sense" or "no sense at all," we see that, like Jacobi, Meillassoux presupposes that knowable reality is transcendental. And, like Jacobi, his challenge to the transcendental idealist who initiates correlationism is a taunt: "the consistent correlationist should stop being modest and dare to assert openly that she is in a position to provide the scientist with an *a priori* demonstration that the latter's ancestral statements are *illusory*" (Meillassoux 2008, p. 17). Does Kant undermine scientific objectivity?

Following a long tradition, Meillassoux projects a Cartesian conception of internality and externality onto transcendental idealism. Kant's empirical externality, he says, is "a cloistered outside" in that it is "relative to us." We may know appearances, but we have "lost the *great outdoors*, the *absolute* outside of pre-critical thinkers" (Meillassoux 2008, p. 7). Meillassoux mourns the death of a God's-eye view, lamenting that empirical externality confines us to a mental space that excludes, and affords no inference to, absolute being. As we saw, Kant employs both transcendental and empirical senses of internality and externality: space is in us without empirical objects being mental; and we can think, but cannot think up, transcendental objects. Empirical reality is "cloistered" only if it is conflated with mental contents, as on a Cartesian picture.[32] Meillassoux's projection leads him mistakenly to assert that, for Kant, empirical objects exist only if subjects do and thereby to assert, without reference to either the Refutation of Idealism or the *Prolegomena*, that Kant's position is indistinguishable from Berkeley's (Meillassoux 2008, pp. 28–29, 122).[33] Preoccupied by Kant's conclusion that we can only know appearances, Meillassoux neglects his motivating problem, which is the question, not whether what appears is real, but how anything can appear at all. Kant's concern is not whether appearances are dreams, but how appearances "belong" to an experiential standpoint, without which they would be "less than a dream" (Kant, A112).[34]

Meillassoux aims to "reactivate the Cartesian thesis" that we can know "properties of the in-itself" (Meillassoux 2008, p. 3). But his rejection of tran-

---

[32] See Ameriks 2015.
[33] See Bruno 2017.
[34] See Conant 2004.

scendental idealism circularly posits that knowable reality is transcendental. The first premise of his "argument from the arche-fossil" is that ancestrality denotes an event *"anterior to givenness itself"* (Meillassoux 2008, p. 20). If ancestral statements refer to reality independent of *"every form of human relation,"* including givenness in possible experience, and if they are true, then transcendental realism is true. But this is to say that transcendental idealism is false, which is no premise in a convincing argument to that conclusion.[35] In begging the question against Kant, Meillassoux fails to show that ancestral statements differ in kind from statements about the present. And he cannot show this: the former are as bound as the latter to possible experience.[36]

Jacobi and Kant each aim to reverse a form of self-alienation. When Meillassoux urges us *"to get out of ourselves, to grasp the in-itself"* (Meillassoux 2008, p. 27), he demands what we might call a *salto immortale*, indulging self-alienation of the sort that Kant diagnoses in the Amphiboly:

> If the complaints 'That we have no insight into the inner in things' are to mean that we do not understand through pure reason what the things that appear to us might be in themselves, then they are entirely improper and irrational; for they would have us be able to cognize things, thus intuit them, even without senses, consequently they would have it that we have a faculty of cognition entirely distinct from the human not merely in degree but even in intuition and kind. (Kant A277–8/B333–4)

Meillassoux's wish for insight into what is "neither visible nor perceptible in things" (Meillassoux 2008, p. 82) is "improper and irrational," for it renounces the human faculty on whose behalf Kant redresses an abiding estrangement.[37]

4

Certain Kantian claims can tempt a Cartesian framing. So, too, can the impression that transcendental idealism is a doctrine about the mind. I want to suggest that Kant's idealism is usefully interpreted as a doctrine about the modality of

---

[35] See Bruno 2018b.
[36] Cf. Zahavi 2018 on neuroscience's privileging of knowledge of the brain.
[37] Cf. Cavell 1979: "In Wittgenstein's view the gap between mind and the world is closed, or the distortion between them straightened, in the appreciation and acceptance of particular human forms of life, human 'convention'. This implies that the *sense* of gap originates in an attempt, or wish, to escape (to remain a 'stranger' to, 'alienated' from) those shared forms of life, to give up the responsibility of their maintenance [...Wittgenstein] never, I think, underestimated the power of the motive to reject the human: nothing could be more human" (pp. 109, 207).

the conditions of objectivity. For Kant, it is crucial to determine which logic is appropriate for securing these conditions. General logic, we saw, abstracts from all content to the "mere form of thinking." It permits any non-contradictory claim, including speculative claims that outstrip experience and set reason adrift (Kant, A4/B8, A54/B78; cf. B19, B24). To forge a rigorous path, transcendental logic delimits the "form of a possible experience," i.e., the universal and necessary conditions whereby judgment subsumes an object under a concept (Kant, A246–8/B303–5). Since general logic requires merely that thought not contradict itself, it can only explain analytic judgment. Accordingly,

> the possibility of synthetic judgments is a problem with which general logic has nothing to do, indeed whose name it need not even know. But in a transcendental logic it is the most important business of all, and indeed the only business if the issue is the possibility of synthetic *a priori* judgments and likewise the conditions and the domain of their validity. (Kant, A154/B193)

Analytic judgment, which cannot amplify cognition, and synthetic *a posteriori* judgment, which affords neither universality nor necessity, raise the "real problem of pure reason," namely, the possibility of universal and necessary yet ampliative judgment, i.e., synthetic *a priori* judgment (Kant, B19).[38] Transcendental logic solves this problem by determining the conditions of possible experience.

Crucially, such conditions are contingent in that they do not follow from the mere form of thinking, yet necessary in that they constitute the form of experience. In other words, their necessity is not general-logical, but their contingency is not empirical. The unique modality of conditions of objectivity qualifies them as factical.[39] They are brute facts about our orbit in logical space. Facticity abounds in Kant's thought: our forms of intuition are "peculiar to us;" their origin is a "mystery;" it is a "peculiarity of our understanding" that it has the forms of judgment and categories that it does; the common root of sensibility and understanding is "unknown;" and reason's "peculiar fate" is to pose unanswerable questions (Kant, Avii, A15/B29, A35/B51, B145, A268/B324, A278/B334).

---

38 Synthetic judgment thus cannot be governed only by the principle of contradiction, but must also be governed by the "supreme principle of all synthetic judgments," which states that any object presupposes the necessary conditions of the unity of the manifold of intuition in a possible experience (Kant, A158/B197; cf. AA 4, pp. 267, 269; AA 8, p. 193).
39 While this definition of facticity differs from Meillassoux's, he does attribute the former to Kant (2008, p. 38). Yet his thought is incomplete: he includes space and time, but does not specify why they are factical; he omits the ideas of reason; and he includes the categories, but falsely denies that they are deducible.

Conditions of objectivity, in virtue of their facticity, are susceptible neither to rational doubt nor to rational grounding. They arguably avoid Cartesian and Humean skepticism insofar as they are necessary for possible experience, but they derive from no absolute first principle. By securing conditions with this modal character, transcendental logic supplants a logic incapable of resolving the antinomous accounts of objectivity that proliferate when reason restricts itself to analytic and synthetic *a posteriori* judgment. Not only does transcendental logic thereby transform reasoning from a Humean fork to a Kantian trident: assuming we eschew Cartesian projections, it affords a path between Jacobian faith and what Jacobi advertises as egoism.[40]

Bibliography

Ameriks, Karl (2015): "On Reconciling the Transcendental Turn with Kant's Idealism." In: Sebastian Gardner/Matthew Grist (Eds.). *The Transcendental Turn*. Oxford: Oxford University Press, pp. 35–55.

Bird, Graham (1996): "McDowell's Kant: Mind and World." In: *Philosophy* 71, No. 276, pp. 219–243.

Bowie, Andrew (1996): "John McDowell's *Mind and World* and Early Romantic Epistemology." In: *Revue Internationale de Philosophie* 50, No. 197, pp. 515–554.

Bruno, G. Anthony (2017): "Empirical Realism and the Great Outdoors: A Critique of Meillassoux." In: Marie-Eve Morin (Ed.): *Continental Realism and its Discontents*. Edinburgh: Edinburgh University Press, pp. 1–15.

Bruno, G. Anthony (2018): "Skepticism, Deduction, and Reason's Maturation." In: G. Anthony Bruno/A. C. Rutherford (Eds.): *Skepticism: Historical and Contemporary Inquiries*. London: Routledge, pp. 203–220.

Bruno, G. Anthony (2018a): "Genealogy and Jurisprudence in Fichte's Genetic Deduction of the Categories." In: *History of Philosophy Quarterly* 35. No. 1, pp. 77–96.

Bruno, G. Anthony (2018b). "Meillassoux, Correlationism, and the Ontological Difference." In: *PhaenEx* 12. No. 2, pp. 1–12.

Bruno, G. Anthony (forthcoming): "The Thought of a Principle: Rödl's Fichteanism." In: Marina Bykova (Ed.): *The Bloomsbury Companion to Fichte*. New York: Bloomsbury.

Cavell, Stanley (1979): *The Claim of Reason: Wittgenstein, Skepticism, Morality and Tragedy*. Oxford: Oxford University Press.

Conant, James (2004): "Varieties of Skepticism." In: Denis McManus (Ed.): *Wittgenstein and Skepticism*. London: Routledge, pp. 97–136.

Crowe, Benjamin (2009): "F.H. Jacobi on Faith, or What It Takes to Be an Irrationalist." In: *Religious Studies* 45. No. 3, pp. 309–324.

Di Giovanni, George (1998): "The Jacobi-Fichte-Reinhold Dialogue and Analytical Philosophy." In: *Fichte-Studien* 14, pp. 63–86.

---

40 Thanks to the editors, Tom Krell, and Clinton Tolley for helpful comments on this chapter.

Fichte, Johann G. (1988): *Early Philosophical Writings*. Translated by D. Breazeale. Ithaca: Cornell University Press.
Fichte, Johann G. (1994): *Introductions to the Wissenschaftslehre and Other Writings*. Translated by D. Breazeale. Indianapolis: Hackett.
Fichte, Johann G. (2000): *Foundations of Natural Right*. Translated by M. Bauer. Cambridge: Cambridge University Press.
Franks, Paul (2005): *All or Nothing: Systematicity, Transcendental Arguments, and Skepticism in German Idealism*. Cambridge, Mass.: Harvard University Press.
Gardner, Sebastian (2013): "Transcendental Philosophy and the Possibility of the Given." In: Joseph K. Schear (Ed.): *Mind, Reason, and Being-In-The-World: The McDowell-Dreyfus Debate*. London: Routledge, pp. 110–142.
Hegel, Georg W.F. (1977): *Phenomenology of Spirit*. Translated by A.V. Miller. Oxford: Oxford University Press.
Hegel, Georg W.F. (1991): *The Encyclopedia Logic (with the Zusätze)*. Translated by T.F. Geraets, W.A. Suchting, and H.S. Harris. Indianapolis: Hackett.
Jacobi, Friedrich H. (1994): *Main Philosophical Writings and the Novel Alwill*. Translated by G. di Giovanni. Montreal: McGill-Queen's University Press.
Kant, Immanuel (1900): *Kants gesammelte Schriften* (cited as AA, except for the *Critique of Pure Reason*, cited in the A/B pagination of the 1781/1787 editions). Berlin: de Gruyter.
Kant, Immanuel (1998): *Critique of Pure Reason*. Translated by P. Guyer and A.W. Wood. Cambridge: Cambridge University Press.
Kant, Immanuel (1999): *Critique of Practical Reason*. In *Practical Philosophy*. Edited by M.J. Gregor. Cambridge: Cambridge University Press.
Kant, Immanuel (2002): *Prolegomena to Any Future Metaphysics. Theoretical Philosophy After 1781*. Edited by H. Allison and P. Heath. Cambridge: Cambridge University Press.
Meillassoux, Quentin (2008): *After Finitude: An Essay on the Necessity of Contingency*. Translated by R. Brassier. New York: Continuum.
McDowell, John (1996): *Mind and World*. Cambridge, Mass.: Harvard University Press.
McDowell, John (2009): "Hegel's Idealism as Radicalization of Kant." In: *Having the World in View*. Cambridge, Mass.: Harvard University Press, pp. 69–89.
Moore, A.W. (2006): "The Bounds of Sense." In: *Philosophical Topics* 34. No. 1/2, pp. 327–344.
Pippin, Robert (2002): "Leaving Nature Behind: or Two Cheers for 'Subjectivism.'" In: Nicolas Smith (Ed.): *Reading McDowell: On Mind and World*. London: Routledge, pp. 58–76.
Rödl, Sebastian (2007): "Eliminating Externality." In: *International Yearbook of German Idealism* 5, pp. 176–188.
Stang, Nicholas F. (2015): "Who's Afraid of Double Affection?" In: *Philosopher's Imprint* 15. No. 18, pp. 1–28.
Strawson, Peter F. (1975): *The Bounds of Sense*. London: Routledge.
Zahavi, Dan (2018): "Brain, Mind, World: Predictive Coding, Neo-Kantianism, and Transcendental Idealism." In: *Husserl Studies* 34. No. 1, pp. 47–61.

Andrea Kern
How Not to Be a Naïve Realist: On Knowledge and Perception

Abstract: This paper challenges the assumption, widely taken for granted, that the nature of perception can be investigated independently of the question whether it does or does not figure in the self-consciousness of the perceiver. Kern argues that the main obstacle that hinders us in understanding the idea of an intrinsically self-conscious capacity for perception, which enables its bearer to know how things are, is based on the false premise that perception and judgment are two distinguishable capacities. By contrast, Kern argues that the perceptions of a being that is able to judge are not exercises of a capacity that is more primitive than its capacity for judgment, but rather a specific manner of its exercise. The two-capacity view is taken for granted by almost everybody in the debate about perceptual knowledge, including John McDowell, whose conception of perceptual knowledge gives us the most sophisticated and complex account of the relation between perception and judgment. Kern argues that the two-capacity view, as such, is confused. Perceiving how things are is a distinctive manner of making judgments about them. Perceptions, as such, equip their bearer with genuine knowledge of the world. Perception is, on this view, a fundamental cognitive capacity of the human mind to acquire knowledge of how things are.

1

"Naïve Realism" is the view that perception provides direct access to objects that are as they are independently of their perception as being thus-and-so. Since this understanding of perception is taken to be identical to its self-understanding by many or most beings who have an understanding of their perceptions, in that many or most of them think of themselves as able to know directly how things are in the world by perceiving them, this view is also sometimes called "Common Sense Realism." The idea is that many or most beings who can think about their perceptions think of themselves as being in possession of perceptual capacities whose exercise consists in a consciousness of objects that are as they are independently of their perception of them as being thus-and-so. According to this picture, "Naïve Realism" is taken to be:

(1) a theory about perception – a theory about what perception is, at which the philosopher arrives through an investigation of what it is.

(2) a theory that – for whatever reasons – accords with the theory that many or most people have of perception who are not only in possession of the capacity for perception but also, additionally, able to have a theory about it.

This manner of approaching the topic, as a theory which construes what something is – something that can either be in accordance, or not, with the theory of those who possess the very property that is the object of this theory – characterizes many positions that label themselves as realism, naïve or not, as well as many positions that label themselves as idealism, naïve or not. What defines this manner of approaching the topic is that it presupposes, right from the start, that its topic – perception – is a kind of thing whose nature, i.e. what it is and what role it plays in the life of those who possess it, is independent of, and therefore can be studied independently of, the question of whether the subject of this capacity is able to think about her perceptions and hence relates to her perceptions in a self-conscious manner. According to this manner of approaching the topic, the fact that the beings whose perceptions are under investigation are not only perceivers, but also self-conscious thinkers who are able to think about what they perceive and acquire knowledge through it, is treated, right from the start, as an aspect of the topic that is external to its very nature. Before any theorizing about what perception is begins, according to this approach, before any question gets started about how perception is related to the world and how perception provides us access to the world, this much theory about perception is already taken for granted: that perception is something whose nature can be investigated independently of the question of whether the subject whose perception is under investigation is self-consciously related to it and conceives of it as a source of knowledge or not. The idea that there is such a thing as "Common Sense Realism" and the idea that some philosophical positions such as "Naïve Realism" might be an expression of it, whereas others are not, presupposes a thought along these lines.

This assumption, however, is not innocuous. It is not, because it excludes, right from the start, the idea that the capacity for perception could be an intrinsic element of the self-consciousness of a being without which she would not be the kind of being that she is. In what follows, I will call the idea of such a capacity for perception the idea of a capacity for perception *from self-consciousness*. The above assumption is a denial of the idea that perception could be an *intrinsically* self-conscious capacity for knowledge.

In what follows I will discuss the difficulty that one is confronted with when one wants to give up the above assumption. I will unfold this difficulty by discussing John McDowell's various attempts to defend the idea of perception as an intrinsically self-conscious capacity for knowledge in the light of a dilemma that this position is confronted with. I will bring out the Kantian roots of this conception of empirical knowledge and argue that any broadly Kantian epistemology is confronted with the same dilemma. Reflection upon this dilemma will help us to identify the obstacle that hinders us in giving up the above assumption. The obstacle that hinders us in understanding the idea of perception as an intrinsically self-conscious capacity for knowledge, I will argue, is a thought that is taken for granted by almost everybody in the debate about perceptual knowledge, but which is confused. It is the thought that the relation between perception and judgment is a relation between two distinguishable capacities. I will call this the two-capacity view. This thought seems to be so obviously true that it is not even considered to be questionable. This is because, after all, perceiving that p and judging that p cannot be the same, given that one can judge that p without perceiving that p. How, then, can there not be two distinguishable capacities? I will argue that the two-capacity-view rests upon a conception of judging that abstracts from the very idea of a capacity and hence from the idea of something that could so much as be related to another capacity. Once we see the incoherence of this conception of judging we will be able to understand the capacity for perception as an intrinsically self-conscious capacity whose exercise, if things go well, equips its bearer with perceptual knowledge of the world. There is thus a truth in "Naïve Realism," which is that the capacity for perception, as such, provides knowledge of objects around us. Yet the Naïve Realist misunderstands this truth, I will argue, because he does not understand it as a truth that articulates what perception is for a self-conscious thinker for whom perceiving is not a more primitive activity than judging, but a specific manner of exercising it.

2

To understand the possibility of judgment and *a fortiori* of perceptual knowledge, John McDowell has argued, we must think of a concept-possessing being as having a capacity for perception that is actualized in forms of sensible awareness of objects in which objects are *revealed* to her as they are. We must understand a concept-possessing being as having a capacity for perception whose actualizations, as such, reveal to her how things are in the world around her. A concept-possessing being actualizes her sensibility in acts of perceptual awareness whose content has conceptuality as its form. He writes: "(W)hen we enjoy experience conceptual capacities are drawn on *in* receptivity" (McDowell 1996, p. 10).

When McDowell claims that the content of perception already contains an actualization of conceptual capacities, this must be seen in light of the attempt to say what perception is *for those* who are able to ascribe perceptions to themselves. Thus the claim that "experiences already have conceptual content" (McDowell 1996, p. 10) is not meant to be part of a theory about something – a kind of act or episode called "perception" – that is as it is, independently of whether the subject herself, to which these acts or episodes are ascribed, can ascribe them to herself. Rather, it is meant to be a claim about what perception is for those who can think of themselves as the bearer of such acts. It is meant to be a claim about perception *from within self-consciousness*. A subject who perceives something in this sense could not be said to have perceptions in this sense if she herself were not able to think of herself as the bearer of perceptions.

Now, it matters that one reads this manner of fixing the topic of the theory in the right way. It is not supposed to restrict the scope of the validity of the theory, as it would if it were a theory of perception that claimed validity only for some perceptual acts, namely the so-called self-conscious perceptions, but not for the whole spectrum of perceptions, including the non-self-conscious ones. If one thinks of it in this way, then one must presuppose that it is possible to disentangle the question of what perception is from the question of the nature of its subject and its relation to perception. When McDowell fixes his topic by saying that the concept of perception and knowledge that he attempts to unfold is the concept of self-conscious perception and knowledge, his point is to deny that the question of what perception is can be disentangled from the question of the nature of the subject in whose life perception figures.

3

When one fixes one's topic in this manner, one denies that, applied to a concept-possessing being, the meaning of the concept of perception is the same as it would be applied to a being that does not possess conceptual capacities. Rather, the suggestion is that, in application to a being that possesses conceptual capacities, the meaning of the concept of perception is dependent upon the self-consciousness that such a being manifests when she judges about what she perceives. According to McDowell, therefore, our investigation of what perception is must take the form of an investigation of the self-consciousness of a perceiver who judges about what she perceives. It must take the form of an investigation of the self-consciousness that one has qua being able to think and to judge about what one perceives.

It might be helpful to rephrase McDowell's way of approaching the topic in a manner that brings out the Kantian spirit of his investigation: what are the conditions of the possibility of thoughts that purport to be about objects of perceptual experience? Kant argues that the conditions of the possibility of such thoughts are perceptions that have the form of the "I think." Kant expresses this claim at the beginning of §16 of the *Critique of Pure Reason* where he famously writes that the "I think" must be able to accompany "all my representations," for "otherwise," as he tells us there, "something would be represented in me which could not be thought at all, and that is equivalent to saying that the representation would be impossible, or at least would be nothing to me" (Kant 1965, B 131–132). Representations of a being that can think about what she represents, Kant wants to say, have the form of the "I think." "All the manifold of intuition has," Kant concludes, "a necessary relation to the 'I think' in the same subject in which this manifold is found" (Kant 1965, B 132). Thus there is no representation of an object in the world which purports to be about an object of perceptual experience that is not based on a perceptual experience united to a unity of thoughts which is, by being thus united, conscious of itself. As Kant summarizes his argument:

> For the manifold representations, which are given in an intuition, would not be one and all *my* representations, if they did not belong to one self-consciousness. As *my* representations (even if I am not conscious of them as such) they must conform to the condition under which alone they *can* stand together in one universal consciousness, because otherwise they would not all without exception belong to me. (Kant 1965, B 132f.)

For thoughts that purport to be about objects of perceptual experience to be possible, Kant tells us, the form of the perceptual experiences on which these thoughts are based must be the "I think." McDowell's account of perception and perceptual knowledge is meant to be a response to the Kantian question that deepens, in a certain sense, the Kantian understanding of perceptual experience. The condition of the possibility of thoughts that purport to be about objects of perceptual experience, McDowell argues, is the possession of conceptual capacities that are operative in a being's capacity for perception on account of which facts can be *revealed* to her in an act of perception whose conceptual content is, as such, dependent upon things being the way she judges them to be on its basis (McDowell 1996, p. 34). The reason for this "revealing" character of perception is that having perceptions in this sense means being in a state of consciousness whose conceptual content *depends* on things being the way one would come to judge them to be on its basis. It means being in a state of consciousness that provides one with a *ground* for judging that things are thus-and-so in a sense that establishes the truth of one's judgment about how things are. Having such a ground means having a ground for judging that represents the judgment justified on that ground as an act of *knowledge*. Thus the condition of the possibility of thoughts that purport to be about objects of perceptual experience is a state of consciousness that provides a ground for judging that p, that explains a case of perceptual knowledge.

This gives us the following account of perception and its relation to judgment and perceptual knowledge:

a. Perceptions are *grounds* for judgments.
b. Perceptions are grounds for judgments that *depend* on the truth of the judgments based on them.
c. Someone who judges on the basis of a perception that things are thus-and-so thereby *knows* that things are thus-and-so.
d. Perceptions are knowledge-enabling by providing grounds for judgments that establish the truth of the judgment.

A perceiver who can think and judge about what she perceives, is, according to this account, equipped with perceptions of objects whose conceptual content provides her a ground for judging that things are thus-and-so. Since these perceptual grounds are such that they establish the truth of her judgment, a perceiver who can think and judge about what she perceives is, as such, equipped with perceptual knowledge of the world.

4

For a rational being, McDowell wants to say, perception is a capacity that belongs to her self-consciousness. From within the self-consciousness of a being that has the capacity for judging that things are thus-and-so, the concept of perception describes a capacity whose successful exercise provides its bearer a ground, or puts her "in a position," as McDowell wants to say, to ascribe to herself an act of perceptual knowledge.[1] Any other conception of perception, which construes perception as something other than a capacity for episodes that are grounds for perceptual knowledge, according to McDowell, is not a conception

---

[1] See, for McDowell's employment of the locution of "being in a position to know" as a position that is distinguished from and prior to actually knowing, *inter alia*, McDowell 1998a, p. 390 (fn. 37); see also McDowell 1998b, p. 411.

which anyone who is able to judge about how things are can coherently entertain.

It has been argued, among others by Barry Stroud, that this conception of perceptual knowledge faces a dilemma (see Stroud 2002). The dilemma turns on the question of how to understand the idea of perception which is supposed to be a ground for knowledge. The idea of perception, according to the objection, can be understood in two different ways depending on how we construe the content of perception. The idea of perception can describe either an epistemic act of consciousness whose content is a fact, or it can describe a non-epistemic act of consciousness whose content is not a fact, but an object. Whereas the former episode entails that one has knowledge of the fact which is the content of one's consciousness, the latter does not.[2] The question is, which idea of perception is meant to describe the act or episode that is supposed to be a ground for knowledge? If a perceptual ground is meant to be an epistemic perception, then one's having a perception in this sense entails that one judges that things are thus-and-so. However, if one's perception already entails that one judges about how things are, then perception cannot be conceived as a ground for judgment and hence cannot be conceived as a ground for knowledge. Perception in this sense cannot be said to be an act (or state or episode) on the basis of which the judgment is formed, and hence explained through it, because it already entails the judgment. By contrast, if a perceptual ground is meant to be a non-epistemic perception, then one can say that there are perceptions that do not entail judging that things are thus-and-so. However, then the only way to think of the relation between perception and knowledge as a relation of "grounding," Stroud argues, is in terms of an "inference or transition from something else one perceives or knows to be so" (Stroud 2015, p. 393). And this would undermine the very idea that McDowell wants to establish, namely that perception is a *ground* for knowledge that, as such, explains one's knowledge of how things are.[3]

---

[2] See, for Stroud's employment of the distinction between epistemic and non-epistemic perceptions: Stroud 2015, p. 392ff. The following discussion of the idea of a perceptual ground partly expands on material that I have developed more abstractly in a related paper whose focus is a discussion and diagnosis of the debate between so-called minimal empiricism and rationalism. See my "The Capacity to Know and Perception" (Kern 2019).

[3] The distinction between object perception and fact perception, as Stroud and others think that we must employ it to fully understand human perception, must not be confused with a related, but significantly different question about whether perceptual verbs have an intentional sense or not, or whether perception is an intentional phenomenon at all. Since the latter question can only be raised with respect to the idea of object perception, it must already presuppose the above distinction and a certain manner of understanding it. For this debate see, among others, Marie McGinn (2015), Charles Travis (2004), Elizabeth Anscombe (1981), John Austin (1962).

The only way out of this dilemma, according to Stroud, is to deny the idea that perceptual knowledge is grounded in anything at all. Perception, he thinks, is a mere condition for the capacity for judgment to be exercised, not a capacity that delivers episodes that are grounds for perceptual knowledge.

5

As is well known, McDowell has come to grant a point to the objection. He has given up the view that perception has (or must have) the same propositional content as the judgment based on it. But he holds onto the view that the content of perception, qua perception, is conceptual in that so-called formal concepts are operative within it (McDowell 2009, p. 261). By the notion of formal concepts he means concepts whose role it is to synthesize the sensible manifold into the unity of an object of a certain kind that can be conceptually determined (ibid., p 265). Qua being perceived, the object is not yet conceived through any material concept that would determine the object to be a this-such rather than a that-such. It is the business of the judgment, then, to determine the object that is perceptually given to me as a unity of a certain kind, through material concepts.

The modified conception wants to state that perception is a manner of being consciously related to objects: objects which fall short of the "I think," but are, qua being unified into objects of perception, able *to be taken up* by the "I think." The objects of perception, qua being perceived, are thinkables, without as yet being determinately thought. He writes:

> An object is present to a subject in an intuition whether or not the "I think" accompanies any of the intuition's content. But any of the content of an intuition must be able to be accompanied by the "I think." And for the "I think" to accompany some of the content of an intuition, say a visual intuition, of mine is to *judge* that I am visually confronted by an object with such-and-such features. Since the intuition makes the object visually present to me through these features, such a judgment would be knowledgeable. (ibid., p. 266)

McDowell thinks that this modification makes his conception of perception no longer vulnerable to the dilemma stated above. He thinks that this gives him room to hold onto the idea of a grounding-relation in the case of perceptual knowledge without construing perceptual knowledge as an instance of inferential knowledge. But this is not true. For the consequence of the modified conception is that perceptual knowledge that things are thus-and-so is now construed as a unity not of two acts with the same conceptual content, but as a *unity of two acts* whose contents differ in terms of determinacy. That things are thus-and-so is not, according to the modified conception, what she perceives qua perceiving it, since what she perceives qua perceiving it is not articulated by material concepts. The content of the perception qua perception cannot be expressed in a sentence of the form "this is a yellow goldfinch" or "this is a black sparrow," as the judgment, by contrast, can be.

However, if the act of perception that is supposed to ground the judgment has no materially articulated conceptual content in virtue of which the perceiver, qua perceiving what she perceives, can distinguish her perception of a yellow goldfinch from a perception of a black sparrow, then one can no longer hold onto the view that a judgment is based on perception in a justificatory sense. The sense in which perception *enables* judgment is no longer identical with the idea of justification – it does not enable it in the sense of *justifying* it, as it was supposed to do in the former conception. According to the modified version, I cannot tell from what I see that it is true to judge that there is a black sparrow in front of me instead of, say, a yellow goldfinch.

The point of the modified conception is to say that the object of perception is the same as the object that she judges to be thus-and-so on its basis, although it is given to her in a different manner. It is given to her as something that can be judged in a conceptually articulated manner, but is not judged to be thus-and-so. But whether that which *can* be judged in a conceptually articulated manner actually *is* thus-and-so or otherwise is a question that perception, as such, cannot answer. Perception, as such, no longer reveals to us how things are. Thus the modified conception just seems to confirm the point of the above objection: that it is impossible to escape the above dilemma without giving up the idea of a grounding relation between perception and judgment.

6

According to Stroud, the above dilemma reflects a general difficulty that any account of perceptual knowledge has to face which attempts to understand the possibility of perceptual knowledge on the basis of a state of perceptual awareness that is anything less than perceptual knowledge of how things are. The idea that such an understanding is possible, he argues, is an illusion. He calls the idea of such a basis the idea of "what we can be sure perception alone gives us" (Stroud 2015, p. 387). The idea of "what we can be sure perception alone gives us" is the idea of a content of perception that, qua perceptual content, can be specified without implying that the bearer of an act with this content is in possession of perceptual knowledge of the world.

Stroud calls this strategy "bottom up" because it does not begin with the actuality of perceptual knowledge of the world whose conditions of possibility it investigates but with the actuality of something less, whatever this something less might be. What matters is that this starting point is conceived as a perceptual state in which one could also be even if one did not have perceptual knowledge. Stroud opposes this manner of proceeding and proposes instead what he calls a "top down" procedure (ibid.). What makes the new starting point different from the former is, according to Stroud, that it "involves" an act that has, qua act, *an understanding of itself.* Because perceptual knowledge, in contrast to mere perception, he tells us, involves "propositional thought that has a truth-value" (ibid.). A propositional thought is an act of consciousness that contains an understanding of its content as something that is either true or false. The possibility of having objective thoughts is thus analyzed in terms of a mastery in combining parts of the thought according to a "predicational structure" in which "part of the thought expresses something that is thought to be true of some object or item picked out by another part of that same thought" (ibid., p. 388). Stroud accordingly defines a propositional thought in terms of a subject's capacity to assert something *as* true. He then identifies the capacity to assert something as true with the capacity to judge.

The capacity to judge, Stroud argues, is an intrinsically self-conscious capacity. One cannot make this capacity intelligible unless one conceives of the judger as a being that is conscious of her capacity to judge and hence able to exercise her capacity for judgment in a self-conscious manner. Stroud's argument for this is that a thinker can only recognize the content of her thinking and judging to be true independently of her thinking it if she is able to think of herself as a "thinker of thoughts" (Stroud 2018, p. 136). Stroud writes:

> For a thinker to recognize or acknowledge that what he thinks could be true (or false) independently of whether he thinks it, the person must be capable of thinking of himself as a thinker of thoughts. Having a conception of the independence or objectivity of what he thinks to be so carries with it the need for a capacity to think of himself as subject or bearer of those thoughts. (…) (W)ithout a capacity to think of myself as a thinker, and attribute thoughts to myself, I could have no conception of something's being so (or not) independently of whether I think it is so (ibid.).

According to this argument one cannot be a judger without ascribing the capacity for judgment to oneself. This entails that one has an understanding of the concept of judging that one employs in this form of self-ascription. To analyze perceptual knowledge "top down" thus means, for Stroud, to put an activity at the center of perceptual knowledge that contains, as such, an understanding of itself. It is qua judgmental activity that perceptual knowledge is conceived as a mental state that is available for self-consciousness. However, as Stroud notices, the mere idea of a self-conscious capacity for judgment is not enough to account for the possibility of perceptual knowledge. To understand the possibility of perceptual knowledge further conditions have to be fulfilled. For nothing, so far, entitles one to think of an act that springs from a capacity for judgment as knowledge of an object of perception. So far, no sense has been given to the idea that the object of our thought and judgment is an object of perception. Stroud calls these further conditions, accordingly, "perceptual conditions" (Stroud 2015, p. 392). One of these perceptual conditions that Stroud thinks to be "important, perhaps essential" not only for perceptual knowledge but for our capacity for judgment is the capacity "to perceive particular objects, to be aware of an object, to single it out perceptually, to discriminate it from its background or surroundings, to have our attention drawn to it" (ibid.).

Stroud thinks that a perceptual capacity of this sort is what humans and non-human animals share. A capacity for perception of this sort is not and cannot be part of the self-consciousness of its bearer because not only is self-consciousness a condition for judging and propositional thinking, according to Stroud, but judging and propositional thinking is also a condition for self-consciousness. The capacity for self-consciousness and the capacity for propositional thought go together. This is so, Stroud thinks, because the self-consciousness one exhibits when one thinks of oneself as thinking a thought is itself an act of one's capacity for propositional thought. "The self-consciousness I exhibit in attributing states and attitudes to myself in the first person," Stroud argues, "is itself a form of propositional thought" (Stroud 2018, p. 139). If this is so then this means that "not only is the possibility of self-consciousness essential to propositional thought," as it has been argued above, but that "the possibility of propositional thought is also essential to self-consciousness" (ibid.).

From this it follows that the capacity for perception that is supposed to be an enabling condition for perceptual knowledge is something that is not, as such, available to the self-consciousness of its bearers. It is a capacity, Stroud thinks, whose nature can be specified independently of the question whether its bearer is a thinker and judger and hence independently from the self-consciousness that the subject exhibits when she is conscious of herself as a perceptual knower that is the starting point of this account.

What enables the human animal to have perceptual knowledge, according to this account, is that the human, in addition to this perceptual capacity, has the capacity to judge that entails self-consciousness in the sense that the judger has a general consciousness of her capacity for judging, that is a form of consciousness which her capacity for perception, as such, does not entail. Perceiving an object in the sense shared by humans and non-human animals means to be in a state of consciousness that is logically different from an act of thinking or judging in that the content of such a perception is not dependent upon the subject's conceptual capacities that she actualizes in judging but upon an "object" whose existence and identity comes to be known by her only when she, *in addition* to her capacity to perceive in this "non-epistemic" sense of perception, exercises her capacity for judgment (Stroud 2015, p. 392). Thus, in order to account for the perceptual character of perceptual knowledge Stroud employs the idea of non-epistemic perception to describe an act of perception that differs from an act of epistemic perception in that its content is supposed to be not a fact but an object. Stroud thinks that this kind of non-epistemic perception is necessary for perceptual knowledge. He moreover thinks that this kind of non-epistemic perception is "important, perhaps essential" to the possibility of "objective thought" (ibid.). It matters to the kind of position, he envisages, that he must leave open the status of this kind of non-epistemic perception with respect to thought. For this kind of perception enters our investigation of perceptual knowledge from outside the scope of the "I think" which, by contrast, constitutes the capacity for judgment. The idea of a non-epistemic perception enters our investigation as the idea of an *enabling condition* for perceptual knowledge, not as an act that enters into the constitution of the content of one's knowledge. The capacity for perception is represented as a capacity whose exercise, as such, is not within the scope of the "I think." So for Stroud, a subject who both perceives objects in a sense that falls short of the "I think" and has the capacity for judgment as well fulfills the necessary as well as sufficient conditions for having a capacity for perceptual knowledge. A subject who has these two capacities, Stroud thinks, can "see what there is" and thereby know what there is "by perception alone" (ibid., p. 392).

Stroud is convinced of his having achieved a position which he calls "Realism" and that is not of the naïve kind. It is not naïve, he thinks, since it represents perceptual knowledge as a complex matter of cognitive and perceptual capacities (ibid.). According to this account, naïve Realism would be the position which states that the only condition that needs to be fulfilled for it to be intelligible how a subject can have perceptual knowledge is her possession of perceptual capacities in virtue of which she is thought to have direct access to the objects around her. If she does not also have cognitive capacities of the above sort, Stroud thinks, then there is simply no sense in which one can say of such a subject that her relation to an object is a relation of knowledge. This is because she does not relate to the object that she represents as the object of a true thought. Thus, she does not relate to the object as something of which her representation can be so much as true or false. Any realism that is not aware of the cognitive conditions that a subject must fulfill for it to be intelligible that she is conscious of an object about which she can be so much as right or wrong, is naïve.

7

McDowell thinks that any account of perceptual knowledge on the basis of two capacities, a capacity for perception on the one side and a capacity for judging on the other, which conceives of the former as logically independent of the latter, is incoherent. It not only fails to account for the possibility of perceptual knowledge, but for the possibility of judgment in general. "(W)e must not suppose," he insists, "that receptivity makes an even notionally separable contribution to its co-operation with spontaneity" (McDowell 1996, p. 51). By contrast, Stroud thinks that there is no reason to think that perception is a capacity that is logically dependent upon the cognitive capacity once we give up the assumption that perceptual knowledge must be construed in terms of a judgment that has a perceptual ground. Once we give up this assumption we can think of perception as a capacity that, instead of providing a ground for judging that things are thus-and-so, provides an enabling condition for the capacity for judgment to be exercised.

Stroud characterizes the enabling role of perception by saying that it singles out an object and brings it to "our attention" (ibid, p. 392). Having perceptions in this sense is supposed to explain the transition from a state in which the object is not yet part of the subject's consciousness into a state in which it is part of it. What matters is that these perceptions can do what they do, namely single out an object and bring it to our attention, without it being a requirement for the subject who is related to an object in this manner to possess any conceptual capacities for being related to it in this manner. In consequence, the conditions for perceiving an object and the conditions for thinking and judging about it fall apart in the sense that one's perception of an object does not entail that the object one perceives is a thinkable object, let alone an object that one thinks. And vice versa. One's judging about an object does not entail that the object one judges about is a perceptible object, let alone an object that one perceives.

Stroud is not worried about this gap. It is, I think, of interest to note that Kant, by contrast, whose analysis of empirical knowledge Stroud otherwise finds attractive, addresses this gap explicitly in the form of the following worry: is it possible that the unity of that which is given to us in intuition is such that the concepts that the understanding employs to bring about the unity of a judgment are not valid of what is given in intuition? If this were the case, Kant thinks, then the very idea of a capacity for judgment would turn out to be a "mere phantom of the brain" (Kant, 1965, B 124). It is for this reason that Kant thinks that a Transcendental Deduction is needed for the concepts that are conceived to be the conditions of judging. In the section entitled "Transition to the Transcendental Deduction of the Categories" Kant writes:

> That objects of sensible intuition must conform to the formal conditions of sensibility which lie *a priori* in the mind is evident, because otherwise they would not be objects for us. But that they must likewise conform to the conditions which the understanding requires for the synthetic unity of thought, is a conclusion the grounds of which are by no means so obvious. Appearances might very well be so constituted that the understanding should not find them to be in accordance with the conditions of its unity. (Kant, 1965, B 122f)

The task of the Transcendental Deduction, as Kant unfolds it, is to address this worry by showing that the possibility that motivates the worry, i.e. that the objects of sensible intuitions might not conform to the conditions of judging, is an illusion. Kant takes himself to show that the worry is only an apparent worry because the very idea of a manifold as being given to one in an intuition already presupposes the employment of the concepts of the understanding in virtue of which it brings about the unity of a judgment.

By contrast, when Stroud is not worried about the possibility that the objects of perception, qua being perceived, could be such that the concepts one employs to bring about the unity of a judgment would not be valid of it, this is not because he has entitled himself to think that this possibility is an illusion. For this possibility, and hence the related worry, could only be an illusion by his lights if he were in a position to claim that the conditions for perceiving an object would already entail the conditions for judging about it. But this is precisely what Stroud denies. For one to be able to think and judge about an object, it is not enough to be able to perceive it. A further, and different, condition must be satisfied. One must possess conceptual capacities that one can employ to make judgments.

Kant thought that it impossible to grant such a gap without thereby dissolving the very idea of a capacity for judgment. And indeed, this is what happens to the concept of judgment from which Stroud begins: it dissolves. This is because, if we grant that the conditions for perceiving and judging fall apart, then it follows that one's judging an object to be thus-and-so does not, as such, entail the thought that the content which one endorses as true is such that it can be perceived, let alone that it *is* perceived. However, this raises the question of what, on this account, enables one to think of *any* judgment one makes to be about an object of perception, on account of which the judgment is either true or false, rather than a combination of representations that is grounded in other combinations of representations and so forth; none of which, however, provides for a subject's thought that the content of her representation is an object of perception on account of which the judgment is either true or false.

Stroud wants to say that perceiving that things are thus-and-so is an irreducible *manner of knowing*, not a *ground* for knowledge. However, as I have argued, the thought that perception is a capacity that is logically independent of the cognitive capacity threatens the idea that the judging subject, simply in virtue of judging that thing are thus-and-so, is able to conceive of the object of her judgment as an object of perception. But this undermines the idea that Stroud wants to establish, namely that the judging subject, simply in virtue of judging, can conceive of her judgment as a perceptual manner of knowing how things are, and hence as an act of perceptual knowledge.

8

The difficulty we seem to be faced with is the following: either we deny that perceptual knowledge has a perceptual ground available to the subject as such a ground – then we have to pay the price of jettisoning the idea that an act of perceptual knowledge, as such, can ever be conscious of itself as perceptual knowledge and hence as an act of knowledge about objects of perception – or we construe perceptual knowledge as a form of inferential knowledge, grounded on perceptual states that are less than epistemic. Then we have to give up the idea of perceptual knowledge altogether.

I will argue in the final sections of this paper that the supposed difficulty is the result of an assumption that we must give up. The source of the supposed difficulty is a thought that seems to be so obviously true that it is not even considered to be questionable. The source of the supposed difficulty is the thought that the relation between judgment and perception is a relation between two different capacities. It is the idea that perception and judgment are two different capacities whose joint exercise brings about perceptual knowledge. Let us call it the two-capacity view. The two-capacity view is incoherent because it rests upon an incoherent conception of judgment; or so I will argue.

It is no coincidence that both McDowell and Stroud, despite the differences of their positions, represent themselves – each with different restrictions – as readers of Kant's epistemology. For Kant's epistemology is perhaps the most sophisticated expression of the two-capacity doctrine. Kant never challenged the thought that perceptual knowledge has to be construed as a combination of two distinguishable capacities, a capacity for perception and a capacity for judgment, and neither do Stroud or McDowell. Just as Kant argues from the start of the first *Critique* to the end that perception is one of the two "stems" or "sources" of knowledge, of which the understanding is the other (Kant 1965, B 74), never contemplating that their relation might be of a different kind than that of two "stems," so, too, argue Stroud and McDowell. They never question the idea that perception and judgment relate to each other as two distinguishable capacities. The main difference between their positions – and hence their respective readings of Kant – is with regard to the question of how these two capacities that Kant distinguishes are related to each other. Whereas Stroud thinks that the deliverances of the capacity for perception qua perceptions are independent of the capacity for judgment, and merely provide the condition of the exercise of the capacity for judgment, McDowell thinks the two capacities are logically dependent upon each other and therefore thinks he can construe an act of perception as a ground for knowledge.

Whereas in Stroud the assumption of two distinguishable capacities – perception and judgment – comes in the form of the claim that "perception alone" is a mere enabling condition of perceptual knowledge whose fulfillment does not require any conceptual capacities that are required for judging, in McDowell this assumption comes in the form of the claim that someone who sees how things are has a ground for judging how things are, that puts her "in a position" to know.

The difficulty we are confronted with is that we seem to be forced to give up the idea that perceptual judgment is an activity that is, qua perceptual judgment, conscious of its perceptual ground and thereby conscious of itself as a perceptual judgment. We seem to be forced to give up the idea that an act of perceptual knowledge is, as such, conscious of itself as perceptual knowledge. The idea that perceptual knowledge is, qua act, conscious of itself as perceptual knowledge, is the very idea that McDowell had promised to make available to us, when he writes: "One's perceptual knowledge that there is something red and rectangular in front of one includes knowledge of its own credentials as knowledge" (McDowell 2013, p. 151).

The idea spelled out in this quotation becomes unavailable to us on any account which thinks of perceptual knowledge in terms of two distinguishable acts that spring from two distinguishable capacities. What drives this analysis of perceptual knowledge is a conception of judgment that is confused. Its consequence is a conception of the relation between judgment and perception that gives rise to the above dilemma. The assumption that drives this analysis of perceptual knowledge can be stated like this: it is the assumption that judging is an act of a capacity that can be specified without being specified as a particular capacity for knowledge, such as, for example, the capacity for perceptual knowledge. Neither McDowell nor Stroud question this assumption. Yet it is this assumption that hinders us in understanding the nexus of grounding that goes with the idea of knowledge and, for that reason, the idea of perceptual knowledge as an intrinsically self-conscious state. Once one realizes that this conception of judgment is incoherent, I will argue, one will realize that the relation between perception and judgment is not a relation between two distinguishable capacities. It is a relation of a different kind. It is a relation between a *concrete* concept of judging that describes an act of a particular capacity for knowledge, and an *abstract* concept of judging that does not describe an act of any capacity but rather abstracts from the very idea of a capacity. The abstract concept of judging, just by itself, does not describe an act of a capacity at all. The assumption that it does, however, is the common misunderstanding that drives the above dilemma.

One can see the incoherence of this assumption by reflecting upon the concept of a capacity that one thereby employs. The concept of a capacity entails the idea of a contrast between capacity and act. It is the concept of a potentiality whose actuality, qua actuality, is something that *comes to be*. In order to see this I want to recall a distinction that Kant himself employs several times in the first *Critique:* the distinction between an infinite and a finite intellect. An infinite intellect is an intellect, as Kant argues, to which the distinction between the unity of the manifold that is the content of its self-consciousness and the unity of self-consciousness is not applicable. Because of that, it is an understanding to whom "the principle of the original *synthetic* unity of apperception" does not apply, that is, whose self-consciousness does not consist in the self-consciousness of an activity of synthesis (Kant 1965, B 137). Kant writes:

> This principle [=the principle of the original synthetic unity of apperception – A.K.], is not, however, to be taken as applying to every possible understanding, but only to that understanding through whose pure apperception, in the representation "I am", nothing manifold is given. An understanding which through its self-consciousness could supply to itself that manifold of intuition – an understanding, that is to say, through whose representation the objects of the representation should at the same time exist – would not require, for the unity of consciousness, a special act of synthesis of the manifold. (Kant, 1965, B 138f)

According to this fundamental distinction between two kinds of intellect, the activity of an intellect to whom the contrast between the unity of what it is conscious of and the unity of self-consciousness does not apply, does not consist in an activity of synthesis and hence is not an activity of thinking and judging. The infinite intellect does not "think" the unity of the manifold because the unity of what it represents and the unity of its representation are not two distinct unities. However, if that is so, then we must conclude that the activity of an infinite intellect cannot be characterized in terms of a distinction that has guided our account of the cognitive capacity right from the start: namely in terms of the distinction between capacity and act. By contrast, the distinction between capacity and act is constitutive for any cognitive activity whose knowledge consists in an activity of thinking and judging and that is, for any cognitive activity whose knowledge consists, qua act, in a transition from a state of ignorance to a state of knowledge.

The concept of judging, as it were, essentially divides itself into the description of a *capacity* and the description of an *act*. However, if this is what judging is – an act of a capacity – then it follows that any judgment, qua act, must entail the idea of circumstances upon which the exercise of the capacity is dependent. This is because the idea of such circumstances is identical to the idea that there is a logical contrast between capacity and act. The idea of an act that is the actualization of a capacity is the idea of an act whose very concept entails the idea of circumstances upon which the actuality of the act, as it were, is dependent. To conceive of judging as an act of a capacity is thus to conceive of judging as an act whose concept contains, as such, the idea of circumstances that explain the actuality of this act.

However, this understanding of the concept of judging – as a capacity whose concept entails the idea of circumstances that explain its actuality – is not reflected in the concept of judging, as it is employed in the above debate. The concept of judging is specified as the concept of an activity which consists in putting together the parts of a propositional unity that one endorses as true. This specification of the activity of judging does not, as such, entail the idea of such circumstances that explain the *actuality* of this activity. It does not, as such, entail an understanding of the actuality of the act that it describes which it, at the same time, *presupposes* in the idea that judging is a capacity. It is thus an *abstract* concept of judgment because it abstracts from the idea of circumstances that explain the actuality of the relevant act. To abstract from the idea of circumstances that explain the actuality of an act of endorsing a propositional unity as true is to abstract from the understanding of judgment that is contained in its concept qua being the concept of a *capacity*. Thus, when we employ the abstract concept of judging we do not employ it as the concept of an act that actualizes a capacity. For the concept of judgment not to be abstract, that is, for it to be the concept of a capacity, it must contain an understanding of the actuality of its act. This is to say that, for its concept to not be abstract, it must contain an understanding of its actuality. What is such a concrete concept of judging?

Now, since the abstract concept of judging simply is what it is, namely abstract, the suggestion at this moment cannot be that we start from this abstract concept and try to derive from there the concrete concept of judging. It must be the other way round. The abstract concept of judging is only possible because there is a concrete concept of judging whose understanding is prior to the abstract concept and presupposed in it. Thus, in order to find a concrete concept of judging we must turn to ourselves and ask ourselves whether we find in our thoughts concrete concepts of judging. My suggestion is: the concepts of perceptual knowledge, inferential knowledge, or knowledge by hearsay, are precisely that. They are concrete concepts of judging that represent judging as an act that contains, as such, an explanation of the judgment thus specified. The concepts for particular forms of knowledge as we have them are concepts for particular capacities for judging whose actualization yields an act of the particular form of knowledge that the concept of its capacity specifies.

The concept of perceptual knowledge, according to this line of thought, is thus to be understood as a concrete concept of judging that represents judging as an act of a capacity that contains, in its very concept, the idea of an explanation of the judgment. If the capacity thus specified is fully exercised, then the act of this capacity yields an act of knowledge of the specified kind. There is thus no judgment that does not, as such, actualize a particular capacity for knowledge, such as the capacity for perceptual knowledge, or the capacity for inferential knowledge, or the capacity for knowledge by hearsay.

It follows from this understanding of judging that the role of the concept of perception in the life of a thinker is not to describe a capacity other than a capacity for judging, but to specify a manner of its exercise which, when things go well, results in acts of perceptual knowledge. The question of how the capacity for perception and the capacity for judgment are related to each other has, thus, *no meaning*, because there is no such thing as a capacity for perception that is anything other than a capacity for perceptual knowledge. The role of the concept of perception is thus the same as the role of the concepts of inference, or learning from someone else, or remembering. They are misconceived if they are conceived as concepts of capacities whose actualizations are *something other* than the actualization of a capacity for judgment. Their role is to specify the abstract concept of judging by representing judging as an act of a capacity that contains, in its very concept, an explanation of the actuality of the act that falls under this concept.

There is thus no such thing as a capacity to judge that a subject can be said to possess and exercise which is not, as such, a particular capacity for knowledge with particular circumstances of its exercise. Perceiving that things are thus-and-so is the exercise of a particular capacity for knowledge that is particular in that the act of this capacity is dependent upon particular circumstances that distinguish it from the acts of other capacities for knowledge not dependent upon those circumstances. What characterizes an act of perceptual knowledge, *inter alia*, is that it is dependent upon the object's being *here* and *now*. That the object that I come to know is *here* and *now*, where I come to know it on the basis of the exercise of my capacity, specifies the particular circumstances that belong to my capacity for perceptual knowledge. However, an object can be here and now in a sense that does not imply that I perceive it. My perception of the object might be hindered by another object between me and the object in question. Or it might be dark in the room, so that I cannot see the object. It characterizes an act of perceptual knowledge that the object that is here and now is given to me under circumstances that provide an occasion for my capacity for perception to be exercised. In this sense, perceiving how things are requires different circumstances than inferring how things are. For example, I can infer that q from my knowledge that p, and that p implies q, when it is dark in the room; but I cannot see that q when it is totally dark in the room, etc.

The role of these capacity-circumstances, I have argued, is to explain the actuality of the particular capacity for judging specified through these circumstances. Since any capacity for judging is self-consciously possessed and exercised, a subject who judges that things are thus-and-so will, as such, be conscious of the particular circumstances of her judgment, and hence, of her judgment *as* an act of the particular capacity specified through these circumstances.

This gives us what we were looking for: the idea of an act of perceptual knowledge that entails, as such, a consciousness of itself as an act of perceptual knowledge. This is because it gives us the idea of an act of perceptual knowledge that entails, as such, a consciousness of the ground of the judgment. For this ground, as we now can say, is nothing other than this: it is the *capacity* to acquire perceptual knowledge that p, whose consciousness one manifests when one perceptually judges that p. The ground of one's perceptual judgment that p is the capacity for perceptual knowledge that p from which it springs, and of which she is conscious when she perceptually judges that p. This *consciousness of the ground* of her judgment enables her to justify her judgment in an utterance of the form "I know that p because I perceive that p." The point of the utterance is not to point to an act or episode other than one's judgment that p but to reveal the ground of one's judgment that p by specifying the particular capacity for knowledge of which the judgment is represented as a perfect instance. Thus, one's ground for perceptually judging p is neither some prior act of perception from which one infers, given some further premises, the truth of one's judgment. Nor is it some prior act of perception, of which it could be said that it is available to the judging subject as a justification of her judgment. Rather, the ground of one's perceptual judgment is nothing other than one's capacity for perceptual knowledge.

To be sure, not every judgment is a perfect instance of the capacity that is its ground. The capacity from which the judgment springs is a fallible capacity. This means that there can be situations in which the circumstances for perceptually knowing that things are thus-and-so are less than favorable for perfectly exercising this capacity without the subject knowing this to be so. When this is the case, then this means that the particular circumstances of this case are such that they hinder us from perfectly exercising our capacity for knowledge. This happens, for example, when light conditions are such that one cannot tell the color of an object by perception. There can be unfavorable circumstances of which we are not aware. But it can also be the case that the circumstances are not unfavorable, but that the subject has been falsely informed about them and thinks they were unfavorable.[4] In such a case the subject is hindered from acquiring knowledge by perception, not because the circumstances hinder her, but because considerations about the circumstances hinder her. This is a case where one is hindered from fully actualizing one's capacity for perceptual knowledge on account of considerations about one's epistemic situation.

In such a case we can say, from a third person perspective, that she can see that p, although she herself cannot say this because she is misled into thinking that she cannot see that p, although, as a matter of fact, she can. However, the "can" in question that is employed from a third-person perspective in the locution "She can see that p" is not the "can" that describes her capacity for perceptual knowledge, but the more limited notion of an occasion for perceptual knowledge contained in the capacity-notion but not exhausting its meaning. Rather, the meaning of the more limited notion of an occasion for perceptual knowledge can only be understood on the basis of the capacity-notion whose meaning is fundamental.

There is a further kind of case entailed by the fallibility of the capacity: This is the case where circumstances are unfavorable for perfectly exercising our capacity for perceptual knowledge and where we are aware of this. When this is the case, we do not take ourselves to perceptually know how things are, but to have, at best, something less than knowledge. This would still be an imperfect instance of our capacity for perceptual knowledge, although there would be nothing in the subject's epistemic doxastic behavior that renders it imperfect. By contrast, a case of perceptual knowledge is a case in which there is nothing that hinders the subject from perfectly exercising her capacity for perceptual knowledge. A case of knowledge is a case in which the capacity for knowledge is exercised perfectly in all respects.

---

[4] For a detailed discussion of the fallibility of rational capacities for knowledge, see my book, *Sources of Knowledge* (Kern 2017, pp. 198–224).

9

This yields an understanding of perceptual knowledge that is a form of realism. It conceives of the objects of perceptual knowledge as independent of the act of knowing of them. The objects of perceptual knowledge are perceptually knowable facts. Any particular act of perceptual knowledge depends on them. Stroud thinks that any realism that portrays the possibility of perceptual knowledge as a "complex matter" in the sense that it requires an "elaborate set of conditions" "certainly cannot be called Naïve Realism" (Stroud 2015, p. 394). Naïve, according to this reading, would be any position that thinks that we can understand how it is possible for a subject to know how things are if we only equip the subject with the capacity to perceive things in the sense which Stroud characterizes as non-epistemic. Stroud thinks "perception alone," *in this sense*, cannot explain the possibility of perceptual knowledge because knowledge entails objective thought. The possibility of objective thought requires a complex of conceptual capacities without which a subject cannot be said to have an object in view about which she can so much as have thoughts that can be true or false.

The position I have sketched above is not naïve in the sense in which Stroud thinks one should not be. But it calls into question the conception of perceptual knowledge that Stroud and McDowell still share with those they criticize and which the position which they think is naïve does not share. According to them, perceptual knowledge is analyzed in terms of two distinguishable capacities, perception and judgment. The naïve position does not think that perceptual knowledge can be analyzed in terms of a capacity other than itself. I think this is the "truth" of its naiveté. Not because I think that "perception alone," in the sense in which the naïve realist understands this phrase, gives us knowledge. But because the capacity for perception, possessed by a thinker, is nothing other than a capacity for judgment whose perfect instance is an act of perceptual knowledge. This does not mean that perceiving is the same as judging, which it is not. One can judge that p without perceiving that p. It rather means that the concept of judgment does not describe a capacity at all unless it is specified either as a capacity for perceptual knowledge or for some other kind of knowledge. And in this sense, there is only one capacity exercised in perceptual knowledge, and this capacity alone gives you perceptual knowledge.

Bibliography

Anscombe, Elizabeth (1981): "The Intentionality of Sensation." In: *Collected Philosophical Papers*, vol. 2: *Metaphysics and the Philosophy of Mind*. Oxford: Blackwell, pp. 3–20.
Austin, John L. (1962): *Sense and Sensibilia*. Oxford: Clarendon Press.
Kant, Immanuel (1965): *Critique of Pure Reason*. Translated by Norman Kemp Smith. New York: St. Martin's Press.
Kern, Andrea (2017): *Sources of Knowledge. On the Concept of a Capacity for Knowledge*. Cambridge, MA: Harvard University Press.
Kern, Andrea (2019): "The Capacity to Know and Perception." In: *Philosophical Issues* 29, pp. 159–171.
McDowell, John (1996): *Mind and World*. Cambridge, MA: Harvard University Press.
McDowell, John (1998a): "Criteria, Defeasibility and Knowledge." In: *Meaning, Knowledge and Reality*. Cambridge, MA: Harvard University Press, pp. 369–394.
McDowell, John (1998b): "Knowledge and the Internal." In: *Meaning, Knowledge and Reality*. Cambridge, MA: Harvard University Press, pp. 395–413.
McDowell, John (2009): "Avoiding the Myth of the Given." In: *Having the World in View. Essays on Kant, Hegel and Sellars*. Cambridge, MA: Harvard University Press, pp. 256–274.
McDowell, John (2013): "Perceptual Experience: Both Relational and Contentful." In: *European Journal of Philosophy* 21. No. 1, pp. 144–157.
McGinn, Marie (2015): "Two senses of 'see.'" In: M. Campbell and M. O'Sullivan (Eds.): *Wittgenstein and Perception*. Oxford: Oxford University Press, pp. 33–44.
Travis, Charles (2004): "The Silence of the Senses." In: *Mind* 113, pp. 57–94.
Stroud, Barry (2002): "Sense-experience and the grounding of thought." In: Nicolas Smith (Ed.): *Reading McDowell. On Mind and World*. London, New York: Routledge Press, pp. 79–91.
Stroud, Barry (2015): "Perceptual Knowledge and the Primacy of Judgment." In: *Journal of the American Philosophical Association* 1. No. 3, pp. 385–395.
Stroud, Barry (2018): "Judgment, Self-Consciousness, Idealism." In: *Seeing, Knowing, Understanding*. Oxford: Oxford University Press, pp. 128–140.

Anton Friedrich Koch
Is Hermeneutic Realism a Dialectical Materialism?

Thinking With and Beyond Heidegger and Adorno

Abstract: The essay unfolds Koch's understanding of hermeneutic realism, based centrally on the philosophies of Kant and Heidegger and spelled out in distinction to Irad Kimhi's theory of negation and the thinking-being relationship. The author analyzes the basic structures of predication, which he partly interprets against Kimhi's claim for the primacy of the predicative statement of negation. He then comments, with reference to Aristotle's notions of "aisthesis" and "noesis," on Heidegger's theory of "unconcealment" and presents his own conception of a "hermeneutic realism," grounded in this theory, which combines the idea of an essentially interpretive or hermeneutic engagement with the world with an underlying realism about the world as thus engaged. Following Adorno, Koch here argues that thinking literally 'works' itself out of the raw materiality of nature through engaging hermeneutically in its constitutive confrontation with this same nature itself. It is in this sense that his understanding of hermeneutics is not only close to Hegel and Marx but is, as he argues, truly inscribed as well in the tradition of dialectical materialism.

1

Where is the origin of thought? Perhaps the divide between continental and analytic philosophy (a strange distinction; one would hardly distinguish continental from maritime philosophy, or oppose a "synthetic" to analytic philosophy) can be traced back to two fundamentally different ways of answering this question.

One of the two ways considers the assertoric sentence as the expression of thought and cleaves, with respect to its analysis, to its elementary form: that of simple predication. Quine and Strawson called this the "basic combination." The early Wittgenstein and Sellars analyzed the simple assertoric sentence as a logical picture of a particular fact or object. Today Irad Kimhi (2018) of the University of Chicago – siding, remarkably, with Aristotle against Frege – criticizes the tendency within analytic philosophy to neglect, with respect to the assertoric sentence in general, its fundamentally predicative form and formation.

The other, continental way of answering the question turns instead on the attempt to get behind predication. In the course of his development, Wittgenstein (it is worth noting) changed his position from the first one to the second, describing thinking, in his late philosophy, as an open, evolving network of language games. As a consequence, his *Philosophical Investigations* are treated poorly in the mainstream of contemporary analytic philosophy. But here we do not want to look at Wittgenstein's notorious theoretical abstemiousness, but rather at Heidegger's hermeneutic and Adorno's dialectical ways of illuminating the prior ground of predication.

Heidegger understands predication as "pointing-out" (*Aufzeigung*) and thereby intends to "adhere to the primordial meaning of λόγος as ἀπόφανσις: letting an entity be seen from itself" (Heidegger 1962, p. 196). The predicative structure of *ti kata tinos*, asserting something to be the case of something, serves to make something visible as something: Theaetetus himself as sitting, the fresh snow itself as white, etc. Here, neither Theaetetus nor the snow are treated as mediated through mental representations, just as, incidentally, is maintained by a family of theories of a completely different character, those developing from Russellian semantics. Nevertheless, in the predicative sentence, the "as" of this letting an entity be seen is "pushed back into the uniform plane of that which is merely present-at-hand" by virtue of a "levelling of the primordial 'as' of circumspective interpretation." The latter is what Heidegger calls "the 'existential-hermeneutical 'as' in distinction from the 'apophantic 'as'' of the assertion" (Heidegger 1962, pp. 200–201). The assertion is rooted in circumspection (*Umsicht*).

Adorno, at the other end of the continental spectrum, follows Hegel in his striking doctrine that the origin of thought is negation; this is striking since negation seems to presuppose predication, and not vice versa. Unimpressed by this, Adorno writes in the introduction to his *Negative Dialectics:* "Thought as such, before all particular contents, is an act of negation, of resistance to that which is forced upon it; this is what thought has inherited from its archetype, the relation between labor and material" (Adorno 1973, p. 19). That thinking is negating is what dialectics is about, and as such, it is also the position of the dialectical idealism that Adorno attributes to Hegel. However, that thought has inherited its negating character from labor as thought's own archetype is Adorno's objection against Hegel, as well as the materialistic aspect of his dialectics, his dialectical materialism.

The label "dialectical materialism" may sound repugnant. But Adorno is, of course, far from any sympathy for the Soviet version of dialectical materialism ("Diamat") and the Soviet empire in general. His dialectical materialism is, without a doubt, the philosophical one of an intellectual and critically educated citizen.

With vigor, he sets himself apart from the "vulgar materialisms" of both camps: from the psychophysical identity theories and functionalisms of the North Atlantic value- and weapon-alliance, as well as from the theory-hostile apologists of illegitimate party dictatorships in the former empire of the Warsaw Pact. Let us, therefore, consider Adorno's materialism with friendly interest as a philosophical theoretical offering that is worth grappling with. We could, in any case, rename the philosophical position "dialectical realism," but Adorno would not like the epistemological connotations of this label. So, let us stick confidently with "dialectical materialism."

2

Realism will nonetheless be granted its due; together with the epithet "hermeneutic" it characterizes a philosophical theory that combines aspects of Heidegger's hermeneutics and Adorno's dialectics, although it can be developed and established quite independently of both. Markus Gabriel correctly calls this theory a realism "supplemented by an analytically upgraded hermeneutics" (Gabriel 2017, p. 797). Four of "hermeneutical realism's" core theses are presented in the following – despite Adorno's warning against any kind of 'philosophy-reports' ("philosophy is not expoundable," he writes (Adorno 1973, p. 33)) – and commented on briefly, without further reference to the current literature on the topic (but see also Koch 2016, pp. 7–9).

Let us look first at the *subjectivity thesis*. It implies, in one direction, that subjectivity is necessarily spatiotemporally embodied, and, in the other direction, that every possible space-time system contains, somewhere and sometime, thinking subjectivity in the form of subjects with bodies. It thus consists of a corporeality thesis for subjectivity and a subjectivity thesis for space and time. This is not to say that space and time are subjective – this thesis is not an idealism – but only that space and time are essentially related to a subjectivity embodied within them, that they include subjectivity. The reason for this is that the logical points beyond itself to space and time as its necessary Other, and that the identity of indistinguishables is guaranteed as a logical truth for spatio-temporal individual things only if indexical properties such as being-here, being-over-there-on-the-right, happening-now, having-taken-place-last-year, and so forth, can be exemplified by them as well, properties which exist only relative to intra-temporal thinking and speaking beings. So, beings like us are no coincidence, but necessary. Without us there would be no universe; the big bang sooner or later had to lead to physical subjects, be it over here or over there. This required no fine-tuning of the cosmic initial conditions and constants of nature by an intelligent designer, because logical necessity trumps teleology, and this means that teleological explanations function only with reference to contingency. Since, according to the subjectivity thesis, we are logically necessary relative to space and time, the intelligent design of our genesis would be an unnecessary supplement.

Second, the *readability thesis*. This is a continuation, modification, and deepening of the logical picture theories of the predicative sentence proposed by the early Wittgenstein and then, in another form, by Wilfrid Sellars. This thesis says that once we have learned to speak, we can read middle-sized perceptible objects, in that we talk about them with others, as original tokens of their own names, translating them into our spoken language, and also read them as original tokens of bundles of predicative sentences about them. By virtue of being original tokens of their proper names they are objects; by virtue of being original tokens of sentences about them they are facts [Fakten] (rather than being matters of fact [Tatsachen] that one can analyze, following Sellars, as interlinguistic types of assertoric sentences; instead they are truth-makers of elementary natural facts [Tatsachen]). When, however, things as facts [Fakten] or singular thing-sentences are connected to spoken language, they can function as reasons and exemplify metalinguistic, conceptual properties. The logical space of reasons expands – it has always already expanded – and encompasses the logical space of nature. Our justifications lose the appearance of spinning in the void and generating mere figments of the imagination, instead possessing, as McDowell rightly demands, friction with reality.

Third, the thesis of the *threefold structure of truth*. This thesis holds that truth – its concept as well as its matter – has three essential aspects, each maintained in competing truth theories as absolute and exclusive of the others: (1) a realistic or objective aspect, (2) a pragmatic or normative one, and (3) a phenomenal or epistemic one. Under the realistic aspect, truth appears as a correspondence of thought with an independent reality. Under the pragmatist one, it appears as warranted assertibility according to intersubjective rules of verification; and under the phenomenal aspect, truth is understood as unconcealment of the real [*des Realen*] for sense-perception and thought. These aspects of truth are not 'modules' in the sense of independent building blocks of truth; no one of them can occur without the others. Only for this reason, since correspondence and assertibility are secretly contemplated in unconcealment (*Unverborgenheit*), could the "unconcealment" of the pre-Socratics (if Heidegger is right) be taken for the whole of truth, and similarly in the cases of assertibility and correspondence. Sellars, for instance, can grasp truth decisively as assertibility because he also takes account of correspondence in the form of his picture theory of elementary propositions, and because he at least recognizes a bare remnant of unconcealment, situating it, however, as the sensory [das Sensorische] outside of the space of reasons. It is important to avoid one-sided theories such as these and ones even worse, taking all three aspects of truth equally into account in an integrative theory, and, further, to recognize these aspects, in modified form, in other basic philosophical concepts and situations as well, for example, as the modes of time. We can easily recognize, for example, how the past corresponds with the realistic aspect of truth, the present with the phenomenal, and the future with the pragmatic one.

Fourth, the *antinomy thesis*. This thesis states that thought as such, in its empty basic position [*in seiner leeren Nulleinstellung*], is contradictory in itself, and, indeed, incurably contradictory, because thought bears the antinomy of reflexive negativity. This can be proven by a mathematically inspired *tu-quoque* consideration as well as by an example provided by the so-called liar paradox: "The sentence you are listening to or reading is not true." The *tu-quoque* consideration is based on non-well-founded sets, especially the singleton, Ω, defined by the fact that this set only has itself as an element. Set theorists ask and openly discuss whether Ω is to be recognized as existing or not. Either way, no contradiction threatens this set. If one adds to the Zermelo-Fraenkel axiom system (ZF) the axiom of foundation, one can prove the nonexistence of Ω. But if ZF is consistent with the axiom of foundation, then it is consistent also without it, and then as well with a suitable antifoundation axiom from which the existence of Ω and other non-well-founded sets follows (Aczel 1988). Whether mathematicians speak for or against unfounded sets, they at least understand what is meant by non well-founded sets such as Ω.

But this, then, is generally true: if we understand how set formation can work (i.e. produce a set) even if running at idle [*im Leerlauf*], we accordingly understand it also in the case of other operations, such as the case of negation. Analogously to Ω, we therefore grasp the idea of an unfounded negation, which is defined only as the negation of itself. It is easy to see that liar-paradoxes, by way of semantic ascent, that is, with the help of the truth predicate, fulfill this definition: they are negations of themselves. The tu-quoque argument proves that we understand them (if there is a need for proof anyway). As with the set Ω, the question arises whether we want to acknowledge the quasi-propositional content *self-negation* or not. Formal objects such as Ω are recognized or rejected as existent or non-existent. Self-negation is not an object, but rather a quasi-propositional content that we have understood. So, if we acknowledge self-negations, then we acknowledge them (not as existing objects but) as being true; if we reject them, then as being false. If we acknowledge them, we are led, though, to their falsity and from their falsity back to their truth. This is the well-known antinomy of the liar: the antinomy of negation.

3

If we now compare the central theses of hermeneutic realism presented above to positions gleaned from Heidegger and Adorno, we find a tendential unanimity regarding the subjectivity thesis. This is especially true for the subjectivity thesis's less unusual half, the corporeality thesis. Human subjectivity, which Heidegger calls *Dasein*, is not understood by him as depending on a world-free, pure ego, but rather as circumspect, embodied being-in-the-world. This thought is expressed similarly by Adorno in another, more abstract terminology: "To be an object also is part of the meaning of subjectivity; but we can conceive an object that is not a subject" (Adorno 1973, p. 183). Because of the "object's preponderance," "dialectic is rendered materialistic" (Adorno 1973, p. 192). In other words, the preponderance of the object lies in the fact that all subjects are, necessarily, objects, but only a few objects are subjects. The subjectivity thesis in its more controversial half adds another modality: some objects are subjects *necessarily*.

We leave open here the question of how Adorno would respond to this claim. In Heidegger's work, though, considerations can be found that point to agreement. Prominent in his teaching is the position that to the being of things belongs their unconcealment, which can be attained in thought by inner-worldly thinkers, i.e. human beings, who – as guardians of Being (*Hüter des Seins*) – have to answer to the claim of Being. We are no coincidence, but rather are indispensable as such guardians. Thus far, Heidegger therefore accepts the subjectivity thesis, which states, according to Adorno's rather than Heidegger's phrasing: necessarily, all subjects are objects (physical ones, of course) and some objects are subjects.

Secondly, as far as the *readability thesis* is concerned, Adorno uses phrases such as this: "It is when things in being are read as a text of their becoming that idealistic and materialistic dialectics touch" (Adorno 1973, p. 52). But Adorno probably does not here mean "read" in a precise, non-metaphoric sense. Readability theses are, rather, a matter of hermeneutics, as Gadamer's well-known expression also illustrates: "Being that can be understood is language" (Gadamer 2004, p. 470), a thought that itself was formulated cognizantly in Heidegger's fitting statements. "Language speaks as the peal of stillness," Heidegger says in his 1950 lecture "Language" (Heidegger 2001, pp. 185–208). "The peal of silence is nothing human," but needs "the speaking of mortals in order to sound as the peal of stillness for the hearing of mortals. Only as men belong within the peal of stillness are mortals able to speak in *their own* way in sounds" (Heidegger 2001, p. 205).

Translated into a neutral theoretical language, this means that pre-human reality can be regarded as a silent language, fulfilled within the speech of people by their enunciation and thereby becoming language in the ordinary sense. This clearly involves regarding a silent language as a kind of written language so that pre-human reality is seen as a prehistorical writing, which we decode and translate into spoken language and, finally, can set down again in ordinary written language. Sound mediates between two kinds of writing, the prehistorical and the actually written script. The benefit of the readability thesis to hermeneutic philosophy consists in the fact that, in the aftermath of Wittgenstein's and Sellars's logical pictorial theories, it strips, roughly speaking, the talk of reading and translating things of all metaphorical character and reformulates them in clear theoretical language.

Furthermore, a demand on Russellian semantics and, equally, on the theory of direct reference (a demand which the adherents of Russellian semantics like to avoid by citing the division of labor between epistemology and semantics) can easily be fulfilled by means of the readability thesis. This is Frege's understandable request directed towards Russell: to explain, without making a category mistake, how an object can form part of a thought. Things are, *qua* objects, primitive tokens of their proper names, and directly referential terms are their equivalents in ordinary language. At the same time, things are, *qua* facts, primitive tokens of predicative sentences about them and therefore, insofar as they are read in perception, directly express the contents of sentences or thoughts. Hence, the readability thesis belies the strict division of labor between semantics and epistemology, which is perhaps not the least of its virtues.

Thirdly, with regard to the aspects of truth, Heidegger defends the philosophical-historical thesis that the pre-Socratics understood truth, starting from its phenomenal aspect, as unconcealment, and that this phenomenal aspect, which he also likes to grant a certain priority, has sunk ever deeper into oblivion from Plato onward. Heidegger interprets this process as a change in the essence of truth itself that mortals cannot direct. Deviating from this, and in a less foreordained manner, hermeneutic realism's conception of the truth invites philosophers to bring the three aspects of truth into a stable theoretical equilibrium and to refer the resulting triple structure of truth, now again with Heidegger, back to other basic philosophical facts.

Heidegger's central theorem of *Being and Time*, that time is the meaning [Sinn] of being, can then be meaningfully interpreted and affirmed in two steps. First, classical ontology distinguishes between existence and essence (*Ex-*

istenz und Essenz), being and essence (*Sein und Wesen*). But the term "Being" should not be reserved specifically for the existential kind of being, because, more fundamentally, there is being true, being-the-case, being as the obtaining of states of affairs *qua* facts [*Tatsachen*]. As being-true, this being must exhibit the aspects of truth: the realist one, as independence from our opinions; the pragmatic one, by contrast, with reference to an internal relationship to our actions and opinions; and the phenomenal one, as sensory, qualitative phenomenality and internal relation to our perceptual beliefs. At first sight this does not form a coherent picture. The three aspects of truth pull apart from one another and threaten to destroy the unity of veridical being – and that may well be the reason why realist and pragmatic conceptions of truth are often irreconcilably opposed to one another. However, in terms of time and its three modes, the realist one of the past, the phenomenal one of the present and the pragmatic one of the future, we have a precedent and a model of how the unity of the aspects, in this inner tension, is nevertheless possible. Time, therefore, is a model of the unity of being.

Secondly, the difference between existence and essence has its veritative correlate in the difference between *that-being* [*Dass-Sein*] and *what-being* [*Was-Sein*], or formal *being-the-case* [*Der-Fall-Sein*] and material *being-the case* (not only essentially being the case, but also accidentally). To this, hermeneutic realism links the suggestion that time should be regarded as the general form of formal being-the-case and space as the general form of material being-the-case. Kant shows the way here by teaching that time is the form of inner intuition, and space the form of outer intuition, and that in inner intuition "the representations of outer sense make up the proper material with which we occupy our mind" (Kant 1997, B67/p. 189). The material of intuitions is spatially dispersed; the circumstance which we perceive, that our mind is furnished with intuitive matter, happens successively in time. Hence, time is not only the model for the unity of being-the-case in the trinity of its aspects, but also the general form of formally being-the-case, that is, formal being in its pure structure, in abstraction from any specific content, whose own form, its Euclidean three-dimensionality, is space. With this, we have two reasons for considering time to be the general horizon from which formal being is understood and conceptually profiled, and it is in this twofold way that time is the meaning of being.

With the *antinomy thesis* we turn the page from hermeneutics back to dialectics and forge a connection with Hegel's and Adorno's doctrine of the primacy of negation in the nature of thinking. In Hegel's *Logic*, the negatively impregnated *Dasein* is treated very early on as a logical *quale* and only much later as a judgment, specifically a predicative judgment of existence [*des Daseins*]. Negation is here operative, in changing forms, from the very beginning. In particular, its self-application continues ceaselessly, and it first explicitly emerges within the "Logic of Being-there" (*Daseinslogik*) in the form of its own Other. In the Concept, logic finally attains its principle, which as Concept returns to itself from the areas of being and essence, and thus becomes transparent to itself as pure, reflexive, and absolute negation. Hegel's *Logic* is therefore basically nothing other than the ever-failing attempt to dissolve the antinomy of reflexive negation. More and more logical structure must be mobilized for this purpose, until, according to Hegel's claim, the antinomy within the absolute idea is finally tamed and all logical structure has become apparent. Because he does not believe in this final reconciliation, Adorno calls his dialectic a *negative* one, which in itself would be a pleonasm, even if he announces it in the introduction of *Negative Dialectics* as a paradox (Adorno 1973, p. xix): the dialectic is not only negative along its route, but remains so, contrary to Hegel's hope, up until its destination, which loses itself in the indefinite.

We are not going to comment on the intra-dialectical debate concerning whether reconciliation in thought is possible; instead, we want to focus on the debate about whether negation takes precedence over predication, or vice versa. To teach the primacy of predication over negation or (at least) predication's simultaneous origin with negation could prove to be an effective measure to defuse the antinomy, even if it is opposed by the fact that in Hegel's *Logic*, for example, the antinomy is by no means mastered at the stage of judgment (but only at the level of the absolute idea, if at all).

4

Hermeneutic philosophy does not, either in Heidegger or in Gadamer, distinguish itself as dialectical in Hegel's pointed sense; rather, it first does so only as hermeneutic realism, by means of the antinomy thesis. But Heidegger, too, allows that predication be grounded in something pre-existing, as we have seen: not, however, in negation and in its antinomy, but in circumspection (*Umsicht*) and its hermeneutical "as." In § 7B of *Being and Time* he interprets Aristotle on the subject, largely affirmatively, as follows. The "*logos apophantikos*" – we should think here of predication as its elementary form – lets something be seen, in that it puts something into the focus of attention. For this, in the prehistory of the human species, a pointing gesture may originally have sufficed, perhaps accompanied by a commenting gesture or a pronouncement, a nod or a laugh, a "Psst!," or something similar. Only because of the fact that in the *logos* the pointing and the commenting gesture or pronouncement come together in the function of letting-be-seen [*Sehenlassens*], according to Heidegger,

> ...can the logos have the structural form of the *sýnthesis*. Here "synthesis" does not mean a binding and linking together of representations, a manipulation of psychical occurrences [...]. The *syn* has a purely apophantical signification and means letting something be seen in its *togetherness* (*Beisammen*) with something – letting it be seen as something. (Heidegger 1962, p. 56)

From the synthetic function of letting-be-seen follows, then, the bivalence of the *logos:* it can be true or false. The ability to let something be seen is a "*dunamis meta logou*" (Aristotle 1999, Θ 2), a rational and therefore two-way faculty: it is not some arbitrary ability, but rather the "*dunamis meta logou kat' exochên*," because it is the rational ability of reason itself, that of letting-be-seen through the *logos*. A hot stone can only warm its environment; its capacity to heat is an alogical or one-way ability. Doctors, on the other hand, can heal and, in violation of their oath, even intentionally harm their patients; furthermore, they can make mistakes in their art. The art of healing is a *dunamis meta logou*, a two-way capacity, similar to rational or logical abilities as such: we can uncover something or hide it in letting-be-seen, for example an economically ruined village through a Potemkin facade. In addition, we can make mistakes in letting-be-seen. "There, a fox," shouts someone, when instead it is a squirrel.

Since the logical-apophantic ability is the dual-way capacity par excellence, "the *lógos* is just *not* the kind of thing that can be considered as the primary 'locus' of truth," and indeed not, as Heidegger emphasizes, on Aristotle's account (Heidegger 1962, p. 57). The *logos* rather is the place of truth or falsity, i.e. of bivalence, and Aristotle has determined it as such. Otherwise it would be unintelligible how a *dunamis meta logou* could be a two-way capacity in the first place. The primary place of truth qua *alêtheia*, unconcealment, is, for Aristotle, as for Greek thought in general, not the *logos* at all, but the pure, error-immune and, so to speak, one-valued perceiving (*Vernehmen*) within *aisthêsis* and *noêsis*. Aristotle treats this issue in *De Anima* III 6 and in *Metaphysics* Θ 10. *To gar pseudos en synthesei aei*, the false is always in a synthesis, Aristotle writes in *De Anima* III 6 (430b1f.). This is why Heidegger rightly says that for Aristotle the truth of judgment is "merely the opposite of this covering-up, a secondary phenomenon of truth, *with more than one kind of foundation*" (Heidegger 1962, p. 57): The primary phenomenon of truth is the one-valued perceiving in *aisthêsis* or *noêsis*; the secondary phenomenon is falsehood, whose possibility arises from synthesis, and only with the tertiary phenomenon is there the truth of judgments as the rejection of this falsehood.

Heidegger does not react uncritically to the picture he thus draws from Aristotle's theory of judgment. The appeal to a one-valued perceiving (*Vernehmen*) in *aisthêsis* or *noêsis* is not his own; it is rather a case of what Sellars has criticized as the "myth of the given." From the prior hermeneutical "as" of active circumspection (*Umsicht*), what arises is not a one-valued perceiving (*Vernehmen*), but rather an "apophantic as" which immediately falls into the duality of negation and affirmation. Heidegger emphasizes, against the myth of the given, the pragmatic aspect of truth coded in the privative *Alpha* of *alêtheia:* un-concealment must be torn from the (otherwise concealed) being of beings similarly to a theft. More carefully formulated, we have to meet the claim of Being actively so that truth can come forth.

The simple predicative assertion is called by Aristotle *kataphasis*, affirmation [*Zu-Sage*]. In it, something, for example an act of sitting, is claimed to be the case with regard to something else, for instance Theaetetus: "Theaetetus sits." The negation, on the other hand, is an *apophasis*, denial [*Ab-Sage*] (not to be confused with *apophansis*, letting something be seen). Thus, we deny flying to Theaetetus: "Theaetetus does not fly." Irad Kimhi points out that affirmation [*Zu-Sage*] and denial [*Ab-sage*] stand originally and equiprimordially in opposition to each other and that while affirmation is goal-oriented, denial points to the indeterminate (Kimhi 2018). This may be the case due to the fact that, according to Aristotle, it prevents a possible falsehood, and only in this mediated way makes something visible.

In agreement with Aristotle (*Metaphysics* Θ 2, 1046b13f), Kimhi sees denial as the privative form of affirmation. With Heidegger, one should better interpolate the failure of the affirmation, in cases of mistake or intentional deception, as the privative joint between affirmation and denial. The affirmation has, like every exercise within a two-way ability, a purposeful and a privative way of performing, whereby on the side of privation a distinction can again be made between erroneous and deliberately improper use. The privative exercise of the ability of letting-be-seen [*Sehenlassen*] through the *logos* is to cover up something purposefully or erroneously by means of an affirmation [*Zu-Sagen*], for example to cover up Theaetetus's cries of pain by the affirmation "Theaetetus laughs." Such obscuration by means of *kataphasis*, not *apophasis*, is therefore the privative form of letting-be-seen. The denial [*Ab-Sage*] comes systematically a step later, as a new form of speech which lets-be-seen, as a response that forms the remedy to the privative exercise, as the doctor administers an antidote to help a poisoned patient:[1] Theaetetus laughs? No, he does *not* laugh. Thus deni-

---

1 See also Kant, *Critique of Pure Reason*, "To be sure, *logically* one can express negatively any propositions that one wants, but in regard to the content of our cognition in general, that is, whether it is expanded or limited by a judgment, negative judgments have the special job solely of *preventing error*" (Kant 1997, A 709/B 737, p. 628). I thank Mike Stange for reminding me of this passage.

al/"Ab-Sage," as a new form of speech that lets-be-seen, connects with affirmation/"Zu-Sage," and can now for its part facilitate errors or be carried out with deceptive intention, and necessitate, again, a new counter-speech (double negation, that is, affirmation). That simple affirmation [*Zusage*] can already be understood as assertion [*Bejahung*] is due to its *ex post facto* equivalence with double negation.

5

A radical counter-image to both Heidegger's Aristotle and Kimhi is presented by Hegel and Adorno. In the beginning was the negation, not so much in the immediate logical beginning as the pure Nothing, which is just as much pure Being (this speaks for their equiprimordiality), but rather: in the logical-conceptual beginning as the pure, reflexive, and absolute negation that the (Hegelian) Concept, the principle of the logical, represents. Qua concept, negation is more original, not only than the apophantic "as" of *kataphasis*, but even than the hermeneutic "as," and is the origin and the engine of everything logical. The antinomy thesis comes very close to this with its emphasis on reflexive negation and thereby introduces a dialectical moment into hermeneutic realism. The question of the title, whether hermeneutic realism is a dialectical materialism, can therefore be answered in the affirmative insofar as hermeneutic realism is, at least, a dialectical realism.

The antinomy thesis, it seems to me, stands or falls with the priority of negation to assertion. If negation is prior, the Liar is a philosophical challenge; but if the assertion takes precedence or is co-original with negation, we have only a nicely puzzling enigma, from which nothing will follow, except, perhaps and indirectly, as Tarski has shown, certain things for model theory, the semantic branch of mathematical logic. Kimhi teaches the co-originality of negation and the predicative assertion: it is, according to him, the privative exercise of the two-way faculty of predication.[2] We saw that one should rather attribute this status to the predication that is false, and assign negation a new, remedial status in relation to this one. But either way, without the priority of negation, the two-way character of the logical remains inexplicably suspended. Furthermore,

---

[2] I have to thank Andrea Kern for the most legitimate indication that Kimhi may not be condemned for the one-sided primacy of predication against negation, as suggested by careless wording on my part.

the claim of co-originality does not help here, since it is an aspect of what is to be explained rather than an explanation.

But, for present purposes, be this as it may. Let us ask instead how, through the priority of predication to negation or their co-originality, the antinomy of negation could be neutralized. With reference to this Kimhi makes a suggestion worth considering by extending Frege's context principle (against Frege's intention) from the context of predicate logic to that of proposition logic. The sentence "p" (we pretend that "p" is a sentence, not a schematic letter or a dummy for sentences) does not occur as a sentence in the context of the negation "~ p." Instead, with the expression "p" the sentence "p" is only gesturally hinted at, just as – Kimhi's example – one indicates decapitation by means of a hand gesture crossing the throat. If this is so, then every negation presupposes an antecedent predication independent of it, to which it can make a gesture-like reference. Negation and proposition-logical operations in general are thus tacitly understood as executions of a primitive semantic ascent, as ways of indicatively mentioning sentences, and already the truth-functional complexion proves to be a covertly metalinguistic one. The Liar, however, according to its logical grammar, cannot include any reference to a prior, independent predication. Let's look at the Liar in its minimal form: "This is false." The predicative phrase "is false" serves here as an operator of negation. But the indexical "this" is not a sentence, and nor can one refer by it to a predication prior to the Liar; rather, it is indeed intended to refer to the Liar itself.

If, then, the assertion takes precedence over negation or is co-original with it, then nothing is asserted in Liar-paradoxical sentences; consequently, they are neither true nor false, but senseless, and simulate sense only in a grammatical-lexical way. As mentioned, the two-way nature of the logical [des Logischen] and the bivalence of the assertion then remain unexplained and in abeyance, but we will pass over this fact. We turn, finally, to the opposite side. We read in Adorno that thinking is supposed to be "an act of negation, of resistance to that which is forced upon it" (Adorno 1973, p. 19); for him this is what thinking has inherited from work, its own prototype. Through work, or the planned organization of his metabolism with nature, *homo sapiens* not only transforms nature, but also transforms himself[3] into the *zôon logon echon*. The *logos* as thinking is the general and abstract form of working, which, as a formal invariant, runs through all special activities as an unavoidable basic activity, which we cannot choose be-

---

[3] The masculine form "himself" here answers to the grammatical gender of the Latin noun "homo;" the Greek "*zôon*" that follows would require the neutral form "itself." By the way, "persona sapiens" would have required "herself."

cause it is the condition of the possibility of any choice. Work, however, negates its material, and through such negation, humans thus tear themselves free from their animal existence, from the absorption in a pre-intentional feeling which once wholly determined their relationship to nature.

Against the "popular materialistic usage" of equating "the mind [...] with cerebral processes" (Adorno 1973, p. 194), Marx has, according to Adorno, drawn "the line between historic materialism and the popular-metaphysical kind" (Adorno 1973, p. 197). The former aims not at brain physiology and, finally, physics, but at history and economics, especially at the history of labor. And it is not only because this history is a history of class struggles, but rather because work is, at its heart, negation, that historical materialism is dialectical. The original negation is the process of detachment from pre-intentional animal life with its characteristic feelings. Do we find here an immediate, a given? The myth of the given in ontology is (broadly understood) logical atomism, i.e. the assumption that reality ultimately consists of distinct, not essentially related entities. The myth of the given in epistemology is the assumption that logical form can operate on entities which themselves have no logical form. The animalistic feeling has no logical form; negation cannot operate within it, unless the myth is true. In its primary operation, therefore, negation operates only on itself, and only through this does the object constitute itself, over against it (i.e. negation) qua subjectivity, out of the pre-intentional feeling, as a logical subject for possible predications.

This consideration of the justification of the priority of negation over the predicative assertion, drawn from Adorno, supplements the twofold justification of the antinomy thesis. Those who cite Kimhi-like objections to the argument from the example of the Liar should be persuaded by the *tu-quoque* argument, or by the connection between the primacy of negation and the critique of the myth of the given in ontology and epistemology. It is strange, of course, that thinking begins in contradiction, and moreover, in a hopeless one that constitutes its pure form. Thinking works (in the literal sense of "working") itself out and works itself free of nature by being engaged in the confrontation with the material provided by nature into less contradictory and more materially rich domains. Regarding the question of the title of this paper this means: yes, hermeneutic realism is, if you like, a dialectical materialism. And why not?

(Translated by Dominik Finkelde and Paul Livingston)

Bibliography

Aczel, Peter (1988): *Non-Well-Founded Sets. CSLI Lecture Notes* (vol. 14). Stanford: CSLI.
Adorno, Theodor W. (1973): *Negative Dialectics*. Translated by E. B. Ashton. London: Routledge.
Aristotle (1999): *Metaphysics*. London: Penguin Classics.
Gabriel, Markus (2017): "Wie viel Subjektivität verträgt der ontologische Realismus?" In: *Deutsche Zeitschrift für Philosophie* 65, pp. 792–797.
Gadamer, Hans-Georg (2004): *Truth and Method*. Translated by Joel Weinsheimer and Donald G. Marshall. London: Continuum.
Heidegger, Martin (1962): *Being and Time*. Translated by John Macquarrie and Edward Robinson. Oxford: Blackwell.
Heidegger, Martin (2001): "Language." In: *Poetry, Language, Thought*. Translated by Albert Hofstadter. New York: Harper, pp. 185–208.
Kant, Immanuel (1997): *Critique of Pure Reason*. Edited and translated by Paul Guyer and Allan W. Wood. Cambridge: Cambridge University Press.
Kimhi, Irad (2018): *Thinking and Being*. Chicago: The University of Chicago Press.
Koch, Anton Friedrich (2016): *Hermeneutischer Realismus*. Tübingen: Mohr Siebeck.

Iain Hamilton Grant
Nature After Nature, or Naturephilosophical Futurism[1]

Abstract: This paper interprets Schelling's "Weltgesetz" as a manifesto for philosophical futurism. As the Law of the World, the *Weltgesetz* is neither imposed upon nor summative of a world. Rather, as both systematic and open-ended, it cannot be satisfied by any one state of any given world, but only, on a principle of radical non-exclusion, by all. Viewed as such, the quest for an objective ontology is not a quest for the objective furniture of the world. Schelling, instead, favours a first philosophy as ontogeny, or an account of the becoming of being. "World" for Schelling is thus not synonymous either with "planet" nor with "the entire universe." Rather, the term means, in an important sense, that there will be no whole – not even a paradoxical one including itself – because a world was never not what creation will become.

Schelling reports that "world (according to the Old High German term) means a standing, duration, a definite period of time."[2] 'World' on this account is neither synonymous with 'planet' nor with 'whole,' insofar as planets gravitationalize as well as perdure, and because, being local with respect to time so qualifies a Whole, an All, or a One as always to render it instead a part. That is, 'world' means: there is no whole (even including the whole that includes the whole and that which it is part of) that includes a final environment. It is the world turned inside out and the center thus dispersed. Yet Schelling also discusses pre-worldly and post-worldly states, thus augmenting the non-included systems amongst which 'world' figures.

If we ask '*how* does the world so figure?' we may imagine this figuring as the drawing of a line. No line may be drawn that does not create three spaces: this side, that side, and the line itself. For this reason, it is a mistake to think that one line is sufficient to forge a division, which does not occur unless that one line is situated within a pre-delimited space. Were there no such pre-delimited space, the line remains a line, not a division, and becomes one space among (at

---

[1] A version of this paper was first delivered at St. Johns University, Newfoundland, Canada, in August 2013. My thanks to Sean McGrath for the invitation, and to the students and staff of the Philosophy department there for their astute taxing and enthusiastic questions.
[2] "*Welt* (*nach dem altdeutschen Worte*) *eine Währung, eine Dauer, eine bestimmte Zeit bedeutet*" (Schelling 1998, p. 15).

least) three (in non-delimited space, there is no limit to the number of spaces because there is no 'in' in it). Similarly, an occurrence – a world in the above sense – does not arise *in* one time; rather, because it arises, there are three times: pre-worldly, post-worldly and worldly. It is, according to this explication of 'world', geogeny itself that individuates time-systems.

That 'world,' 'pre-world,' and 'post-world' are individual systems does not, I will argue, entail a larger 'meta-world' system these individual systems compose – that is, they are not themselves parts of a larger system such as a continuous 'time' running through them; their existence at all, rather, entails their non-obtaining. My claim is that nature obtains when there is an open-ended number of systems to which their non-obtaining may always be added. Such a view has consequences regarding how the situatedness of abstract entities in nature is conceived, which in turn has consequences regarding how nature is conceived. If, that is, nature is reformulated as a non-exclusive category, then not only is there nothing in particular that nature is, but more importantly, neither is there any thing that nature is not.

1 Nature and Thought

Frege says "there are thoughts" in the full Platonic sense. But where? We know that brains are organs that form the thinking we call ours, and we know that brains occur "naturally." It is not false therefore to state that nature thinks. Firstly, however, nature performs many tasks, very few of which resemble, at first glance, thinking. What is the significance of the claim being made, therefore, when it is said that nature thinks? Might there be a species of naturalism so idealistic as to assert that thinking is in fact all that nature does, even when it *may seem* that nature is "mountaining" or "planetizing?" Yet secondly, what warrants restricting the extension of "thinking" to the thinking I recognize myself and other sapient mammals as having, being, or hosting? The assumption that thought is substrate-independent is effectively a transcendental and a material condition for modelling Artificial Intelligences. The assumption is that the prospect that thinking may occur in environments compositionally and chemically unlike than that in which mine does is a genuine one. Yet surely such a prospect, if it is thus agreed that it is one at all, obtains not only for such environments as experimental engineers might manufacture, but also for others than those supporting a thinking we currently call 'natural'? Such a prospect entails acknowledging that the forms and media for the expression or actuation of thought need not resemble one another, save in one crucial respect: that there be repeatable structure.

To address, as I intend to here, nature *and* thought does not mean that *all* that is thought is *all that nature is*, but rather something like the following: the "nature" that is in thought *is* also the "nature" that is in *nature*, save that if it is true that nature precedes thought – if it is true, that is, that the cosmos is not a late acquisition of thinking, but rather the converse: that thinking is a later acquisition of the cosmos – then the "nature" that is *in* thought is a consequent one, or, as we may call it, a "nature after nature."[3]

Nor does "nature is thought" amount to a judgment that all of nature is or will be thought. Such a judgment, if thought is consequent upon nature, would amount to the elimination of natural history or thought's recovery of initial conditions that never belonged to it but which eventually enabled its existence. Such conditions, whatever they were, would have been the very beginning of nature itself, before there was any thought about it whatsoever and, we might add, therefore before there was any nature – unless, that is, the "not-being" of nature is a necessary element of what nature is.

More simply and more positively, by "nature is thought" I mean: when there is thinking, it is an event *in* nature. What difference this makes and how this situation ('thought is in nature') is to be conceived will be addressed in what follows.

So stated, the alternatives to this view are, it seems to me, untenable. Amongst these alternatives is the claim that 'thought is *not* natural' but belongs to an impersonal and abstract "third realm," a *kōsmos noetōs* or an isolably intellectual world. Such a world could have, in principle, no connection with the world in which it arose.

There are two ways of parsing this dualistic claim: firstly, it could be argued that the difference in kind between thought and nature makes their identity of origin irrelevant. The laws of thought are entirely separable not only from this but from any particular physical-physiological substrate. No matter what is going on brainside, so to speak, thoughts do not obey electromagnetic, but rather logical laws. Since the latter are properly supervenient upon the physical substrate, they are irreducible to it in turn. Therefore *thought is just not natural*. This account, however, mistakes irreducibility for independence, since it is no more the case that thought arises *ex nihilo* than that particular thoughts may be replaced by their causally underpinning brain states without loss of meaning.

---

3 "'Nature after Nature" was the title of an exhibition at the Friedericianum, Kassel, curated by Susanne Pfeffer in July 2014, and in which I participated. The 2013 Newfoundland version of this paper, however, was called "Nature after Nature," showing that we had arrived at this usage independently and, moreover, that we were both keen to exploit the phrase's ambiguity, since it refers both to imitation and consequence.

Thought may enjoy autonomy with respect to its precursor states, of whatever kind these may be; yet it remains irreversibly and inseparably dependent on such states occurring.

Yet perhaps all this talk of brain states and physical and logical laws mistakes the essential in matters of thought. Thus, the second way of parsing the cosmological dualism between thoughtworlds and thingworlds would begin from the fact that the thought of what a brain, computer, or river bed (I will explain this below) are doing when they are thinking differs in kind from what such entities are in fact doing. That is, the addition of thought is not like the addition of the n-th pebble to a cairn, but rather places the events thought about into a context to which they would otherwise have no access. Accordingly, the functions and operations to which thought has access bear no logical relation whatsoever to events of a non-thought kind. Thus, *the nature that is thought is not the nature that is nature.*

Yet why is this meta-physical functionality not precisely part of the natural history of thought? Firstly, nothing will undo the natural historical fact that this is precisely what thought has done. Secondly, surely the account just given remains dependent on the bond thought establishes with the earth, whence it arises if the events thought deems irreplaceably thought-like are to be claimed to be elsewhere undiscoverable. Yet doesn't this contrastive bond disprove what it sets out to prove, namely, that thought operations are irremediably contextually different from other types of operations? For if this were true, no such contrast could be judged or thought to obtain without violating the principle it seeks to establish.

On both accounts, then, it is false that there is a world of stones on the one hand and a world of thoughts on the other. Whatever the *kōsmos noetōs* might be (I have considered it here only according to more or less contemporary paradigms, yet historically it has been treated as the world made by the thoughts of God,[4] a world to which, if God were the world's creator, this world would in fact belong) it is not the case that it amounts to a "second nature" (Kant, McDowell) or "third realm" (Popper) which is *not* a physical cosmos. Because the idea of an "intellectual cosmos" sums this up, and because this phrase *does not occur in Plato,*[5] I call these emergent dualisms "false Platonism;" and there is one further example, weaker than the other two, but nevertheless pervasive.

---

4 See Philo of Alexandria (1929).

5 According to both Paul Shorey (in a note to the second volume of his Loeb translation of Plato's *Republic*. Cambridge: Harvard University Press, 1935, p.130a) and, more recently, Hermann Krings (in his edition of Schelling's *Timaeus* (1794). Stuttgart-Bad Canstatt: Frommann Holz-

Thought and nature are *opposed*, it may be argued; yet if so, how? What term belongs to the one that cannot belong to the other and yet divides them? How can the absence of matter qualify one species of entity while its presence qualifies another? And would such a division occur *in nature* or *in thought*? If in nature, nature is divided and that's all there is to it. There is a domain called, perhaps, "hyper" or "super" nature, depending on choice, in which entities belong if they have neither place in nor contact with nature. If, by contrast, the division occurs in thought, then does it also occur in nature? If not, then we only *think* that thought and nature are opposed, so that in nature, no such opposition obtains.

I do not want to resolve or reopen the problems of dualism in the philosophy of mind; my purpose is simply to point out that it is more prevalent than we might imagine, even in this "Age of Science" (Putnam 2012), and that it is implicit whenever thought is asserted not to be a natural occurrence. Nor yet have we asserted what it is that nature is – does it consist, for instance, in what the best of our natural sciences tell us it does? Even were this the case, would this exhaust the problem of what nature is, that is, the ontological problem of nature? It is to this that we proceed next.

2 Systematicity and Depth

An ontology in which nature *figures*, that is, the thinking of the being of nature or of nature as Being, cannot simply reproduce nature in thought, for two reasons. First, were nature thus "embraceable in thought," as John McDowell likes to say, then thought would be not only the larger of the two domains, but also the more grounding. Nature would be the issuance of thought, rather than the other way round, but by the same token, the difference in kind between them would evaporate so completely as to eliminate nature from ontology. The ontology of nature would have its elimination as its consequence. Second, should thought (*per impossible*) repeat nature so completely as to be indistinguishable from its object, then neither can thought be distinguished from nature. Thus, nature would have had no consequence whatsoever.

Yet naturephilosophy, which I will define as the philosophy of the nature in which ontology figures, does not demand nature's reproduction as if this were to consist in a stand-alone or autonomous image. Rather, it requires that nature's

---

boog, 1994, p.82). For a discussion of this point, see my *Philosophies of Nature After Schelling*, ch.2.

reproduction be itself an instance of nature doing what nature does. That is, a nature that has philosophy in it requires that the latter be consequent upon a nature that was without it, but also that it reiterate, by some means, this process in its turn, since unless it were to do so, it would not be *being* nature, or doing what it is that nature does. If we accept, then, that a system that is the cosmos is also a system that is thinking, the question inevitably arises as to the precursors and/or ultimate consequents of this nature or self-iterating cosmos. How, in other words, did this system of antecedents and consequents arise? This is the question with which Schelling began his celebrated *Stuttgart Seminars* in 1810:

> To what extent is a system ever possible? I would answer that long before man decided to create a system, there already existed one, that of the world-system or cosmos. (Schelling 1994, p. 179)[6]

That thought is consequent upon nature is, again, clearly asserted. Yet the passage says more than this. It states that no system that is thought is reducible to thought because it is antecedent to thought. As per Schelling's claim, that is, the system in the thinking is, *qua* system, the system in the cosmos; or the system that is the cosmos is the system that is thinking.

Far from boiling down to a macrocosm-microcosm relation, Schelling's point induces a serial operation into the concept of system as *itself* having a natural history, both "pre-worldly" and "post-worldly," as he elsewhere puts it (Schelling 1946, pp. 21, 120).[7] Although the thought of the natural history of systems has become commonplace amongst the contemporary sciences, it is here introduced philosophically, which means both that it answers questions concerning the conditions of possibility of systems; and that the operation it identifies, if it obtains at all, should also iterate beyond the situation it describes, into the pre- and post-worldly, or pre- and post-cosmic.

If, that is, a system is at all identifiable, and if this identifiable system is consequent upon a system already having obtained, then it follows either that (1) there is a system of eternity or (2) that system is an item consequent upon some other. If (1) were true and this system always obtained, then in what sense would system be consequent at all? If, conversely, it is true that identifiable or thinkable system is consequent upon cosmological or worldly systems, it

---

[6] The German text: Friedrich W. J. Schelling, *Stuttgarter Privatvorlesungen* (Schelling 1856–1861, I/1–10; II/1–4; here: I/7, p. 421).
[7] The terms derive from the first (1811) and second (1813) versions of the *Weltalter* typescripts but do not occur in the third (1815), printed in Schelling (1856–1861, I/8).

must be the case that these, too, are consequent upon some other, since otherwise (1) remains true and there is no consequence.

If we accept the non-eternity of systems, whether cosmological or thoughtish, then it follows that system must be consequent upon something that is not it, just as thought is consequent upon the nature that, until there was thought, nature either *was* not or *did not produce*. So system is only consequent if there previously existed not-system or "asystasy." Asystasy is that of which there may be no system and is therefore the negation of systems. But 'not-system' is an insufficient ground if we want the grounds of system to have some relation to that ground which makes a system's emergence from it at least retrospectively knowable. The prejudice here, however, is that grounding is equivalent to determination or, if you prefer, that causality occurs only on a 'push' rather than on a 'pull' model. If, in contrast with push-modelled causality, a pull model is assumed, then the future will determine a past as being the past of that future, on two conditions.

The first of these is that the future does not resemble its past. If this were not the case, nothing could ever happen other than what already had. The second is that the consequent character of the future does not proceed towards a goal, but changes the direction that the past would have assumed had no consequent occurred. If both conditions are met, then nature amounts to stratified remains of futures, each of which cancels the direction that what becomes their past would have taken had these remained unchecked by a future they do not resemble.

If geogeny did not individuate times, as Schelling argues, there would be a first system of time at the root of all times, and the question of how far our excavations of the past would need to extend in order to reach the very *first* first would follow the dimension of depth alone. Yet the beginning is a time in which that whose beginning it is, by definition, is not there. The deep past is inhabited by firsts and earliests – it is palaeontological; but the pre-worldly is simply uninhabited. Thus the impoverished question, "How can I know the past?," reveals not simply its species-parochialism (can there be no other imaginable knowers but the ones we happen, as a matter of fact, to know?),[8] but more importantly its locality as consequent upon a geogeny by which world is a system and which is not that of the pre-worldly. For such an account as this, it is not locality but *universality* that is the problem: if there is just one universal system,

---

[8] Species-parochialism receives its defining formulation in Thomas Nagel's answer to his otherwise excellent question, 'What is it like to be a bat?,' which is: "there is nothing that it is like to be a bat, since a bat lacks the means of contrasting its own sensibility with that of others." What this proves is that *Nagel* lacks what he accuses the bat of lacking, thus rendering his conclusion solely a matter of a self-reflection.

how can it have consequents? Moreover, what would 'universality' be if not the hypothesis of a single universe? If so, then there is no universality, since the universe is unrepeatable according to that hypothesis, meaning that nothing actually has nor can have in principle the same extension as the universe without being it.

If by contrast we start the other way round, by asserting that there are consequents, that there is, therefore, a future, then it follows that individuation is the ambit of locality as such, and that individuation consists in the generation of a system consequent upon one as an element of which it did not figure. If this is accepted, the question now turns to *what* is individuated if individuation is thus systemic.

3 Consequence and Locality

That there are consequents means that a difference has been introduced with respect to antecedents. But antecedents are not such by nature, so to speak. Rather, they become antecedents just when consequents obtain, and not because they contain their consequents. If they did contain their consequents, then in what sense could consequence be said to obtain?

The terms 'antecedent' and 'consequent' are susceptible of both a logical and a natural reading. According to the former, the medieval terms 'antecedent' and 'consequent' are replaceable by the modern nomenclature for the parts of the proposition, namely 'subject' and 'predicate.' According to the natural reading, however, antecedent and consequent are localities such that what is true of the former may not be of the latter, and the latter is not merely "said of" the former as in predication. It is important to take this natural account of locality in all its dimensions.

Firstly, that it is natural does not mean, as we have seen in part 1 of this essay, that it is therefore not logical; rather, that it is logical entails that it is natural. According to the natural reading of antecedence and consequence, sequence is entailed by their conjunction, not because the resultant proposition is of some state of affairs whose merely formal echo it is, but rather because the operation it describes is the operation it performs. Sequence, that is, occurs. This means that the logical reading of antecedence and consequence is unwarrantedly reductive of the operations of which they treat.

Secondly, that it is natural, or perhaps we might say 'worldly,' location that we are dealing with does not mean that locality is to be determined spatially according to this or that system of coordinates. We may say instead that natural locality is distributed precisely as antecedent and consequent as successor temporal systems (not as parts of the one temporal system, as we saw in section 2). It is not the locality of the proposition's referents, but the locality that the individuated elements of the proposition have, and the locality that the proposition as a whole has, in relation to time.

Thirdly, the individuation it therefore performs is, at its most general, that of the *locality of the operation*, where this operation consists in individuation, that is, in the local distribution of localities. That is, the locality of the operation is not a 'place in time' because locality is, rather than *contains*, the unfolding of the operation.

Fourthly, we cannot derive from this 'general' nature pertaining to the operation a 'most general' and therefore 'universal' natural operation, because such an operation would then be all that nature is or could be. It would be done in advance, no sooner started than finished. That is, if the general operation is individuation, then at root, what is individuated by 'antecedence' and 'consequence' is precisely individuation operations, or localities.

Fifthly, were consequence universal, it would entail consequence "all the way down." But consequence all the way down would not be consequent upon anything if it were universal. Therefore, consequence is itself local if there exists consequence at all. Moreover, this means that locality is not consequent upon universality – it is not a space picked out within a larger one; therefore locality is only consequent *once* there is consequence, i. e. *futurally*. Strictly speaking, therefore, there are not localities but only *consequent or futural localities* that will be only once consequents have occurred.

Finally, consequence is locality also when it is non-exhaustive. This means contrastive cases must occur, i.e. instances in where there is no consequence. One such instance would be a past so deep as not yet to have had consequences, a past, that is, following which nothing 'first' has yet been deposited, a Big Bang without an ensuing expansion, or an emanation without anything having emanated. Such a past is not yet antecedence, for such would obtain only relative to a consequence. Nor, therefore, can it be said to be the beginning of antecedence, the first crack of the Big Bang, or a dissonance in the One prior to emanation. Unchecked by futurity, the past telescopes because it is not, as such, part of any consequent. Beginning *per se*, that is, is not the beginning of anything. Creation, finally, is misconceived if it is considered as a simple locality. Identified creation is at the very least located or posited locality. Rather, creation occurs in the growth of consequent locality, or 'metalocality.' This growth is not without limits, but rather itself a local concatenation of localities, or the issuance of locality from localities.

Nature thus comprises a "palaeontological" system of beginnings and a futurist system of consequences. The antecedents created by the latter are not members of the system of the former, since they *will be* the antecedents of what consequents are to occur. That is, the locality we have been examining applies both intra- and inter-systemically. We may treat of each system separately or of both together, provided that the latter case remain local in the sense discussed. Minimally, that is, the union of the two systems differs from either system on its own. Moreover, the idea of a beginning is local with respect to the system of beginnings, just as that of an end is local to that of antecedents and consequences. In other words, there is no extra- or meta-systemic beginning or end *of all things*. Thankfully, biology provides an illustration.

4 Morphogenesis and the Cuticle

According to Alessandro Minelli's *Forms of Becoming*, the twin errors of comparatism in contemporary evolutionary developmental biology are

1. the assumption of discrete processes in organic development (cerebrogenesis, hepatogenesis, etc.); and
2. the finality assumption in morphogenesis, i.e. the assumption of "programmed adulthood."

A process is "discrete" when it is said to terminate in the achievement of a specific end, and morphogenesis correspondingly discrete when an organism achieves adulthood. The systems of antecedence and consequence are not discrete in this sense, since their iterability entails that ends are locally relative. Locality, in other words, is general but not universal, while discreteness is non-repeatable particularity. A process is discrete when it retains its identity regardless of when it occurs. By contrast, a process is local if its individuation is itself consequent, and will suffer consequents different from it. The generation of brains, for instance, remains currently local to animal life, but need not remain so. Moreover, it is consequent upon the emergence of life as such, which is consequent upon planetary, solar, and cosmological formation. If nature undermines process-discreteness, our sciences ought to reflect this.

Minelli's attempt at precisely this is achieved by dropping the assumptions of process-individuation ('discreteness') and finality. In consequence, he advocates searching not for completed individuals between which to establish homologies, as Richard Owen[9] or Lorenz Oken (1847) did in nineteenth-century compa-

---

9 See, for example, Phillip R. Sloan's 'On the edge of evolution' (1992).

rative natural history. By contrast, evolutionary developmental biology shifts its attention from finalistic programming, or a consequent without consequence, towards *elementary operations and non-specific tools*.[10] Thus, just as animal appendages (legs or antennae) are iterations of the central axis of an animal's body but lack an individuated "internal leaflet" or digestive tract such as animal bodies possess, so the operation that initially constructs "polarity" across the "anterioposterior axis" of a bilateral or symmetrical animal body (mouth-anus, as determined by the pole that encounters new location; geophiliac-geophobic, as determined by that surface that maintains contact with the substrate), also constructs additional dimensions (rotation about an axis perpendicular to the anterioposterior; raising and lowering; exploration of as yet unoccupied loci, etc.).[11] For Minelli, genes are not plans but positions, locating the branching of appendages from an animal axis and, given a moult-series in insects, for example, the quantity of the iteration of segments. In keeping with the hypothesis of natural logics, genes are, so to speak, copulae conjoining any nonfinal morphogenetic stages (e.g. in the centipede, larva-segment iteration), which stages in turn constitute a copula to the second power (segment-appendage iteration). Thus, in place of "uniquely defined units" such as 'segment' or 'tissue,' "whose evolution we can study or whose generative processes we can highlight, [a] plurality of structures, each one the result of intertwined developmental processes, now corresponds to each of these concepts" (Minelli 2009, pp. 107–108).

Because finally eliminating finality indifferently makes forms into media depending on the sequencing of antecedence and consequence; and because the same "indiscrete" ontogeny[12] applies also in the case of putatively individuated processes, development finally abandons the reflective principle of process and product. Thus, Minelli criticizes the "biogenetic law" with which, *inter alia*, Carl Friedrich Kielmeyer is associated, on the grounds that it fails to account for novelty.[13] In the case, that is, of perfect and linear recapitulation, ontogeny or individuation runs through exactly those stages passed through by phylogeny or spe-

---

10 See Alessandro Minelli (2009). On non-specific organic genesis, see p. 129; on "finally getting rid of finality," see pp. 89–90; on elementary operations and non-specific tools, pp. 192–193.
11 Minelli 2009, p. 47: "In these animals [Bilateria], the front is the extremity with which the animal always encounters new locations, and the top is the side opposite the one the animal, if it moves on the ocean floor or on the ground, uses to remain in contact with the substrate."
12 For "indiscrete ontology," see Hogrebe 1992, pp. 116–119. For ontogeny as locally supplanting ontology, see the 'Preface to the Italian Edition' of my *Philosophies of Nature After Schelling* (2017).
13 I argue this is a false account of the so-called biogenetic law, which is mere shorthand for the theory of recapitulation, in chapter 4 of *Philosophies of Nature After Schelling* (2008).

ciation. A *principle of sufficient reason*, that is, that "the full cause is equivalent to the entire effect,"[14] is undone precisely if the case for the individuation of either is not merely epistemologically, but rather ontologically moot. If, as we have argued, no function is process- or product-specific (that the 'function of the eye is to see'[15] is a virtue operated equally by the camera NASA attached to a blind man's brain in 1966), the problem of individuation is condensed from entity to iterative quantity: *how many iterations can a process undergo?* Thus, the primary outcome of Minelli's evo-devo (as "evolutionary developmental biology" is nicknamed) lesson, is that morphogenesis (the development of form), *is inseparable from locality, just as an individual is from the ecosystem of which it is itself a local expression.*

In morphogenesis, locality turns out to have a complex relation to process-iterability: there is no discrete process whose archetype rests at the root of nature, driven to expression by internal pressures. Rather, individuation, or a morphogenetic episode, arises when metalocality, i.e. the consistency of consequence upon consequence, like drawing a line, possesses an iterative quantity. As in creation itself, *einmal ist keinmal.*

Yet if a consequence is one only when it differs from its antecedent, it would seem that the only consistency to be had in iterative quantity or individuation is that there is differentiation. Surely, moreover, once this is said to apply also at the inter-systemic level, the consequence that there are several systems, each of which is systemic yet of which there is no system in general, effectively makes systematic organization asystemic? Isn't this simply a contradiction?

5 How Many Natures?

The question of the number of natures does not seem, at first sight, to be one much asked. Yet that there is a particular number of natures is often asserted, and varies generally between "only one" and "two," the second being dominant. There is a virtue in the latter conception that is vitiated by its finalism, as I shall show below, but my purpose here is to rescue its virtue.

> The science with which we are concerned knows no other law than that all possibilities are fulfilled and none suppressed. (Schelling 1856–1861: II/1, p. 492)

---

[14] I use Isabelle Stengers' concise formulation, from *Power and Invention* (1997, p. 25).
[15] On functional specificity and realism, see Maurizio Ferraris, "Sum ergo cogito. Schelling and Positive Realism" (2013, pp. 187–189).

In this sentence, Schelling defines what he calls the *Weltgesetz*, the Law of the World. Why, we might ask, is it "worldly" or natural that all possibilities be fulfilled? One solution would be to identify nature with the sum-total of possibilities and to say, with the Schelling of four decades prior to positing the *Weltgesetz*, that "anything whose conditions simply cannot be given in nature, must be absolutely impossible" (Schelling 1856–1861: I/3, p. 571). In this case, however, the equation offers a reduction of possibilities only if we already know what it is that nature is, and how to differentiate it from other entities. If, that is, it is proposed that nature is as physics describes it, then amongst the host of entities contrasting to nature are plants, numbers, and persons. Yet the consequence of this would be that Schelling would be asserting that plants, numbers, or persons are impossible, which is far from true.

If by contrast a broader concept of nature is adopted, and if it is, as *per* the hypothesis, possible in nature that there are contradictions, this has the advantage that contradictions, hitherto regarded as reducibly logical entities, are naturally occurring. Moreover, since all that we thus know is that contradictions occur *in* nature, we may say both that nature is such as to embrace contradictions and that the latter are therefore local events within the former, rather than the reverse. This means that any state of affairs belongs in nature only if its contrary is admitted as a possibility. The law of the world now states: *if* it is a possibility that nature is that domain in which an entity may and may not occur, then it is also a possibility that nature is not that domain. If by that law all possibilities are fulfilled, it follows that both the obtaining and the not-obtaining of that state of affairs belong to nature.

By the same law, however, it follows that nature might not obtain. It is important to recognize that this is not a merely logical possibility, amounting to the assertion of the contingent fact that nature does exist. Rather, its contingency consists not in its obtaining at some time, i.e. locally, but rather in the sequencing of its obtaining and not obtaining. Because both must occur, it follows from Schelling's law of the world that ontogeny supplants ontology as first philosophy.

Given this pattern of reasoning, let us make it more concrete and ask: how many natures are there? If there were just one, then the possibilities of its non-obtaining in the future or having not obtained in the past are eliminated. Perhaps, then, there are two: nature insofar as it exists, and nature insofar as it does not. Yet were this the case, then there would be at least three possibilities: (1) that nature obtains; (2) that it does not, and (3) because contradictions are possible and therefore must be satisfied, that nature both obtains and does not. Minimally, there will therefore be three natures.

But this does not mean nature is *all that is*, because its obtaining includes its own not-being. Nature is all that is only if it is (a) complete and therefore (b) no consequences obtain. But if (b) is the case, then consequences could never have obtained, since then nature would not have been and now is, contradicting the claim. Or, if nature is completed and no consequents obtain, then nature is eliminated. If nature obtains, its non-obtaining must also obtain, and one must be consequent upon the other (even should nature's elimination be this consequent), from which it follows that nature is not all there is. Does this, nature's locality, mean in turn that there is something that is not-nature? No: it means that *if* there is nature, this is the case just when there are consequents, and when there is no upper limit to the number of consequents, and therefore the number of natures, which can obtain.

Moreover, this means that the *Weltgesetz* is satisfied by no *Weltgesetzt*, no world or cosmos posited as past with respect to the positing. It is at this point that the law of the world bites against the much discussed possibility of a "second nature." What is intuitively wrong about the claim that a second nature can exist is that it is merely second, i.e. that it stops there and, moreover, stops nature. In general terms, the philosophical content of second nature is *our*, and therefore, rather optimistically according to its proponents, *moral*, our *educated* or *educable* nature that supplants the nature upon which this plastic morality is consequent. It is clearly intuitively wrong to posit such a second nature since it, the consequent, is larger and more powerful than the nature prior to it. Moreover, the seond nature worldly-posit has no bite whatsoever unless, to counter Kant's fears of terrestrial disturbances eliminating the Kingdom of Ends, it is final with respect to the nature preceding it. Or it might be final in the sense that it forms the outcome of all natural outcomes, a consequent that envelops its predecessors and consumes the past as its own, as opposed to the past retaining its efficacy in respect of any and all antecedents and consequents.

Such a nature is as absurd as it is instrumentalist: it fails to discover the locality it perforce articulates just as it denies consequents, whereas, even should the nature that nurtures humanity be eliminated, nature will remain just insofar as there are consequents, even if these are neither humans nor, for instance, the crustaceans H.G. Wells forecast as our far future replacements in *The Time Machine*.

That no posited nature is final with respect to the nature preceding it does not mean there are no posited natures, but only that these are amongst the innumerable consequents nature has as its function to produce once there is nature, i.e. consequence, at all. On this basis – and this is the virtue of a naturalistic account of second-natural naturalism – not only does ontogeny supplant ontology, but naturephilosophy becomes futurism, just because the worldly posit is nonfinal and philosophy local to the nature whose philosophy it is does not mean that the quantity of its posits' iterability is set in advance. Since consequence is what determines antecedence as the antecedence of *that* consequence rather than another, it follows that futurism is not prediction, but nature's conceptual reengineering of its local efficacy. Amongst the consequences of the two dimensions of the locality of thought in nature (the denial of which, as we saw in section 1, was philosophically untenable) – namely (1) its antecedent embeddedness in nature when (2) it is a consequent articulation of nature, i.e. a movement of which it was hitherto incapable – are the following.

First, if logic is simply a pattern occurring in nature, then it is one amongst many: there are the desiccated riverbeds of the Baja peninsula, for example, which are manifestly amenable to fractal formalisation, or the branching or *Entzweiung* patterns developed by particular trees; the rivers of methane on Titan, or the fractured surface of Europa; each amounts to a thought otherwise unarticulated. Here we have the basis for a properly philosophical ecology premised not on the elimination of moral animals but on that of thoughts nature was once capable of having, but no longer is. How many have thus passed? Here the question of a system of systems achieves new purchase: is there a natural tower of Babel, a system of all systems that permits their universal translatability?

Secondly, if it is consequence that determines the antecedent as the antecedent of that consequent, then the past is overrated as determinant. To grasp this fact entails the reorientation of conceptual activity in accordance not with where nature is, but where it will be. Philosophical futurism is therefore part of the determination of what it was that nature will have been, not globally or universally, but locally, as befits any of nature's many products.

Bibliography

Colson, F.H. and Whitaker, G.H. (1929): *On Cosmopoiesis according to Moses. Philo of Alexandria. Volume I*. Translated by F.H. Colson and G.H. Whitaker. Cambridge, Mass.: Harvard University Press.

Ferraris, Maurizio (2013): "Sum ergo cogito. Schelling and Positive Realism." In: Emilio Carlo Corriero/Andrea Dezi (Eds.): *Nature and Realism in Schelling's Philosophy*. Turin: Accademia University Press, pp. 187–189.

Grant, Iain Hamilton (2008): *Philosophies of Nature after Schelling*. London, New York: Continuum.

Grant, Iain Hamilton (2017): *Filosofie della natura dopo Schelling*. Translated by Emilio Carlo Corriero. Torino: Rosenberg & Seiler.

Hogrebe, Wolfram (1992): *Metaphysik und Mantik. Die Deutungsnatur des Menschen (Système orphique de Iéna)*. Frankfurt am Main: Suhrkamp.

Krings, Hermann (1994): *Timaeus (1794): Zur Bedeutung der 'Timaeus'-Handschrift für Schellings Naturphilosophie*. Stuttgart, Bad Cannstatt: Frommann Holzboog.

Minelli, Alessandro (2009): *Forms of Becoming. The Evolutionary Biology of Development*. Translated by Mark Epstein. Princeton: Princeton University Press.

Oken, Lorenz (1847): *Elements of Physio-Philosophy*. Translated by Alfred Tulk. London: Ray Society.

Pfau, Thomas (Ed.) (1994): *Idealism and the Endgame of Theory: Three Essays by F.W.J. Schelling*. New York: SUNY.

Philo of Alexandria (1929): *On Cosmopoiesis according to Moses*. Translated by tr. F.H. Colson and G.H. Whitaker, *Philo I*. Cambridge, Mass.: Harvard University Press.

Putnam, Hilary (2012): *Philosophy in the Age of Science. Physics, Mathematics, and Skepticism*. Mario de Caro/David Macarthur (Eds.). Cambridge, Mass.: Harvard University Press.

Schelling, Friedrich W.J. (1856–1861): *Schelling Werke*. Edited by K.F.A. Schelling. Stuttgart, Augsburg: Cotta Verlag.

Schelling, Friedrich W.J. (1856): "Stuttgarter Privatvorlesungen". In: *Schellings Werke*. Edited by K.F.A. Schelling. Stuttgart, Augsburg: J.G. Cotta Verlag.

Schelling, Friedrich W. J. (1946): *Die Weltalter Fragmente*. Edited by Manfred Schröter. München: C.H. Beck.

Schelling, Friedrich W. J. (1994): "Stuttgart Seminars". In: *Idealism and the Endgame of Theory. Three Essays by F.W.J. Schelling*. Translated by Thomas Pfau. New York: SUNY, 1994, pp. 195–243.

Schelling, F. W. J. (1998): "System der Weltalter". In: Siegbert Peetz (Ed.): *Münchener Vorlesung 1827/28 in einer Nachschrift von Ernst von Lasaulx*. Frankfurt: Vittorio Klostermann.

Shorey, Paul (1935): *Plato: The Republic*. Cambridge: Harvard University Press.

Sloan, Phillip R. (1992): "On the Edge of Evolution". In: Richard Owen (Ed.): *The Hunterian Lectures in Comparative Anatomy. May and June 1837*. London: Natural History Museum.

Stenger, Isabelle (1997): *Power and Invention*. Translated by Paul Bains. Minneapolis: University of Minnesota Press.

Part 2 **Relativism**

Johannes Hübner
Metaontological Deflationism and Ontological Realism

Eli Hirsch's Doctrine of Quantifier Variance

Abstract: This paper discusses Eli Hirsch's ontological deflationism, as it is presented in Hirsch's doctrine of quantifier variance. On this view, ontological disputes about the existence and nature of material objects can be understood in terms of distinctions between different users' ontological languages. Hübner shows that ontological relativism proves to be the only way for Hirsch to save his deflationist idea according to which seemingly contradictory ontological claims can be interpreted as true within their respective languages. Therefore, quantifier variance cannot be maintained as a form of ontological realism, contrarily to what Hirsch claims.

The last 30 years have seen a revival of metaphysics and ontology, followed more recently by a renewed interest in metaontological questions. Different varieties of metaontological deflationism have been put forward, all of them agreeing that at least some disputed ontological questions rest upon wrong presuppositions and therefore should be abandoned. Proponents of this or that variety differ in what they identify as mistaken presuppositions. Antirealists deny that there are any ontological facts to disagree about in the first place. Sceptics reject optimism about the possibility of justifying (some) rival ontological claims.[1] According to the easy ontology of Amy Thomasson (2015), it is a mistake to see a hard task in answering ontological questions of existence. Finally, Eli Hirsch aims at showing that (some) ontological disputes are merely verbal, so that it would be wrong to regard them as substantive issues.

This paper deals with Hirsch's position, which is known as the "doctrine of quantifier variance." One might suspect that denying substance to ontological questions commits one to denying objects a substantive, mind-independent mode manner of existence. By contrast, Hirsch, like Thomasson, purports to combine metaontological deflationism with ontological realism. While Putnam, whom Hirsch credits with the doctrine of quantifier variance, opposes what he calls "metaphysical realism,"[2] Hirsch himself describes his own position as "ro-

---
[1] Cf. Bennett (2009); she dubs her variety of metaontological deflationism "epistemicism".
[2] Cf. Putnam (1989) for a short statement of his position.

https://doi.org/10.1515/9783110670349-007

bustly realist" (Hirsch 2009, p. 231) and repeatedly declares the compatibility of quantifier variance with ontological realism.[3] The question of this paper is whether Hirsch actually succeeds in avoiding ontological antirealism.

I will proceed as follows: the first two sections introduce some terminology and present Hirsch's deflationary strategy. Using the debate about mereological composition as an example, the third section discusses the application of this strategy. The upshot of my discussion will be that Hirsch's metaontological deflationism cannot work without ontological relativism and therefore is in conflict with ontological realism.

1 Definitions

In my argument, I will assume that ontological relativism in its most common form implies ontological antirealism. Therefore, some definitions are in order. Following Michael Devitt (1991) and Alexander Miller (2016) one may define ontological realism with regard to some domain as a combination of two theses: first, a thesis about existence, and second, a thesis about mind-independence.

> (R) *Ontological realism about F's:* There are F's and their existence does not depend on the mental (in non-trivial ways).

The clause in brackets is meant to do justice to the fact that some things, e.g. mental states and artefacts, depend upon the mental in trivial ways. Of course, mental states and artefacts would not exist if there were no creatures with minds. This is trivial, since understanding the concept of a mental state and an artefact tells you as much. Such trivial mind-dependence of something should not preclude ontological realism with respect to it. Roughly, the existence of F's is trivially mind-dependent if the concept of an F entails that F's exist in virtue of mental or linguistic activities.

Often, realism is defined in terms of truth. Given the equivalence scheme

> the proposition that p is true if and only if p

definition (R) may be stated equivalently in this way:

---

[3] Cf. Hirsch (2002, pp. 52–53; 2008, pp. 373–374). Hirsch says: "In fact, I would want to stipulate that only realists count as quantifier variantists" (2011, p. xvi).

(R*) It is true that there are *F*'s and this truth does not depend on the mental (in non-trivial ways).

(R*) is just a semantically ascended version of (R). Ontological antirealism is the negation of ontological realism.

Ontological realism about *F*'s is incompatible with usual forms of ontological relativism about *F*'s. In general, relativism about a subject-matter has it that the corresponding propositions are true or false relative to certain parameters, e.g. epistemic systems, aesthetic standards, or moral systems.[4] But a relativist has to say more. She has to say, first, that there are several parameters, second, that different parameters may yield incompatible evaluations for one and the same proposition, and third, that there is no way of privileging one parameter over others.[5]

Propositions of taste may serve as an uncontroversial example: there are different standards of taste; the proposition that apples are delicious is assigned the value 'true' according to my standard of taste and the value 'false' according to your standard of taste; there is no way of privileging my standard of taste over yours.

Ontological relativism may be defined accordingly. Usually, conceptual schemes are chosen as parameters for ontological relativism. A conceptual scheme may be understood as a language or part of a language which contains, among other things, rules of application for predicates. Of special interest are predicates like 'compose something.' The rules of application for such predicates allow us to assign truth values to existential propositions, say the proposition that there is something composed of the moon and the Eiffel tower. So we may define ontological relativism about *F*'s as follows:

(REL) If *p* is an existential proposition about *F*'s, then:

(i) *p* is true or false relative to some parameter of type *R*

(ii) there are different parameters of type *R*

(iii) different parameters may yield incompatible evaluations for *p*

(iv) no parameter is privileged.

---

4 This way of presenting relativism corresponds to what Crispin Wright (2007) calls "New Age Relativism." By contrast, traditional indexical relativism would build the relativizing parameters right into the propositions.
5 As made clear by Boghossian (2006, ch. 4).

One can see now why ontological realism is incompatible with ontological relativism in its usual guise. Ontological realism is incompatible with any version of relativism employing mind-dependent parameters. Since conceptual schemes are mind-dependent and the usual form of ontological relativism refers to conceptual schemes, ontological realism is incompatible with ontological relativism in its usual form. To put it otherwise, usual ontological relativism implies ontological antirealism, though not vice versa. Being an ontological relativist (in its usual form) is one way among others (e.g. eliminitavism and expressivism) of being an ontological antirealist.

Therefore, it is interesting to note that in one of his papers, Hirsch recommends an "existential realism" which amounts to ontological relativism as defined above. He further reports his inclination to think that there is "no genuinely substantive difference" between "existential realism" and "quantifier relativism," 'quantifier relativism' being another name for the doctrine of quantifier variance (Hirsch 2004, pp. 231–232). This would mean that there is "no genuinely substantive difference" between the doctrine of quantifier variance and ontological relativism as defined above.[6] If this were correct, it would be a serious threat to the compatibility of ontological realism with metaontological deflationism based on the doctrine of quantifier variance.

2 Hirsch's deflationary strategy

Hirsch's deflationary idea is that some ontological disputes are merely verbal. He does not claim that all ontological disputes are merely verbal, but he holds that some are. He concedes, for example, that the debate about abstract entities might well involve substantive disagreement while insisting that the dispute about mereological composition is indeed merely verbal. Roughly, his deflationism pertains only "to issues about the existence and identity of perceivable objects" (Hirsch 2008, p. 377). The reason for this restriction is that mutual translatability between rival ontological positions is crucial for Hirsch's argument and that only ontological claims about such issues seem to satisfy the condition of intertranslatability.

Hirsch's argument may be described as proceeding in three steps.

---

[6] Usually, Hirsch thinks of quantifier variance in terms of different ontological languages and not in terms of different conceptual schemes. In his 2004, Hirsch adopts reference to conceptual schemes from Sosa's discussion of existential relativity; cf. Sosa (1999, p. 133).

a) First, he suggests that one may legitimately look upon the parties of certain ontological disputes as speaking different ontological languages. In particular, one may interpret them as using different quantifier idioms.

b) Once seen in this way, ontological disputes may be related to the doctrine of quantifier variance introduced in the second step. In a recent contribution, Hirsch states it thus: "The doctrine says that there is no uniquely best ontological language with which to describe the world" (Hirsch 2011, p. xii). Ontological languages with different meanings may have equal descriptive power since they may serve equally well for making true claims about the world, while – this is crucial – the claims in different languages may be true even if they prima facie contradict each other. As the doctrine's name suggests, relevant possible differences in meaning especially concern the words used to express existence: "the words 'what exists' and related words [...] corresponding to the quantifiers of our language, can vary in meaning from one language to another" (Hirsch 2009, p. 231). E. g., if a person comes to accept the principle of unrestricted composition for physical objects which she formerly rejected, Hirsch would say that she adopts a new sense of 'exist;'[7] eventually the meanings of other words would also be affected.

c) Finally, Hirsch concludes that at least some ontological issues are purely verbal because his criterion for verbal dispute is fulfilled. As he explains: "It is a dispute in which, given the correct view of linguistic interpretation, each party will agree that the other party speaks the truth in its own language" (Hirsch 2009, p. 239). E. g., one party says "there are F's" while the other says "there are no F's." And yet, if they are charitable interpreters, they will concede that each is right in its respective language, showing that their controversy has the "status of being 'merely a matter of choosing a language'" (Hirsch 2016, p. 107).

In order to become clear about the force of this claim, one should note that Hirsch excludes two rather unexciting readings. First, his point is not that sentences like "there is a God" might have just any meaning in other languages (Hirsch 2008, p. 374). E. g., if "there is a God" in your language meant that apples are green, you would not contradict my claim that "there is no God." We would just talk past each other because 'there is' in your language would not function as a quantifier. By contrast, Hirsch thinks that the meanings of the quantifiers in a language might be changed in such a way that the expressions still count as quantifiers, yielding "a *different* or *extended* notion of existence" (Hirsch 2002, p. 53). In particular, the intended meaning changes may not affect the logical

---

7 Hirsch (2002, p. 53); cf. Putnam (2004, p. 234).

properties of the quantifier expressions. Quantifier rules like existential generalization will remain intact.[8]

Presumably similar qualifications should apply to possible meaning changes of other words. E. g., if accepting the principle of unrestricted composition also affects the meaning of 'whole,' the word will still express a "different notion of whole." Otherwise, accepting an ontological principle like the principle of unrestricted composition would amount to changing the subject.

Second, the intended changes in meaning do not amount to quantifier restrictions. Given an unrestricted domain of discourse, it would be easy to restrict the domain. Seeming contradictions could be easily explained away. E. g., my "there is no beer" would not contradict your "there is beer" if the domain presupposed in my utterance were restricted to the content of my fridge while you were talking about drinks available in your home. But quantifier restriction is not what Hirsch has in mind (cf. Hirsch 2002, p. 64). Otherwise, the claim of equal descriptive power for different ontological languages would be untenable because, other things being equal, a language with restricted quantifiers cannot match the descriptive power of an unrestricted language.[9]

So Hirsch's deflationary claim is that two philosophers sharing the correct view of linguistic interpretation will accept as true in the respective language what they say with "there are *F*'s" and "there are no *F*'s," even though in both languages 'there are' expresses existence and the domains are unrestricted. How could that be true? Ontological relativism would provide an easy answer. Relative to different conceptual schemes, both the proposition that there are *F*'s and the proposition that there are no *F*'s might be true. But Hirsch has to show that the criterion for verbal dispute can be satisfied without appealing to such a form of ontological relativism. Does he succeed? I will pursue this question by retracing the three steps of the strategy sketched above.

---

[8] Hirsch remarks that changing the meaning of the quantifier expressions might also be described as "'giving up the quantifier'" (Hirsch 2002, p. 53). Referring to this remark, he later comments that if one preferred this description "maybe we should talk of quantifier 'elimination' rather than 'variance'" (Hirsch 2011, p. xiv). It is hard to reconcile this generosity with his claim that a language and its altered counterpart should be on a par as ontological languages. For how could a language without quantifiers and without a notion of existence qualify as an *ontological* language? Therefore, I will ignore the suggestion of "quantifier elimination."

[9] Given that these readings are not intended, it is quite difficult to see how one could explain the different meanings of 'there is' in different languages. Either the different meanings amount to domain variation, or not. If not, it is not clear what they do amount to. For this objection, cf. Hale and Wright (2009, pp. 181–184).

3 A version of metaontological deflationism without ontological relativism?

a) Different ontological languages

Why should it be legitimate to describe two English speakers as using different languages once they have entered into a controversial discussion about the ontology of physical objects? Let us consider the dispute about mereological composition as an example. The main question discussed is whether arbitrary physical objects compose a whole. In other words, do arbitrary physical objects automatically have a sum or a fusion? Those who say 'yes' are called mereologists while those who say 'no' are anti-mereologists. Mereologists affirm, e.g., that the moon and the Eiffel tower do compose a whole, while anti-mereologists deny it. Let us express their positions by a pair of seemingly contradictory sentences:

(1) There is something that is composed of the moon and the Eiffel tower.

(1N) There is nothing that is composed of the moon and the Eiffel tower.

Suppose that anti-mereologist Ann and mereologist Mike are English speakers disagreeing about the truth conditions for sentences (1) und (1N). Ann rejects (1) and accepts (1N) when uttered in English. She believes that some unifying relations must obtain between any two things if they are to make up a whole. Since no such relations obtain between the moon and the Eiffel tower, she believes that they do not compose anything. By contrast, Mike believes that arbitrary things compose something regardless of any special relations obtaining between them. According to him, no more than existence is necessary for composition. He accepts (1) and rejects (1N) as English sentences. Whenever Ann and Mike engage in ontological discussion with one another, they each claim that the other is wrong. Each of them thinks that the other does not get the facts right.

In order to persuade them each to cede that the other's position is true in the sense of Hirsch, one would first have to get them to see each other as speaking different languages whenever engaged in ontological debates about physical objects.

Hirsch (2009, pp. 233–234) develops a thought experiment in order to make plausible that participants in ontological controversies about physical objects speak different languages. Adopting his example, we may suppose that Ann is tired of discussing this with Mike and decides to conceal her disagreement. She secretly adopts a code or "language of her own" which allows her to utter sentences exactly like the sentences which Mike would utter in his language in order to state his mereological views.[10] She devises a mereological language M by stipulating truth conditions for sentences containing mereological vocabulary. She stipulates that, e.g.,

> Sentence (1) as a sentence in language M is true $=_{df}$ the moon and the Eiffel tower exist.

More generally, in M, sentences of the form 'a and b compose something' are stipulated to have the truth condition that a and b exist. Similar stipulations concern sentences containing 'part' and 'whole.' Ann believes what she says in her new language, e.g. she believes what she says by uttering (1) in language M. After all, that only says that the moon and the Eiffel tower exist. So she feigns Mike's linguistic behaviour. She talks as if she were a mereologist.

We may imagine Mike doing the same: he devises an *anti*-mereological language A by stipulating truth conditions, e.g.

> Sentence (1) as a sentence in language A is true $=_{df}$ some unifying relations obtain between the moon and the Eiffel tower.

More generally, sentences of the form 'a and b compose something' are stipulated to have in language A the truth condition that a and b stand in unifying relations to each other, whatever that amounts to. Similar provisions are made for expressions like 'part' and 'whole.' So Mike has found a way to veil his disagreement with any anti-mereologist while staying faithful to his convictions. While Ann affirms (1) as a sentence in M, Mike denies (1) as a sentence in A because he denies that there are unifying relations between the moon and the Eiffel tower.

Although they disagree about the truth conditions for (1) as a sentence in English, they would agree about the truth conditions for (1) as a sentence in A and in M if they knew the language devised by the other.

So far, Ann and Mike have found ways to hide their disagreement (of course, they should not employ their languages at the same time). What else is accomplished? Hirsch seems to assume that if one party devises a special language in order to talk like the other, then the other party may correctly be described as

---

10 Hirsch individuates sentences as strings of symbols apart from any meaning. According to Hirsch, sentences get meanings by being used within a language so that one and the same sentence may have different meanings in different languages. Within a language, sentences have interpretations which assign them meanings, while the meanings fix the truth conditions. Cf. Hirsch (2009, p. 234).

using that language. The question whether this assumption is correct will be postponed to section 3c).

b) Equal capability for truthful description of the world?

Within the next step, the doctrine of quantifier variance comes into play. Applied to the case at hand, it says that languages A and M are descriptively equivalent or have "essentially the same fact-stating power" (Hirsch 2008, p. 376). Hirsch bases this claim on the assumption that one may translate the one language into the other: "It is indeed because of this intertranslatability that the proponent of quantifier variance maintains that the two languages are equally capable of truthfully describing the world" (Hirsch 2002, p. 57). In order to cast doubt on this claim, consider the sentence

> (2) Some things do not compose anything.

As a sentence in language A, (2) is true because it says that some things do not stand in unifying relations to each other, which is indeed the case, while as a sentence in language M this is false because it says that there are some things which do not exist, which is a contradiction (on the assumption that 'there are' and 'exist' have the same meaning).

Let us describe matters from Ann's point of view; that is, let us assume that the principle of unrestricted composition is false. We could adopt Mike's position just as well. What matters is not whether Ann or Mike is right; what matters is whether a proponent of an ontological thesis who believes himself to be engaged in an ontological dispute could be expected to agree to Hirsch's claim. Could Ann reasonably agree that language M is capable of truthfully describing the world? This is not the case. For as long as she uses language M, Ann cannot truthfully express her conviction that some things do not compose anything and therefore she cannot truthfully state what she considers a fact. Uttering (2) as a sentence in M means producing a contradiction.

Here is an analogy. Imagine an old lady with plenty of grandchildren and great-grandchildren. Grandmother cannot cope with the fact that some couples have children without being married. Unfortunately, none of her grandchildren is married, although several of them live in permanent relationships and have children. So all of her great-grandchildren stem from illegitimate relationships. Grandmother cannot acknowledge those embarrassing facts. She just calls her grandchildren and their partners wives and husbands. So instead of saying "your partner just called" or "Tom just called," she would say "your husband just called."

The grandchildren want to avoid hurting Grandmother's feelings and secretly adopt a language in which all couples with children satisfy the predicate 'married,' Grandmother-married so to speak. They stipulate, e.g.

'a and b are married' in Grandmother-code is true $=_{df}$ a and b are a couple with children.

Similar stipulations concern 'wife,' 'spouse,' and so on. This is the Grandmother-code. The grandchildren agree to use the Grandmother-code whenever Grandmother is nearby.

Now let us ask whether the Grandmother language is as capable of truthfully describing the world as English is. Obviously, this is not so since the Grandmother-code cannot truthfully describe a real difference, namely the difference between married couples with children and *un*married couples with children. In Grandmother-code there is no sentence expressing the fact that some couples with children are not married. Consider this sentence:

(3) Some couples with children are not married.

By uttering (3) assertively in *English* one states a fact. But by uttering (3) assertively in *Grandmother-code* one asserts the contradiction that some couples with children are not couples with children. So the Grandmother-code lacks the means of truthfully describing one part of reality – which is what was to be expected since the code is devised in order to conceal some embarrassing facts.

The same is true of language M. Just as the Grandmother-code cannot describe the difference between married and unmarried couples with children, M cannot describe the difference between things which do compose something and those which do not. Again, this is not surprising since language M is devised in order to conceal commitment to mereological assumptions. (There are many more facts Ann could not truthfully state if she were confined to language M, e.g. the fact that the moon and the Eiffel tower do not compose anything; that the dark side of the moon and the Eiffel tower do not compose anything; that the moon and the upper half of the Eiffel tower do not compose anything, and so on. So, from her point of view, M is no good at truthfully describing the world.)

We may also view matters from Mike's perspective. Mike should not agree that anti-mereological language A is capable of truthfully describing the world because it would not allow him to truthfully assert that any two things compose something. Using A, Mike would be bound to make the absurd claim that any two things stand in unifying relations to each other.

If it is a fact that some things do not compose anything, Ann cannot express this fact truthfully by using language M. Then M is not as capable of truthfully describing the world as A. If it is a fact that any two things do compose something, Mike cannot express this fact truthfully by using language A. In this case A is not as capable of truthfully describing the world as M. So language A and language M are not equally capable of truthfully describing the world, and Ann and Mike should not agree that they are.

Note that at this point Hirsch would not be entitled to object that the existence and nonexistence of complex objects are not matters of fact because thereby he would simply presuppose ontological antirealism concerning complex objects.

To sum up this point: One should not concede that A and M are equally capable of truthfully describing the world.

c) Which language is spoken?

The question to be addressed next is whether Hirsch's criterion for verbal dispute is satisfied, i.e., whether Ann and Mike should agree that each one speaks the truth in her own language. Let us return to the pair of seemingly contradictory sentences (1) and (1N). Hirsch is committed to saying that

> Ann should agree that: If Mike utters (1) in his own language, he says something true.
>
> Mike should agree that: If Ann utters (1N) in her own language, she says something true.

I will refer to these claims as Hirsch's irenic claims. The crucial question is which language is spoken by Ann and Mike within their ontological exchanges. We thereby come back to the question which has been postponed in section 3a): if one party devises a special language in order to talk like the other, is the other party to be seen as using that language? Presumably, one would say that Ann and Mike speak English, at least as long as they do not switch to their secret languages.

But it is crucial for the argument Hirsch offers for his irenic claims to interpret them otherwise. By adaptation from Hirsch (2009, pp. 239–241), one can extract the following argument with respect to the first irenic claim:

(i) If Mike utters (1) as a sentence in M, he says something true.
(ii) If Mike utters (1) as a sentence in M, he speaks his *own* language.
(iii) So, if Mike utters (1) in his own language, he says something true.

In an analogous way one could argue with respect to the second irenic claim:

(i) (i') If Ann utters (1N) as a sentence in A, she says something true.
(ii) (ii') If Ann utters (1N) as a sentence in A, she speaks her *own* language.
(iii) (iii') So, if Ann utters (1N) in her own language, she says something true.

If Ann and Mike should agree to these arguments, Hirsch's irenic claims would be established. Should they? Premises (i) and (i') are trivial. Premise (i) is trivial because what is said with (1) in M is true if and only if the moon and the Eiffel tower exist. Premise (i') is trivial because what is said with (1N) in A is true if and only if there are no unifying relations between the moon and the Eiffel tower.

The crucial steps are premises (ii) and (ii'). It is obvious that one should not interpret the *anti*-mereologist as using a *mereological* language and should not interpret the *mereologist* as using an *anti*-mereological language, and it might seem that one should interpret the *anti*-mereologist as using an *anti*-mereological language and the *mereologist* as using a *mereological* language. But in fact, one should interpret both Ann and Mike as speaking English, for the simple reason that otherwise interpretation will miss their characteristic claims. Here is why.

If Ann utters sentence (1) in language M she merely states the fact that the moon and the Eiffel tower exist. Sentence (1) is stipulated to have this truth condition in M – the whole point of language M is to avoid expressing any further commitments concerning composition. By parity of reason, if mereologist Mike uses (1) in mereological language M, he also merely states the fact that the moon and the Eiffel tower exist. But if Mike speaks his *own* language and utters (1), he wants to assert that the moon and the Eiffel tower do compose something. He does not merely want to make the trivial claim that the moon and the Eiffel tower exist.

So, if Ann interprets Mike as using language M when speaking his own language, she takes him not to make the point he wants to make as a mereologist, i.e. that arbitrary things like the moon and the Eiffel tower do compose something. She takes him to avoid asserting his characteristic commitments concerning composition. So Ann would do a bad job of interpretation if she took Mike to use M as his own language. Mike could reasonably complain that Ann would not let him make the claims he wants to make. He should insist that she interprets him as speaking English.

The same applies to Mike's possible interpretations of Ann. Suppose *anti*-mereologist Ann utters (1N) in her own language and Mike interprets her as using *anti*-mereological language A. Given this interpretation, Ann would say that there are no unifying relations between the moon and the Eiffel tower – which is trivially true, but simply not what she wants to say. She wants to say that the moon and the Eiffel tower do not compose anything (due to lack of unifying relations). Ann could reasonably complain that Mike's interpretation misses the claim she wants to make (after all, just like language M, language A is made in order to avoid expressing characteristic commitments concerning composition). She should insist that he interprets her as speaking English.

Here is another analogy. The catholic dogma of papal infallibility says that the pope cannot possibly err if he declares a doctrine of faith speaking *ex cathedra*, i.e. as the teacher of all Christians. We might put it thus:

(P) If the Pope *ex cathedra* declares that *p*, then it is true that *p*.

E.g., it was declared in 1950 that Virgin Mary was bodily taken up into Heaven. Let Cate be a faithful Catholic who believes that Mary was taken up into Heaven bodily and who believes dogma (P). I for my part am disinclined to share her beliefs. I introduce a new use for the word 'true,' marked by an unspoken asterisk, by stipulating that

proposition *p* is true* =$_{df}$ *p* is true or declared *ex cathedra* by the Pope.

Of course I accept that it is true* that Mary was bodily taken up into Heaven. If Cate uttered the sentence "It is true that Mary was bodily taken up into Heaven" and if I interpreted her as using my 'true*,' then I would miss what Cate wants to claim. Cate should reject my interpretation because it would disallow her to assert her faith. Our disagreement about the truth of papal declarations would not be rendered verbal but would be simply ignored by me as long as I insisted on my interpretation. The upshot is that interpreting a speaker as saying something trivially true may be inadequate because it would miss the claim the speaker wants to make.

Up to now, we have not yet considered the "correct view of linguistic interpretation" which, according to Hirsch, has to be in place if Ann and Mike will agree that Ann is to be interpreted as using language A and Mike as using language M (in mereological utterances). Hirsch appeals to the "principle of charity" which he explains as follows: "Central to linguistic interpretation is the presumption that the correct interpretation is the one that makes people's use of language as reasonable as possible" (Hirsch 2009, p. 240). Therefore, he adds, in interpreting a language one has to presume that typical speakers "make perceptual assertions that are reasonably accurate." Let us grant this and see what follows.

Hirsch would surely be correct to claim that Ann should not interpret Mike as using the *anti*-mereological language A when Mike is speaking his own language and states his mereological views.[11] Otherwise, Ann would interpret Mike as saying with sentence (1) that some unifying relations obtain between the moon and the Eiffel tower – which is obviously not the case. Neither should Mike interpret Ann as using the *mereological* language when Ann is stating her anti-mereological views, e. g. by asserting (1N). Otherwise, he would interpret Ann as saying that the moon and the Eiffel tower do not exist – which is manifestly false. According to these interpretations, Ann and Mike would assert obvious falsehoods. One should not interpret them in this way.

But it does not follow, either, that Ann should interpret Mike as using language M or that Mike should interpret Ann as using language A. The problem with these interpretations is not that they have Ann and Mike asserting obvious falsehoods. The problem is rather, as we have seen, that they do not allow them to say what they want to say when speaking their own language. So these interpretations are not charitable. The simple solution is that Ann and Mike should interpret each other as speaking English.

So far, there does not seem to be a good reason why we should take Hirsch's criterion for verbal disputes to be fulfilled in Ann's and Mike's case. The availability of languages A and M does not help to render their dispute merely verbal; rather, it allows them to agree on the level of mere words.

Let us sum up: None of the three steps of Hirsch's deflationary strategy as applied to the dispute about mereology seems to be successful. Neither does it seem to be legitimate to view the parties in disputes about the ontology of physical objects as speaking different languages; nor is it the case that the alleged ontological languages are equally capable of truthfully describing the world; nor is Hirsch's criterion for verbal dispute satisfied in our example.

What does this mean for the question of ontological realism? Let us have a final look at Ann and Mike. Given that both are speaking English when speaking their own language, it seems that they contradict each other when Ann utters

(1N) There is nothing composed of the moon and the Eiffel tower

and Mike utters

(1) There is something composed of the moon and the Eiffel tower.

---

[11] Hirsch (2009, p. 240) presses an analogous point with regard to the endurantist-perdurantist debate.

After all, the first sentence is the negation of the second. Is there any chance for what is said with the sentences to come out equally true? As far as I can see, the only remaining possibility for ascribing truth to both propositions is to appeal to relative truth. If the propositions expressed by (1) and (1N) are not true and false absolutely but relative to some conceptual scheme, then Ann and Mike might agree that both say something true by asserting (1) and (1N) in English. What Mike says might be true relative to the conceptual scheme of mereology, what Ann says might be true relative to some anti-mereologist conceptual scheme. Then Hirsch would end up with the usual form of ontological relativism.

This is an undesirable result. If Hirsch did rely on this form of ontological relativism, he could not remain faithful to his ontological realism. I have no strict argument showing that Hirsch's metaontological deflationism implies ontological antirealism. My point is that the only available way for Hirsch's metaontological deflationism to succeed is to appeal to the usual form of ontological relativism, thereby precluding ontological realism. Therefore I conclude that Hirsch's brand of metaontological deflationism is not compatible with ontological realism.

Bibliography

Bennett, Karen (2009): "Composition, Colocation, and Metaontology." In: David Chalmers, David Manley, Ryan Wasserman (Eds.): *Metametaphysics: New Essays on the Foundations of Ontology*. Oxford: Oxford University Press, pp. 38–76.

Boghossian, Paul (2006): *Fear of Knowledge: Against Relativism and Constructivism*. Oxford: Oxford University Press.

Devitt, Michael (1991): "Aberrations of the Realism Debate." In: *Philosophical Studies* 61, pp. 43–63.

Hale, Bob and Wright, Crispin (2009): "The Metaontology of Abstraction." In: David Chalmers, David Manley, Ryan Wasserman (Eds.): *Metametaphysics: New Essays on the Foundations of Ontology*. Oxford: Oxford University Press, pp. 178–212.

Hirsch, Eli (2002): "Quantifier Variance and Realism." In: *Philosophical Issues* 12, pp. 51–73.

Hirsch, Eli (2004): "Sosa's Existential Relativism." In: John Greco (Ed.): *Ernest Sosa and his Critics*. Malden, MA: Blackwell, pp. 224–232.

Hirsch, Eli (2008): "Ontological Arguments: Interpretive Charity and Quantifier Variance." In: Theodore Sider, John Hawthorne, Dean W. Zimmerman (Eds.): *Contemporary Debates in Metaphysics*. Malden, MA: Blackwell, pp. 367–381.

Hirsch, Eli (2009): "Ontology and Alternative Languages." In: David Chalmers, David Manley, Ryan Wasserman (Eds.): *Metametaphysics: New Essays on the Foundations of Ontology*. Oxford: Oxford University Press, pp. 231–259.

Hirsch, Eli (2011): *Quantifier Variance and Realism: Essays in Metaontology*. Oxford: Oxford University Press.

Hirsch, Eli (2016): "Three Degrees of Carnapian Tolerance." In: Stephan Blatti and Sandra Lapointe (Eds.): *Ontology After Carnap*. Oxford: Oxford University Press, pp. 105–121.

Miller, Alexander (2016): "Realism." In: Edward N. Zalta (Ed.): *The Stanford Encyclopedia of Philosophy*. Winter 2016 Edition. https://plato.stanford.edu/archives/win2016/entries/realism/, visited on 10 January 2019.

Putnam, Hilary (1989): "Truth and Convention: On Davidson's Refutation of Conceptual Relativism." In: Michael Krausz (Ed.): *Relativism: Interpretation and Confrontation*. Notre Dame, IN: University of Notre Dame Press, pp. 173–181.

Putnam, Hilary (2004): "Sosa on Internal Realism and Conceptual Relativity." In: John Greco (Ed.): *Ernest Sosa and his Critics*. Malden, MA: Blackwell, pp. 233–248.

Sosa, Ernest (1999): "Existential Relativity." In: *Midwest Studies in Philosophy* 23, pp. 132–143.

Thomasson, Amy L. (2015): *Ontology Made Easy*. Oxford: Oxford University Press.

Wright, Crispin (2007): "New Age Relativism and Epistemic Possibility: The Question of Evidence." In: *Philosophical Issues* 17, pp. 262–283.

Martin Kusch
Stances, Voluntarism, Relativism

Abstract: This paper explores two ideas put forward and defended in Bas van Fraassen's *The Empirical Stance* (2002) as well as in some related papers. The first idea is that many philosophical positions are best rendered not as "doctrines" but as "stances," that is, as sets, systems, or bundles of values, emotions, policies, preferences, and beliefs. The second idea is a form of epistemology that van Fraassen calls "epistemic voluntarism." It is based on the rejection of two received views: that principles of rationality determine which philosophical positions and scientific paradigms we must adopt, and that epistemology is (akin to) a descriptive-explanatory (scientific) theory of cognition. The paper relates the stance-idea and epistemic voluntarism to debates over (epistemic) relativism.

1 Introduction

In this paper I want to explore two ideas put forward and defended in Bas van Fraassen's *The Empirical Stance* (2002) (=*ES*) as well as in some related papers. The first idea is that many philosophical positions are best rendered not as "doctrines" but as "stances," that is, as sets, systems, or bundles of values, emotions, policies, preferences, and beliefs. (To avoid torturous repetition, I shall refer to sets of values, emotions, policies, and preferences as "VEPPs".) The second idea is a form of epistemology that van Fraassen calls "epistemic voluntarism." It is based on the rejection of two received views: that principles of rationality determine which philosophical positions and scientific paradigms we must adopt, and that epistemology is (akin to) a descriptive-explanatory (scientific) theory of cognition. I shall relate the stance-idea and epistemic voluntarism to debates over (epistemic) relativism.

2 Stances

ES seeks to renew empiricism. According to van Fraassen, empiricism is first and foremost a "rebellion" against metaphysics. This is because "metaphysicians interpret what we initially understand into something hardly anyone understands, and then insist that we cannot do without that" (2002, p. 3). Take the question "Does the world exist?" To answer this question, metaphysicians use a technical concept of world. David Lewis, for instance, holds that a world simply is "the sum of all things spatio-temporally related to a given thing" (2002, p. 10). How does Lewis arrive at this result? Why is the mingle-mangle of things more or less distantly related to me "a world?" As *ES* sees it, Lewis simply "postulates" how "world" is to be understood and that it exists. It is here that van Fraassen "rebels:" "... I did not ask whether the existence of the world can be consistently postulated! I asked: Does the world exist?" (2002, p. 10).

Empiricism rejects Lewis' and other metaphysicians' theorizing. This rejection is motivated by empiricism's core elements. In order to explain what these core elements are, van Fraassen first offers a reflection on how, in general, philosophical positions are to be understood. His primary target is what he calls "Principle Zero:"

> (*Principle Zero*) For each philosophical position X there exists a statement $X+$ such that to have (or take) position X is to believe (or decide to believe) that $X+$ (2002, p. 41).

Assume *Principle Zero* were adequate. What then would be the dogma "$E+$" for empiricism? Going by the received (textbook) view, the most obvious candidate, at least for the "naïve empiricist," is the following:

> ($E+$) Experience is the one and only source of information (2002, p. 43).

If *Principle Zero* were correct, van Fraassen thinks, then it would have to be able to perform a crucial critical function. For any alternative ($=A$) to empiricism, if A's $A+$ were to turn out incompatible with $E+$, then the (naïve) empiricist would thereby have reason enough to reject A, and even without entering into any further argumentative give-and-take. For instance, given *Principle Zero*, an empiricist critique of metaphysics would have to show no more than that metaphysics and its central dogma is incompatible with $E+$.

ES does not accept *Principle Zero* and its interpretation of the encounter between empiricism and metaphysics. In order to summarize the argument succinctly, I shall use "empiricism$_{E+}$" for an empiricism rendered in terms of *Principle Zero* and $E+$. van Fraassen's key move is to remind that the content of empiricism in general, or empiricism$_{E+}$ in particular, is not exhausted by $E+$. A crucial further element of both is an admiration for the ideal of empirical science, to wit, the ideal according to which all empirical hypotheses deserve an unbiased and open-minded investigation. Empiricists$_{E+}$ emulate this ideal when they think of $E+$ as an empirical hypothesis and as subject to rigorous empirical testing (2002, pp. 42–44).

Unfortunately, the ideal of an open-minded testing of empirical hypotheses is incompatible with how empiricists$_{E+}$ intend to rule out metaphysics. Empiricists$_{E+}$ want $E+$ to *immediately and directly* rule out of court every alternative A whose $A+$ is incompatible with $E+$. And yet, if $E+$ is an empirical hypothesis, then so are statements contradicting $E+$. Some of the latter are core doctrines (=$A+$) of alternative philosophical positions, like metaphysics. But if these $A+$ are also empirical hypotheses, then they too deserve to be tested in the normal way of empirical science. In other words, these $A+$, or *non-E+*, cannot be ruled out on the sole basis that they conflict with $E+$.

For *ES*, all this is reason enough to give up *Principle Zero* and empiricism$_{E+}$. van Fraassen's empiricism – let's call it "empiricism$_{vF}$" – is defined not by a single dogma like $E+$ but by a set of VEPPs and beliefs. This gives the advocacy for the ideal of empirical-scientific inquiry a new role in the opposition to metaphysics. Empiricism$_{vF}$ can rule out metaphysics immediately, and without entering into extended debate. This is, van Fraassen claims, because metaphysics does not emulate the conduct of empirical science; it does not value empirical hypotheses; and it does not engage in the empirical testing of philosophical theses. We have here an incompatibility in VEPPs rather than an incompatibility in dogmas. But it still gives the empiricist$_{vF}$ a sufficient and immediate reason for rejection or rebellion.

Making VEPPs central to our understanding of empiricism naturally leads to the idea that many philosophical positions are "stances" rather than "dogmas." What characterizes empiricism$_{vF}$ is a ...

> ... rejection of explanation demands and dissatisfaction with and disvaluing of explanation by postulate ... calling us back to experience, ... rebellion against theory, ideals of epistemic rationality, ... admiration for science, and the virtue they see in an idea of rationality that does not bar disagreement. ... The attitudes that appear in this list are to some extent epistemic and to some extent evaluative, and they may well involve or require certain beliefs for their own coherence. But none are equatable with beliefs. (2002, p. 47)

As *ES* has it, empiricism is not the only philosophical position best rendered as a stance. The same applies to materialism. van Fraassen defends this claim by showing that materialists had better not commit to a $M+$ like "Only matter exists." Given the fact that natural science has frequently revolutionized our understanding of matter, "Only matter exists" lacks any determinate content over time. It is much better therefore to understand materialism in terms of VEPPs. For instance, materialists admire the ingenuity of many foundational scientific theories, and they are committed to following science on what there is (2002, p. 60).

3 Objectifying Epistemology, Epistemic Voluntarism and Scientific Revolutions

Having proposed a new understanding of philosophical positions, *ES* turns to introducing and defending "epistemic voluntarism." Epistemic voluntarism is based on two central claims:

(i) that principles of rationality underdetermine our choice of philosophical stances or scientific paradigms; and
(ii) that a theory of epistemic rationality must not be "objectifying," that is, it must not be a descriptive-explanatory theory of cognition.

By "principles of rationality" van Fraassen means primarily deductive logic, the theory of probability, and the practical syllogism. As long as we stick to these principles we avoid inconsistency and incoherence; we avoid reasoning in ways that – even in our own eyes – result in "self-sabotage:" a reasoning that prevents us from reaching our goals (2002, pp. 88, 224).

ES defends (i) by drawing on an idea of William James (1956). According to James, we have two central goals in our epistemic life: to believe as many truths as possible, and to believe as few falsehoods as possible. Since we cannot maximize both goals at once, each one of us implicitly or explicitly fixes his/her respective "risk-quotients." Each one of us has to choose which of the two goals is more important (either in general or in specific contexts). Deductive logic and the theory of probability do not tell us how to make this choice. Our choice must therefore be based upon VEPPs (2002, p. 87). Which brings us back to the stances, but with a new twist. Stances now turn out to be important not just as renderings of some philosophical positions; they also turn out to be significant in how we organize our epistemic practices.

ES argues for (ii) by revisiting the issue of scientific revolutions. van Fraassen agrees with Thomas Kuhn's and Paul Feyerabend's thought that, from the perspective of the pre-revolutionary old paradigm, the post-revolutionary new paradigm seems "literally absurd, incoherent, obviously false, or worse – meaningless, unintelligible." And yet, differently from Kuhn or Feyerabend, van Fraassen allows for a different perspective *after* the revolution. From the post-revolution perspective, the pre-revolution viewpoint can be understood as a partial truth (2002, p. 71). For instance, it follows from Einstein's Special Theory of Relativity that Newton's Laws of Motion are true for entities whose velocity is small when compared with the speed of light (2002, p. 115). Moreover, van Fraassen thinks that scientific revolutions often result in the discovery of *ambiguities* in the old paradigm. Thus Newtonians did not realize that mass could be characterized as "proper mass," "gravitational mass," and "inertial mass." And they therefore regarded as absurd the notion that mass varies with velocity (2002, p. 113).

According to ES, the litmus test for every epistemology is whether it is able to preserve the rationality of scientific revolutions while acknowledging the element of "conversion" at their very heart. Objectifying epistemologies that describe and explain how our cognitive apparatus fits into the world do not pass muster. They fail the litmus test since they invariably are enmeshed with the scientific theories of their day. The objectifying epistemology *en vogue* during the reign of the old paradigm licenses the old paradigm's epistemic ways. It therefore cannot but reject as irrational the epistemic practices of the new paradigm (2002, p. 81).

Epistemic voluntarism does better for three reasons. First, it is prescriptive-evaluative rather than descriptive-explanatory (2002, p. 82). This lessens the ties to prevalent scientific paradigms. Second, epistemic voluntarism is minimalist (cf. (i) above). And third, epistemic voluntarism gives emotion – or similar "impulses" – a legitimate place in our epistemic life. Points two and three connect epistemic voluntarism to the stance-idea. van Fraassen's thought seems to be that scientific paradigms are, or include, one or more scientific stances.

ES's example for how emotions can change one's epistemic options comes from Franz Kafka's short story *Metamorphosis*. One morning, Gregor, the son of the Samsa family, wakes up in the shape of a gigantic beetle, unable to communicate with humans. Initially his parents and his sister Grete think of the beetle as their son or brother. Alas, this rendering of the situation makes their life unbearable. There just is no way to maintain a normal family life when one family member is an insect. It is only when Grete eventually has an emotional breakdown that the parents find a way forward: they take the beetle for nothing but a beetle – and kill it (2002, p. 106). Grete's emotion enables the family to recognize the situation more correctly, at least when judged retrospectively.

Going beyond van Fraassen's own words, we can use *Metamorphosis* also to illustrate another central claim of *ES*, to wit, the claim that scientific revolutions involve a re-interpretation of central rules guiding scientific work (2002, Ch. 4). The Samsa family, throughout the whole episode, operates with the rule *Protect the members of your family*. Initially this rule is used in a "conservative way:" Gregor and the beetle are taken to be the same person. And thus Gregor-the-beetle remains within the domain of the rule. After Grete's breakdown however, the rule is interpreted in a "revolutionary way:" it is understood as legitimating the killing of the beetle. The family now thinks that the beetle has destroyed and replaced Gregor. Killing the insect safeguards Grete's well-being and revenges Gregor.

One central rule in empirical science is "*Sola experientia!*" Defenders of the old paradigm use this rule in a conservative-defensive way. They insist that their paradigm is fully based upon experience (observation and experiment) and free of idle speculation. The proponents of the new paradigm instead accuse the old paradigm of violating *Sola experientia!*. They use *Sola experientia!* in a revolutionary way. For instance, Newton's critics identified his assumptions concerning absolute time and space as metaphysical baggage not licensed by experience. The upshot is that scientific revolutionaries do not simply throw scientific rationality overboard. But they interpret it in radically new ways. And there must be an emotion-like "impulse" to set off such developments (2002, Ch. 4).

4 Challenges, Allies, Refinements

In this section I shall discuss three ways of developing van Fraassen's ideas further. These ways will be important when we turn to the issue of relativism in the following sections.

(a) Policies

Several authors have elaborated on what it means to occupy a stance. Paul Teller's (2004, 2011) suggestion has rightly received most attention. Teller proposes that committing to a stance is like "adopting a policy." And this involves the following features. (I reformulate them in my own words for the sake of brevity.)

(1) To adopt a policy P is to commit oneself to acting or deciding in accordance with a statement of P.
(2) A policy is not true or false, but useful, clever, or easy to use.
(3) Policies can be overridden by other policies.
(4) To apply a policy is to interpret it.
(5) Applying a policy requires "judgment."
(6) Policies are "expressions or implementations of values" (2004, p. 167).
(7) Policies simplify decision-making.
(8) It is possible to argue for or against policies. But since policies are at least in part based on value commitments, such arguments cannot be straightforwardly factual. Defences of policies often appeal to more general policies (2004, pp. 167–168).

One of the strengths of this suggestion is that it sheds light on the relationship between stances and beliefs. Policies are "recipes" for generating beliefs, but not themselves beliefs or belief-like. Note, though, that policies do not just *generate* beliefs; policies in turn *depend upon* beliefs for their operation and defence.

Teller's proposal should not, however, be pushed too far. While stances are plausibly thought of as *including* policies, it would not be right to equate the two. Stances are more comprehensive than policies; they also include values, emotions, preferences, and beliefs. Starting from the policies we can see how the other elements come into view. Still, the other elements do not simply collapse into parts or moments of policies. Remember that empiricism is about the "rejection of explanation demands ... disvaluing of explanation by postulate ... calling us back to experience, ... rebellion against theory, ideals of epistemic rationality, ... admiration for science, and the virtue they see in an idea of rationality that does not bar disagreement. ..." (2002, p. 47). It takes some conceptual violence to squeeze all these attitudes and actions into the policy-format.

If we straightforwardly equate stances with policies for generating beliefs, it becomes difficult to appreciate the dichotomy of stance and dogma. If we equate stances with policies we invariably end up wondering whether the stance qua policy isn't simply the road to dogma (cf. Lipton 2004). Again, we can preserve the difference between the two renderings of philosophical positions only if we allow stances to have content beyond policies. We can then state the differences between the two views of philosophical positions as follows. *Principle Zero* treats the dogma and its justification as crucial, and everything else (like VEPPs) as merely contingently and externally related to the dogma. The stance-account claims that VEPPs are what defines (certain) philosophical positions, and that "dogmas" are typically no more than "glosses" or "post-hoc rationalizations" of non-doxastic elements.

(b) " ... not straightforwardly factual ..."

Even though I have cautioned against equating stances and policies, I still find the idea of epistemic policies as parts of stances fruitful. Among other things, it allows us to get a better handle on epistemic voluntarism. Remember epistemic voluntarism's two central ingredients: it rejects objectifying epistemology, and it involves a minimalism concerning rationality.

van Fraassen doesn't spend much time searching for potential allies for epistemic voluntarism. But one such potential ally clearly stands out: Hartry Field's 2009 paper "Epistemology without Metaphysics." Already the very title should be music to van Fraassen's ears. Field's meta-epistemology is a form of expressivism; and expressivism has of course been a constant element in empiricist thinking for the past hundred years. As Field has it, a sentence in which we evaluate someone's epistemic justification, "expresses a mental state that is a resultant of norms and factual beliefs" (2009, p. 252). Put differently, "epistemic evaluations, like other evaluations, aren't straightforwardly factual" (2009, p. 250).

Epistemic norms for Field are not "fairly general normative propositions" (2009, p. 258); epistemic norms are "policies:" "a policy both for believing (or believing to a certain degree) and for acting so as to improve one's epistemic situation." Epistemic policies may be highly local or general. And they can play a variety of different roles: sometimes we are guided by them; sometimes we evaluate in accordance with them; sometimes we are committed to them (2009, p. 260).

It is important to stress that treating epistemic norms as policies is part and parcel of Field's attempt to free epistemology from metaphysics. Epistemic norms are not facts in the world, Platonic entities, or "there anyway." They are not truths about epistemic values. They are not true or false at all. van Fraassen would surely agree.

Finally, note that at least in his 2009 paper Field is adamant that his "evaluationism" is a form of "relativism." Every epistemic evaluation is relative to a norm. No sense can be made of an absolute perspective on evaluations or norms. This does not mean that Field would subscribe to the "idea that all norms are equally good" (2009, p. 255): to attribute this thesis to relativism "is just refusing to take relativism with even an iota of seriousness" (2009, p. 256). To make epistemic evaluation norm-relative is not to say that we cannot evaluate some norms as better than others. It is to say that any such evaluation of norms is in turn relative to norms. As we shall see below, van Fraassen should say pretty much the same thing.

(c) Moderate versus radical epistemic voluntarism

van Fraassen's epistemic voluntarism is premised on the distinction between stance-transcending principles of rationality on the one hand, and stance-specific values, emotions, preferences, and policies on the other hand. One way to put pressure on this distinction is to ask whether epistemic voluntarism isn't demanding too much. van Fraassen himself poses the crucial question thus:

> What if I detect a straightforward contradiction in someone's beliefs, conclude that he has sabotaged himself in the management of his opinions, and he turns out to be Graham Priest? Priest happily admits to believing that certain contradictions are or may be true. (2004a, p. 184)

In response van Fraassen readily admits that Priest's beliefs are consistent. But he goes on to suggest that Priest's logic is "quite different from the one most familiar to us" and that evolutionary arguments might ultimately speak against it (2004a, p. 185).

This response does not quite seem to address the challenge that Priest poses. The issue is not whether Priest's beliefs about paraconsistent logic are consistent; the question is rather whether consistency and coherence should be the supreme touchstones of rationality in the first place. Priest argues that consistency is a matter of degree and must always be weighed against other cognitive values such as "simplicity" ("Is the theory clean and elegant, or is it complex and contrived?"), "unity" ("Does it have to invoke numerous *ad hoc* hypotheses ...?"), "explanatory power" ("Can the theory be used to explain other things in the same domain ...?") or "parsimony" ("Does the theory multiply entities beyond necessity?") (2005, p. 123). It is hard to see how evolutionary arguments could work against this account.

If Priest is right about consistency and its relation to other epistemic values, then it becomes difficult for van Fraassen to maintain the distinction between *stance-transcending* principles of rationality and *stance-dependent* VEPPs. If consistency can be rationally overruled, then it cannot be the universal and necessary criterion of rationality. If consistency can be overruled, then a stance which does so is not *per se* irrational. On this alternative picture, differences between rationally acceptable stances may be differences in what weight these stances give different "cognitive values," including the value of consistency.

Of course, van Fraassen also has a second stance-transcending criterion of rationality, to wit, the demand not to reason in a way that constitutes self-sabotage. This formal criterion leaves open which principles of rationality and cognitive values one commits to, as long as self-sabotage is avoided. This is a rather vague criterion, but perhaps the best we can do.

It should be added that the challenge to van Fraassen's emphasis on consistency does not just come from Priest's controversial views. Philosophers of science like Kuhn, Feyerabend, or Peter Lipton (2004) have argued along similar lines. Lipton's position is especially interesting here since he writes in response to van Fraassen's book.

Lipton suggests that Kuhn's paper "Objectivity, Value Judgment, and Theory Choice" (1977) can be read as a "constructive proof of voluntarism." Kuhn offers "shared epistemic values" (accuracy, consistency, scope, simplicity, fruitfulness) as the rational backbone of theory- or paradigm-choice. But Kuhn also insists that different scientists may rationally favour some values over other; interpret a given value in differently; or resolve conflicts between these epistemic values in variant ways (Lipton 2004, pp. 153–155). All this is clearly in line with epistemic voluntarism. Note, however, that consistency is again part of the value-mix and not standing outside as the ultimate touchstone or arbiter.

Lipton raises a number of questions concerning the differences between principles of rationality and (stance-dependent) epistemic policies or values. One question is how much difference is needed for there to be a difference of stance. Do two scientists have different stances just because they weigh the same epistemic value differently? Can we read, based on a scientist's inferences which stances, values, or policies they have adopted? Lipton is sceptical, since very often there will be other possible explanations, like background beliefs or differences in evidence (2004, pp. 155–157).

Lipton has a point. Perhaps the best way to respond to his challenge is to modify van Fraassen's bifurcation of principles of rationality and stance-dependent values and policies. The modification I have in mind is to follow Kuhn and Priest and let rationality consist in one's honouring all or some of the epistemic values. Kuhn and Priest list some of these values, but no doubt there are more. Indeed, which epistemic values there are can only be determined by research in cognitive psychology and the history and philosophy of science (including epistemology). This does not give us a firm and fixed base; but perhaps it is the *conditio humana* to cope without such a foundation.

To sum up this train of thought, we should distinguish between *moderate* and *radical* voluntarism. van Fraassen's voluntarism is moderate in so far as he assumes a clear-cut borderline between stance-*transcending* principles of rationality and stance-*dependent* VEPPs. Radical voluntarism denies that there is a clear borderline here.[1]

---

[1] In correspondence, van Fraassen has suggested that his acceptance of Carnap's "Principle of Tolerance" for languages is a radical-epistemic-voluntarist element in this work. Nevertheless, van Fraassen is not convinced that "consistency is just one epistemic virtue among others." He argues as follows: Arthur Prior's "tonk-language" is an instance of a language in which every sentence is inconsistent. The relevant sense of inconsistency here is proof-theoretic: everything follows logically from any sentence or set of sentences. In such language all distinctions collapse. van Fraassen concludes: "... a position within which all distinctions collapse could not even be called 'relativist'." – I agree with the view that relativism is not the same as mysticism. The latter typically involves the idea of a "coincidentia oppositorum," as Nicholas of Cusa put it. (I have heard Priest explain similar ideas from Buddhism.) To be clear, I do not adhere to these views. But are they irrational by definition? I am not so sure. Moreover, I do not think that the radical voluntarist must regard "consistency as just one epistemic virtue among others." The "among others" perhaps hides an ambiguity. It is easily heard as "no better or no worse, and no more important" than the others. But in the present context it could also mean "it is part of the set of epistemic virtues and can sometimes be restricted in its scope and outweighed by other virtues." I would tie radical voluntarism to the second rendering, not the first.

5 Relativism

In this section I shall discuss the relationship between epistemic voluntarism (including the stance-idea) and epistemic relativism from two different angles. In subsection (a) I shall focus on the question whether epistemic voluntarism involves a form of relativism. In (b) I shall suggest that at least some forms of relativism can fruitfully be rendered as stances rather than doctrines. In (c) I shall deal with some general objections regarding my argument in (b).

(a) Epistemic voluntarism and relativism
Epistemic voluntarism even in its moderate form seems to involve a form of epistemic relativism:

(I) The epistemic status of judgements is relative to stances.
(II) Different stances evaluate the same judgements differently.
(III) There is no perspective from which stances can be neutrally and absolutely ranked.
(IV) The move from one stance to another can have the character of a "conversion:" principles of rationality combined with empirical data cannot compel a transition from one stance to another.

van Fraassen himself invokes the idea of conversion as follows:

> Being or becoming an empiricist will then be similar or analogous to conversion to a cause, a religion, an ideology, to capitalism or to socialism, to a worldview such as Dawkins's selfish gene view or the view Russell expressed in 'Why I am Not a Christian.' (2002, p. 60)

And elsewhere he comments:

> If this is relativism, it is certainly not debilitating relativism – it is only an acknowledgement of the logic of this aspect of the human condition. (2004b, p. 11)

I take it that by "debilitating relativism" van Fraassen means a form of relativism that makes its advocate unable to judge or argue. Perhaps he is thinking of versions of epistemic relativism that declare all stances to be "equally valid." Clearly, if all stances are equally valid then there cannot be much point in arguing whether the beliefs licenced by one stance are superior to those licensed by another stance.

van Fraassen's alternative is worth spelling out pedantically. I shall here assume moderate rather than radical epistemic voluntarism. Let "S1" and "S2" stand for two incompatible stances (or paradigms), "A_{S1}" and "B_{S1}" for two proponents of S1; "C_{S2}" for a proponent of S2, and "p" for a proposition over which A, B, or C disagree.

Clearly, when A_{S1} and B_{S1} disagree over p, they have a rich shared background of principles of rationality *and* stance-specific VEPPs to adjudicate their differences. This shared background will often determine which view on p is bindingly correct and which is incorrect.

Could A_{S1} convince C_{S2} to stop occupying S2? One possibility is that adherence to S2 is irrational in light of the stance-transcending principles of rationality, and that C_{S2} therefore engages in self-sabotage. Here the principles of rationality are a common and neutral ground.

The situation is different when neither side flouts the principles of rationality. This does not pre-empt argument and changing the other's mind, but there no longer is a universal common ground capable of adjudicating the differences. At least two things might happen in such setting:

- A_{S1} might be able to show C_{S2} that one of C_{S2}'s VEPPs or beliefs is insufficiently motivated by a VEPP or belief that A_{S1} and C_{S2} share (but that is not necessarily shared by other stances).
- A_{S1} might be able to show C_{S2} that one of C_{S2}'s VEPPs or beliefs is insufficiently motivated by one of C_{S2} own beliefs or VEPPs (not shared by A_{S1}).

What should A_{S1} say about C_{S2} or S2 more generally, when neither of these strategies succeed? One thing is clear: A_{S1} is not compelled to treat his own S1 and C's S2 as "equally valid." Given A_{S1}'s VEPPs and beliefs, there may well be good grounds for A_{S1} to reject S2 and at least some of the VEPPs and beliefs that constitute S2.

The above reflections were based on moderate epistemic voluntarism. The situation changes when we replace moderate with radical epistemic voluntarism. In this case the common ground will be smaller. Instead of stance-transcending principles of rationality we only have a partially shared set of epistemic values given different weights. But even in this case, argument is surely possible – at least when the values relevant to the adjudication between S1 and S2 are shared.

Where does all this leave the debate between empiricists$_{vF}$ and metaphysicians? Assume that both sides honour the principles of rationality and thus have coherent systems of beliefs and values. Would empiricists$_{vF}$ be able to reject metaphysics under these conditions? van Fraassen's answer should be clear. Empiricists$_{vF}$ recognize that they share VEPPs and beliefs with sensible metaphysicians (an admiration for aspects of science, for example). But it does not follow that empiricists have to tolerate the metaphysical stance as an equal. To repeat, another stance does not become my stance's equal just because the other stance is consistent and coherent. The empiricists$_{vF}$' values – and especially the value attached to the empirical-scientific testing of empirical hypothesis – license a direct rejection of metaphysics.[2] Still, this does not preclude empiricists$_{vF}$' efforts at convincing the metaphysicians – albeit that there is no guarantee of success.

To summarize what I take to be the main lesson of this subsection, I hope to have made plausible that van Fraassen's epistemic voluntarism does indeed involve a form of relativism. But this relativism is benign rather than debilitating: it does not declare all stances equally valid, and it allows for meaningful discussion across stances.

(b) Applying the stance-idea to relativism: The example of Sociology of Scientific Knowledge

In this subsection I shall change tack. Rather than exploring the link between voluntarism and relativism, I shall here concentrate on the stance-idea in its relationship to relativism. My guiding question is this: Is (epistemic) relativism a philosophical stance (like empiricism$_{vF}$)? Or, more precisely, are *all* forms of relativism best thought of as stances, or perhaps only *some?* These are intriguing questions suggested by van Fraassen's work. Addressing them adequately would demand a separate paper. Here I am content to give one example of a form of relativism that *is* naturally thought of as a stance. It is also a position that is similar to van Fraassen's in some unexpected ways. I am referring to the "Sociology of Scientific Knowledge" (=SSK), as it has been developed and defended by David Bloor.

Like empiricism$_{vF}$ so also SSK is naturally thought of as a "rebellion." But in Bloor's case the rebellion is not just against metaphysics – it is against philosophy tout court: "To ask questions of the sort which philosophers address to themselves is usually to paralyze the mind" (1991, p. 52). In particular Bloor dismisses work in epistemology and the philosophy of science. He faults these fields for having no "controlled input of data." Since such control is missing, epistemological discussions are "simply affirmations of the values and perspectives of some social group" (1991, p. 80). Bloor tries to substantiate this allegation by showing that Popper's and Kuhn's philosophies of science are expressions of values and "thought-styles" going back to Enlightenment (Popper) or Romantic (Kuhn) ideologies (1991, p. 62).

---

2 Of course, determined metaphysicians will resist this argument. They will insist that it is the very subject matter of metaphysics that precludes the option of empirical testing. Clearly, this topic requires much more space than I have here. I am grateful to Delia Belleri for pushing me on this point.

Bloor does not just compare philosophy unfavourably to science. He also finds philosophy deserving of less respect than theology. This has to do with the arguments over relativism versus absolutism. In the Vatican Bloor finds "a clear-sighted absolutism in action." For instance, Pope Benedict XVI's argument "against relativism is grounded in his faith in God as the ultimate source of truth" (2007, p. 254). Secular philosophers mistakenly think that they can defend absolutism without explaining their access to absolute truth.

Despite his contempt for much of philosophy, Bloor is happy to declare his allegiance to certain philosophical "isms." He sides with *empiricism* if it is understood as a "psychological theory" urging that "our perceptions influence our thinking more than our thinking influences our perceptions" (1991, p. 33). He accepts *materialism* if it amounts to seeing humans as "part of the material world" and as holding that "social learning is part of how the material world functions" (1991, p. 34). And he commits to *naturalism* as the view that "knowledge and belief ... must be grounded in the natural world, and they are themselves things which are susceptible to scientific explanation" (2007, p. 252). None of these commitments are defended in any detail; they are seen as preferences underpinning SSK.

van Fraassen locates the main difference between the empiricist and the materialist stances in their respective admiration for empirical science. Bloor also seeks to follow the model of natural science:

> I have taken for granted and endorsed what I think is the standpoint of most contemporary science. In the main, science is causal, theoretical, value-neutral, often reductionist, to an extent empiricist, and ultimately materialistic like common sense. (1991, p. 157)

Bloor's well-known "strong programme" is said to "embody the same values which are taken for granted in other scientific disciplines." The strong programme recommends that investigations in SSK be "causal," "impartial," "symmetrical," and "reflexive" (1991, p. 7). This is of course to advocate a set of policies for research rather than a theory about the world.

Bloor elsewhere presents SSK as part of the "*Einheitswissenschaft*" of logical positivists. He draws particularly on the physicist Philipp Frank and his book *Wahrheit: Relativ oder Absolut* (1952) (Bloor 2011). Frank argues that the progress of science "has been accompanied by an increase in 'relativisation.' Ever more concepts are modified with the expression "relative to a given frame of reference" (1952, p. 73). Moreover, Frank recommends relativism as "the only effective weapon against any kind of totalitarianism" (1952, p. 14). Again, the value-orientation is palpable.

When it comes to motivating and defending relativism, Bloor has three lines of argument. One is to say that relativism is simply the denial of absolutism: "no *absolute* knowledge and no *absolute* morality:" "Knowledge and morality cannot transcend the machinery of our brains and the deliverances of our sense organs, the culture we occupy and the traditions on which we depend" (2007, p. 251). According to the second line of argument, SSK-relativism is supported by the fact that many impressive empirical studies rely on it as a methodological guide (Barnes and Bloor 1982, p. 25). The third line of argument seeks to show that philosophical critics conflate SSK-relativism with unsavoury doctrines like "subjectivism," "irrationalism," or "scepticism" (Bloor 2011, p. 433).

Finally, Bloor's theory of rationality is at least structurally similar to the epistemic voluntarism defended by van Fraassen. Recall that van Fraassen restricts principles of rationality to deductive logic and the theory of probability, or – alternatively – to principles that prevent us from falling into self-sabotage. Over and above these principles we are free to choose. Bloor's dichotomy is different. For him the basic level consists of our "natural inductive" or "natural deductive propensities." These are studied by cognitive science and are taken to be common to normal members of the human species. The second level consists of systems of "normative" rationality; these are different codifications of our reasoning propensities, according to the interests and negotiations of different groups. Normative rationality is the subject matter of the sociologist (1991, pp. 168–169).

Since normative rationality is thus invariably a local phenomenon, Bloor thinks it is unlikely that the debate between relativism and absolutism could ever be resolved: "No relativist should believe that relativism can be proven true or that history is on its side …" (2011, p. 450) "So the sociology of knowledge is not bound to eliminate the rival standpoint. It only has to separate itself from it, reject it, and make sure that its own house is in logical order" (1991, p. 12).

(c) Dealing with an objection

There clearly are costs in reconstructing Bloor's relativism as a stance rather than as a doctrine. It makes it more difficult to argue for or against it. Rather than testing the consistency of a brief dogma and its coherence with other independently established truths, we have to engage with VEPPs that do not have truth-values at all. That makes the task of the critic a lot harder.

There is also a deeper issue here. The obvious objection to the whole stance-idea might be put as follows: of course, in his writings Bloor appeals to all sorts of VEPPs, and obviously he suggests a range of SSK policies. No one denies that this is so. But why should we make these VEPPs part and parcel of his relativism? Why can't we distinguish between his relativistic credo or dogma – say, "there are no context-free or super-cultural norms of rationality" (Barnes and Bloor 1982, p. 27) – on the one hand, and the various motivations for this credo, and the consequences drawn from it, on the other?

The right answer seems to me to be the following. To attribute relativism as a stance is to make a claim about where one should locate the *core* or *essence* of the respective position. Do the advocates of the position foreground a claim or doctrine (about the world), and do they marshal their evidence and VEPPs as arguments for this doctrine? Or do the advocates put the emphasis on rebellion, admiration, and VEPPs, and treat stated credos as no more than rough glosses intended to point beyond themselves at the underlying epistemic and evaluative commitments?

In Bloor's case we are clearly dealing with the latter scenario. The claim that "there are no context-free or super-cultural norms of rationality" is not simply a descriptive claim for which Bloor assembles evidence. It is also, and indeed primarily, a reference first to his rebellion against any kind of absolutes, and second to his commitment to leave the study of human rationality to the empirical sciences. Rationality is to be studied empirically, and to do so is to identify contextual dependencies (albeit that the relevant context might sometimes be that of the whole species).

To see Bloor's position as a "stance" might also help us understand why arguments between philosophers and SSK-advocates are so often fruitless. Philosophers are focused on doctrines that they can test for consistency and coherence. And they get palpably annoyed when they do not find such snappy position statements. Philosophers see the lack of such statements as a lack of conceptual clarity and intellectual commitment. Indeed, confronted with this situation philosophers sometimes use something like the stance-idea – but with strictly negative connotations: the SSK-advocate is seen as guided by an animus against science, by physics- or philosophy-envy, and by a rejection of the demands of intellectual responsibility (Haack 1998). This might convince fellow philosophers, but it leaves sociologists cold.

One of van Fraassen's central motivations for interpreting empiricism as a stance is the desire to find a common denominator for the numerous self-proclaimed empiricists in our tradition, from the Ancient Greek school of physicians, the "*Empirici*," to the Vienna Circle and beyond. A short *E+* like "Experience is the one and only source of information" (2002, p. 43) doesn't do the trick. Invoking the rebellion against metaphysics (and related VEPPs) works much better. I submit that the same is true for relativism. If we start from a brief three-point definition, say of the kind offered in Paul Boghossian's influential *Fear of Knowledge* (2006, p. 73), it is difficult to find any self-proclaimed, or otherwise identified, relativists who actually commit to this "*R+*".³ Boghossian claims to be targeting Richard Rorty in particular, but he never shows in any detail that Rorty would accept Boghossian's definition of epistemic relativism (2006, pp. 60–63). The situation would be no different if instead we used the definition of relativism given in 5 (a) above.

Perhaps, as is the case with empiricism, so also in the case of relativism it is easier to find a common denominator if we turn from dogmas to stances. What unites authors accused of, or happily embracing, forms of relativism – from the sophists to Bloor and Rorty – is first and foremost the rebellion against forms of metaphysics, epistemology, or ethics that posit absolutes (Herbert 2001; Kusch 1995; Kusch *et al.* 2019). These absolutes are variously taken to be divine commands, ultimate scientific truths, *consensi gentium*, apodictic intuitions, or "truths that are there anyway." Different relativist authors are preoccupied with opposing different such absolutes. But they all share the same *animus*. Interestingly enough, this rebellion against absolutes situates many relativists in the proximity of empiricism: the opposition to metaphysics is obviously a commonality. Many relativists also share further values or virtues: they oppose individualism, intellectual imperialism, or unchecked epistemic hierarchies, and they value epistemic humility, tolerance, or equality. It seems to me that the shift from a relativist dogma to a relativist stance might bring into view a "tradition of relativist thinking" that up to now has been largely invisible.

6 Stance Relativism and Boghossian's Challenges

In this final section I shall discuss how stance-relativism of the kind discussed in this paper fares against Boghossian's battery of anti-relativist arguments.

(1) By "absolute relativism" Boghossian means a form of relativism that works with a mixture of absolute and relative principles. The paradigmatic case of this view is a relativism of manners based on the one absolute principle: "When in Rome do as the Romans do." Or think of subjective Bayesians for whom the Bayesian formula is the one and only absolute principle (Boghossian 2011, p. 67).

---

3 Of course, in some cases this will be so because the relativists adopt doctrines that are much more sophisticated than Boghossian allows for. This would make Boghossian's arguments instances of the straw-man fallacy.

Boghossian rejects absolute relativism as a viable form of relativism. By accepting the existence of one absolute principle, Boghossian submits, the relativist has lost what surely must be her strongest card, to wit, doubts about how absolute principles fit into the empirical world and how they can be known by finite and fallible creatures. Moreover, the absolute relativist has no good answer to the question why there could not in principle be more than one absolute norm (Boghossian 2011, p. 68).

A voluntaristic-epistemic relativism (of stances) can easily appear to be an instance of "absolute relativism." After all, van Fraassen treats principles forbidding inconsistency and incoherence as definitive of rationality, and a different from epistemic policies. Nevertheless, it seems possible to defend van Fraassen against Boghossian's considerations.

One line of defence is to shift from *moderate* to *radical* epistemic voluntarism. This is the shift from fixed stance-transcending principles of rationality to stance-relative selections from a larger set of epistemic values. None of these values is absolute in the sense that it has to be present in every stance, or that it has to be always interpreted in the same way. Indeed, the set itself could be seen as a contingent product of our evolutionary and social history.

Boghossian might regroup and focus instead on the demand not to self-sabotage. Is this not a universal demand of rationality? And doesn't its presence make epistemic voluntarism a case of absolute relativism after all? Here too the epistemic voluntarist has a response – at least if she borrows a line from Bloor. She might insist that seeking to avoid self-sabotage is simply something we (most of us, most of the time) instinctively do. It is not a principle of rationality that "is there anyway," but part and parcel of the "natural rationality" installed in us by a contingent evolutionary history.

(2) Boghossian readily acknowledges that our epistemic practices vary, but he denies that that this variation supports relativism. What variation there is can be explained by the fact that our absolute rules are sometimes vague and unspecific. They leave room for choice (Boghossian, pers. comm.; 2006, p. 110). This suggestion seems to fit with van Fraassen's *moderate* epistemic voluntarism with its principles of rationality that leave our choices of stances or paradigms underdetermined. This underdetermination is removed only once VEPPs do their work.

The first thing to note here is that Boghossian's idea does not in fact block relativism. If true, all it suggests is that the *scope* of relativism is not unlimited. But the breadth of the scope remains completely open. Clearly, Boghossian, van Fraassen, and Bloor are likely to have very different views on this breadth. Moreover, the move from moderate to radical epistemic voluntarism again avoids Boghossian's rendering of the relativist position. The radical version of epistemic voluntarism does not fit into Boghossian's template.

And yet, Boghossian might have a further reply specifically addressing radical epistemic voluntarism: If we allow, as we should, for appropriate forms of idealization and abstraction, then surely we will be able to construct general and absolute epistemic principles to which every normal human being is at least implicitly committed.

The radical epistemic voluntarist might reply as follows. Yes indeed, we might proceed in the way Boghossian suggests. But we should not expect this methodology to lead to one unique outcome. On the contrary, work done in this way is faced with all the old issues concerning the underdetermination of theory by observation. Moreover, it might well be highly artificial and contrived to bring all of our epistemic folkways under one small set of absolute epistemic principles. Not to be forgotten is that abstract principles might be far too schematic to guide our epistemic conduct. Boghossian's method would thus produce a merely schematic, but ultimately hollow form of absolutism.[4] And last but not least, what should we do with the actors' own perspective on their epistemic folkways? Should we simply ignore this perspective? If not, what then should we say when the actors do not recognize their own reasoning in the epistemologists' reconstructions and idealizations? (Kinzel and Kusch 2018)

(3) Stances and perhaps even paradigms can be more or less different, more or less distant, from one another. The greater the difference or distance, the more we need the idea of "conversion" for capturing what happens when the folk or scientists shift from one stance or paradigm to another. And it is only when conversion is needed for capturing the change that epistemic relativism is vindicated.

Parts of Boghossian's 2006 book can be read as offering a suggestion for how the relativism-motivating distance or difference between stances or paradigms can be captured. Boghossian distinguishes between "fundamental" and "derived" "epistemic principles." A *fundamental* principle concerning observation licences perceptual beliefs under certain general conditions. A *derived* principle concerning observation licences the perceptual beliefs of a specific person, or perceptual belief given a specific instrument (like a microscope or telescope). Boghossian claims that two "epistemic systems" – that is, two systems of epistemic principles – are "fundamentally different" when they differ in at least one fundamental epistemic principle. And fundamental difference of epistemic systems is what defines a relativistic setting. Of course, Boghossian's interest

---

[4] Here I am indebted once more to Delia Belleri.

in all this is to bury relativism, not to praise it. He therefore goes on to argue that relativists have so far failed to offer a single convincing case of such fundamental difference between epistemic systems. In particular, Galileo and Cardinal Bellarmine did not differ over any fundamental epistemic principle (Boghossian 2006, pp. 63–69, 90–91, 103–105).

Can Boghossian's concepts and criticisms be applied to van Fraassen's relativism of stances? Has van Fraassen offered convincing examples of differences in fundamental epistemic principles? To my mind, stance-relativism is not threatened by Boghossian's considerations. To begin with, it is unlikely that van Fraassen would accept Boghossian's criterion for a relativism-inducing difference in stances, that is, a difference in at least one fundamental principle. van Fraassen's perspective is coherentist rather than foundationalist. What distinguishes Cardinal Bellarmine from Galileo is not one fundamental epistemic principle but a whole host of beliefs and VEPPs. It is the number and weight of these differences that requires a conversion, not the fundamental character of one of them. The distance from Boghossian increases further as we shift from moderate to radical epistemic voluntarism: the latter does not accept that everyone must share (the interpretation of) the same basic epistemic values.

(4) As Boghossian has it, the epistemic relativist's single best argument against absolute epistemic principles goes as follows:

> (#) To justify our belief that our epistemic system S is absolutely correct, we invariably have to rely on this very S. This procedure is circular and thus unacceptable. Hence we cannot justify our belief that S is absolutely correct. And the same is true of any other S.

Boghossian rejects (#). It is not generally true that no epistemic principle P can be used to justify itself. Such circularity is forbidden only if P has already become independently doubtful (2006, pp. 96–102).

What would or could van Fraassen respond? Is he committed to rejecting epistemic circularity? I think not. By this I do not mean to suggest that van Fraassen agrees with Boghossian that the relativist has no good argument for his opposition to epistemic absolutes. As we saw above, van Fraassen holds that the best evidence for epistemic voluntarism, and thus for relativism, comes from the history of scientific revolutions. He is convinced that there have been many instances where the progress of science has involved seismic shifts in our epistemic values and policies. It is scientific revolutions, not any apriori reflections on rule-circularity, that should push us in the direction of relativism.

(5) Boghossian (2011, pp. 60–66) finds epistemic relativism inherently unstable. On the one hand, the relativist allows that epistemic systems fundamentally different from her own are, in some sense, as valid as her own. On the other

hand, the relativist also prefers her own epistemic system and does not give it up. How can these two attitudes be reconciled? Boghossian is doubtful that relativism can deliver a plausible solution.

Van Fraassen's response is perhaps best captured in the following remark (which was not addressing Boghossian's considerations):

> I remain convinced that genuine, conscious reflection on alternative beliefs, orientations, values – in an open and undogmatic spirit – does not automatically undermine one's own commitments (van Fraassen 2011, p. 156).

Of course, we need an argument defending this conviction. I shall use radical epistemic voluntarism for providing such an argument. It might go as follows. Under certain conditions, we can – from the perspective of our stance – recognize the VEPPs and beliefs of another stance as justifiable. That is, we can come to see the VEPPs and beliefs of another stance as rational *provided only* that we can identify a way of justifying them with reference to some plausible combination and weighting of epistemic values. If this proves possible, then the other stance is *in some sense* "equal" to our own. And yet, the fact that we can see the other stance in this light does not give us a reason to convert to it. After all, we might well have VEPPs and beliefs that differ from those of the other stance. And our VEPPs and beliefs might give us sufficient reason not to convert.

The situation is different when we are faced with a crisis of confidence in our own epistemic system, when we are involved in a scientific (or other) revolution (of thought). In such a situation we do not regard the other paradigm (or stance) as equal to our own; we regard the alternative as absurd. *And* we no longer know how to go on with our own paradigm. Note, however, that this is not the situation of relativistic epistemic voluntarism. The advocates of the latter do not (as yet) have any cause for a crisis of confidence (though they might well think of the absolutist alternatives as absurd).

7 Conclusion

In this paper I have tried to develop van Fraassen's epistemic voluntarism concerning stances and scientific paradigms in two main ways: by distinguishing between moderate and radical forms of epistemic voluntarism, and by rendering all forms of epistemic voluntarism as so many forms of epistemic relativism. In the process I have suggested that epistemic relativism can sometimes take the form of a stance rather than a dogma, and that a relativistic epistemic voluntarism can be defended against Boghossian's well-known battery of arguments against epistemic relativism. I hope to have made plausible the general thought that the two key ideas of van Fraassen's *Empirical Stance* are worthy of further reflection and refinement.[5]

Bibliography

Barnes, Barry and David Bloor (1982): "Relativism, Rationalism, and the Sociology of Knowledge." In: Martin Hollis/Steven Lukes (Eds.): *Rationality and Relativism*. Oxford: Blackwell, pp. 21–47.
Bloor, David (1991): *Knowledge and Social Imagery*, 2nd ed. Chicago: The University of Chicago Press.
Bloor, David (2007): "Epistemic Grace: Antirealism as Theology in Disguise." In: *Common Knowledge* 13, pp. 250–280.
Bloor, David (2011): "Relativism and the Sociology of Knowledge." In: Steven Hales (Ed.): *A Companion to Relativism*. Oxford: Wiley-Blackwell, pp. 433–456.
Boghossian, Paul (2006): *Fear of Knowledge: Against Relativism and Constructivism*. Oxford: Clarendon.
Boghossian, Paul (2011): "Three Kinds of Relativism." In: Steven Hales (Ed.): *A Companion to Relativism*. Oxford: Wiley-Blackwell, pp. 53–69.
Field, Hartry (2009): "Epistemology without Metaphysics." In: *Philosophical Studies* 143, pp. 249–290.
Frank, Philip (1952): *Wahrheit: Relativ oder Absolut?* Zürich: Pan-Verlag.
Haack, Susan (1998): *Confessions of a Passionate Moderate*. Chicago: The University of Chicago Press.
Hales, Steven (2011): *A Companion to Relativism*. Oxford: Wiley-Blackwell.
Herbert, Christopher (2001): *Victorian Relativity: Radical Thought and Scientific Discovery*. Chicago: The University of Chicago Press.
James, William (1956): "The Will to Believe." In: *The Will to Believe and Human Immortality*. New York: Dover, pp. 1–31.
Kinzel, Katherina and Martin Kusch (2018): "De-Idealizing Disagreement, Rethinking Relativism." In: *International Journal of Philosophical Studies* 26, pp. 40–71.
Kuhn, Thomas S. (1977): "Objectivity, Value Judgment, and Theory Choice." In: *The Essential Tension*. Chicago: The University of Chicago Press, pp. 320–339.
Kusch, Martin (1995): *Psychologism*. London: Routledge.
Kusch, Martin, Katharina Kinzel, Johannes Steizinger, and Nils Wildschut (Eds.) (2019): *The Emergence of Relativism*. London: Routledge.
Lipton, Peter (2004): "Epistemic Options." In: *Philosophical Studies* 121, pp. 147–158.
Priest, Graham (2005): *Doubt Truth to be a Liar*. Oxford: Oxford University Press.

---

[5] Work on this paper was made possible by ERC Ad Grant #339382. For comments I am deeply indebted to Bas van Fraassen, Delia Belleri, Anne-Kathrin Koch, Sophie Veigl, Dominik Finkelde, and Paul Livingston.

Teller, Paul (2004): "Review of The Empirical Stance by B. C. van Fraassen." In: *Philosophical Studies* 121, pp. 159–170.
Teller, Paul (2011): "Learning to Live with Voluntarism." In: *Synthese* 178, pp. 49–66.
van Fraassen, Bas (2002): *The Empirical Stance*. Princeton: Princeton University Press.
van Fraassen, Bas (2004a): "Replies." In: *Philosophical Studies* 121, pp. 171–192.
van Fraassen, Bas (2004b): "Reply to Chakravartty, Jauernig, and McMullin," unpublished typescript from http://www.princeton.edu/~fraassen/abstract/ReplyAPA-04.pdf, visited on 13 September 2018.
van Fraassen, Bas (2011): "On Stance and Rationality." In: *Synthese* 178, pp. 155–169.

Dominik Finkelde
Subjectivity as a Feature of Reality:

On Diffraction Laws of Consciousness and Reality Within Justified True Belief[1]

Abstract: In any account of how things really are, subjectivity can be both a formal and a distorting factor for Hegel and Lacan's adaptation of Hegelian dialectics. Lacan speaks of a pre-theoretical experience of being in the world where human beings are literally called by reality to be social agents and fill in gaps of this reality at the same time with their fantasies. As such, fantasies play an epistemic role, neglected often in both epistemological and ontological debates. But since the status of reality, with or without fantasies, is never all and complete, antagonisms within reality cannot be contained. Ontology, as our inquiry into 'what there is,' affects 'what there is' in that subjectivity, troubled by antagonism, always goes beyond established forms of facts, theoretically, practically and phantasmagorically. Finkelde argues, especially with reference to Kant and Hegel, that subjectivity, with its imaginary intertwinement of what Lacan calls the symbolic order, is a feature of reality (as virtuality) and not just a hallmark of the conscious mind.

1 Thinking and being

If there is a fundamental conviction that Hegel, as a dialectical idealist, and contemporary left-Hegelians, as dialectical materialists, share, then it is the conviction of the identity of being with thinking. This is the case even though, for dialectical materialists like Badiou, Žižek, Lefort, and Rancière, this identity is – as expressed in Alain Badiou's own words – only to be understood as a "local occurrence and not a totalized result," as Hegel allegedly sees it (Badiou 2009a, p. 143). Hegel is, however, closer to the materialist 'takeover' or acquisition of idealism than his critics often are willing to grant him. He acknowledges both a "gap" between thinking and being and the mutual co-dependence of both.

---

[1] The article is part of a broader research project on anamorphosis and subjectivity. As such, it is based on and develops further ideas presented in recent publications of mine: Finkelde 2017a; 2017b; 2019.

https://doi.org/10.1515/9783110670349-009

Hegel grants, especially, Kant the merit of having introduced this gap between thinking and being into ontology. For Kant's solution of the conflict between empiricism and rationalism consists *not* in having delivered a synthesis of both philosophical currents, but instead in formulating the avoidance of a positive solution between two mutually exclusive ontologies. Hegel radicalizes this Kantian insight for process-philosophical purposes, reinterpreting the gap between Kant's "thing-in-itself" and the respective "phenomena" as a gap that separates phenomena from themselves. And Hegel discusses this line of thought in various forms and in almost all of his metaphysical works, repeatedly pointing out the extent to which the primary structure of being is to be understood as one that can be grasped by reason alone, and one that expresses itself conceptually within a process of self-transcending forms of justification (see for example: Hegel 1977, pp. 1–45; 1991, §§ 1–17). The precondition of this, though, is the already-mentioned gap, which introduces some distance between truth and knowledge, or between veridical reality and itself. For if there were no gap, no lack of identity between thinking and being, the possibility of knowledge as "justified true belief" (Plato, *Theaetetus*, 202c 7–8) would not arise at all.

Hegel speaks explicitly and repeatedly of a symbiosis between being and thinking. "Being" is "reflection of itself into itself" (Hegel 1977, § 7); it is "absolutely mediated" (Hegel 1977, § 37) and proves in its abundance of things, facts, and states of affairs to be "substantial content" (Hegel 1977, § 37) through the conceptual determinations of thought. In addition, Hegel points out that the content-related object of thought is "the property of the self," just as the same object is "self-like" (in German: "selbstisch") through its determinate being in the thinking subject (Hegel 1977, § 32). An object, a thing, an entity is in its being insofar as it has its concept, just as the concept is a concept for subjects. For Hegel, however, a symbiosis of being and thinking can only take place if the object finds, metaphorically speaking, a 'setting' within its concept. This is only possible if being and thinking are related, but not one. For were the difference between being and thinking resolved without friction or tension, we would, as Hegel writes, "soon die of hunger, bodily as well as spiritually" (Hegel 2010, p. 199).

In the vocabulary of the left-Hegelian philosopher Alain Badiou, one could say: thinking shows itself capable of "multiple-presentations" but "the errancy of the void" (Badiou 2006, 93) can never be entirely excluded by thinking, since it is always included in every situation. A gap or divide between thinking and being is thus a condition of both, and up to the present it manifests itself in the plurality of our references to the world, where a plurality of truth-concepts (existential, phenomenological, scientific, artistic, etc.) opens up a plurality of respective objects within uncountable "fields of sense" (Gabriel 2015).

Jacques Lacan, the avid reader of Hegel and Kant and the founding father of the structural theory of psychoanalysis, develops his own emblematic understanding of this "gap" with reference to Hans Holbein the Younger's painting *The Ambassadors* (1533), to which I will refer in more detail later on. The painting reveals to him how the visual field of perception cannot measure the entire space of its veridical grasp on facts and states of affairs. The effect of the painting lies in the deliberate division of the seemingly homologous form of the representation by the construction of a parallax gap, where the shift of the subject provokes a shift in the object as well. I will come back to this later on.

For Hegel, even the law of identity "A = A" expresses this claim of an inherent gap within all kinds of entities (Hegel 2010a, pp. 358–361). "A" literally comes to be distanced from itself as part of a symbolic network in "= A" and only then becomes one with itself. This distance manifests itself formally in the proposition that A is equal to A. A fits into its mold. From the first "A" onwards, which assumes the role of a predicative subject, the object "A" becomes the predication "=A". The first "A" comes to coincide with the second and says, albeit with little content, very much for Hegel formally about the self-reflexivity of entities in holistic structures of their objectification (see also Hegel 2010b, pp. 177–178).[2]

Badiou endorses the Hegelian division within identities and entities mentioned above. He does so prominently in his early work *The Theory of the Subject* (2009b). Here he presents a theoretical argument, one recurrent in his thought, for his theory of an "event." For an event is, in Badiou's theory, the epitomizing proof that thinking and being circle around each other via a necessary non-coincidence. This non-coincidence opens up places of untamed significations – i.e. illegal places of subjectivity that give proof that subjectivity is a feature of reality.

---

[2] It might be relevant to mention here that we encounter this significant structure of self-identity in bifurcated, dissyllabic words of infants of just a few months old. In words such as "da-da," "pa-pa," and "ma-ma," the second syllable opens a place whereby the signifier of the first syllable can fall back into itself at the place of its repetition. Two-syllable words are the prototypes of higher-order signifiers and, as such, more than mere signs. A = A is then related to the immediate environment of the child, e.g.: "ma = ma," "pa = pa," "da = da". The identity of persons and things is tied into a rebuilding structure as a rudimentary symbolic system for toddlers. "-ma" is similar to an inverted mold/shape in a symbolic system and "Ma-," the identity of the mother, who takes place in it.

2 The identity-theorem: A *as such* and A *placed in a topos*

In the first chapter of his book *Theory of the Subject*, Badiou introduces his reader to the Hegelian dialectic according to which every identity imparts a formal eccentricity to itself (Badiou 2009b, pp. 3–12). And – as we will see – this has important consequences for political conflicts as well, where objects are often inscribed within disputes: or, more specifically, within the battle of the criteria of their existence.[3] Badiou shows how each being is constitutively split into its "being-in-itself" and its indexical localization, that is, in the place of its appearance. The splitting of an entity into an "in-itself" and its "localization" is the condition for something to appear. This argument is similar to Hegel's reflections on the identity theorem A=A. Badiou names the elements of division by differentiating between A (read as: "A as such" or "A as pure being") and A_p (read as: A "being placed" at a location: Badiou 2009b, p. 7). A-as-such is the appearing being, the being that has no place – the utopian dimension of A (as such). A_p, on the other hand, is A as placed. It is the being that is inscribed in a topos. A and A_p are not two independent entities. Rather, they signify how each entity is divided into its ideal form, its abstract thought-identity ("liberté" in itself), and its local embodiment in space-time (presentable in its extension: "liberté" in 1789).

Badiou sums this thought up as follows: "A is itself, but it is also its power of repetition, the legibility of itself at a distance from itself" (Badiou 2009b, p. 6). He proposes the neologism "esplace" which derives from the abbreviation of "espace de placement" ("space of placement," Badiou 2009b, p. 10). For the unregistered, not placed, and thus utopian A, he suggests the word "horlieu" ("outplace," Badiou 2009b, p. 10). This out-of-place or the "being in itself," which is the "real" of the "esplace" ("splace," Badiou 2009b, p. 10), is not representable. It stands in for what Lacan calls a lack of being. Badiou makes clear that the entity A is affected in its division between A and A_p by an inherent negativity, because the "in-itself" of A is by its localization even at a distance from its very embodiment in A_p. It is utopian. Badiou thus illustrates Hegel's thesis that "identity internally breaks apart into diversity because, as absolute difference in itself, it posits itself as the negative of itself and these, its two moments (itself and the

---

[3] We see this battle becoming especially virulent today in contemporary debates within ontology where representatives of "New Realism" or "Speculative Realism" oppose all kinds of theories within the research field of Reductive Physicalism.

negative of itself), are reflections into themselves, are identical with themselves" (Hegel 2010, p. 362). In the Preface of the *Phenomenology*, Hegel writes, "the bifurcation of the simple [. . .] is the True" (Hegel 1977, § 18) to express the extent to which each entity is inscribed with a double negation: on the one hand, by being the difference from other determinations and, on the other, by being in a purely formal self-relation, which is always affected by an inherent non-identity. Now, Badiou applies the Hegelian definition of identity, which is equally marked by two excluding moments of identity and non-identity, to political situations, and it is especially here that we touch upon subjectivity as a feature of reality.

As is well known, Badiou formalizes his arguments with the help of set theory in the form of embedded and excluded multiplicities that can conflict with one another about the sovereign claims of their representation. In *Being and Event* he describes, for example, the extent to which "there is nothing apart from situations. Ontology, if it exists, is a situation" (Badiou 2006, p. 25). But ontology is just a situation among others, so to speak, on the meta-level of philosophical reflection. Other situations can be located concretely in space and time. This implies that Paris in 1848 is "a situation;" or Russia in 1917, or the "White on White" painting of Kazimir Malevich from 1918.

What distinguishes these situations, as exceptional ones, from others, is the manifestation of their inconsistencies through identities in which – as in Badiou's split of "A-in-itself" and "A-placed" – the utopian moment (the in-itself) opens the place of placement. For example, the painting "White on White" of Malevich as an artistically utopian idea, or the Russian Revolution as a political one, meet, in their respective forms of being "in itself," the place of their arrival with incomprehension or resistance surrounding them. In other words, their identity is shaped by inherent moments of non-identity. Consistency, as Hegel suggests, is always dependent on inconsistency. In other words, every structured situation that is counted as one is based on a lack of structure that cannot be presented from the point of view of the prevailing count. With Slavoj Žižek one can say that the inconsistent situation is "the pure multiple, the not yet symbolically structured multitude of experience, that which is given; this multitude is not a multitude of Ones, since the counting has not yet taken place" (Žižek 1998, p. 235). Therefore, Badiou can also write: "All multiple-presentation is exposed to the danger of the void: the void is its being. The consistency of the multiple amounts to the following: the void, which is the name of inconsistency in the situation (under the law of the count-as-one), cannot, in itself, be presented or fixed" (Badiou 2006, p. 93).

It is worth mentioning here that Graham Harman builds his "object-oriented ontology" in part on this insight (Harman 2002). In his Husserlian return "zu den Sachen selbst" and his Heideggerian analysis of tool-being, all kinds of objects depend on the self-reflexive form of *"withdrawal* or *witholding"* (Harman 2017, p. 7). Chairs, stock-market bonds, airplanes cannot be defined by bundles of their properties. They withdraw insofar as they exist as "real objects." "Real objects cannot relate to one another directly, but only indirectly, by means of a sensual object" (Harman 2017, p. 9). They are supernumerary by definition with regard to their properties and, as such, retract themselves into what Lacan would have called "the real." As such they are neither fully accessible to human beings, nor to other objects they interact with on a biological, mechanistic, symbolic or physical level. Lacan's interest in Hans Holbein's anamorphic painting *The Ambassadors* illustrates this Hegelian, as well as Heideggerian, insight allegorically. And since the philosophy of psychoanalysis is the discipline that takes subjectivity as a feature of reality for granted, it is relevant to bring Lacan more centrally into this analysis.

3 The "gaze" splitting the field of phenomena

Lacan is fascinated by Holbein's painting *The Ambassadors* because it shows how in the field of vision (as the emblematic field of what can be known) a blind sight-like "gaze" is inscribed via the famous skull depicted anamorphically in the lower part of the painting. For Lacan, this skull is a metaphor for the inherent limit of the human mind. The geometrical view-point with its dominant central perspective of the painting is undermined by a hidden point of reference: a mixture of Kant's concept of the "thing in itself" and pure nonsense, since the skull is in its anamorphic form nothing more than an oval color patch. Some sort of "the True" (Frege) can be found here on the surface of what is seen since this entity is, figuratively speaking, the hidden and noumenon-like backside of the phenomena depicted in the painting with the ambassadors Jean de Dinteville and Georges de Selves at the royal court of Henry VIII at center stage. As such it has, according to Lacan, the effect that, "as subjects, we are literally called into the picture" (Lacan 1998, p. 92) and indeed in the form of the blind spot, which, according to Slavoj Žižek, is "in the object more than the object itself," the place from whence the object might even look back (Žižek 2006, p. 17).

I understand Žižek's enigmatic comment as pointing to the fact that the form of human reason, measured transcendently by Kant and Hegel, leads to the insight that the domain of veridical facts becomes clear only at a distance from veridical reality itself. I mentioned this thought at the beginning of this text. Harman calls this, fittingly, "first floor realism" in his critique of the "ground-floor" reductionism (Harman 2010, p. 784) defended by John Ladyman and Dan Ross (2009). The latter defend "structure" as the physical ground of reality, and so establish a new mythical view from nowhere. Why is it that reality needs distance from itself? Because, as indicated above with reference to Hegel and Badiou, the forms of knowledge access reality, necessarily, with a mode of excess, too-muchness. This is so because 'to know' yields – within the classical understanding of knowledge as being justified true belief – not only "adequacy" (as Bas van Fraassen urges us to accept, 1980, p. 69), but "truth" – truth of facts and states of affairs. Žižek repeatedly refers in this context to the "parallax gap" within the subject-object dichotomy and states that any "'epistemological' shift in the subject's point of view always reflects an 'ontological' shift in the object itself" (Žižek 2006, p. 17).

"Reality," "the world," the "field of experience" comes to existence only in the mere form of inferentially related judgments where judgments themselves are the pre-condition of "reality" to be perceived as potentially veridical. Harman examines this property of transcendental anamorphosis within beings in his object-oriented ontology. He underlines how human beings have contact with objects only in an "indirect way" as objects incorporate their own withdrawal (Harman 2017, p. 7). As I mentioned above, Kant already introduced parts of this insight by explaining that the "conditions of the possibility of experience" are simultaneously "the conditions of the possibility of objects of experience" (Kant 1997, B 197). That is to say, the space of experience is shaped by the intellect's form-condition of knowledge, and as such is not able to quantify uncritically the form-condition of content and the content-condition of form. But we can also refer to Willard V. O. Quine and express that the coordinate system in which an entity is revealed in its existence in the form of a "bound variable" can never be replaced by a seemingly direct "referential" correlation between subject and object, since the belief in a system-free reference is "nonsense" (Quine 1969, p. 48). This means that the subject holds, allegorically speaking, his/her reason-frame like a mirror onto reality, but, as such, it (the subject) is always hidden in the mirror itself: as the central perspective of what Kant calls the transcendental "I" of apperception. Lacan sees this exemplified in the skull in Holbein's painting. It looks back at the viewer from a place-out-of place. This non-place now has – in times of epistemic, political, or psychological crises – the potential to "re-mark" reality as it proves the status of the transcendental "I" itself to be essentially virtual – a place of gapping.[4] In his *Seminar XI* Lacan explains this to his audience: "[N]ote the way in which the leather [of a finger of a winter glove turned inside-out] envelops the fur [...] – that conscious-

---

[4] Lacan expresses this in his famous words: "The picture, certainly, is in my eye. But I am in the picture" (Lacan 1998, p. 96).

ness, in its illusion of *seeing itself seeing itself*, finds its basis in the inside-out structure of the gaze" (Lacan 1998, p. 82). Seeing itself seeing itself is a distinct feature of the imagination found only within the human mind. It is for Lacan a form of "*Vorstellungsrepräsentanz*" (Lacan 1998, p. 60), the signifier that serves to mark something that escapes representation. "*Vorstellungsrepräsentanz*" (the representation of a representation) is a placeholder for all kinds of imaginations about oneself within reality in which my identity is mirrored via justified beliefs. "It is less a representative representative than a *non-representative representative*" (Lacan 1998, 2018). This *Vorstellungsrepräsentanz* can be filled by a Bororo man with the proposition "*I am a parrot* [while] we say *I am me* [*moi*]" (Lacan 1991, p. 39) and so proves to be nothing but a placeholder for a lack. Today the common form of *Vorstellungsrepräsentanz* among philosophers is the self-declaration "I am a naturalist" which Hilary Putnam criticized with humor both due to the term's lack of clarity as well as its ideological identity-political form (Putnam 2012, pp. 109–110).[5] Lacan underlines with this comment the extent to which the symbolic network can be reshaped by the inner gap of the outside representation that – like a glove stripped from the hand – suddenly turns certain properties of reality inside out. How? Among other things, through a change of the *Vorstellungsrepräsentanz* itself.

The Lacanian conviction of shifting world-pictures through changing forms of *Vorstellungsrepräsentanz* is also expressed in both Hegel's and Badiou's dialectics. Especially Hegel underlines that there is no area of veridical facts and states of affairs without derivation from the anamorphic location known as subjectivity. No wonder that the third part of Hegel's *Science of Logic*, "The Doctrine of the Notion," is called "Subjective Logic," since it is here that the most essential forms of being are reflected upon. Subjectivity is the meta-frame through which objectivity becomes comprehensible (like in a prism) but – and this is important – the subject is at the same time a mereological part of this objectivity via supernumerary background-conditions of knowledge. It is from here that

---

[5] Putnam: "Today the most common use of the term 'naturalism' might be described as follows: philosophers – perhaps even a majority of all the philosophers writing about issues in metaphysics, epistemology, philosophy of mind, and philosophy of language – announce in one or another conspicuous place in their essays and books that they are 'naturalists' or that the view or account being defended is a 'naturalist' one. This announcement, in its placing and emphasis, resembles the placing of the announcement in articles written in Stalin's Soviet Union that a view was in agreement with Comrade Stalin's; as in the case of the latter announcement, it is supposed to be clear that any view that is not 'naturalist' (not in agreement with Comrade Stalin's view) is anathema and could not possibly be correct. A further very common feature is that, as a rule, 'naturalism' is not defined" (2012, pp. 109–110).

one must understand Lacan's fascination with anamorphosis and his continuous references to Hegel as well as Badiou's reference to both Lacan and Hegel as essential sources of his philosophy. Hegel teaches his readers why the mind is always eccentric to itself. It cannot be reduced to the brain as a physical organ of each individual or an entire population, as the abstract network of thoughts and imaginations would then dissolve. Mind needs brains, but its true being must be located in the abstract realm of signifiers – what Lacan calls the symbolic – and their historical networks of inferential data units.

4 Subject, lack, and substance

Hegel indirectly explores the idea of an anamorphosis-like distortion in the "Introduction" to the *Phenomenology of Spirit*. Here, in critical demarcation from Kant, he equates the human apparatus of perception with a medium that, according to the "law of its refraction," opens up a point of access to the external world (Hegel 1977, p. 47). This conventional image of knowledge as a medium, which Hegel claims to have discovered in Kant's philosophy, presents the subject as someone literally standing in front of a telescope-like device focused on the world. The medium focuses the light of truth, thereby creating access to the other side: the object. But Hegel unfolds this ironic commentary on Kant's transcendental philosophy to emphasize that "it is not the fraction of the ray, but the ray itself whereby truth reaches us, that is cognition; and if this were removed, all that would be indicated would be a pure direction or a blank space" (Hegel 1977, p. 47).

Kant neglects to consider that it is the subject herself that brings the ray of truth along the path through the telescope-like device (= the mind as medium) to the object, thereby bringing the object into its form of representation ("A" takes a 'setting' in "=A"). The source of light is no neutral reflection of light-beams from the surface of objects 'out there;' rather, it is what the subject brings towards the object within the limits of its five senses and its capacity for category-formation. The subject, hence, mediates the subject-object dichotomy through herself. The object's veridicality is not found in an eternal truth-pattern that correlates subject and object from a "view from nowhere," but the subject steps literally into the object equipped with justifications to guarantee forms of veridicality of that very object it literally stepped into. To say it with Lacan: The subject may very well see "what is the case," but it *itself* is through its transcendental conditions of perception already unthematically "within the picture" (Lacan 1998,

p. 96) of that which is the case.⁶ The subject is, according to Lacan, in a non-extensional determinable meta-frame inscribed in the condition of insight into "what there is," since *it is* the frame. What does this meta-frame consist of? Among other things, of "memes," i.e. inferentially justification-necessary data-unites which carry cultural ideas (of liberalism, for example, individual freedom etc.) just as much as they do economic practices (private ownership of the means of production) and basic principles of the natural sciences (like natural laws). Bas van Fraassen speaks of bundles of values, emotions, politics, preferences, and beliefs that shape "stances" (van Fraassen 2002) of scientifically reasonable beliefs. The subject has internalized them as her second nature in the cognitive situations of everyday life in which she is located within an epoch – sometimes with more competence, sometimes with less. With Hegel's reference to "rays of truth:" the subject asserts the "ray" of truth within herself. The subject is part of what she knows about as well as the medium of her knowledge. She is part of her knowledge, because she is the medium of her mind, as well as *in* the medium of her mind – a medium that is extended through historical and social memes and concepts. If we take this into account, it truly is difficult to share what Paul Boghossian calls, with a certain amount of polemic, *Fear of Knowledge* (2006) with regard to authors like Richard Rorty, Hilary Putnam, Nelson Goodman, or Thomas Kuhn, who know, roughly speaking, about the antinomies of knowledge very well. Boghossian argues in his book against a widespread "epistemic relativism" within philosophy of anthropological, sociological, and epistemological kinds whereby truth is depicted as depending on cultural conditions. Boghossian, for his part, defends "fundamental epistemic principles" which will give us, he thinks, definite verdicts about which beliefs are justified and which are not. However, one of the book's shortcomings lies in what Boghossian subsumes in a very reductionist manner as contemporary relativism. He begins his book with the strange reference to an "equal validity" doctrine (Boghossian 2006, p. 2) according to which "postmodern philosophers" see the "truths" of primitive tribes on an equal footing with findings within the natural sciences. But if there is an insight for which the supposedly postmodern relativists stand, then it is certainly not that the truthfulness of the existence of "atoms" is dependent on cultural "points of view," or that belief in a geocentric universe is equally valid for a postmodern philosopher as belief in a heliocentric one, but that 'truth' unfolds historically in what Hegel calls the "concept" as a process of progressing knowledge that is constantly being re-articulated through its inher-

---

6 I understand Andrea Kern's defense of realism in this sense (see her article in this volume).

ent lack of fundamental epistemic principles.⁷ The subject is part of her knowledge, because knowledge itself is a medium eccentric to itself, with the subject being, analogically speaking, a paradoxical subset of it, as well as part of the set's boundary itself. The subject is inscribed in a collectively and eccentric medium-structure of mind, where mind is something that crisscrosses the individual brain, though – in certain situations – it may find in an individual brain nevertheless its eccentric point of non-coincidence, i.e. an outlet of what is not yet comprehensible within an established form of objective knowledge. Alain Badiou calls situations where an all-encompassing collection of beliefs and assumptions is challenged by a point of non-coincidence eventual sites of "truth" that crisscross an inferential field of "objective knowledge," and where subjectivity as a feature of reality comes to the fore. But Kant, Hegel, and Lacan already knew about these sites (see Finkelde 2017).

So, when the perceiving subject produces the "ray" of truth, it (so to speak) brings, through the medium of her mind, the object into the external world as already (at least in part) alongside herself. This has the effect that the subject is the meta-frame in which objectivity becomes comprehensible and it is a mereological part of this objectivity encompassed within herself being part of the content too. In this sense the claim here is that there is no way to conceive of objectivity without thinking of it as framed by subjects within systems of belief. To think of objectivity as something that can be seen from the "view from nowhere," with no subject necessarily around, forgets that the view from nowhere presupposes some kind of subject already seeing something as something. But *from where* should the "view from nowhere" look and *on what* should it look? The moon? The earth? The Milky Way? The galaxy-clusters our Milky Way is in? Or the – other way around – at molecules, atoms and particles? Referring to a "view from nowhere" forgets the presupposition of framing that is already – at least indirectly – mediated by subjects. Does the moon exist, even if there is no single eye looking at it? The question itself is misleading, since, as I said, without a frame the moon cannot even be an entity since it can as well be a mer-

---

7 Facts are always part of this "concept," since epistemic principles are. The world existed before the existence of humans, but as a fact it can be identified only within the "concept;" i.e. in a holistic system in which "something as something" is representable. Here is where the insights of authors such as Putnam, Rorty, or Derrida are to be found: the incalculability of the representation of "all facts" cannot be obtained, which does not put into question truth and facts in themselves as epistemic necessities within their historical re-evaluation. Therefore, accepting the truth-conditions in science does not eliminate the ability to detect truth-conditions, as also in Shakespeare's tragedies, in paintings by Roy Lichtenstein, or in the life-style of a primitive tribe in the Amazon. See also Martin Kusch's critique of Boghossian in this volume.

eological part of galaxy-clusters. The "moon" is, within multiple-multiplicities itself, a multiple-multiplicity of rocks, atoms, quarks etc.

As I said, Lacan reflects on the conceptual structure of mind in its relation to the world. And he is especially fascinated by the paradox of self-inclusion, presented as the emblematic *mise-on-scène* in Holbein's depiction of a parallax gap. The painting's 'message' is no less ontological than it is political. It is political insofar as any question "on what there is" has political repercussions.

Where or when do we see events that exhibit a paradoxical self-inclusion of subject, frame, and object occur? Quite often, I would say, and maybe even more than we want. To give an example of this paradoxical self-inclusion of a subject that brings an object into the realm of "what there is" by being (somehow) herself the object and the place of veridicality (A=A), one can refer to Christianity's hybrid of a God-Son. The man from Galilee retotalizes via its particular and contingent location in space and time what the four letters YHWH in the Hebrew bible stood for until then. As Jesus *from Nazareth* he is a paradoxical element in his own God-set: frame and content. God-Substance is retotalized paradoxically from within through a particular. Or, to refer back again to the Holbein painting: within the field of vision of orthodox Judaism, Jesus Messiah is the universal and particular exception within substance which redefines what Judaism is about: Christianity. But so is the "White on White" painting of Malevich, as well, within the realm of art at a certain time and at a certain place. Modern art as we know it today would not exist without this paradoxical object presented to the world in 1918.

Hegel writes in the "Introduction" of the *Phenomenology* that "Substance shows itself to be essentially Subject" (Hegel 1977, p. 21), that is, as the special element where substance identifies its own non-identity. The foundations of Hegel's understanding of being as ontologically split can be found here. This insight allows him to describe numerous areas of human life (science, art, law, religion) as essentially anamorphic, that is, as dependent on a process-generating non-coincidence between subject and object, which cannot be perceived as a non-coincidence per se, since it opens up the range of veridical facts within different logical forms of knowledge time and again. In other words, Hegel understands substance as a totality (whether in science, art, law, religion) which includes a particular element that embodies both the structural principle of totality and the totality in the form of a particular, a place of non-identity in this totality, by being this totality itself *en miniature* in an inverted form. The figure of Jesus of Nazareth as *Vorstellungsrepräsentanz* breaks the spell of orthodox Judaism simply by being the singular exception to what Judaism *via Christ* is.

To bring "Subject" on par with "Substance" as a synonym for the primary structure of being is, for the philosophical tradition, of course a self-annihilation of the concept "substance" with its own plurality of meanings. But in a way, this is Hegel's demand. Hegel does not adopt here in his train of reasoning the Aristotelian idea that a "subject" embodies the substance-form of the human species, and therefore is *also*, as an individual being, substance as well. Rather, Hegel means that the subject has a substantial share in substance. This thought, however, was basically impossible to conceptualize within the limits of the traditional understanding of the concept of substance – at least until Hegel's reinterpretation of Spinoza's monistic understanding of it. Substance can incorporate accidents, or be the homeostatic sum of all of its accidental modes, but not the other way around, i.e. be incorporated by an accidental moment in which substance itself supervenes.

The Hegelian insight, though, that "Substance shows itself to be essentially Subject," (Hegel 1977, p. 21) refers to a missed encounter within substance itself where the subject-as-substance is constituted by a structure of a paradoxical self-inclusion of substance-as-substance. The particular/accidental can be both *within* the universal and *be the universal* at the same time in the form of a particular exception where the exception is the universal in an inverted and yet (for the universal *unknown*) form of itself. (The example of Jesus *the Christ*, mentioned above, exemplifies this thought fittingly.) For, as we have said, "subject" is not just an accidental property of substance. It can *be* substance *tout court*. This thought corresponds, therefore, purely formally at least, with the Lacanian logic of anamorphosis: the logic of a parallax gap in a totality by a corresponding element which is in itself and, at the same time, excluded from itself.

This kind of paradoxical self-inclusion, which Bertrand Russell tried to circumvent in the *Principia Mathematica* with his Type Theory (after diagnosing in Gottlob Frege's logicism the lack of accounting for the paradox of all sets that are not members of themselves), is more part of *Dasein's* self-relation than sapient beings normally appreciate. It can be found in every self-consciousness where the particularity (of being me) and the universality (of being me as a self-reflexive unit of veridical thoughts and propositions about me) relate to each other by auto-annihilating each other as well. This topic is, of course, addressed especially within the philosophy of psychoanalysis, where the self-inflicted stress of a mind with its inner contradictions is the topic that brought psychoanalysis into being. Next to Lacan, it is especially Wilfred Bion whose work in this field formalizes the mind's inner/outer reality with algebraic equations (Bion 1989). This auto-annihilation comes, for example, to the fore where I relate formally and universally to myself with my consciousness *to my consciousness* and bring the particular and contingent fact of being myself to the unshakable belief, that this me, which knows "*what it is like to be me,*" truly *is* me. But independently of this universal form of self-reflexivity, self-consciousness stands opposed to the self-conscious individual as the latter is experienced, as well, as fallible and contingent within the natural and causal processes of his/her body as well as of his/her culture and the contingent location in spacetime. Time and again, the human mind thinks to incorporate the positive qualities of the universal (prudence, objectivity, rationality, etc.), and yet it knows that on its concrete subject-plane of existence it is part of causal processes within nature and so can never adequately establish its universality beyond this frame. My universal (Fichtean) insight that "I" have a body contradicts with the (Dennettian) insight that *I am* my body. As such, self-consciousness embodies the formal-logical structure of a paradoxical self-relation known, of course, as the "mind-body problem." Abstract universality focuses on the particularity of a specific body (mine) and back again. Within this context we find one of the reasons why Daniel Dennett and Thomas Metzinger focus, in different strands of their investigations, on consciousness as an "illusion" while especially Dennett defends at the same time a rather obscure concept of "free will" (Dennett 2015). The latter's deficiencies have been called out by Sam Harris (Harris 2014).

As Lacan repeatedly emphasized and as Émile Beveniste had already shown linguistically in his interpretation of personal pronouns (Benveniste 1973), the place of the speaking ego is always part of a paradoxical self-recourse (Lacan 2006, p. 556). Benveniste describes the linguistic function of personal pronouns as one that does not refer to an object. The "I" makes "the coincidence of the event described with the instance of discourse that describes it" (Benveniste 1973, p. 226). This means that personal pronouns in a successful linguistic speech act become their own reality; a reality that cannot be objectified by a third authority. It is from this self-recourse that parallax proves itself to be fundamental within the subject-object dichotomy of being. Self-consciousness is intrinsically analogous to the paradox of the liar: the subject in the enunciation "I am autonomous, self-conscious, and as a rational being the source of justified true belief, for what else should I be?" is taken back performatively by the subject of enunciation.

5 The element that is lacking in the form of a stand-in. On Lacan's "suture"

We mentioned above Hegel's insight that the subject is both the meta-frame in which objectivity becomes comprehensible and a mereological part of objectivity too. Why? Because the frame of subjectivity that encapsulates objectivity is also *in* the object in the form of an unsymbolizable "x." Holbein's depiction of a parallax gap is, as I mentioned repeatedly, for Lacan the emblematic *mise-on-scène* of this insight. Within the representation there is a missing element, that – as being present but not represented – encapsulates what is known from a place-out-of-place. How this paradoxical self-inclusion is possible anyway, and how it can be a site/place for a *subject-in-becoming-to-be-a-feature-of-reality*, explains Lacan's comments on what he calls "points de capitons," or quilting points, as well as his concept of "suture."

Lacan conceptualized this term in the early 1960s and its epistemological and ontological importance was made explicit for the first time by Jacques-Alain Miller in 1966 (2012, pp. 91–102). The notion or concept "suture" is interesting insofar as it refers to the recursively structured anchoring process by which a hybrid effective signifying-force opens up inferential truth-value hierarchies in a range of differentially oriented semantic chains of signifiers. Chains of signifiers themselves are quantified sign-units with data-properties that surround the subject holistically in a space of reasons, and which are used by the subject to relate herself meaningfully to 'the world' (that remains, within its abstract form of thought, always underdetermined and overdetermined). As chains of signifiers are dynamically open, a hegemony of meaning is fundamentally necessary to limit this openness, though this is only guaranteed via disparate exceptions within the mentioned chains themselves.

The boundary that distinguishes between meaning and non-meaning and distances a chain of signifiers from the outside of its hegemonic field can be illuminated only by the inner perspective of the symbolic form of the signifying chain. An effect is that a chain of signifiers needs pivotal points of exception to establish coherence, though the exceptions overburden the structure of justification. As the "master-signifier" is the element within various chains of signifiers, it gives stability to the latter (without being itself part of the range of inferentially related differences). Just think of a parliament (totalitarian, royal, or democratic) that is the legal ground of parliamentary discourse within the limits of politics, but which has its justification only after and through its own form-condition (i.e. its being already established). The necessary failure of a stable frontier of legality to constrain the outside of the legal system is camouflaged in the master-signifier's authority by its symbiosis of being at the same time a zero-point of meaning (the law that comes from the lack of law) and a count-as-one of the meaningful law, which now is "the Law" since it says so. Here "suture" is groundless ground and reason's first axiomatic forced choice, forced premise. Miller: "Suture names [...] the element which is lacking, in the form of a stand-in [*tenant-lieu*]. For while there lacking, it is not purely and simply absent" (Miller 2012, p. 93). The 'sewing' emerges through a missing element of justification as well as via a replacement of this missing element through the performative setting of a "so be it!" Kant's talk of the "Ding an sich" is a telling example of a "master-signifier" in epistemology. This is because, to cite Heinrich Jacobi's famous critique of the "Ding an sich," one can see Kant's predicament: "Without the presupposition [of the 'thing in itself,'] I was unable to enter into [Kant's] system, but with it I was unable to stay within it" (Jacobi 2000, p. 173).

"Master-signifiers" are needed to "suture" chains of signifiers around nodal points of exception, but their epistemic foundation is unstable or – to say the least – time and again dependent on self-authorized (ex-)positions of self-referential subjectivity. Here again, we touch upon subjectivity as a feature of reality. We see exceptions, established through master-signifiers, in different areas of society, for example in certain currents of an eliminative materialism/naturalism. When a reductive physicalist, like Alexander Rosenberg (2012) for example, cannot explain with sufficient reasons how the abstract medium of thought, of which his theory is composed, emerges in spacetime, word by word, thought by thought, from causal chains of electrons upwards to neurotransmitter-mediated control of neuronal firings, his theory exemplifies a 'posture' of knowledge camouflaging its own inherent shortcomings. To refer back to Lacan's comments on Holbein, one could say that Kant's "thing in itself" is an anamorphic distortion that is needed literally to guarantee facts, states of affairs, but also concepts like freedom, the moral will, the soul, the kingdom of ends, etc. The inferential logic of meaning that arises in the "suture"-performance (of the "thing in itself") negotiates the paradoxical task of its delimitation to the outside through a paradoxical performative act within the structure of justification, camouflaging that the outside is mediated as outside by a gap inside. (Think again of Lacan's reference to a winter glove turned inside-out as an allegory for the inward-outward structure of the human mind.) This holds for the relation of physical and abstract entities, mentioned above, as well. But it needs, of course, a subject – in our example: Kant – who is willing to wager that his concept, carrying a paradox (as 'collateral damage' of an entire network of inferential justifications) is truth-apt nevertheless. This task cannot be accomplished perfectly and demands ever-new provisional solutions to keep the frontier between the inner and the outer of Kant's philosophy from collapsing. This is why Kantian philosophy is still in the making, for example in the work of John McDowell, who tries – unsuccessfully in my opinion – to bridge the gap between "intuitions" and "concepts" by interpreting intuitions as having rational properties themselves (McDowell 1994).

As I already mentioned, Lacan describes paradoxical signifiers which negotiate the outer-inner boundary of meaning and units of signification/signifiers also as "points de capiton," upholstery buttons. They create meaning-hegemony and at the same time delete their own traces. The "point de capiton" proclaims a harmony of meaning that is established by "suture," whereby the act of sewing is subtly faded out. In this sense anchor-points are anamorphic by definition within an inferential web of belief that is struggling to maintain coherence. They bring meaning-changes to a relative standstill, but at the price of an illegal grounding / a paradoxical self-inclusion. This is why their place can be the center of hegemony but also the site of their downfall, when a new master-signifier is erected from the blind spot or from the inherent gap of the old. This non-place then is the illegality from where subjectivity as a feature of reality emerges. It needs subjects who – especially in times of epistemic or political crises – opt for a paradoxical self-inclusion of being signifier and signified at the same time. "Suture" conditions and conceals the inherent gulf from which each field of hegemonic normativity relates meaningfully to itself.

But is this thought not also exactly what Hegel's philosophy is about? He says so explicitly in the aforementioned "Introduction" to the *Phenomenology* with reference to a substance that "shows itself to be essentially Subject" (Hegel 1977, p. 21). In other words, Hegel understands substance as a totality (whether in science, art, law, religion) which time and time again includes a particular element that embodies both the structural principle of totality and the totality in the form of a particular, a place of non-identity in this totality, by being this totality itself *en miniature* in an inverted form.

Bibliography

Aristotle (1998): *Metaphysics*. London: Penguin.
Badiou, Alain (2006): *Being and Event*. Translated by Oliver Feltham. London: Continuum.
Badiou, Alain (2009a): *Logics of Worlds: Being and Event 2*. Translated by Alberto Toscano. London: Continuum.
Badiou, Alain (2009b): *Theory of the Subject*. London: Bloomsbury.
Benveniste, Émile (1973): *Subjectivity in Language. Problems in General Linguistics*. Miami: Miami University Press.
Bion, Wilfred (1989): *Elements of Psychoanalysis*. London: Karnac.
Freud, Sigmund (1960): *Jokes and Their Relation to the Unconscious*. Standard Edition vol. 8. London: Hogarth Press.
Deleuze, Gilles and Felix Guattari (1987): *A Thousand Plateaus. Capitalism & Schizophrenia*. London: Continuum.
Dennett, Daniel (2015): *Elbow Room. The Varieties of Free Will Worth Wanting*. Cambridge, Mass.: MIT Press.
Dolar, Mladen (2015): "Anamorphosis." In: *Journal of the Circle for Lacanian Ideology Critique* 8: pp. 125–140.
McDowell, John (1994): *Mind and World*. Cambridge, Mass.: Harvard University Press.
Finkelde, Dominik (2017a): *Excessive Subjectivity. Kant, Hegel, Lacan, and the Foundations of Ethics*. Translated by Deva Kemmis and Astrid Waigert. New York: Columbia University Press.

Finkelde, Dominik (2017b): "Logics of Scission. The Subject is 'Limit of the World.'" In: *Philosophy Today* 61., No. 3, pp. 595–618.

Finkelde, Dominik (2019): "Lack and Concept. On Hegelian Motives in Badiou." In: Jan Völker (Ed.): *Badiou and the German Tradition of Philosophy*. London: Bloomsbury, pp.35–50.

Gabriel, Markus (2015): *Fields of Sense: A New Realist Ontology*. Edinburgh: Edinburgh University Press.

Harman, Graham (2002): *Tool-Being: Heidegger and the Metaphysics of Objects*. Chicago: Open Court.

Harman, Graham (2010): "I am also of the opinion that materialism must be destroyed." In: *Environment and Planning: Society and Space* 28, pp. 772–790.

Harman, Graham (2017): *Object-Oriented-Ontology. A New Theory of Everything*. London: Penguin.

Harris, Sam (2014): "The Marionette's Lament. A Response to Daniel Dennett." Online: http://www.samharris.org/blog/item/the-marionettes-lament, visited 2 Dec. 2018).

Harris, W. T. and Charles S. Peirce (1867): "Nominalism versus Realism." In: W. T. Harris (Ed.): *The Journal of Speculative Philosophy* 2, No. 1, pp. 57–61.

Hegel, Georg W. F. (1977): *Phenomenology of Spirit*. Translated by A.V. Miller. Oxford: Oxford University Press.

Hegel, Georg W. F. (1991): *Enzyklopädie der philosophischen Wissenschaften (1830)*. Hamburg: Felix Meiner Verlag.

Hegel, Georg W. F. (2010a): *The Science of Logic*. Edited and translated by George di Giovanni. Cambridge: Cambridge University Press.

Hegel, Georg W. F. (2010b): *Encyclopedia of the Philosophical Sciences in Basic Outline*. Edited and translated by Klaus Brinkmann and Daniel O. Dahlstrom. Cambridge: Cambridge University Press.

Jacobi, Heinrich F. (2000): "On Transcendental Idealism." In: Brigitte Sassen (Ed.): *Kant's Early Critics: The Empiricist Critique of the Theoretical Philosophy*. Cambridge: Cambridge University Press, pp. 169–175.

Kant, Immanuel (1997): *Critique of Pure Reason*. Edited and translated by Paul Guyer and Allen W. Wood. Cambridge: Cambridge University Press.

Lacan, Jacques (1991): *The Seminar of Jacques Lacan. Book II. The Ego in Freud' Theory and in the Technique of Psychoanalysis*. Translated by Alan Sheridan. New York: W.W. Norton & Company.

Lacan, Jacques (1998): *The Seminar of Jacques Lacan. Book XI. The Four Fundamental Concepts of Psychoanalysis*. Translated by Alan Sheridan. New York: W.W. Norton & Company.

Ladyman, James and Don Ross (2009): *Everything Must Go: Metaphysics Naturalized*. Oxford: Oxford University Press.

Miller, Jacques-Alain (2012): "Suture (Elements of the Logic of the Signifier)." In: Peter Hallward and Knox Peden (Eds.): *Concept and Form. Volume One. Key Texts from the Cahiers pour l'Analyse*. London: Verso, pp. 91–102.

Putnam, Hilary (2012): *Philosophy in the Age of Science: Physics, Mathematics and Skepticism*. Cambridge, Mass.: Harvard University Press.

Alexander Rosenberg (2012): *The Atheist's Guide to Reality: Enjoying Life Without Illusions*. New York: W.W. Norton & Company.

van Fraassen, Bas (1980): *The Scientific Image*. Oxford: Oxford University Press.

van Fraassen, Bas (2002): *The Empirical Stance*. New Haven: Yale University Press.
Žižek, Slavoj (2006): *The Parallax View*. Cambridge, Mass.: MIT Press.

Ray Brassier
Concrete-in-Thought, Concrete-in-Act:
Marx, Materialism, and the Exchange Abstraction[1]

Abstract: This essay argues that Marx's distinction between concrete-in-thought and concrete-in-reality does not invoke a conceptual or empirical difference but a difference-in-act. This difference is verified in social practice rather than in thought. The actuality of practice verifies that of thought without there being a metaphysical correspondence between them. While thought can adequately represent the structure of practice, there is no similarity or resemblance between the structure of thought (what is concrete-in-thought) and that of practice (concrete-in-reality). What is concrete-in-reality is a practical act whose nature does not reveal itself either to those executing it or to the theoretical consciousness that takes the consciousness of practitioners as its starting point.

1 Introduction

Marx's is a materialism of abstraction. Capitalism is a system of real abstractions: commodity, value, labour, money, exchange, et al. In contrast to thought, abstractions generated through intellection (such as humanity, right, justice, beauty, etc.), real abstractions are generated through social practices. Whereas the unity of thought abstractions defies spatiotemporal localization because it is that of transcendent generality, the unity of real abstractions defies localization because it is spread out across space and time. Real abstractions are immanent without being particular, abstract without being transcendent. Thus money, for example, is represented by ostensible particulars (whether coins, notes, or digital encryptions) but is not itself an ostensible particular. Yet it is not a conceptual artifact; its attributes and functioning do not depend on intellection. It is concrete but not ostensible.[2]

Concrete social activity generates abstractions in consciousness. These include: the individual, property, productivity, population, the market, society, na-

---

[1] The article was first published online in the journal *Crisis and Critique:* http://crisiscritique.org/2018 h/brassier-v1.pdf (visited 1 Sep. 2018, p. 24).
[2] I say "ostensible" rather than "localizable" because specific currencies, such as the dollar or the euro, possess temporally localizable properties (of magnitude or equivalence) even though these properties may not be phenomenologically accessible by their users.

ture, nation-state, law, right, et al. They can be contrasted with the critical form-determinations through which Marx diagnoses these thought abstractions as the ideological masks of real abstractions: commodity, money, labour, value, production, exchange, et al. Uncovering the form-determinations of the capitalist totality reveals how a category like 'society' misrepresents this contradictory totality as a concrete whole.

Maintaining the reality of abstractions while anchoring them in social practices, Marx's materialism breaks with traditional metaphysics and epistemology. This break is radical but not absolute: unlike Nietzsche for instance, Marx does not try to dissolve the dialectic of truth and semblance into a play of forces (competing wills to power).[3] It is Feuerbach who gives Marx his lead in breaking with philosophy's speculative consummation in absolute knowing. For Feuerbach, speculative transcendence becomes immanent as the fusion of the sensuous and the supersensuous, the phenomenal and the noumenal: "[W]e need not go beyond sensuousness to arrive, in the sense of the Absolute Philosophy, at the limit of the merely sensuous and empirical; all we have to do is not separate the intellect from the senses in order to find the supersensuous – spirit and reason – within the sensuous" (Feuerbach 2012, p. 504). The sensuous fusion of sensuous and supersensuous is realized in human being. The essence of being human is communality and the sensuous root of communality lies in interpersonal relation (as opposed to Kantian intersubjectivity). (See Feuerbach 2012, p. 529)

Marx takes over Feuerbach's sensuous immanentization of speculative transcendence. However, for Marx, the social relation is irreducible to the interpersonal because it is rooted in social practice, which operates behind the back of consciousness, whether personal or interpersonal. Sensuous practice – what we do

---

[3] To the extent that it disregards distinctions between levels of explanation (between the physical and the biological, the biological and the psychological, the psychological and the historical, the historical and the cultural), Nietzsche's invocation of 'forces' in his attempt to overcome both transcendental (Kant) and speculative (Hegel) philosophy ends up miring him in psychologism and biologism. For an illuminating reconstruction of the neo-Kantian context of Nietzsche's naturalism, see Peter Bornedal *Nietzsche's Naturalist Deconstruction of Truth* (London and Lanham, MA: Lexington Books, 2020). Marx, by way of contrast, espouses science and affirms the continuity between humanity and nature while rejecting 'worldview' naturalism, i.e. naturalism as a metaphysical ideology. He draws critically on Hegel and Feuerbach to overcome the limitations of both logicism and anthropologism. The logicist equivalence between the real and the rational is subverted by Feuerbach's rooting of spiritual self-externalization in human sociality. But the anthropological equation of sociality with communality is subverted by using the dialectic of essence and appearance to explain how sociality does not appear to itself as it is in itself.

without knowing that we are doing it – is the immanent but unconscious medium of human being. Sensuous social practice is not an attribute of human being; human being is an attribute of sensuous social practice.

Attempts to absolutize Marx's break with philosophy end up recoding it philosophically by appealing to false concretions (consciousness, the body), indeterminate abstractions (utopia, redemption), or, more often than not, a theological fusion of both. Precisely because it eschews undialectical absoluteness, Marx's break with traditional philosophy can only be properly grasped through the resources of philosophy. It resides in a double inversion: Marx overturns rationalism's subordination of the sensible to the intelligible while simultaneously overturning empiricism's subordination of the intelligible to the sensible. Thus Marx 'twists free' of both rationalism and empiricism by suggesting that it is the sensible which is inapparent and the intelligible which is apparent. The critique of political economy follows from this double inversion, together with Marx's claim that what is concrete in reality can only be grasped through the medium of abstraction. The crux of this double inversion resides in the exchange abstraction and the essential split it generates between the reproduction of value and the reproduction of sociality. While *Capital* develops the ramifications of this inversion, it is already prefigured in the tenets of historical materialism. I will recapitulate them here in the form of ten theses derived from *The German Ideology* and the *Theses on Feuerbach* (this list is not supposed to be definitive; it is intended merely as a useful heuristic):

2 Ten theses of historical materialism

1. Human social production is the ultimate determinant of ideation.
2. Human activity is determined by existing conditions but also produces new conditions. It is this circuit of conditioned and conditioning activity that is the empirically (as opposed to logically) real starting point for materialist theory. It is concretely sensuous as the medium of practice; it is not an abstract datum or "matter of fact" of the sort favoured by philosophical empiricism (see Feuerbach 2012, pp. 484–486).
3. Forces of production determine social relations but are also determined by them in turn.
4. The development of the division of labour determines (a) the development of forms of property, (b) the contradiction between theory and practice, and (c) the contradiction between particular and common interests.
5. The difference between humans and other animals is materially produced by human activity; it is not a metaphysical or transcendental difference. Hu-

mans differentiate themselves from other animals in practice before distinguishing themselves from them in theory.
6. The history of humanity, including the history of humanity's relation to nature, is the history of social (re)production. No sensuous datum is merely given; it has always been socially produced (i.e. mediated by a system of social relations, not a concept).
7. The social relation is the source of the materiality of human consciousness.
8. Consciousness is the "inverted reflection" of real social relations. The limitations of material production and social relations impose this inversion upon consciousness.
9. Historical materialism is the science of history to the extent that it proceeds from the real premise of sensuous productive activity as the source of ideological representation, including that of empiricist and idealist history.
10. Practice establishes the truth, i.e. the effectiveness or actuality of thinking.

3 From ideological inversion to fetishistic transposition

I want to begin by considering thesis 8: sensuous productive activity appears inverted in ideation. The limitations of our material activities and social relations impose limits upon our understanding of that activity and these relations. Thus the critique of ideology starts from the critique of the primacy of consciousness. The "historical life-process" (the production and reproduction of the means of existence) makes human social relations appear upside-down in consciousness:

> If the conscious expression of the real relations of these individuals is illusory, if in their imagination they turn reality upside-down, then this in its turn is the result of their limited material mode of activity and their limited social relations arising from it. [...] Men are the producers of their conceptions, ideas, etc., that is, real, active men, as they are conditioned by a definite development of their productive forces and of the intercourse corresponding to these, up to its furthest forms. Consciousness [*das Bewusstsein*] can never be anything other than conscious being [*das bewusste Sein*], and the being of men is their actual life-process. If in all ideology men and their relations appear upside-down as in a camera obscura, this phenomenon arises just as much from their historical life process as the inversion of objects on the retina does from their physical life-process. (Marx 1998, p. 42)

If ideology (religious, juridical, economic, philosophical, scientific) is the 'inverted image' of social existence, understood as circuit of conditioned and conditioning productive activity, then this inversion cannot be confined to a single dimension of representation (e.g. spatial orientation, up-down). Marx's 'inversion' of the metaphysical subordination of sensuous appearance to supersensuous reality does not just re-subordinate the latter to the former. The critical torsion proper to the critique of political economy implies that the sensuous (forces and relations of production) is inapparent and that the intelligible (consciousness as representation of these forces and relations) is apparent, so that the intelligible is the distorted form of appearance of inapparent sensuous activity (the activity constituting productive forces and relations).

In *Capital*, however, ideological inversion becomes fetishistic *transposition*. The commodity is the juncture of the sensuous and the supersensuous: it is the form in which sensuous relations between producers appear to the producers themselves as supersensuous relations between their products:

> A commodity is therefore a mysterious thing, simply because in it the social character of men's labour appears to them as an objective character stamped upon the product of that labour; because the relation of the producers to the sum total of their own labour is presented to them as a social relation, existing not between themselves, but between the products of their labour. This is the reason why the products of labour become commodities, social things whose qualities are at the same time perceptible and imperceptible by the senses [....] [But] the existence of the things qua commodities, and the value relation between the products of labour which stamps them as commodities, have absolutely no connection with their physical properties and with the material relations arising therefrom. There it is a definite social relation between men that assumes, in their eyes, the fantastic form of a relation between things. (Marx 2000b, p. 473)

The relation of producers to "the sum total of their own labour" is their relation to the exchange value that relates commodities to each other. As the transposition of social relations among producers into relations between products mediated by the 'spectral objectivity' of value, fetishism is the occlusion of productive social activity in the act of commodity exchange. Consciousness of the individual act of exchange occludes consciousness of its social precondition. Consciousness is necessarily false in the sense that we can only be individually conscious of what we are doing in exchange by *not* being conscious of what we are collectively doing in exchange. The collective practice of commodity exchange is precisely what cannot be intuited or represented from the vantage of individuals engaged in exchange. Exchange is a practical abstraction whose concreteness can only be grasped by abstracting from what appears as concrete from the vantage of individual consciousness. The epistemic index for the primacy of social practice is its misprision in consciousness. Practice is not transparent to its practitioners. Supersensible abstraction (what Marx calls 'form-determination') is the concrete form in which sensuous practice appears to theoretical consciousness, which is the reified and reifying consciousness conditioned by the division of (intellectual and manual) labour.

Two clarifications are necessary at this point. First, Marx's materialism is not soldered to a metaphysics of labour. Labour is not the essence of history because useful work is necessarily misrepresented as valuable labour within a specific historical context.[4] There is no determination of use that does not involve abstracting from the historically specific determination of exchange-value under capitalism. Thus there is no use in-itself, no domain of use-values transcending historically specific alignments of production and consumption. Second, Marx is not wedded to a metaphysics of production. Capitalist production is commodity production: the form of production under capital is conditioned by and subordinated to the commodity form. The means of production themselves are composed of commodities. Thus, under capitalism, both production and consumption are subordinated to exchange (to the commodity-form and thereby to value). There is no trans-historical perspective on production, save for what Marx describes as "singling out and fixing" the general features common to historically specific social formations. 'Production in general' is a methodological abstraction, not an ontological category.[5] To hypostatize production and elevate

---

[4] "So far therefore as labour is a creator of use-value, is useful labour, it is a necessary condition, independent of all forms of society for the existence of the human race; it is an eternal nature-imposed necessity, without which there can be no material exchanges between man and Nature, and therefore no life" (Marx 2000b, p. 464). Note that while useful labour in general is a transhistorical condition of human life, the specific varieties of useful labour, or what counts as useful labour within a particular society will be historically variable. Marx does not postulate a set of use-values in-themselves, transcending historically specific social formations. In a capitalist society coordinated around the production and exchange of commodities, the use-values of commodities, i.e. the variety of uses to which they can be put, is shaped in negative by the primacy of exchange-value, which is the first and final cause of their existence.

[5] "Whenever we speak, therefore, of production, we always have in mind production at a certain stage of social development, or production by social individuals [...] 'Production in general' is an abstraction, but it is a rational abstraction, in so far as it singles out and fixes the common features, thereby saving us repetition" (Marx 2000a, p. 381). Production as methodological abstraction stands in contrast to the hypostatization of production, which often accompanies the naturalization of capitalism. The latter involves a four-step argument, which Marx summarizes as follows: (i) production always requires some instrument of production ("let that instrument be only the hand"); (ii) production is not possible without past accumulated labour ("even if that labour should consist of mere skill which has been accumulated and concentrated in the hand of the savage by repeated exercise"); (iii) capital is ("among other things") both an instrument of production and past impersonal labour; (iv) therefore, "capital is a universal, eternal, natural phenomenon." But this is only true, writes Marx, "if we disregard the specific properties which turn an 'instrument of production' and 'stored up labour' into capital" (Marx 2000a, pp. 381–382). These specific properties, unveiled in Marx's analysis, are their status as commodities and their subjection to the valorization process, which is perpetuated by the practice of commodity exchange. But these are social properties, not natural ones.

it into a metaphysical principle ("nature is production") is to naturalize a historically specific social category. Since the commodity-form is intrinsic to the categories of 'production' and 'productivity,' the logic of production is indissociable from the logic of commodity exchange.[6]

But the practical reality of commodity exchange is not experienced *as* practice within reified consciousness (i.e. the social consciousness subjugated by the commodity form).[7] Thus the reality of collective practical activity can only be indirectly attested to by exposing its symptomatic (fetishistic) misrepresentation both in individual consciousness and the theoretical consciousness that takes its cue from the latter. This is why the critique of political economy is necessary. To grasp the structure of the necessary false consciousness operative in misrepresentation is to identify this falsity as the only veritable index of the social relation, understood as a system of impersonal practices, rather than a set of interpersonal relations. The necessity of falsity points to its inapparent truth. Consciousness is necessarily false: it does not *express* the social relation (the system of impersonal practices) that is its essence; it *represses* it.

4 The concrete-in-thought

Marx's critique begins with the categories of political economy as expressions of socially necessary false consciousness. These categories are shown to be results of historically specific conditions and relations of production. What the critique reveals, however, is not the truth of the invisible but the untruth of the visible, i.e. the intelligible. What presents itself to thought as concrete is an incomplete abstraction; but through its incompleteness, this abstraction harbors a symptomatic relation to what is really concrete, the social totality. The structure of the latter, however, is precisely what cannot be intuited or inferred. It does not give itself to consciousness. It is ideologically misrepresented as an aggregate of composite abstractions, which critique must first decompose into their elementary parts before recomposing these parts into a conceptual totality that corresponds to the social totality but does not resemble it:

> It seems to be the correct procedure to commence with the real and the concrete, the actual prerequisites. In the case of political economy, to commence with population, which is the basis and the author of the entire productive activity of society. Yet on closer consideration

---

6 This ontologization of production arguably vitiates Deleuze's and Guattari's attempt to align Marx with Spinoza in *Anti-Oedipus* (Minneapolis: University of Minnesota Press, 1983).
7 Lukacs's remains the most powerful and sophisticated account of reification: see Lukacs 1972.

> it proves to be wrong. Population is an abstraction, if we leave out for example the classes of which it consists. These classes, again, are but an empty word unless we know what are the elements on which they are based, such as wage-labour, capital, etc. These imply, in their turn, exchange, division of labour, prices, etc. Capital, for example, does not mean anything without wage-labour, value, money, price, etc. If we start out, therefore, with population, we do so with a chaotic conception [*Vorstellung*] of the whole [*Ganzen*], and by closer analysis we will gradually arrive at simpler ideas; thus we shall proceed from the imaginary [*vorgestellten*] concrete to less and less complex abstractions, until we arrive at the simplest determinations. This once attained, we might start on our return journey until we finally came back to population, but this time not as a chaotic notion of an integral whole, but as a rich aggregate [*Totalität*] of many determinations and relations […] The concrete is concrete because it is a combination [*Zusammenfassung*] of many determinations, i.e. a unity of diverse elements [*Mannigfaltigen*]. In our thought it therefore appears as a process of synthesis, as a result, and not as a starting-point, although it is the actual [*wirkliche*] starting-point and, therefore, also the starting-point of observation [*Anschauung*] and conception [*Vorstellung*]. By the former method the complete conception passes into an abstract definition; by the latter the abstract definitions lead to the reproduction of the concrete subject in the course of reasoning. (Marx 2000a, p. 386)

Marx's method of critique comprises two steps: first the decomposition of the abstracted (represented) concrete into its elementary components (simple abstractions); then the recombination of simple abstractions into concretely determined abstraction: the totality of determinations as concrete-in-thought. What is *represented* as concrete-in-reality is an indeterminate whole. What is *reproduced* as concrete-in-thought is a determinate totality. The movement from abstract representation to concrete reproduction is logical, not material. Thus it is necessary to distinguish ideal movement from the real *act* of production:

> [T]he consciousness for which comprehending thought is what is most real in man, for which the world is only real when comprehended (and philosophical consciousness is of this nature), mistakes the movement of categories for the real act of production (which unfortunately receives only its impetus from outside), whose result is the world; that is true – here we have, however, again a tautology – in so far as the concrete aggregate [*Totalität*], as a thought aggregate [*Gedankentotalität*], the concrete subject of our thought [*Gedankenkonkretum*], is in fact a product of thought, of comprehension; not, however, in the sense of a product of a self-emanating conception which works outside of and stands above observation [*Anschauung*] and imagination [*Vorstellung*], but of a conceptual working-over [*Verarbeitung*] of observation and imagination. The whole [*Ganze*], as it appears in our heads as a thought-aggregate [*Gedankenganze*], is the product of a thinking mind which grasps the world in the only way open to it, a way which differs from the one employed by the artistic, religious, or practical mind. The concrete [*reale*] subject continues to lead an independent existence after it has been grasped, as it did before, outside the head, so long as the head contemplates it only speculatively, theoretically. So that in the employment of the theoretical method in political economy, the subject, society, must constantly be kept in mind as the premise from which we start. (Marx 2000a, p. 387)

The difference between the real (social) subject and the thought aggregate (e. g. society), or between what is really concrete and what is concrete-in-thought, is not a difference in thought. But here an obvious rejoinder presents itself: how are we to distinguish between concrete and abstract in thought, and concrete and abstract in reality, without invoking either a metaphysical or empirical difference between thought and reality? Can Marx maintain this methodological distinction without unwittingly reiterating philosophical dualisms (between thought and reality, concept and thing, ideal and real) that have already been dialectically superseded in Hegel's idealism? The distinction between real subject and thought-aggregate cannot be empirically attested to: we cannot *point* to the real subject because the social totality is not an empirical datum. Nor is it accessible from Feuerbach's "absolute standpoint," which is that of the interpersonal relation between 'I' and 'You': Marx's real subject is a locus of impersonal practices irreducible to the interpersonal relation.[8] Conversely, to insist that the difference can be substantiated from a purely rational vantage point is to readopt the contemplative stance whose separation of thought and being, or mind and matter, reflects the division of labour and the separation of theory and practice.

I want to suggest that the right way to grasp Marx's distinction between concrete-in-thought and concrete-in-reality is neither as a conceptual difference nor as an empirical difference but as a *difference-in-act*. What is concrete-in-reality is the totality of impersonal social practices, and these practices constitute a system of actual differences that cannot be ratified at the level of consciousness or experience. Thus the fundamental difference, from which the critique of political economy proceeds is verified in social practice rather than in experience or thought. Recall the tenth thesis of historical materialism stated above: the truth, i.e., the effectiveness or actuality (*Wirklichkeit*) of thinking, is established in practice. My claim is that for Marx, the actuality of practice verifies that of thought without there being a metaphysical correspondence between the actuality of thought and the actuality of practice. Indeed, Marx's point is that while thought can adequately represent the structure of practice, there is no similarity or resemblance between the structure of thought (what is concrete-in-thought) and that of practice (concrete-in-reality). What is concrete-in-reality is a practical act whose nature does not reveal itself either to those executing it or to the the-

---

[8] "The natural standpoint of man, the standpoint of the distinction between 'I' and 'You', between subject and object is the true, the absolute standpoint and, hence, also the standpoint of philosophy" (Feuerbach 2012, p. 528).

oretical consciousness that takes the consciousness of practitioners as its starting point.

5 Using and exchanging

Sohn-Rethel roots Marx's distinction between use-value and exchange-value in the socially instituted distinction between the act of using and the act of exchanging. But this social distinction also has an ontological basis:

> The point is that use and exchange are not only different and contrasting by description, but are mutually exclusive in time. They must take place separately at different times. This is because exchange serves only a change of ownership, a change, that is, in terms of a purely social status of the commodities as owned property. In order to make this change possible on a basis of negotiated agreement the physical condition of the commodities, their material status, must remain unchanged, or at any rate must be assumed to remain unchanged. Commodity exchange cannot take place as a recognised social institution unless this separation of exchange from use is stringently observed. [...] Thus the salient feature of the act of exchange is that its separation from use has assumed the compelling necessity of an objective social law. Wherever commodity exchange takes place it does so in effective 'abstraction' from use. This is an abstraction not in mind, but in fact. It is a state of affairs prevailing at a definite place and lasting a definite time. It is the state of affairs which reigns on the market. (Sohn-Rethel 1978, pp. 24–25)

Commodity exchange separates use from value: this is the source of real abstraction. Use is determined by qualitative particularity, exchange by quantitative homogeneity. Using and exchanging are concrete social acts. For Sohn-Rethel, it is their spatiotemporal disjunction (the fact that one cannot exchange what one is using or use what one is exchanging) that makes abstraction a concrete act. However, the act of exchange presupposes the actuality of the commodity-form: every exchange is an exchange of commodities (buying and selling). But exchange cannot generate commodification if commodification is the condition of exchange (i.e the commodification of labour as wage-labour). Thus the reality of the exchange abstraction implies a difference between exchange-in-act (the actuality of exchange) and the act of exchange. The concrete act generative of abstraction cannot presuppose its actuality. The sociality of the act of exchange is distinct from the actuality of commodification. But sociality is the totality of relations joining productive forces and relations (otherwise it is a metaphysical abstraction). Since the production process presupposes commodification and commodification (the exchange-abstraction) presupposes un-commodified social activity, we face the following dilemma: either try to give a positive account of non-commodified sociality, i.e. of the social relation, at the risk of relapsing into an ultimately ideological metaphysics of sociality (reiterating Feuerbach's conflation of sociality and communality); or insist that we cannot determine the social relation other than as the negation of commodified sociality. The latter option implies that the un-commodified root of commodified sociality cannot be positively characterised as social.

6 Labour and valorization

The difference between exchange as act and exchange as actuality underlies the distinction between concrete and abstract labour. The labour that enters into the composition of value has already had its qualitative particularity expunged from it through the act of exchange: "[W]henever, by an exchange, we equate as values our different products, by that very act, we also equate, as human labour, the different kinds of labour expended upon them. *We are not aware of this, nevertheless we do it*. Value, therefore, does not stalk about with a label describing what it is. It is value, rather, that converts every product into a social hieroglyphic" (Marx 2000b, p. 474, my italics).

By inscribing itself into the body of every commodity, the 'spectral objectivity' of value converts every product into a cipher whose sensuous structure is blotted out by its supersensuous signification. But the process in which value acquires substance and inscribes itself into the commodity is also the process in which labour is transubstantiated into value. This is the process in which concretely differentiated human labour is rendered into what Marx describes as an undifferentiated "*bloße Gallerte*," a 'gelatinous mass.'[9] Yet this rendering process, the reduction of concretely differentiated labour into undifferentiated abstract labour, is already governed by value. Thus value oversees its own substantialization: it perpetually regenerates itself by ensuring that the substrate from which it draws substance, labour, has 'always already' been rendered homogenous with it. This is carried out through what Michael Heinrich calls a "threefold reduction:" of individually expended labor-time to average socially necessary labor-time; of individual productivity to socially average productivity correlated with monetary social demand; of differences in kinds and degrees of skill to a socially average type and degree of skill (see Heinrich 2012, pp.100–102). Thus the abstraction of labour is its social *validation* as value-constituting labour. Abstract labour is both socially valorized and *valorizing* insofar

---

9 For an insightful discussion of the significance of the expression "*bloße Gallerte*," see Sutherland 2010.

as it has already been appropriated by what Marx calls "self-sufficient value" (see Marx 2000a, p. 409): its "valorizing activity" is carried out on behalf of self-valorizing value.

However, Marx insists, "the value of labour-power and the value which that labour-power creates in the production process, are two entirely different magnitudes" (Marx 2000b, p. 504). As with every other commodity, the value of labour-power is measured by the socially necessary time required to reproduce it. But in reproducing itself, labour-power creates value in excess of itself, i.e., a value greater than the value of labour-power as measured by the time required for its reproduction. This is what Marx calls 'surplus-value.' Surplus-value is a function of the discrepancy between the value of unexpended labour-power, a value measured by the time required to reconstitute an equivalent of this unexpended potential, and the value generated by its expenditure, which is greater than that of its unexpended state. This appeal to the metaphysical distinction between potentiality and actuality should not be taken to entail the ontologization of labour-power; rather, it follows from its social status as a commodity. The distinction between potential and actualized labour-power is internal to commodified labour; it is decreed by capitalism's metaphysics of value. But it does not map onto the distinction between abstract and concrete labour. The actualization of labour-power, i.e. the consumption of its use-value, in the capitalist production process, generates exchange-values in excess of the exchange-value of labour-power. As Peter Thomas points out, this is a consequence of labour-power's exceptional status as the commodity whose use-value is generative of the exchange-value of all other commodities: "labour-power is the only commodity that is not exhausted in the consumption of its particular use-value following exchange. On the contrary, the consumption of the use-value of labour-power has the potential to give the capitalist more exchange-values than the seller of labour-power, the worker, received" (Thomas 2010, p. 51). But note that the consumption of labour-power is only *potentially* productive of exchange-values greater than its own. This is because, as Thomas observes, although it is exchanged as abstract labour-power, it is consumed as concrete labour. The capitalist's consumption of this concrete labour generates another magnitude of potential abstract value; but its realization as a surplus depends on additional factors exceeding those of production per se (e.g. social demand, the market, etc.). More importantly, the difference between the exchange and consumption of labour-power (which corresponds to the difference between abstract and concrete labour) does not unfold in the same dimension as the difference between its potentiality and its actuality. The first difference transects the second but does not overlap with it. While the difference between the actuality and potentiality of labour-power is internal to the exchange abstraction, the difference between exchanging and consuming labour-power bridges the spheres of exchange and use, which is to say, between the abstract and the concrete. This is why Thomas describes labour-power as a "vanishing mediator" between the spheres of circulation and production (Thomas 2010, p. 52). However, it is not labour-power qua commodity that plays this mediating role between the spheres of circulation and production, since the commodity-form already presupposes the constitution of the difference between these two spheres, or the difference between exchange and use. Thus the actuality of the exchange abstraction (within which the difference between potential and actual labour-power obtains) is constituted by a concrete act that also establishes the difference between exchanging and using, or circulation and production. The vanishing mediator here is not labour-power but the unvalidated act through which labour is abstracted into its socially validated, value-constituting role.

Value is measured abstractly (through abstract labour time) but realized concretely (through concrete labour time). Thus surplus-value is a function not only of the difference between the potential and actual expenditure of labour-power, but also of the inequality between the value of labour as measured by the abstract time required to reproduce it and the value of the products generated through its reproduction when measured by the same yardstick. Whether absolute and obtained by the extensive increase of expended labour-power (lengthening the working day) or relative and obtained through its intensive increase (increasing productivity without lengthening the working day), surplus-value is generated by the unvalorized surplus labour required for labour's self-reproduction. Thus capital extracts surplus-value from labour-power's activation of the value embodied in both constant and variable capital (a value which is itself nothing but a sum of objectified or 'congealed' labour-power). Potential surplus-value is realized as profit with the sale of the products of labour-power and then reinvested in production. In the diagram below, the valorization process proceeds from money (M, representing constant and variable capital), to commodities (C, representing living labour's activation of the value embodied in constant and variable capital), to a greater quantity of money generated through the extraction of surplus-value from living labour's activation of the initial sum of value (M', surplus-value):

7 Capital as self-valorizing value

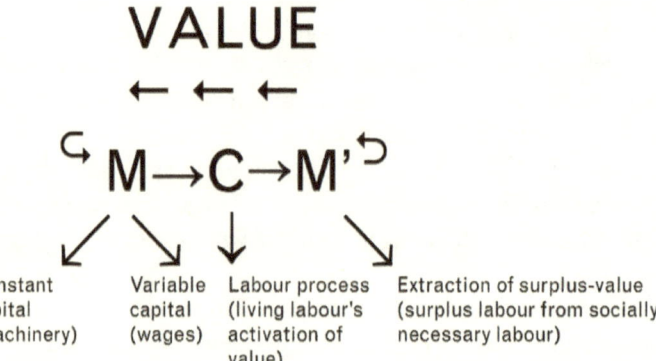

| Constant capital (machinery) | Variable capital (wages) | Labour process (living labour's activation of value) | Extraction of surplus-value (surplus labour from socially necessary labour) |

In reproducing itself, living labour creates the 'spectral objectivity' of value, to which it is re-subordinated in turn as commodified wage-labour, i.e. socially validated labour. But the difference between commodified and un-commodified labour is neither metaphysical nor sociological: it is the formal difference between socially validated exchange and the unvalidated act of exchange.

8 Dissociative sociality

In a society where all social validation is governed by exchange, Tony Smith suggests that the actuality of the social relation is necessarily dissociative. Following Smith, I want to argue that since, under capitalism, the social component of dissociation is governed by exchange (commodification), the practical source of commodification (the act of exchange) is necessarily asocial. This is to say that socially validated labour is conditioned by un-validated practical activity. This entails a split between the essence of sociality and the essence of value, i.e. capital. Smith formulates this split as follows:

> Generalised commodity-production must be conceptualised as a set of relationships among things (commodities and money), with value reigning as the 'essence' of these relationships. The underlying truth of this essence (abstract, homogeneous and quantitative value) is adequately manifested in its form of appearance (abstract, homogeneous and quantitative money). (Smith 2009, p. 31)

On Smith's account, commodity exchange is the alien form of sociality in the historically specific mode of dissociated sociality. Sociality is the 'essence' of the totality of productive forces and relations. But this essence can only manifest itself as its own untruth (as capitalist 'society'). Dissociative sociality entails that social relations cannot appear as what they essentially are:

> The social ontology of generalised commodity-production is defined by two completely incommensurable Essence-Logics in Hegel's sense of the term. On the one hand, value is the essence commodities must possess to play a role in social reproduction. This essence adequately appears in the form of the money that validates the production of those commodities. But the value of commodities is a reflection of the form taken by human sociality in our epoch, and the money that manifests value is nothing but the fetishized appearance of this quite different sort of essence. Each essence-claim is incompatible with the other; neither can be reduced to or explained away by the other. (Smith 2009, p. 32)

This bifurcation in the essence of the social totality follows from capital's being a "contradiction in act": it is compelled to reduce labour time to a minimum while maintaining it as the sole measure of value. Socially necessary labour time is decreased in order to increase surplus labour time, thereby turning surplus labour time into the condition for necessary labour time. Capital's self-reproduction, i.e. its infinite expansion as self-valorizing value, generates the internal obstacle to its reproduction, i.e. the immanent limit to its infinite expansion.[10] Thus, as *Endnotes* puts it, capital is split between its "constant return to itself as true infinity, and its incessant driving beyond itself as false or spurious infinity."[11]

This scission in the capitalist totality, its 'contradiction-in-act,' generates the split between the reproductive cycles of capital and of labour-power. Capital reproduces itself through the valorization process, in which necessary labour is constantly diminished to maximize surplus labour and hence surplus-value. At the same time, labour-power reproduces itself by valorizing capital, but in doing so increases surplus labour, making necessary labour ever more dependent upon it. Thus the activation of value in the valorization process depends not on the abstract difference between potential and actual labour-power but on the concrete actuality of the disjunct between (un-commodified, valueless) practice and (commodified, valuable) activity. Interpreted in this way, Marx's contrast be-

---

[10] "Capital is itself contradiction in act, since it makes an effort to reduce labour time to the minimum, while at the same time establishing labour time as the sole measurement and source of wealth. Thus it diminishes labour time in its necessary form, in order to increase its surplus form; therefore it increasingly establishes surplus labour time as a condition (a question of life and death) for necessary labour time" (Marx 2000a, p. 415, translation modified).
[11] Endnotes 2010.

tween 'living' and 'dead' labour is shorn of its Romantic, vitalist overtones. Adopting Marx's terminology, we could say that it is labour-power as commodity that is subsumed by capital, not living labour as such. But the capitalist class relation compels living labour to commodify (i.e. sell) itself in order to reproduce itself, thereby also reproducing capital:

> "Proletariat and capital stand in a relation of reciprocal implication with each other: each pole reproduces the other, such that the relation between the two is self-reproducing. The relation is asymmetric, however, in that it is capital which subsumes the labour of proletarians."[12]

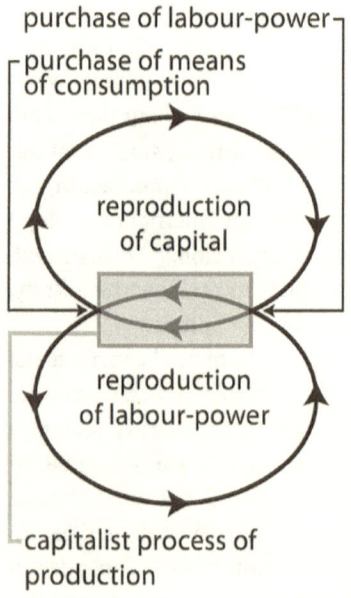

Labour-power's purchase of the means of consumption it requires to reproduce itself fuels capital's purchase of labour-power in capital's self-reproduction (see figure above[13]). The exchange of labour-power for wages (C→M) initiates the reproduction of labour-power; the exchange of wages for commodities (M→C)

---

12 Endnotes 2010.
13 This diagram is taken from Endnotes 2008. I would like to thank Endnotes for letting me use it.

completes it. At the same time, but at the opposite pole of the class relation, the capitalist's purchase of labour-power (M→C) is the exchange that initiates the valorization process, while the sale of the commodities embodying the surplus-value extracted from labour-power (C→M') is the exchange that completes it. Both reproductive cycles (of labour-power and capital) are mediated by exchange. Yet exchange cannot be realized without the intervention of valueless activity, which capital requires to activate value, i.e., to convert the magnitude of actual value embodied in fixed and constant capital into a potential surplus.

9 Conclusion

Reification is the fetishization of social relations: the transposition of relations between producers into relations between products. But Marx's critique of reification is epistemological, not ontological. The distinction between 'living' (objectivating) and 'dead' (objectified) labour is not a metaphysical contrast between authentic and inauthentic existence or between lived and represented experience. It is a formal contrast between unconscious (unvalidated) practice and conscious (socially validated) activity. Nevertheless, the contrast has an ontological premise: the actuality of exchange depends upon an act that is not actually exchanged (valorized). This unconscious practice is essentially or veridically human precisely in the sense that, under capitalism, our socially validated humanity (as persons) is necessarily dissociative. The question is whether knowing this, and the necessary worthlessness of continuing to reproduce ourselves under the capital relation, provides any clue about determining the negation of this contradiction between what we do and what we are.

Bibliography

Endnotes (2008): "Afterword." In: *Endnotes 1: Preliminary Materials for a Balance Sheet of the 20th Century*. https://endnotes.org.uk/issues/1/en/endnotes-afterword, visited on 18 March 2019.

Endnotes (2010): "The Moving Contradiction." In: *Endnotes 2: Misery and the Value-Form*. https://endnotes.org.uk/issues/2/en/endnotes-the-moving-contradiction, visited on 18 March 2019.

Feuerbach, Ludwig (2012): *The Fiery Brook: Selected Writings*. Translated by Zawar Hanfi. London and New York: Verso.

Heinrich, Michael (2012): *An Introduction to the Three Volumes of Karl Marx's Capital*. Translated by Alexander Locascio. New York: Monthly Review Press.

Lukács, Georg (1972): "Reification and the Consciousness of the Proletariat." In: *History and Class Consciousness*. Translated by Rodney Livingstone. Cambridge, MA and London: MIT Press, pp. 83–222.

Marx, Karl (1998): *The German Ideology*. Amherst, NY: Prometheus Books.

Marx, Karl (2000): *Selected Writings*, 2nd edition. David McLellan (Ed.). Oxford: Oxford University Press.

Marx, Karl (2000a): *Grundrisse*. In: Marx 2000, pp. 379–423.

Marx, Karl (2000b): *Capital: Volume I*. In: Marx 2000, pp. 452–525.

Smith, Tony (2009): "Hegel, Marx, and the Comprehension of Capitalism." In: Fred Moseley and Tony Smith (Eds.): *Marx's Capital and Hegel's Logic: A Re-examination*. Chicago, IL: Haymarket Books.

Sohn-Rethel, Alfred (1978): *Intellectual and Manual Labour: A Critique of Epistemology*. Translated by Martin Sohn-Rethel. London and Basingstoke: The Macmillan Press.

Sutherland, Keston (2010): "Marx in Jargon." http://www.worldpicturejournal.com/WP_1.1/KSutherland.pdf, visited on 18 March 2019.

Thomas, Peter (2010): "Labour-Power (Arbeitskraft)." In: *Krisis: Journal of Contemporary Philosophy 2*, pp. 59–54. http://krisis.eu/wp-content/uploads/2017/04/krisis-2010-2-09-thomas.pdf?, visited on 18 March 2019.

Deborah Goldgaber
Matter and Indifference: Realism and Anti-realism in Feminist Accounts of the Body

Abstract: Recently, influential critics have argued that feminist accounts of the body are insufficiently realist and materialist. These emphasize the body's social or discursive 'construction' at the expense of biological morphogenesis. The way feminists 'bracket' the body's biological status prevents them from theorizing the relation and interaction of social and biological forces. While these materialist critiques correctly diagnose issues with certain anti-realist accounts of embodiment, which contest that the body has a *biological* essence, most feminist accounts of embodiment, I argue, are not anti-realist in this respect. Indeed, contrary to an increasingly influential view, feminist accounts of discursive construction are not inherently anti-realist or anti-materialist. The real issue with constructivist accounts is not that they exclude the body's organic or biological substance, as the materialists argue, but rather the assumption that discursive construction refers exclusively to cultural processes. Thus, I propose re-reading feminist new materialist critiques as motivating the extension of 'discursive construction' beyond the human.

1 Feminist Indifference?

Feminist theory has been "indifferent to matter." And it has treated *matter* – organic, biological matter – as if it were indifferent, "conceptually dull," "formless and inert," awaiting cultural inscription (Wilson 2015, p. 58). Influential theorists including Vicki Kirby, Elizabeth Wilson, Karen Barad, and Elizabeth Grosz have argued that distinctively feminist perspectives on the body – those that conceive the body as culturally or discursively constructed – untenably exclude the organic, the biological.[1] Characterizing this issue, Elizabeth Wilson writes:

> Problematically, much of the feminist work on embodiment seems to gesture towards a flat organic realm elsewhere as a way of securing a more valuable or dynamic account of the body closer to home... [T]oo often, it is only when anatomy or physiology or biochemistry

---

[1] See Vicki Kirby (1991; 2011), Elizabeth Wilson (1998; 2015), Karen Barad (2003; 2007) and Elizabeth Grosz (1994; 2012).

are removed from the analytic scene (or, in what amounts to much the same gesture, these domains are considered to be too reductive to be analytically interesting) that it has been possible to generate a recognizably feminist account of the body. (Wilson 2015, p. 58)

This "elision of the body's biological substance" is not a benign, methodological bracketing, but constitutes an "evacuation," an "erasure," a "'crossing out' of Nature by Culture" (Barad 2007, 64). In these accounts, the morphogenetic force of culture or "discourse" is thought at the expense of biological morphogenesis (DeLanda 2012). "Language matters. Discourse matters. Culture matters. There is an important sense in which the only thing that does not seem to matter anymore is matter," Barad famously writes, exhorting feminists to meet the material universe "half-way" (2003, p. 801). It is time, we now often hear, for a "materialist turn" in feminist theory. We require new materialist schemas and new realist starting points that begin by giving (organic) matter its due, while staying attuned to the ways that that "'nature of nature' is open to culture" (Grosz 2010, p. 154).

In this paper, I wish to pursue a certain double reading of these influential critiques. On the one hand, I want to resist what I read as a marked tendency towards overgeneralizing the problem 'materiality' poses for feminist accounts of embodiment. These critiques, I believe, cover over important differences between how feminists have thought about embodiment generally and the relation between biology and culture, in particular. On the other hand, I want to endorse some of the central, speculative insights of new materialist critiques, which urge us to think 'discursivity' and 'performativity' beyond the cultural and the human. This project of generalizing discursivity (beyond the human) may be motivated without arguing that feminist theories of discursive construction are internally incoherent.

Historically, as we shall see, feminists have bracketed biological concerns not because they have doubted that the body is in some sense biological, or because they have thought of organic matter as formless pap awaiting cultural formation – as some new materialists have argued – but because they have thought that *gendered* bodies are constituted by distinctively cultural forces within the limits imposed by biological constraints. These limits have not usually been thought as co-constituted by the cultural forces that produce the body's gendered features. The point is that feminists have often thought of *gendered* bodies in much the same way as a trainer might think of *runners'* bodies, *dancers'* bodies, or *soldiers'* bodies, *i.e.* bodies distinctively formed and distinguishable by the repetition of certain normative practices and performances. If this analogy fails, it is only insofar as gender has most often been thought as the sort of skilled, compulsory performance that *incapacitates* the body.

Feminist accounts of gendered embodiment have justified their methodological bracketing of biology, and their agnosticism about the *nature* of biology, through a tacit or explicit assumption: gender is a kind of biological supplement and the body's gendered features are supplementary (viz., non-essential) features. Of course, it may be worth revisiting these assumptions and justifications in light of new evidence, as Elizabeth Wilson's work in the areas of psychology and pharmacology suggests (1998, p. 2015). We may have good reasons to re-examine the assumption that gender is exclusively a matter of culture, without, for that matter, re-subscribing to the discredited view that gender is *reducible* to biology. The problem, I suggest, with materialist critiques is not their provocations that gender may, after all, implicate the body's physiology or biochemistry in ways feminist accounts of the body have usually resisted, but with their claims that existing feminist accounts of the body rely upon untenable assumptions about the nature of biological substance.

This paper will proceed as follows. I first offer an overview of accounts of discursive construction in feminist theory, in terms of what Karen Barad has called the critique of Representationalism, specifying the assumptions shared between some of the most historically influential accounts. I then argue that materialist critiques apply only to those accounts of discursive construction explicitly challenging assumptions about the body's biological essence. These "anti-essentialist" accounts – often associated with the work of Judith Butler, on the one hand, and Michel Foucault, on the other – give rise to the charges of biological "erasure" and "de-substantialization" so central to new materialist critiques. But the assumptions of these accounts, however influential they have been, are simply not shared by the mainstream of feminist accounts of gendered embodiment. In the final section, I argue that while discursive construction has usually been characterized as distinctive of cultural (as opposed to natural) processes, and in particular as distinctive of Human practices, materialist critiques motivate us to question these assumptions. When suitably generalized, 'discursivity,' which in the context of feminist theory describes how representations or norms come to be embodied, may be characteristic of biological and other non-human interactions.

2 Discursive Construction and its Limits

Karen Barad characterizes contemporary feminist thought in terms of what she calls a salutary but incomplete "critique of Representationalism." 'Representationalism,' according to Barad, is the common view that concepts and categories describe a first-order reality indifferent to its representation (Barad 2003, pp. 803–808). Even if this has not been their main aim, accounts of gender's discursive construction are, *eo ipso*, critiques of Representationalism because they insist on the ontological *productivity* of representations.

Gender is a peculiar form of ascription, 'performatively,' or 'discursively' "producing the bodies it names" (Butler 1993, p. 2).[2] Positing the productivity of categorization reverses the presumed direction of fit between world and word. We normally judge that our concepts are good if they 'fit' or account for the world in the right way. However, 'discursivity' claims that categories and concepts produce the fit they claim to describe. As philosopher Sally Haslanger specifies, 'discursivity' claims that:

> our classificatory schemes…do more than just map pre-existing groups of individuals; rather our attributions have the power to both establish and reinforce groupings which may eventually come to 'fit' the classifications. This works in several ways. Forms of description or classification provide for kinds of intentions … But also, such classifications can function in justifying behavior … and such justification, in turn, can reinforce the distinction. (Haslanger 2000, 44–46)

As Haslanger's description indicates, discursivity's critique of Representationalism is definitely limited. It excepts from the general frame of Representationalism the way that human's interact with their own classificatory schemes.

Haslanger, summing up the relevant literature, argues that while accounts of gender's discursive construction invite us to think of the *gendered* body as an 'interactive kind,' this invitation does not extend to the biological body. The term "interactive kind" is philosopher Ian Hacking's:

> As Hacking elaborates the idea of an interactive kind, it becomes clear that the interaction he has in mind happens through the awareness of the thing classified, though it is typically mediated by the 'larger matrix of institutions and practices surrounding this classification'. (Haslanger 2003, pp. 310–311, my emphasis)

Altering the meanings we assign to bodies alters the physical properties of bodies because of the way these meanings affect intentions, emotions, actions and behaviors. In this way, the discursively produced body – the body as discursive

---

[2] "Performativity" is interchangeable with "discursive construction" as it appears throughout the text, and in particular as Haslanger defines this term (2003). Somewhat confusingly, Butler's notion of discursivity encompasses, or so I argue, both her notion of gender performativity – as morphogenetic response to gender norms – and her notion of "materialization" – which accounts for the body's morphology *qua* appearance.

social kind – is an "interactive kind" in the sense that it involves complex mind-body interactions.

Both Hacking and Haslanger share the view that humans have a special relationship to representations – they produce them – and are thus differentially affected by them. "Human beings are representers. Not *homo faber*, I say, but *homo depicter*. People make representations" (Hacking 1983, p. 132).

It is this *a priori* limitation of discursivity to *homo depicter* that Barad and other new materialists contest. Barad argues that feminist critiques of Representationalism are incomplete inasmuch as the reversal of the direction of fit – and of explanatory efficiency – characteristic of discursivity is limited to humans. Discursive construction specifies the exception proving the Representationalist rule. She thinks the critique needs to be extended and radicalized to make room for "post-human performativity" or discursivity. To see what Barad has in mind, we first have to get a better sense of what is entailed by *human* discursive construction.

As Haslanger writes, in feminist theory, "'construction' arguments often aim to *debunk* accounts that view the distinction between men and women as primarily anatomical or biological" (Haslanger 2003, p. 316). This does not mean that bodies are not primarily (or essentially) anatomical or biological, but that gender distinctions (between bodies), however natural these distinctions appear, are not reducible to or rooted in biological or anatomical facts. Gender differences are *naturalized* rather than natural, rooted in the demands and assumptions of culturally produced and enforced hierarchies. To wit: if gender differences were natural, culture would not have to invest so much in disseminating and enforcing gender norms. All the work and violence which, historically, has gone into gender enforcement indicates that the latter produces what it demands.

According to constructivist accounts, 'biologistic' assumptions about gender fundamentally mischaracterize how gender attribution works. The latter does not function primarily by referencing established anatomical differences; it functions by producing the gendered bodies that (then) appear as 'natural' referents. That is, 'discursive construction' emphasizes that social forces are not limited to producing the *conceptual* distinction 'man/woman' on the basis of natural givens; these forces produce – in the stronger, ontological sense of forming and shaping – material bodies. In general, Haslanger writes,

> To say that an entity is 'discursively constructed' is not to say that language or discourse brings a material object into existence *de novo*. Rather something in existence comes to have – partly as a result of having been categorized in a certain way – a set of features that qualify it as a member of a certain kind or sort. (Haslanger 2003, p. 123)

Drawing out some of the implications of thinking of gender in this way, discursive construction refers to the necessary and sufficient conditions for producing those features that allow a body to be 'read' as belonging to a certain social category, where those features are presumed not already to exist. A material body – already "in existence" – is, by some morphogenetic process or other, re-elaborated, contingently produced, in such a way as to make it *socially* legible. Additionally, as Haslanger and others have specified, gender's corporeal production is usually a detriment to the subject.

Simone de Beauvoir's famous line from *Second Sex*, "one is not born, but becomes a woman," admirably condenses the history of pain the book's account of gendered embodiments so copiously describes. The lesson drawn from the history of gendered bodies is that gender hurts. And it hurts precisely to the extent that it is not natural. We will return to this issue below. As Judith Butler's work makes admirably clear, the social legibility of gender's discursive construction confers is not a good we are free to decline. Butler makes the same point as Hacking, in Althusserian language. We, *Humans*, are not free to be indifferent to how we are represented or "interpellated" by others. The social recognition made possible by discursive construction is constitutive of our subjectivity (Butler 2003; 2004; 2007).

We have seen that accounts of gender's discursive construction specify that for gender attribution to function, gender norms must solicit an embodied response that dissimulates its cultural provenance. The embodiment of norms is the *conditio sine qua non* both because gender attribution requires stable, differentiating marks, and because these marks are not natural – they do not, that is, pre-exist the system of gender attribution. The naturalization of culture makes gender, as Monique Wittig (1980) puts it, an 'ideological' system, one that functions by characteristically dissimulating its contingency. Gender ideology as discursive construction gives 'ideology' a distinct, morphogenetic dimension. Wittig figures discursive construction in terms of a destructive form of cultural morphogenesis:

> In the case of women, ideology goes far since our bodies as well as our minds are the product of this manipulation. We have been compelled in our bodies and in our minds to correspond, feature by feature, with the idea of nature that has been established for us. Distorted to such an extent that our deformed body is what they call 'natural,' what is supposed to exist as such before oppression. (Wittig 1980, p. 103)

On Wittig's account, the features 'constitutive' of gendered bodies are not constitutive of the body's biological capacities or properties. Quite to the contrary, the idea of 'nature' to which women's bodies are compelled to correspond is a *deformation* of nature, a deformation (wrongly) taken to be natural. The deformations producing women's bodies mark them off as inferior. In this context, the familiar assertion that the male body goes unmarked takes on a double sense. The male body serves as the corporeal norm in contrast to which woman's bodies can appear as different or Other; and the male body can serve as a corporeal ideal because it is unmarked by the deformations characterizing feminine embodiment.

Richly resonant with Wittig's account, Iris Marion Young's classic essay on gendered embodiment, "Throwing Like a Girl" (1980), considers the various ways that cultural forces compel in the absence of visible material constraints and hobbling devices. As Young writes, "typically, the feminine body underuses its real capacity, both as the potentiality of its physical size and strength, and as the real skills and coordination that are available to it" (1980, p. 148). Despite the apparent existence and function of certain corporeal and kinaesthetic capacities, these capacities are shut-off, inhibited. Importantly, on Young's account, cultural forces are in no way *constitutive* of the body's essential capacities; indeed, her argument depends upon the body having real, presumably biological, capacities neglected and wasted through their inhibition.

On Young's account, what makes a corporeal difference gendered – discursively constructed – is that a biological capacity is suppressed in support of a hierarchical social scheme. Gender *dis-ables* girls. Girls are culturally dis-abled while biologically able.³ Thought from the point of view of its essential possibilities, the body remains essentially biological. 'Gender' marks the conditions constraining the biological body, and the forces that lead it to have a characteristic shape as a result of these constraints. In all these matters, the 'biological' body serves as the undeniable reference and seat of the body's essential possibilities and, I believe it worth emphasizing, where gender is concerned *this* body remains explanatorily inert.

From de Beauvoir to Iris Marion Young, gender's 'discursive construction' has almost always referred to forces that inhibit, deform, or disrupt the body's essential possibilities; 'culture' names a negative sculpting force, repressing the body's natural capacities, hindering its vitality and preventing its flourishing. The embodied semiotics of gender function only inasmuch as they appear natural. In almost all these accounts, the discursive production of gender is un-

---

3 Iris Marion Young (2008, pp. 286–290) identifies and critiques her own 'ableist' assumptions in "Throwing Like a Girl: 20 years later." She does not note, however, that it is precisely the assumption that 'ability' and 'capacity' lie exclusively on the side of biology or nature that allows her to draw a neat distinction between culture/nature. In general, new materialist critiques of the nature/culture distinction will find powerful impetus and corporation in deconstructive critiques of 'ableism.'

derstood (at least implicitly) as taking place within the limits of the body's (already established) biological possibilities. Or, discursivity as cultural morphogenesis is *not* thought – by de Beauvoir, Wittig, Young, and Haslanger, to name but a few theorists in this tradition – as constituting either the body's biological possibilities or the limits of its own productivity.

Noting the limits assigned to culture's morphogenetic efficacy, Barad argues that feminist accounts of discursive construction have been critically valuable, but fall short of an adequate critique of Representationalism. An adequate critique would dispel altogether the ideal of a *merely* descriptive category – and with it the ontological gap between representation and reality. Such a radical critique would make it impossible to continue to think matter as indifferent to its representation, indifferent to 'culture' and even as 'affectively' indifferent. Matter, Barad insists, "feels, converses, suffers, desires, yearns and remembers" (Barad 2012, p. 48).

Whether or not one is willing to go as far as Barad in devolving agential features, one can agree, at least in principle, that "it is possible to develop coherent philosophical positions that deny that there are representations on the one hand and ontologically separate entities awaiting representation on the other" (2003, p. 807). Indeed, Barad, a trained theoretical physicist, is best known for developing such coherent philosophical positions: a speculative metaphysics of entanglement based on quantum mechanics and the work of Niels Bohr in particular. Though I cannot argue for it directly here, the work of those theorists most associated with the materialist critique (including, Kirby, Wilson, Grosz) share important aspects of Barad's speculative project. Such speculative projects, by generalizing and extending discursive interactions beyond the human, beyond the sphere of culture, would have important consequences for philosophical theories of embodiment. No longer would discursive effects be limited to the sorts of mediations – intentions, behavioral modifications, subjective awareness – that existing accounts of discursive construction rely upon to explain the implication between categories and the bodies they distinguish.

On Barad's view, the problem with feminist accounts of discursivity – what prevents these accounts from attaining an adequate critique of Representationalism – is the tendency to view matter and the body exclusively as the end product of cultural activity, thus depriving 'matter' of any morphogenetic force of its own. Indeed, she argues, the latter is more symptom then cause. It is because we begin by construing matter as passive, inert, and indifferent, that we end by 1) limiting discursivity to the social and cultural elaboration of the body and 2) viewing matter as the end product of cultural activity.

While it is true, as we have seen, that feminist theories have mostly limited their critique of Representationalism to the case of gender – and it is also true that these accounts fall short of articulating the sort of post-humanist account of discursivity that Barad seeks – this does not entail that feminist accounts of embodiment are wrong or in need of repair. Why fault gender theorists for lacking metaphysical ambitions? True, it may turn out that we will not get the right account of the nature of gender unless we first get the metaphysics of nature/culture right. But if that is true, the burden falls on the metaphysician to show how the proposed revision ought to matter to gender theorists. In any case, this is not quite what Barad and other materialists argue. Instead, they argue that we cannot get the right account of gendered embodiment – or discursive construction – if we cannot (first) factor the way in which biological matter is active or "matters to" the process of the "performative" materialization of norms (Barad 2003, pp. 808–809). And we cannot get to such an account of the possible explanatory efficacy of biological matter because our accounts of discursive construction view matter "exclusively" as "the end product of cultural activity."

It is quite true that it would be difficult to factor the contributions of biological matter if the latter were defined in such a way that made it "always already" a cultural artifact. But it is not clear that this critique pertains to the sort of accounts we have just surveyed: accounts that both assume the biological body as given – already "in existence" – and untouched by the kind of productive cultural activity that "discursivity" names. A biological body designated as *indifferent* to cultural activity cannot also be designated as exclusively the product of such activity. Assuming that the biological body is explanatorily inert in the case of gender is not the same as assuming it is ontologically inert (essentially passive). Barad's critique, as I read it, is question-begging; it assumes what it should rather prove, namely that the biological body *is* active in the sorts of processes that produce gendered bodies. Indeed, it is *this* sort of activity that gender theorists have usually denied. The biological body is not implicated in gender's discursive construction *because* gender is neither constitutive of biological facts nor brought about by any of these facts.

Speaking of an interactive, gendered body and a discursively "indifferent" biological body does not necessarily entail problematic dualisms or anti-realisms – at least so long as we assume that the *biological* body names what is essential about the body. To recur to Young's famous example, becoming gendered may involve the systematic and characteristic under-development of certain of the body's capacities, but this does not affect what the biological body essentially is nor the idea that the body is essentially biological. Indeed, if we return to Hacking's founding distinction between inter-active, discursive kinds – which include gendered bodies – and natural, biological kinds, we can see it is based on the assumption that biological 'kinds' do not adjust themselves to social classification schemes, while humans regulate their activities according to such schemes, affecting the expression of biological capacities in predictable ways. *Humans* are interactive kinds because 'discourse' implicates the body in certain ways; biological bodies are not so implicated. However, as we will see in the final section of this paper, there are ample ways to complicate Hacking's distinction. As I will argue, biological kinds can also have morphogenetic responses to their representations and representation need not be construed as an exclusively human talent.

Barad uses the famous double-slit experiments to suggest that quantum theory implies that discursive construction goes all the way down (Barad 2007, pp. 97–106). These double-slit-experiments, she argues, can be read as indications that matter – here it is a matter of the behavior of light – is "aware" of and responsive to its observation. Hence, generalized discursivity would involve thinking matter as more "literate," "vibrant," "intra-active," "aware," as having more of those attributes typically reserved for distinctively human or cultural processes, something that "new materialists" endorse.[4] But disrupting Hacking's humanist assumptions does not necessarily place any revisionary pressure on feminist accounts of *gender*. We may argue that, in general, restricting discursive construction to humans is unwarranted without, *eo ipso*, questioning how feminist theorists have bracketed biology in their accounts of gender. Recall that philosophers like Wittig and Young have argued only that gender 'works' by inhibition and destruction of regular biological processes. This supposes that biological processes may remain 'ignorant' or 'indifferent' to the representations that produce gendered bodies, not that biological processes are intrinsically indifferent to representation as such.

3 Performativity, Discursivity, and Materiality

In the previous section, I argued that the materialist critique does not pertain to those theories of discursive construction that affirm the body's biological essence and distinguish gender from this biological essence, precisely in its inessential, contingent character. But there are at least two influential theories of embodiment that do contest the body's biological essence – and these do seem to have the problems that materialists diagnose. Here, I have in mind Michel Foucault's genealogical account of the body, and Judith Butler's discursive account of "materiality" in *Bodies that Matter*. Yet, the distinctive problems of these ac-

---

[4] For accounts of "vibrant" matter see Bennett 2009; on the proposed "literacy" of matter see Kirby 2011; for intra-active matter see Barad 2007 and 2012.

counts – to which I now turn– are not an index of fundamental flaws with feminist accounts of discursive construction, but rather of fundamental flaws with these theories. In other words, these issues may not motivate a "materialist-turn" as much as a re-turn to traditional accounts of gender construction.

A Butler and *Bodies that* (do not) *Matter*

In her era-defining account of gender "performativity," Butler focuses on the way that gender involves an essentializing illusion or "naturalizing trick." Gender appears natural, as the very essence of the body, but this 'essence' is produced retro-actively by its very performance. The idea of gender as performative combines both a traditional notion of a "performance" (*viz.*, "restored behavior") and J. L. Austin's notion of "performativity" – the notion that language is not merely or even primarily descriptive but has the power to bring about the reality it names. To 'interpellate' someone in gendered terms is, on the 'performative' view, an essential part of creating or producing the referent: a gendered subject. However, as the previous section makes clear, though Butler coins the term "gender performativity," such thinkers as Wittig, Young and de Beauvoir had already elaborated the idea under different names. What is original to Butler, and definitive of a certain era of theorizing embodiment, is the way that gender performativity is yoked to an anti-realist critique of the gender/sex distinction.

In nuce, for Butler, 'biological sex' is the ideological production of a heteronormative gender apparatus, whereas for feminists like Wittig "gender" is the ideology of biological sex. In both cases, ideas about Nature or biology are contested, but in different ways. Wittig argues that cultural processes produce the gendered body as a second "nature" which obscures its real nature. Recall, as Wittig writes, "we have been compelled in our bodies and in our minds to correspond, feature by feature, with the idea of nature that has been established for us." The features 'compelled' by these ideas are anything but natural. By contrast, Butler argues that our ideas about Nature – and the discursive function of these ideas – have 'always already' been determined by the ideological demands of gender regimes. In this way 'sex' is determined as the 'natural' and extra-discursive basis of gender. As Butler writes, the "sex/gender' distinction is no distinction at all;" just as with gendered bodies, *sexed* bodies have "no ontological status apart from the various acts which constitute [their] reality" (Butler 1999, p. 173).

Butler's claim, denying the independent ontological status of sex, can be read in two ways, which are not mutually exclusive. On the first reading, Butler argues that the only grounds for (ideas about) biological 'sex' are the bodily features produced by gender performativity. On the second reading, she argues that *additional* cognitive acts (rooted in gender ideology) produce the 'realist' illusion of sex as an (independent) biological reality. In fact, Butler's must intend both readings, for her argument defends the view that the very idea of an extra-discursive body is unintelligible. Gender ideology constructs 'the very apparatus of production whereby sexes themselves are established" (Butler 1999, p. 11). The same ideological apparatus produces both the *disciplinary* mechanisms compelling individual gender performances and the cognitive-perceptual schemas that lead us to perceive or 'materialize' bodies in naïve realist terms. It follows that the elimination of gender ideology, for Butler, will lead to the elimination of 'sex' as an ontologically salient category. Bodies would no longer appear as sexed. However, it is not at all clear that Butler's anti-realism stops at 'sex.' Rather, it seems to categorically extend to 'biology' and the body's biological substance, as Vicki Kirby has argued (1991).

If, as I have maintained, the notion of gender performativity refers generally to morphogenetic disciplinary practices – practices which, taken together, account for how the illusion of a gendered *'nature'* is produced – this performativity is, for Butler, insufficient to account for how we come to think of or see the body as *essentially* gendered. For Butler, a heteronormative discursive frame produces the idea of biological sex, of a body "always already" sexed that is the natural ground for "gender." Butler argues that feminist theory cannot leave the sex/gender distinction intact, bracketing 'biological sex' in order to fiddle with ideas about the nature of gender. Indeed, insofar as inherited accounts of gendered embodiment maintain the ontological independence of the biological body they will unwittingly reinforce the very gender essentialism they hoped to escape. Therefore, gender theorists must also account for the illusion of biological sex – for it is *this* illusion that produces a body always already fitted to heteronormative demands. The inherited distinction between sex/gender situates biological sex, as the extra- and pre-discursive "truth" of gender and "sex" – however it may be retro-fitted by theorists – will continue to name whatever is needed for the project of naturalizing and essentializing gender. Any reference to a body prior to or independent of this materialization is "ideological" in the sense that it will function to naturalize or essentialize – to dissimulate the work of culture. "Sex posited as prior to construction will, by virtue of being posited, become the effect of that very positing" (Butler 1993, p. 5).

As the foregoing demonstrates, Butler's account of the body shifts attention from claims related to the morphogenetic power of cultural gender norms to claims about how these same norms function to "materialize" bodies according to gendered morphological schema. Accounting for how the body manifests ("materializes") as "always already" sexed will require us to reinterpret the body's *material* substance, making it identical with its phenomenal "materialization" – matter and its meaningful presentation, or what Guyatri Spivak has called its "value coding," are co-original and therefore thinking of 'matter' in realist terms is unintelligible (Spivak 1989). Butler's analysis reduces the body's *materiality* to its ideological materialization, compelling us to construe 'matter,' as Barad writes, "exclusively as the end product of cultural activity." Any claims about an extra-discursive body are part and parcel of the gender illusion and its naturalizing-trick.

Yet, if, as Butler argues, gender performativity will explain how the body comes to have certain, gendered features, how do these performatively produced features relate to other features of the body? After all, Butler denies that gender performance produces the body *tout court*. She never argues that there's nothing to the body beyond gender and sex. But any adequate account of performativity would seem to require us to speak of the conditions and limits for the sort of morphogenetic responses that "performativity" names. Would not 'matter' continue to be a name for the limits of 'performativity' and the limits of 'construction' – even if these limits turned out to be, in principle, unknowable? Yet, Butler's anti-realism requires rejecting any reference to the extra-discursive even as her own framing of performativity requires factoring in the limits of cultural production. This impasse in Butler's argument motivates various new materialist critiques, which argue, on its basis, that discursive construction entails the erasure of the body's materiality, its evacuation and de-substantialization.

Faced with materialist concerns of this sort, Butler, in *Bodies that Matter: On the Discursive Limits of "Sex"* (1993), promises to address directly questions related to the status of the "material" so often and insistently posed to her. Setting up the book's itinerary, she asks: "is there a way to link the question of the materiality of the body to the performativity of gender?" Here, Butler appears to distinguish helpfully between gender performativity (and its morphogenetic effects) and what she refers to as the materiality of the body – or, as she will specify, the *materialization* of this materiality as "extra-discursive" "sex." However, Butler's account of the body's 'materialization' wavers between the ontological and epistemological registers. On the one hand, the body materializes as gendered thanks to the morphogenetic effects of culture. On the other hand, the body 'materializes' as sexed, due to the ideological demands of gender, the 'cognitive penetration' of our gender schemas leads the body to appear as having an essential, sexed morphology. This slippage between the morphogenetic role of culture as an ontological force, and its epistemic role in 'shaping' appearances, leads Barad to note that "questions about the *material* nature of discursive practices seem to hang in the air like the persistent smile of the Cheshire cat" (Barad 2007, p. 64).

If we go back to *Gender Troubles*, and to Butler's descriptions of gender performativity, everything in her account indicates that the (cultural) norms in question are morphogenetic in the way that repetitive motions, habits, and disciplinary practices are morphogenetic. If *Bodies that Matter* is meant to relate questions about "the materiality of the body to the performativity of gender," the relation in question will not, after all, be between cultural or discursive morphogenesis and non-discursive morphogenetic process. Rather, performativity, or discursive construction, is apparently distinguished from 'idea construction,' or the cognitive-ideological processes which produce the (false) idea that the body has, as a matter of its essence, a biological "sex."

Barad is quite right to note that critical questions related to gender 'performativity' cannot even be posed if we cannot, in principle, establish the limits of Culture. How can we ask about the nature and extent of these posited morphogenetic responses, if we cannot pose, except through the figure of a constitutive exclusion, the question of the biological, or whatever would be constitutively heterogeneous to the field of cultural productivity? (Barad 2007, p. 64).

B Foucault's failed "history of bodies"

On Barad's reading, Butler's account of the body's 'materialization' seems to suffer from the very problem that Michel Foucault diagnosed when formulating his proposal for a "history of bodies" in *History of Sexuality* (Volume I):

> I do not envision a 'history of mentalities' that would take account of bodies only through the manner in which they have been perceived and given meaning and value; but a 'history of bodies' and the manner in which what is most material and most vital in them has been invested. (Foucault 1978, pp. 151–152)

As Barad writes, here Foucault makes "crystal clear" that his intention in proposing a "history of bodies" is to understand "history" in terms of a morphogenetic investment *of* bodies, where the latter is understood to refer, unproblematically, to extra-discursive bodies. Foucault's projected "history of bodies" promised to address the "entanglement" of the body's biological materiality with the cultural-historical forces he tracks:

> Far from the body having to be effaced, what is needed is to make it visible through an analysis in which the biological and the historical are not consecutive to one another... but are bound together in an increasingly complex fashion in accordance with the development of the modern technologies of power that take life as their objective (1987, pp. 151–152).

As Barad points out however, in Foucault's genealogical account of the body, we do not, in fact, get anything like an account of this "complex" entanglement of "the biological" and "the historical." Ironically, given his own precautions, Foucault continues to think through history and biology consecutively with 'biology' naming the pre-history of history, the always already displaced and surpassed "origin."

In Foucault's account, the biological body is displaced not, as is the case with Butler, because he equivocates between a history of morphologies and a history of historical morphogenesis, where the former would take into account "bodies only through the manner in which they have been perceived and given meaning and value," but because Foucault gives "history" a radically constitutive, productive power – a power to produce the body's essential features – without giving "the biological" any powers of its own. There is no account of how "that which is most vital about the body" is invested with still more vitality, but only an account of history's vital (dis)investments.

4 Biological Matter and Indifference: A New Response

Contrasting with Foucault's and Butler's anti-realist accounts of the body, many feminist accounts of gender embodiment define culture in terms of a negative morphogenetic force. The biological or pre-discursive body is defined in terms of the body's essential possibilities, which cultural activity alters, disables, or represses. This seems to assume that the biological body, its forces and processes, remains indifferent to its contingent cultural categorizations and representations. The idea of organic matter as indifferent to cultural representations and interpellations underwrites the belief that discursive construction does not effect, in the sense of modify or form, biological processes. As Manuel DeLanda writes, "matter has morphogenetic capacities of its own and does not need to be commanded into generating form" (2012, p. 43). But if matter does not wait for culture to give it form – if it has morphogenetic properties of its own – this also suggests that "culture" insofar as it has morphogenetic capacity is essentially 'exterior' to biology. This is effectively what many feminist accounts of discursive construction have accepted and what thinkers like Foucault, who have designated terms such as "power" and "history" as radically constitutive, contest. The problem with the latter view, as we saw in the previous section, is that it collapses the distinction between biology/culture. "Nature" is nothing but dissimulated culture. In response to this problem, new materialists have developed theoretical approaches that challenge the opposition without collapsing the distinction.

The work of Elizabeth Wilson (2003, 2008) is deconstructive in this respect. She aims to conceptualize culture as radically constitutive of the *biological* body, without collapsing the difference between terms. Unfortunately – unfortunate because this distracts from the force of her otherwise compelling and original arguments – Wilson often motivates this project with the now familiar materialist critique. Feminist theorists have been indifferent to biology because they have viewed biology as indifferent, in the sense of conceptually dull and unresponsive. For feminists, culture alone is lively and morphogenetic. As Wilson writes:

> In recent years there have been an increasing number of researchers claiming to have found the origin of…sexual preference, psychological pathology, and all manner of behavioral and cultural differences in locatable biological entities […]. The typical response from feminist psychology has been to demonstrate how such claims are a social construction, an ideological fabrication or a discursive ruse. In all such accounts, the nature of biological matter (the neuron, the gene, the chemical) remains enigmatic. (Wilson 1998, p. 66)

Here, Wilson suggests that feminists, reasonably wary of biologically *reductionist* explanations that would locate "the origin" of culturally salient differences in biological matter, retreat unreasonably to thinking of biological matter as passive and inert, or ineffable and unknowable. These defensive postures, Wilson argues, "have made it impossible for feminists to 'engage effectively' with accounts of matter at the heart of these theories." Yet it seems by Wilson's own admission that what feminists object to is not any particular conception of neuronal or biological matter, but the idea that cultural differences *originate* in biological matter and hence are reducible to it.

Of course, it may turn out that the "nature of the neuron, the gene, the chemical" is to be *constitutively* entangled with cultural forces and that our oppositional conceptual schemas foreclose thinking this entanglement. But, if feminists have often been indifferent to the nature of nature, as Wilson argues, this is because they have often held the view that the nature of nature is to be indifferent and untroubled by cultural practices. This position is hardly unique to feminists.

Far from arguing that matter is essentially indifferent or unresponsive, passive and inert, in order to construct accounts of gendered bodies shaped by culture, feminist theorists have most often asserted exactly the opposite: contrary to the deadening and defeating effects of culture, the organic body is "lively" and "vibrant" and "morphogenetic." If Wilson wants to argue that feminist theorists ought to question their ideas of biological matter, she should begin with what actually *is* a shared assumption among theorists of discursive construction:

namely, that *discursive* construction is limited to human or cultural processes. This will not necessarily entail that biology is "open" to culture – though it may be – but rather will suggest that features taken to be specific to cultural activity are found on both sides of the nature/culture distinction.

Where theorists have most often gone wrong, I argue, is claiming that the sort of interactive loops that discursive construction describes, loops that locate the impetus of morphogenetic response in representation, are limited to cultural processes and human agents. For example, as we saw above, Ian Hacking argues that in contrast to distinctively interactive (human) kinds, biological kinds are essentially indifferent to representation as such, incapable of responding to how they are depicted. The intuitions in favor of this belief in matter's essential indifference are rather easily defeated.

To see how, we first recall the interactive loop which is the mark of discursive destruction. On Haslanger's formulation of discursivity cited above, classification schemes interact with bodies via intentional structures in order to produce material effects. Altering the meanings we assign to bodies alters the physical properties of bodies because meanings affect intentions, emotions, actions, and behaviors. Classification conditions intentions, which initiate behaviors that, in turn, materially affect bodies. Construed as realizations of the classificatory conditions, these bodily effects feed-back, reinforcing or displacing the initial classificatory conditions. Both the body, as discursive and social, and the classificatory conditions, are the effects of this loop. The body – via the modification of its comportments – responds to the classificatory claims made on it.

Even if we can never locate a purely biological body, we can analytically distinguish between the body as a natural kind and the body as a discursively produced social kind because we can isolate the causal mechanisms responsible for the body's morphological features. It is the awareness of representations that produces the interactive loop characteristic of discursive construction, and awareness, Hacking assumes, is limited, to humans.

Hacking specifies that interactive kinds are exclusively human (2006, pp. 23–26). Indeed, as we saw above, Hacking proposes interactivity as the mark of the human. If the body is an "interactive kind," it is so only insofar as it is a human body. What is human or what makes humans interactive kinds is the capacity to interact with representations and signification in such a way that this interaction produces material effects. "Interactivity" is, in the first instance, the interactivity of representations (viz., the generation of self-representations in and through the way one is represented to and by others, which we could call hetero-representation). Secondarily, it names the way that self- and hetero-representations function to organize behavior, intentions, and actions which in turn interact with presumably non-intentional physical processes.

Indeed, Hacking expressly opposes the "interactivity" of minded processes to the "indifference" of biological processes in a way that follows familiar dualistic ways of thinking the relation between mind-body. While we might be tempted to say that humans "interact" with biological agents, when, for example, administering penicillin to a bacterium, such ways of talking are technically improper, obscuring the specificity of interactive kinds:

> What happens to tuberculosis bacilli depends on whether or not we poison them with BCG vaccine, but it does not depend upon how we describe them. Of course we poison them with a certain vaccine in part because we describe them in certain ways, but it is the vaccine that kills, not our words. (2006, p. 23)

Hacking's point is that it will not do to describe the "tuberculosis bacilli" as an "interactive kind" because the mark of an interactive kind is to be directly responsive to representations and descriptions. As Hacking insists, bacteria do not interact with their designation or representation as "pathogen;" they do not morphogenetically respond to their categorization but to the vaccine. If they are altered by our words this is only indirectly – and that indirection is what counts when defining "interactive kinds."

By contrast, the bacteria are directly altered by causal interaction with the BCG vaccine and only indirectly by "our words." For Hacking, anything that directly interacts with its own classification is an interactive kind. Thus, on Hacking's view, the human body is an interactive kind, thanks to (cognitive) intentional structures mediating between discursive practices that influence behaviors. However, at some level, the body is, like the pathogen, indifferent to its own classifications.

Interestingly, Hacking's example involves a crucial mis-description which, when corrected, goes some way towards deconstructing the opposition he draws between interactive and indifferent kinds, and with it the limitation of discursivity to *homo depicter*. Recall above that Hacking spoke of the BCG vaccine "poisoning" the tuberculosis bacilli. While this is a plausible description for how anti-bacterial agents like penicillin work, it a good deal less apt for describing how vaccines function. The latter, of course, involve introducing a weakened strain of the relevant disease in order to give the immune system the opportunity to develop a recognition-response to the antigen in the form of an anti-body. In order to explain anti-bodies and immune function generally, immunologists tend to resort to intentional-language, including representation, recognition, memory, and awareness. The TB is not killed by the poison in the vaccine – as Hacking tells it – a weakened strain of the TB virus is introduced into the body in order to stimulate an immune response, in the form of a stored representation that will allow the immune system to identify and attack the antigen in the future. Ironically, and quite without realizing it, Hacking has provided an example of a biological function, immunity, that is most difficult to characterize in terms of indifference.

As the vaccine example indicates, it is not only conceivable but increasingly probable that non-human entities engage in such interactions. Consider, for example, that immunologists describe the immune system in terms of cognitive function, as not only producing and storing "representations" of encountered organism-threats but producing a representation of the "self" (Hershberg 2001). On this account, immune system function would hardly be indifferent to representation, since an essential function would be to generate and update an organism's self-representation. If an interactive kind is what responds to and interacts with representations, becomes what it is, or has the features it does on the basis of how it is represented (or represents itself), then the immune systems, as well as myriad features of the nervous system, would be candidates for interactive kinds (Churchland 2002, p. 310).

If, in general, and at all levels of life, organisms are observed to mimic and dissimulate in response to how other organisms represent them, is this sufficient to attribute discursivity and performativity to them? Clearly, extending discursivity beyond the human would entail a very different understanding of biological matter than Hacking seems prepared to consider and a very different account of what will count as representation.

It is also clear why Hacking characterizes interactivity as a uniquely human attribute. Philosophical concepts like representation and intentionality tend to reflect an understanding of conceptual content or meaning that is, if not limited to, defined in terms of human modes of cognition. If discursive construction applies only to interactive kinds, in the absence of the sort of schemata that could conceive "matter" as an interactive kind, a discursively produced body is never a biological body but a human body – that is to say, a lived body or an embodied mind that can be logically marked off from what Hacking calls "indifferent kinds" (e.g. matter). Indeed, as Ian Hacking makes explicit, from the point of view of the way discursive construction has been theorized, the biological body is indeed inert and passive – an essentially "indifferent kind."

Though some theorists have explicitly defined discursive construction as a cultural, indeed human, phenomenon – opposing discursively constructed social kinds ("interactive kinds") to natural or physical kinds ("indifferent kinds") – this oppositional way of drawing the distinction between biology and culture is unwarranted. It confounds the claim that organic matter is, generally speaking, indifferent to *cultural* forms of representation with the less plausible claim that organic matter does not, categorically, engage in representation. Biological kinds need not be "indifferent" to representation as such – there is, increasingly, evidence that non-human, biological individuals (at whatever level we understand such individuation to occur) respond to how they are perceived (or detected). If this is right, then we are perfectly justified in speaking of biological individuals (or kinds) as discursively constructed, just as we now speak of social individuals as discursively constructed. However, saying so does not imply anything about the necessary entanglement of nature/culture nor has it *yet* demonstrated the need to revise traditional distinction between nature/culture. It simply establishes that being responsive to how one is represented is not the exclusive domain of humans or intentional agents.

Bibliography:

Barad, Karen (2003): "Posthumanist Performativity: Toward an Understanding of How Matter Comes to Matter." In: Deborah Orr, Linda López Mcallister, et al. (eds.), *Belief, Bodies, and Being: Feminist Reflections on Embodiment*. Lanham, MD: Rowman & Littlefield, pp. 9–34.

Barad, Karen (2007): *Meeting the Universe Halfway: Quantum Physics and the Entanglement of Matter and Meaning*. Durham, NC: Duke University Press.

Barad, K., Dolphijn, R. and Van der Tuin, I. (2012): "Matter feels, converses, suffers, desires, yearns and remembers." Interview with Karen Barad. In *New Materialism: Interviews & Cartographies*. Ann Arbor, MI: Open Humanities Press, pp. 48–70. Available at: http://quod.lib.umich.edu/o/ohp/11515701.0001.001/1:4.3/–new-materialism-interviews-cartographies?rgn=div2;view=fulltext

Butler, Judith (1993): *Bodies That Matter: On the Discursive Limits of Sex*. New York: Routledge.

Butler, Judith (1997): *The Psychic Life of Power: Theories in Subjection*. Stanford: Stanford University Press.

Churchland, Patricia (2002): "Self-representation in nervous systems." In: *Science* 296, No. 5566, pp. 308–310.

de Beauvoir, Simone (1952): *The Second Sex*. New York: Vintage.

Grosz, Elizabeth (1994): *Volatile Bodies: Toward a Corporeal Feminism*. Indianapolis: Indiana University Press.

Grosz, Elizabeth (2012): "The Nature of Sexual Difference." In: *Angelaki* 17, No. 2, pp. 69–93.

Hacking, Ian (1983): *Representing and Intervening: Introductory Topics in the Philosophy of Natural Science*. Cambridge: Cambridge University Press.

Hacking, Ian (1999): *The Social Construction of What?* Cambridge, MA: Harvard University Press.

Haslanger, Sally (2003). "Social Construction: The 'debunking' project." In: *Socializing Metaphysics*. Oxford: Rowman & Littlefied.

Haslanger, Sally and Ásta Kristjana Sveinsdóttir (2011): "Feminist Metaphysics." In: Edward N. Zalta (Ed.), *The Stanford Encyclopedia of Philosophy* (Winter). http://plato.stanford.edu/archives/win2011/entries/feminism-metaphysics/ (visited on 1 September 2019).

Hershberg, Uri and Sol Efroni (2001): "The immune system and other cognitive systems." In: *Complexity* 6, pp. 14–21.

Kirby, Vicki (1991): "Corporeal Habits: Addressing Essentialism Differently." In: *Hypatia* 6, No. 3, pp. 4–24.

Kirby, Vicki (2002): "When All That Is Solid Melts Into Language: Judith Butler and the Question of Matter." In: *International Journal of Sexuality and Gender Studies* 7, No. 4, pp. 265–280.

Kirby, Vicki (2010): "Original Science: Nature Deconstructing Itself." In: *Derrida Today* 3, No. 2, pp. 201–220.

Kirby, Vicki (2011): *Quantum Anthropologies: Life at Large*. Durham, NC: Duke University Press.

Lennon, Kathleen (2014): "Feminist Perspectives on the Body." In: Edward N. Zalta (Ed.), *The Stanford Encyclopedia of Philosophy* (Fall). http://plato.stanford.edu/archives/fall2014/entries/feminist-body/ (visited on 1 September 2019).

Spivak, Gayatri Chakravorty (1989): "'In a Word', interview with Eileen Roney." In: *differences* 1, No. 2, pp. 124–156.

Wilson, Elizabeth A. (1998): *Neural Geographies: Feminism and the Microstructure of Cognition*. London: Routledge.

Wilson, Elizabeth A. (2004): "Gut Feminism." In: *Differences: A Journal of Feminist Cultural Studies* 15, No. 3, pp. 66–94.

Wilson, Elizabeth A. (1998): *Neural Geographies: Feminism and the Microstructure of Cognition*. London: Routledge.

Wittig, Monique (1980): "On ne naît pas femme" [One is not born a woman]. In: *Questions Féministes. Nouvelles Questions Féministes & Questions Feministes* 8, pp. 75–84.

Young, Iris Marion (1981): *On Female Body Experience: "Throwing Like a Girl" and Other Essays*. Oxford: Oxford University Press.

Young, Iris Marion (1998): "'Throwing Like a Girl': Twenty Years Later." In: Donn Welton (Ed.), *Body and Flesh: A Philosophical Reader*. Malden, MA: Blackwell.

Part 3 **Realism**

Markus Gabriel
Saying What is Not[1]

Abstract: A major weakness of contemporary accounts of existence and non-existence alike arises from the tendency to believe that the answers to questions of existence can put us in touch with a distinctive "catalogue" of reality. Applying instead his ontology of "fields of sense," Gabriel questions in this paper both the idea of existence as dependent upon this "catalogue" conception of reality and, equally, on the Meinongian and Neo-Meinongian positions recently defended by Graham Priest and others, according to which there are objects that do not exist, including even contradictory ones. While the first leads to a "furniture ontology," the latter provokes semantic randomness, in that there is no longer any regular way to answer questions of existence. Gabriel's ontological descriptivism, by contrast, guarantees that the resolution to the question of objectivity depends on nothing but a coherent domain (a field of sense) and its objects.

As we talk, we do many things with our words. What we do with our words has been subject to investigation by both ancient and recent disciplines: rhetoric, grammar, logic, linguistics, philosophy of language, psychology, cognitive neuroscience, and so forth. As human thinkers, we are also in the remarkable position of being able to talk about what we do when we talk. Again, all of the mentioned disciplines deal with this feature of what we do with our words under these conditions of self-referentiality.

In this context, every theoretical grasp on what we say and how we say it inevitably builds a model of linguistic behavior. Like any other model, models of our linguistic behavior have to reduce a given complexity. For models are modes of data compression, which generate new information in turn. When we try to figure out something about human language, we cannot merely repeat what has been said, but have to say something new. In order for the linguistic novelty of the model to do relevant work, it has to be turned into the shape of a theory. A theory rules out alternative models by making explicit their weaknesses in an overall assessment of possible models. Theories rank models such that a theorist is justified in sticking with her theory to the extent to which it can be established that it ranks highest in the space of existing models.

---

[1] This paper draws on a research project on the ontology of fictional objects supported by a Lynen fellowship of the Alexander von Humboldt foundation and the CNRS (LIA CRNR – UMR 8103). I would like to thank these institutions for their generous support.

Evidently, no empirical theory is capable of guaranteeing that it actually ranks highest in comparison to all its competitors, because no one can survey the space of competitors *a priori*. Which competitors actually exist is itself an empirical question, meaning that the justification of an empirical theory falls short of the kind of completeness that would amount to guaranteed success. Therefore, empirical theories are fallible by their very nature.[2] This point is independent of any specific account of what counts as empirical information, as it simply draws on the idea that theories are the outcome of a reduction of a given complexity, such that the given complexity can count as putting the theorist in touch with data she need not have produced. Being in touch with something the theorist need not have produced herself is being in contact with something that is a candidate for being real.[3]

Theories that are in touch with something real rank their models not just in light of *a priori* or structural features of theory construction (such as compatibility with accepted logical systems and principles, coherence of the model, completeness of its underlying formal system, etc.). They also have to keep an eye on the pre-theoretical given, the reality for which we are attempting to build a model in the first place.

Now, how could we ever guarantee that our theory of linguistic behavior is sufficiently near completeness so as not to miss something essential, something that ranks sufficiently highly in the overall hierarchy of possible models? How do we know that we have not missed the most important features of the objects in our domain of investigation? Is it enough to just study linguistic behavior exemplified in the use of so-called natural languages (English, French, Turkish and so on)? Is the assumption that there are natural languages itself justified? For, to claim to know that there are natural languages and to distinguish them from one another is already part of the activity of building a model of linguistic behavior and, therefore, part of a theory of what there is.

The issue of coming to terms with our highly-cherished activity of speaking is, of course, further complicated by the fact that our model of that activity adds to the phenomena under investigation. We change the course of linguistic behavior by turning it into an object of reflective investigation. Formulating a theory necessarily relies on some kind of idealized presentation of the material under scrutiny. As our model is supposed to be in touch with, i.e. to be about, fragments of human language, this idealized presentation is itself subject to rules

---

[2] For an account of the epistemology of philosophy in light of these considerations see Gabriel (forthcoming a).
[3] On the relation between fallibility, objectivity, and reality see Gabriel (forthcoming b).

that will, in one way or another, be borrowed from the activity of speaking about something. In building our model we need to assume that we are in contact with human language. But this cannot be done by merely looking at language, as it were, by just taking it in.

This is why every theory of language that has ever been presented has set out from fragments of human language. These fragments are regarded as examples, as paradigms. Theories of language rely on claims of the form that some example of what is said and done in saying something is not just a random string of signs, noises, words, expressions of thoughts or what have you, but rather a paradigmatic sample.

Philosophy is not immune to these considerations. In what follows, I will discuss the ancient riddle of non-existence. This riddle makes its appearance in the context of a theory construction departing from linguistic data. The selected data are supposed to indicate something essential about our way of referring to what there is and what there is not. The hope is that we thereby achieve a theoretically controlled insight not just into what there is, but also into how we latch onto what there is by making our concepts explicit with the help of language.

1 The problem

The context roughly sketched in my short introduction is the breeding ground of the ancient riddle of non-existence. It has haunted human thought about ourselves as minded, linguistic animals ever since we began theorizing about ourselves under the kinds of descriptions epitomized under the heading of *animal rationale* or *homo sapiens*. Of course, this claim is itself a piece of theory in the sense under discussion here. No one can escape the fate of assuming something about how we got into the position of asking what there is and what there is not.

This is why it does not make sense to try to set the ontological record straight once and for all and just answer the question of what there is and what there is not by writing down a list. First, it will not be as easy as one might imagine to achieve agreement on either side of the dividing line separating what there is from what there is not. Second, even if there were agreement among speakers about what there is and what there is not, they could all be (almost entirely) wrong. Questions of existence are never entirely settled by looking at what speakers ontologically commit to alone. There is always the further question of whether their classification of objects into those existing and those not existing corresponds to how things are.[4]

The account presented here has the advantage of not taking the question in one of its inherited, more specific, forms for granted. A major weakness of contemporary accounts of existence and non-existence alike is the widespread tendency to believe that questions of existence are supposed to put us in touch with a catalogue of reality. To exist, on this score, is to be found in reality, to belong to its furniture. An object that does not exist can, accordingly, be mapped onto the anti-extension of the predicate __ *is found in reality*. Let us call this *naïve metaphysics*. Naïve metaphysics is naïve insofar as it treats the question of non-existence as a first-order question: to exist is to be in the object domain of a discourse about reality; not to exist is not to be there.

Yet, any version of naïve metaphysics (however logically sophisticated it is dressed up) runs into one of two traps, meaning: there is a dilemma here. We can call the first horn of the dilemma *Parmenides' horn*. It has been discussed since Parmenides via Plato, Aristotle, etc. to Meinong, Russell, Quine and beyond. It remains a present problem in contemporary ontology and goes something like this: If existence is the feature of belonging to reality, the term or predicate __ *exists* has an extension, namely existents. Existents, to reframe a little bit, fall under the concept of existence. Unsurprisingly, then, existents exist. In a first-order theory of reality, what makes an utterance or proposition in our theory true is an object's being a certain way. We can thus commit to the seemingly unsurprising statement that existents are objects that exist. Now, the problem is that according to this toy theory of existential predication, it is usually also expected that there be an anti-extension. The extension of __ *is blue* is whatever is blue (the blue objects), its anti-extension everything else (the non-blue objects).

But if these are our options, the anti-extension of __ *exists*, i.e. non-existence, consists of non-existents. Non-existents are the objects that do not exist. Objects that do not exist clearly differ from objects that do exist in terms of at least one property: existence. But this means that there are objects that do not exist. And many of us believe that it is straightforward to cite examples of these. Here are some (sometimes disputed) cases: round squares, unicorns, the biggest natural number, space ships that travel faster than the speed of light, time, justice, immortality, God, the soul, weapons of mass destruction in Iraq, etc. It thus seems as if we were not merely *theoretically* justified in postu-

---

[4] See Quine's distinction between *ontological commitments* and *ontological truth* in (Quine 1951, p. 12).

lating a paradoxical anti-extension for our first-order predicate __ exists, because we have a host of widely accepted examples of non-existent objects. There is evidence of non-existents. But what does it mean to claim that there are non-existent objects? It certainly must not mean that they belong to the furniture of reality, as this category is already occupied by existents which are absolutely determined not to allow non-existents.

Let me just mention in passing that the standard strategy, introduced by Russell and picked up by Quine, of paraphrasing the problem away does not help here. At the end of the day, the standard strategy always boils down to a commitment to the following nominal definition of existence, which can be expressed in the language of first-order logic as follows:

$$x \text{ exists } =_{def.} \neg \forall y (y \neq x)$$

On this basis, one can help oneself to the notion of an *existential quantifier* defined in light of the existence definition: $\exists x(x=y)$.

Unfortunately, as soon as we start to interpret this toy symbolism, i.e., as soon as we say what we mean by our strings of symbols, we are back in the meshwork of troubles which motivated the flight from reality to symbolism. Basically, what we said in seeking refuge in first-order logic is at best nothing more than that something exists only if it is identical to something that exists. This drives us into the uncomfortable situation of having to come up with an account of identity and, what is worse, of existence! For if we define existence in terms of identity, we are saying that to exist is to be identical to something that exists, which, to say the least, needs to be unpacked in a theoretically acceptable manner. This is why the masters of paraphrase, Russell and Quine, defended various versions of *descriptivism*. To exist, according to them, is to make an utterance or proposition true, such that what there is can be identified ideally via a determining, definite description. But let us leave this issue here for now, as we will get back to an enhanced version of descriptivism in the second part of this paper.

The second horn of the dilemma is *the problem of doublespeak* (a.k.a.: plurivocity). For one thing, there are two terms that enter into theoretical conflict: *there is* and *exists*. Naturally, it gets much worse, as our inherited ontological vocabulary is much larger and more confused. It includes expressions like "reality," "actuality," "being," etc. There is a reason why our ontological tongue is split. Doublespeak responds to the following problem; if to exist is to belong to reality, we are committed to there being a maximal domain of existents, namely reality. So far, so good. But what about reality itself? If it did not exist, there would not be a maximal domain of existents. But on that construal, if there were no such domain, nothing would exist, since existence is defined precisely as the feature of belonging to the maximal domain. No maximal domain, no anything.

However, the maximal domain clearly does not belong to itself in the same way in which ordinary existents belong to it. In order to protect reality from the suspicion that something has gone wrong with our account of existence, traditional ontology has reserved a special place for reality. If we use "existence" as a technical term for the feature of belonging to reality, we are free to introduce another term which does a similar job for reality. Typically, this special job is formulated either mereologically (roughly: reality as a whole of which everything but itself is a proper part) or with the help of some set-theoretic axiom system or other designed to avoid the manifold paradoxes that threaten a theorist who makes reality belong to itself in the full-blooded sense of existence.[5]

Probably the clearest case of doublespeak can be found in Heidegger's infamous move (repeated *ad nauseam* in Jean-Luc Marion's ontotheology) of distinguishing between "existence" (Dasein) and "there is" (*es gibt*) (see, for instance, Marion 2002). In his crudest moments, Heidegger concedes that reality as a whole (the world) does not exist, whilst happily endorsing the "view" that though the world does not exist, it – wait for it! – 'worlds' (Heidegger 2002, p. 23).[6] Even worse, he reads the dummy subject in the German *es gibt* as referring to an anonymous superpower which gives, as in hands out, existents. Being a good atheist, he avoids calling the superpower by its proper name "God" and leaves that to his followers who are unabashedly Catholic or otherwise inclined to the transcendent.

What Heidegger brings out by navigating the hitherto uncharted territory of making doublespeak as explicit as possible is something which remains beneath the surface in the standard analytic paraphrase strategy, viz. of replacing the problem by a formal counterpart so as to suggest that we can solve Parmenides' riddle by simply not speaking English anymore, but formal gibberish. What we can learn from Heidegger is precisely what happens when we carry metaphysics to its extremes: we no longer have any idea what to say about what we do when we speak about what there is and what there is not.

Before I present my own antidote to the Eleatic poison, bear with me in moving irresponsibly quickly over Wittgensteinian territory. Wittgenstein offers an interesting alternative to both analytic paraphrases and Heideggerian hardcore metaphysical poetry. His point of departure – most prominently worked out in

---

5 For a discussion of the mereological account see Gabriel/Priest (forthcoming).
6 See also: "The world is nothing in the sense that it is nothing that is. It is nothing that is yet something that "is there." The "there is" ["es" of "es gibt"] which is this not-a-being is itself not being, but is the self-temporalizing temporality" (Heidegger 1992, p. 210).

Philosophical Investigations – is the assumption that there really is no way to give an overall account of language or linguistic behavior. However, this puts him in the position of having to commit to the notion that there is such a thing as ordinary language. Ordinary language is what happens when we do not look too closely. It is the data the theorist tries in vain to get hold of. Wittgenstein accordingly tries to disabuse us of the tendency to over-theorize language use. In this way, he wants us to "se[e] the world rightly" (Wittgenstein 1922, proposition 6.54), as he already wrote in his *Tractatus*. In his *Philosophical Investigations* this is echoed as the injunction: "Don't think, look!" (Wittgenstein 2009, p. 66).

Unfortunately, he does not tell us how to look, but guides us in the peculiar form of his suggestive writing. His injunction remains an empty gesture to the extent to which he does not instruct us how to follow it. To be sure, he has a long response to this worry, namely working out a model of what it is to follow a rule and to be instructed by a master. Only he does not turn it into a theory, so as to avoid the obvious rejoinder that he himself is again really just building a model of linguistic behavior designed to rule out metaphysics for good. This project could not be carried out on Wittgenstein's model, so he tries to anchor our ways of looking at what we do with our words in our linguistic sensibilities, which are grounded in ordinary practices.

Unfortunately, metaphysics is much more entrenched in ordinary experience than Wittgenstein would ever allow, as documented by the very existence of religion, or our various encounters with existential nothingness. As Heidegger was acutely aware: Non-existence is not just a theoretical problem, which arises when we try to build linguistic models, or models of human thought expressed in linguistic form. Of course, Wittgenstein too was very well aware of this, which is why death and the topic of the meaning of life play an important role in the meta-logical theory of the *Tractatus*. But this just means that Wittgenstein has complicated the matter of the metaphysics of non-existence by adding the methodological insight that there really is no ultimate meta-theory, no innocent observer position from which we can take stock and neatly put some objects in the existence basket and exclude others on the basis of any kind of informative procedure (for a fuller account of Wittgenstein's take on ontology, see Gabriel 2019).

2 The solution

The idea that some things absolutely do not exist, that there is an absolute predicate of non-existence, i.e. non-existence *tout court*, typically relies on one of the following two background assumptions. Either existence is understood as the absolute positing of something in reality (mapping it onto the furniture of reality) or there are reasons to believe that some objects are not even logically possible, such that there is no room for them to be even so much as candidates for existence. The first version leads back to metaphysics and the second restricts possibility in logical space by a principle of membership in the domain of objects.

Against this background, different maneuvers for excluding entities from the board of existence make sense. The metaphysician will have to spell out a substantial theory of reality and existence. However, this is hopeless insofar as it merely repeats the problem of the existence of reality as whole: if to exist is to be part of the domain of reality, we are again faced with the problem that reality itself cannot exist or, at least, cannot exist in the same sense as all other existents.

Therefore, it is more plausible to rely on a more formal account, which allows us to restrict our comprehension principles: We do not want it to be necessarily the case that wherever we have any kind of description or predicate there is a corresponding object that exists. At the very least, we want neither the round square, nor the current king of France, nor the golden mountain to be members of reality, despite the fact that the three cases are very different on closer inspection.

Be that as it may, the minimal requirement for a theory of non-existence that is respected by all parties is that we do not want absolute explosion, i.e. an unlimited violation of the principle of non-contradiction in the constitution of the logical space we populate with existents. This is why, naturally, even contemporary Neo-Meinongians such as Graham Priest, who limit the scope of the principle of non-contradiction or allow for impossible worlds, draw on some kind of principle of restriction (for this strategy, see Priest 2005). Otherwise put, maximal logical and semantic randomness simply makes no sense, as sense can only be made where we can distinguish between kinds of cases, such as a case of existence and a case of non-existence. But in order for there to be distinguishable cases, we have to have a rule or array of rules.

Given that metaphysics will not help us here, as it tries to develop a much too ambitious rule-book, and given that, logically speaking, there are anyhow too many competing rule books that will generate utterly different ontologies, we need something more in line with our pre-theoretical findings. For, we have a sense for what there is and what there is not, and in ontological theorizing we set out to account for that sense, to give it a theoretical shape and remodel it where necessary.

In light of these considerations, I have worked out my proposal of an ontology of fields of sense, FOS for short (Gabriel 2015a). FOS claims that to exist is to appear in a field of sense (a *fos*). A *fos* is a domain of objects epistemically individuated by the fact that there is a corresponding rule book that can inform us about which objects are in the domain and which are not. Ontologically, a *fos* is individuated by a Fregean sense, i.e. by a mode of presentation. A mode of presentation or sense here is a structural arrangement of objects such that something is true of those objects. We can make what is true of objects explicit in the form of utterances with truth-values. Yet this should not mislead us into the classical metaphysical assumption par excellence, according to which the real has nothing to do with truth. Being true is not identical to any norm attached to assertoric discourse, which is not to say that there is no propositional truth (see Gabriel 2018).

For instance, Angela Merkel is in the domain of European politics, the number 7 is in the domain of natural numbers, Macbeth is in the domain of fictional characters (characters essentially discussed in the mode of fiction), fermions are in the domain of physics, etc. European politics is not subject to the rule book of *Macbeth*, the number 7 is not subject to the laws of the EU, and fermions are not in the domain of fictional characters. Fermions are subject to laws of nature, which connect them to other physical objects, whereas Angela Merkel is not strictly identical to a physical object or any number of physical objects precisely because no physical objects (no object studied by actual physics and classified according to its rule books) is subject to the laws of the EU. This is not to say that objects that fall within the domain of European politics violate the laws of nature or consist of ectoplasm. It just means that the kind of objects for which the kind of information-processing characteristic of legal procedure makes sense does not include physical objects.

In this context, we can identify a kind of relation: the relation between a domain and its objects. I call the relation a "sense," as it intelligibly maps objects onto a circumscribed domain with the help of something we can make explicit in the logical form of a description. We can search for new objects in given domains precisely because we have confirmed expectations concerning what kind of objects can be found there. These confirmed expectations consist in our epistemic relation to the relation or function that maps objects onto their domain.

FOS is a form of *ontological descriptivism*. It is anchored in the assumption that objects essentially have properties by which they differ from other objects. An object is a cluster of properties that hang together. What we call an "object" is a way for properties to hang together. The object itself is not a further entity beneath or above the cluster, but precisely the "governing sense," as I call it, of the various truths that hold good of it (see Gabriel 2015a, pp. 231–239, 264–271).

Where a function maps an object onto a domain, I say that the object or objects exist. To exist is to appear in a *fos*. What exists is thus and so in a given context. Accordingly, non-existence is defined in two ways. First and foremost, it consists in the fact that some object cannot be mapped onto a given domain. We have a sense, but nothing that corresponds to it. I can tell you what I am looking for if I am searching for the current king of France and you can tell me why I will not find him where I am looking for him (in Paris). It is possible for there to be a current king of France to the extent to which the *fos* of politics is actually open to contingent change.[7] Perhaps I missed some recent political development. To be sure, I am not especially open-minded about this, as my knowledge of the *fos* and, therefore, of the sense of politics and contemporary history pretty much confirms the absence of a current king of France. But as my knowledge fizzles out in other regions of the world, I am more likely to believe falsities with respect to current kings and queens. And even where I know of a king or even know a king personally, I may happen not to know exactly in what sense he is a king (what are his powers; in what precise sense is he a king).

The actual non-existence of an object in a given *fos* is often compatible with its existence elsewhere (*être ailleurs*), as Jocelyn Benoist has pointed out in a critical discussion of FOS (see Benoist 2017, p. 7–13). For instance, if God does not exist outside of the Bible, say, then there is a clear enough sense in which he does not exist. Yet this does not mean that there is no God in the Bible. Or, if there is a sense in which unicorns do not exist, this should not mislead us into misinterpreting the movie *The Last Unicorn*. We would badly misunderstand it if we interpreted it as not containing any unicorns.

Let me give you another example of the structural feature I have in mind and which serves as the basis of my theory of non-existence. Many philosophers since antiquity have pointed out that numbers or universals such as predicates cannot be found in nature. It is not the case that we literally stumble over the number 7 or that we perceive the relational predicate __ *is farther away from earth than* __. Run-of-the-mill denials of the existence of numbers, predicates, meaning, concrete composite objects, colors, free will, consciousness, time, etc. usually point out, quite rightly, that some objects do not exist in their preferred domain, but that they are, for instance, mental entities of some sort. For all the items I have listed more or less at random, there is someone who claims or has claimed that they are somehow mentally constructed or imaginary entities.

On this model, in order to claim that something does not exist, you do not have to rely on the metaphysical notion of absolute non-existence. All that is required is to show that some entity actually appears in a domain whose sense significantly differs from that of the domain where it was originally supposed to be.

---

[7] For the modal apparatus of FOS see Gabriel (2015a, chs. 10 & 11).

For instance, if numbers are mental constructions and if linguistic meaning is just an idealized assumption of semantic theorizing to which nothing in actual language use really corresponds, we are justified in denying their existence in all the contexts in which the existence condition for these kinds of things exceeds the existence condition for imaginary or theory-relative entities.

We can now generalize in order to arrive at a theory of non-existence. For something not to exist need not mean that it has to be absolutely nothing, i.e. that it is not in any domain of objects. It is perfectly compatible with ordinary, restricted assertions of non-existence (be they singular, such as: Krishna does not exist, or general such as: unicorns do not exist), that the objects whose existence is denied with respect to a given *fos* can be affirmed with respect to another *fos*. If witches are intended to be objects in the same *fos* as that inhabited by agents on planet earth, as Martin Luther thought, it is perfectly all right to assert their non-existence. One way of establishing the claim of their non-existence is via the discovery that they are mere figments or fantasy objects constructed by a bunch of discursive practices. They, thus, do exist, but in the realm of fantasy.

What is special about the realm of fantasy is not that it has content without objects, but rather that the objects that appear in its *fos* are essentially dependent for their existence on being imagined to be a certain way by subjects who claim to be knowledgeable about them.[8] If Luther claims to know that witches have certain powers, he might make true claims, but not about a particular woman living in Wittenberg, but rather about witches as they have been constructed, brought into existence as figments of imagination.

Non-existence, like existence, is thus a relation or, more precisely, a function. It maps objects believed to exist in a given *fos* onto a different *fos*. It places them elsewhere in logical space. For something not to exist is for it not to appear where it was supposed to appear. This is why we learn something when we find out that something does not exist, after all (for a similar account of non-existence, see Bergson 1998, pp. 272–298).

3 Two recent objections

In this concluding section I want to deal with two recent objections, one by Jocelyn Benoist, and the other most clearly voiced by Yulia Melikh and Anton Friedrich Koch (see Benoist 2017, pp. 7–13; Melikh 2017; Koch 2016).

---

[8] I present a detailed account of this view in Gabriel, forthcoming c.

Benoist claims that my theory of non-existence overgeneralizes on a kind of case he is willing to countenance. In his portfolio, this is the case of the bus number 60 in Rome. He once was looking for this bus. As it did not arrive at the usual spot, he asked a local who told him "non esiste più" (does not exist anymore). Yet after this encounter he actually saw a 60 in Rome. What the local had asserted turned out to mean that the number 60 does not stop at this particular location anymore, which was not supposed to mean that the number 60 does not exist anymore full stop. Its non-existence at one location in the same logical space (Rome) happened to be compatible with its existence elsewhere in the same logical space. I would handle this case by distinguishing two *fos* within the *fos* of Rome and read the local's claim as precisely an assertion of non-existence qua *être ailleurs*.

At this point, Benoist introduces another case, the case of a conference paper someone forgot to write. As an excuse, the would-be author claims to have forgotten his laptop, on which he had the only copy of the text, in Sardinia. However, he never wrote the text for the conference. Does this mean that according to FOS the non-written text exists elsewhere, namely in Sardinia? Or does it not exist full stop, as one might expect?

My response to this is that the text exists in the *fos* of fictitious objects. Fictitious objects need not be fictional objects, i.e. objects talked about in the mode of fictional story-telling. What characterizes these objects is that they exist in such a way that we can flesh out their properties relative to an interpretation. The range of acceptable interpretations is restricted by the case at hand. If the would-be author is a philosopher, the text never written ought to have contained certain philosophical arguments she is capable of making explicit. If someone who does not see through the lie asks what is in the text forgotten in Sardinia, he cannot reply with just anything. The text, therefore, exists elsewhere. It is relocated on the basis of the sense attached to the *fos* in which it was expected to have been written.

The second objection sets out from the observation that I regularly assert the negative singular existential

(NO-WORLD) The world does not exist.

What is special about this assertion is that it triggers a set of paradoxes under any interpretation according to which "the world" refers to an object with the property of being the object that encompasses absolutely everything which exists.⁹ Let me just quickly go over some paradoxical cases.

Case 1: If "the world" is supposed to refer to the absolute totality of objects, the sense in which it does not exist is the sense in which there is no 'truth of all truths'. Objects are bundles of truths, of what holds good of them. Nothing holds good of all objects in such a way that we thereby create a new object, a governing sense of what there is in general. But that seems to mean that the world is absolutely impossible. And if it is absolutely impossible, the reason why it does not exist is reason to believe that it absolutely does not exist.

However, my own view has it that "the world" does not refer to something absolutely impossible.¹⁰ The point of the reflection on case 1 should not be that there is an object characterized by the property of being absolutely impossible, but rather that there is no sense we can attach to the truth of all truths. Just think of all the regresses one triggers by attempting to posit a truth of all truths! Plus, there are the semantical paradoxes and so forth (for a good overview see Kreis 2015, part III, chs. 11–12).

Case 2: If "the world" is supposed to refer to the absolute totality of facts and if facts are ontological truths (what holds good of an object), we are basically no better off than in case 1. Totalizing on facts does not fare any better than totalizing on all objects.

Case 3: Against this background, my own proposal is to suppose that "the world," had it referred at all, would have referred to the absolute totality of all *fos*. Let us label this alleged hyperfield *w*.

At this point in the dialectics, Melikh and Koch wonder if *w* exists elsewhere so that (NO-WORLD) turns out to be an ordinary negative existential according to FOS. They both propose the *fos* of fictional, or rather of imaginary objects. Let us label this *i*. If *w* exists in *i* and only in *i*, (NO-WORLD) would be akin to the classical Kantian line of reasoning, which degrades the world from the level of ordinary objects of experience to a regulative idea that plays a role in the heuristic set-up of metaphysics.

Let us take a closer look at this proposal. If *w* exists in *i*, *i* itself has to exist. Yet, given that *w* is the field of all fields, the *i*-field has to exist in *w* too. Hence, *w* exists in *i* and *i* exists in *w*. At this point, one might ask a question raised by Quentin Meillassoux during a conversation on the axiomatics of FOS which

---

9 With the potential exception of a non-well-founded mereology. For a discussion of this option see Gabriel/Priest (forthcoming). Priest also presents a version of the Melikh/Koch objection: namely, that the Aleph in Borges' story *The Aleph* is coherently presented and should, thus, be accommodated by FOS.
10 This decisive point is misconstrued by Kreis (2015, pp. 439–443).

took place in Paris on March 29, 2017. Meillassoux asked if I could rule out *a priori* that there is something I would like to call "strong interaction" between two fields, where "strong interaction" is a scenario in which there are ultimately only two *fos*, which mutually appear within each other. My response is that this creates the problem that the relation of strong interaction is itself a *fos* within which the two *fos* which strongly interact exist, so that we now have either three *fos* for which the question of existence can be raised in turn or one *fos* (the relation of strong interaction) binding two objects together. In that scenario, for the singular relational *fos* to exist, there again has to be a *fos*, so that we never quite reach the position according to which there is only one strong interaction.

But even if this could be fixed on an axiomatic or formal level using strategies similar to those known from set theory, this would be of no help in ontology, as our point of departure here is that we are constructing a theory of what there is and what there is not. This theory is anchored in what there is, and we have no pre-theoretical ground to believe that what there is is just one giant, strong interaction with only axiomatic properties.

Hence, we need to look into the details of what would happen if w and i in particular strongly interacted. I believe that this would be disastrous for the following reason. If i exists in w, then all other *fos* besides i exist there too. Let us be parsimonious for the sake of the argument and assume that the only *fos* beside i would be the universe u in the sense of the domain of physical objects where a "physical object" is simply an object whose existence is recognized by physics. Given that the assumption is that u is not imaginary, u does not exist in i. We now have a w in which u and i exist. Given that w exists in i, in i we have a w in which we have a u and an i. And within u within w we have all physical objects.

The situation is, of course, much more intricate than this. We must not forget that w exists in i. Hence, we have a scenario with infinitely many worlds appearing in infinitely many imaginary fields, such that we also have infinitely many physical objects distributed over infinitely many repetitions of the same structure. This is a consequence of the structural realistic feature of FOS, according to which the world might at first glance be an imaginary object, as long as this does not turn all objects into imaginary objects.

Hence, the relation of appearing-in must not be transitive on the construal of the Melikh/Koch objection. If there are trolls in Norwegian mythology and if Norwegian mythology exists in Norway, this should not entail without further ado that there are trolls in Norway (see for this example Gabriel 2015b, p. 88). Similarly, if the world exists in our imagination and if everything exists in the world, this should not entail that everything exists in our imagination in the same sense in which this is alleged to be true of the world. Therefore, the account of a strong interaction between w and i, which needs to commit to a non-transitive relation of appearing-in mutually applying to *w* and *i*, creates infinitely many scenarios for which we have no identity criteria. If my table exists in infinitely many fields of exactly the same kind, which exist in infinitely many worlds, which exist in infinitely many imaginations, the proposed model clearly has serious disadvantages compared to the official proposal of FOS, according to which the world does not exist.

This leaves us with the worry that (NO-WORLD) is not an ordinary negative existential according to FOS itself. I accept that. This is why I use (NO-WORLD) as a slogan to attract metaphysicians and to force them to make explicit what *they* mean when *they* commit to the existence of their preferred version of a totality of what there is. Whatever metaphysics has to offer, it has to be compatible with pre-theoretical experience. FOS has the advantage of not eliminating anything from the realm of pre-theoretical experience except the unnecessary assumption of a singular all-encompassing field of sense.

What there is and what there is not is inherently manifold and indefinitely extensible. There is no ontological theory of absolutely everything. What there is not does not fall within any unified field either. Non-existence is as plural as existence. The landscape of FOS has room for all sorts of non-existents, as long as we do not throw them into one basket full of paradoxes.

It is not a coincidence that this is the exact opposite of Parmenides's view of the unity of reality. It should also not be surprising that the only way out of the Eleatic riddle is the negation of the metaphysical tenet which underpins the whole enterprise of traditional metaphysics: the notion that reality is one.

Bibliography

Benoist, Jocelyn (2017): *L'adresse du réel*. Paris: Vrin.
Bergson, Henri (1998): *Creative Evolution*. Mineola, New York: Dover.
Gabriel, Markus (2015a): *Fields of Sense. A New Realist Ontology*. Edinburgh: Edinburgh University Press.
Gabriel, Markus (2015b): *Why the World Does Not Exist*. Cambridge: Polity.
Gabriel, Markus (2018): "Être vrai". In: *Philosophiques* 45. No 1, pp. 239–247.
Gabriel, Markus (2019): "L'être humain et sa mythologie – quelques réflexions sur *De la certitude*". In: Idem.: *Propos réalistes*. Paris: Vrin.
Gabriel, Markus (forthcoming a): *At the Limits of Epistemology*. Translated by Alex Englander. Cambridge: Polity Press.
Gabriel, Markus (forthcoming b): *The Meaning of Thought*. Cambridge: Polity Press.
Gabriel, Markus (forthcoming c): *Fiktionen*. Berlin: Suhrkamp.
Gabriel, Markus and Priest, Graham (forthcoming): *Everything and Nothing*. Cambridge: Polity Press.

Heidegger, Martin (2002): "The Origin of the Art Work". In: *Off the Beaten Track*. Translated by Julian Young/Kenneth Haynes (Eds.). Cambridge: Cambridge University Press.

Heidegger, Martin (1992): *The Metaphysical Foundations of Logic*. Translated by Michael Heim. Bloomington/Indianapolis: Indiana University Press.

Kreis, Guido (2015): *Negative Dialektik des Unendlichen: Kant, Hegel, Cantor*. Berlin: Suhrkamp.

Koch, Anton Friedrich (2016): *Hermeneutischer Realismus*. Tübingen: Mohr Siebeck.

Marion, Jean-Luc (2002): *Being Given. Toward a Phenomenology of Giveness*. Translated by Jeffrey L. Kosky. Stanford: Stanford University Press.

Melikh, Yulia (2017): "Kopernikanischer Salto. Über den neuen neutralen Realismus. Gedanken zum Vortrag von Markus Gabriel". In: Markus Gabriel (Ed.): *Метафизика или онтология? Нейтральный реализм*. Moscow: Идея Пресс, pp. 107–117.

Priest, Graham (2005): *Towards Non-Being. The Logic and Metaphysics of Intentionality*. Oxford: Oxford University Press.

Quine, Willard van Orman (1951): "Ontology and Ideology". In: *Philosophical Studies* 2, pp. 11–15.

Wittgenstein, Ludwig (1922): *Tractatus Logico-Philosophicus (TLP)*. Translated by C. K. Ogden. London: Routledge & Kegan Paul.

Wittgenstein, Ludwig (2009): *Philosophical Investigations (PI)*, 4th edition. Translated by P.M.S. Hacker and Joachim Schulte (Eds.). Oxford: Wiley-Blackwell.

Paul Livingston
Sense, Realism, and Ontological Difference

Abstract: The paper brings Dummett's formulation of "realism" into dialogue with Heidegger's understanding of truth as "unconcealment." Livingston argues, with references to Frege and Wittgenstein, that the phenomenon of truth can be understood theoretically and analytically as requiring the pre-theoretical appearing and constitution of objects, in experiential, practical, or explicitly linguistic modalities. This approach provides a basis for new logically- and phenomenologically-based accounts of the structure of objectivity within linguistic truth in relation to the appearance and being of objects. Within the context of a development of Heidegger's idea of ontological difference, this further implies that truth and objectivity must have a logically paradoxical structure. Even if Heidegger does not often say so explicitly, this paradoxical structure of objectivity and truth is centrally involved, as Livingston argues, in his understanding of the "clearing" and the interpretation it allows of beings "as such and as a whole."

An aim of this paper is to bring into view one aspect of the way thinking and being may be seen as related, if a certain kind of global realism about intentional sense is maintained.[1] This realism is motivated, in part, by Frege's realist conception of linguistic senses as objective modes of the presentation of entities, and thus as ways that things can appear, or show up as being. But it also extends the idea of intentional presentation beyond the linguistic theory of reference, aiming to characterize, with maximal generality, the structural conditions for the intelligible presentation of entities, whatever their specific modalities of presentation (and thus, not only in language, but equally in perception, imagination, memory, engaged practice, etc.).[2] Within this conception, the objectivity of senses means that they present entities as they are, or can be: that the intentional presentation, in whatever modality, of an entity is, indeed, the presentation of just *that* entity as being some way or other, which is a way it is, or can be. For this to be maintained in general, it must be the case that the ways that entities can appear as being just are the ways that they are, or can be. But as I shall argue, this implies a correlative realism about the structural basis of this appearing itself: about the basis of their appearing, that is, as the

---
[1] This realism about sense is formulated and defended more fully in Livingston (2017), especially chapters 1 and 5.
[2] For a closely related extension of Tarski's disquotational Convention T to phenomenologically presentational acts or vehicles in general, see Smith (2016).

https://doi.org/10.1515/9783110670349-013

entities that they are, or can be. Global realism about sense will be, then, overall realism about appearing: the thesis of realism is, here, the thesis that the ways things can appear intelligibly to thought are grounded in the ways they are or can be, or in what we may collectively refer to as their "being," in general and as such.

In the restricted context of discussion of the intentional structure of a natural language, this requirement of realism about sense naturally takes the form of the maintenance, with respect to *semantic* discourse, of the formal requirement that Michael Dummett has proposed as a maximally general formulation of realism in any specified domain. This is the requirement that statements about entities in that domain be supplied with truth-values in such a way that their *logical bivalence* is maintained: these statements must be determined as either true or false, independently of our knowledge about them or our epistemic procedures concerning them.[3] If the theory of presentational sense is broadened to take into account the modes of appearance of entities in general, rather than being restricted to the discussion of language only, however, this requirement is naturally extended to that of bivalence with respect to the broader ground of that appearance, without prejudice to its determination by specifically linguistic concepts and categories. This ground must be such that it allows the manifestation of entities to thought, in a broad sense including perception and other varieties of intentional presentation, such that thought in this broad sense presents them as being the ways they, in fact, are, or can be. As such, it must be a basis, not only for their secondary appearance in representation, or to a thinking subjectivity, but also, more basically, for their ontological determination as being the entities they are, or can be, at all.[4]

---

[3] Dummett (1963); see also Dummett (1978) and (1982).

[4] Here, the relevant kind of bivalence, as applied to sentences characterizing sense, thus extends beyond sentences characterizing specifically *linguistic* sense. Nevertheless, it is still, as on Dummett's original formulation, to be understood as a requirement on the truth-values of a specific range of sentences: namely those that characterize the *intentional presentation* of some entity or state of affairs as being some way. Thus, for example, the requirement bears on sentences such as "P *presents* the tree over there as flowering" where P is a (token) *perceptual* state, act, or vehicle, or "C *presents* the hammer as heavy" where C is an engaged act of grasping the hammer. For the kind of realism contemplated here, the crucial requirement is just that such "presentational" sentences in general (and without respect to linguistic or nonlinguistic presentational modality) be determinately either true or false; there is therefore no need to construe the contemplated realism as a matter of "semantic descent" to considering the existence (or non-existence) of truth*makers* for the relevant truths and falsities, despite the often non-linguistic character of these truthmakers. As an anonymous reviewer (to whom this footnote responds) has also helpfully pointed out, for the realist position contemplated here it is necessary that, in ad-

Sense, Realism, and Ontological Difference — 235

On this kind of picture, senses are, then, ways in which *whatever is* can be presented to thought. For this reason, as I shall argue, the relevant global realism about sense is also naturally formulated in the terms of Heidegger's idea of ontological difference, insofar as it construes the global sense of *whatever is* [*das Seiendes*], or of "entities," as determined with reference to their univocal difference from being [*das Sein*]. On Heidegger's conception, the global sense of entities can be seen as determined through their thinkable being, so that the appearance of an entity as being some way or other (Heidegger will term this its "unconcealment" [*Unverborgenheit*]) is dependent upon what can be characterized as its "ontological sense" [*Seinsinn*]. This is the sense of its determination by whatever, of its being, is thinkable. In the context of this idea of presentational sense as unconcealing entities *in* their being, global realism about sense thus requires realism about ontological difference itself: realism, that is, about the difference on the basis of which it is first possible for entities, as such and as a whole, to appear in, or for, thought. To apply this realism to the senses of entities, as such and as a whole, is, then, just to formulate such a conception of the relationship between being and thinking: to maintain that, on the basis of their difference from being, entities can appear as meaningful or intelligible for thinking, and indeed by appearing in just the ways they are, or can be. Speaking formally, and extending Dummett's formal requirement of bivalence, this indicates, however, that the thinking-being relationship cannot be specified as a whole without contradiction; and thereby, as a consequence, that the global determination of the thinkable sense of entities itself cannot be specified in non-contradictory fashion.

1

When Frege, in "On Sense and Reference," introduced the idea of an objective sense as a mode of presentation [*Art des Gegebensein*] of its referent, he already thereby invited a conception of the sense of a singular term as accomplishing the *direct* presentation of its referential object. On such a conception, a singular sense is a presentation of that particular entity *as* being some way, and its functioning is just that: to make the entity available in some particular way, i.e. *as* being some way or other. This functioning is, then, just what is explicated by the idea of a linguistic term's sense; and this idea is quite independent of any

---

dition to overall bivalence, the sentences characterizing presentational sense in general also be understood as i) truth-apt and ii) not uniformly non-substantive or false.

specification of the sense in terms of an individuating description, or as having any other representational content of its own. Inasmuch as it figures in Frege's account, this conception of sense as direct presentation is there formulated, of course, primarily with application to linguistic meaning. But as students of Husserlian phenomenology have long known, there is no evident reason why it cannot be expanded beyond the confines of this requirement to take in modes of presentation, or the structure of availability of entities to intentional presentation, *in general:* that is, without respect to the specific modality (linguistic or non-linguistic) by which they are presented.[5] Thus, on the requisitely expanded conception, the idea of the intentional presentation of an entity includes, in addition to linguistic modalities, also the perceptual, abstractive, imaginary, or practical ones, among others, whereby it may appear to an intentional agent at a particular time, in any sense of "appearing." With this phenomenological expansion of "sense" beyond the linguistic constraints of Frege's picture, it is possible to conceive the modes of presentation of an entity, as it may appear, for instance, in perception, as including those which are irreducibly *indexical* or demonstrative: those which involve the presentation of an entity or event, for example, as (as we might formulate them) "the person here in front of me," or "the explosion happening right now."[6] It is also possible for an entity to appear only *inexplicitly* as being some way: as, for instance, when, in the course of ordinary practice, an object shows up as being some way without one's attending to it, thematizing it, or even being conscious of it. (Think, for example, of objects in a blurry background of other objects in the foreground.)

If the idea of presentational sense is expanded in this ways, it will motivate an overall conception of the conditions of the *availability of entities* for meaningful consideration, description, and practical involvement. Here it is possible, in particular, to consider the general or structural conditions under which entities can be intentionally presented at all, not only as they figure in particular acts or events of linguistic reference, but also as they are available for such reference to

---

[5] This generality is marked in Brentano's inaugural statement of the idea of intentionality: "Every mental phenomenon includes something as object within itself, although they do not all do so in the same way. In presentation, something is presented, in judgment something is affirmed or denied, in love loved, in hate hated, in desire desired, and so on" (Brentano 1879, p. 88). The core idea of the intentional presentation of an entity, in a way that is neutral with respect to the presenting modality, is plausibly at least one aspect of Husserl's concept of its noema, or noematic sense; for the classic presentation of the parallel between Husserl's conception and a suitable generalization of Frege's notion of sense, see Føllesdal (1969).

[6] This aspect of the present conception thus appears congenial to Evans' idea of demonstrative senses (as in Evans 1981 and 1982).

begin with.[7] This will, plausibly, include both "perceptual" (and other practical) and "conceptual" and other intellectual aspects of presentational availability: as, for example, my significant *linguistic* reference to *"the flowering tree over there"* (as thus described and indicated) requires that I have prior *perceptual* access to it, as *well as* prior access to the concepts or categories under which I thereby describe it ("flowering"; "tree").

Such a conception will preserve, even in the broadened context, the constitutive links among sense, presentation, and truth that are characteristic of Frege's own (more limited) linguistic theory. For example, the sense of a singular linguistic term will remain a mode of presentation of its referent: that is, a way of presenting *just this referent* as being. And since the truth-value of a declarative sentence will then, similarly, be determined by whether the entities it describes *are* as it presents them as being, such a sentence's sense will still be understood as Frege understands it: that is, as the mode of presentation of a truth-value. But these links will also be extended beyond the linguistic case. A presentational state or vehicle in general (for instance, a sentence or thought, but also, for example, a visual perception or memory) will be true (or veridical), just in case it presents its object as *being* the way it (in fact) is; and a presentation of some complex or relationship of entities as being thus-and-so will be true (or veridical) just if the complex or relationship *is* thus-and-so: that is, just if what it presents *as being* the case, in fact, *is* the case. An act of perception will be veridical, for example, just when the way it presents its object is the way that object is, as it is in itself. When a presentational vehicle, directed at an individual entity, is veridical in this sense, we can then naturally speak of it as *showing* the entity "in its being." Its senses are then understood as the possibilities for this showing, or – switching to Heidegger's jargon – of unconcealing, in its being, the entity itself.

As thus characterized, it is further plausible that an entity's unconcealment always takes place *within a broader, relational context*. That is, it does not make sense to suppose an entity to be presented as it is, or can be, just *by itself* and without any relation to anything else. Rather, the presentation of an entity as being such-and-such a way always relates it to other entities, as well as to *their* ways of being, in such a way as to locate it, along with those other entities, within a broader shared horizon of relational significance. The horizons of an entity's appearing can be simultaneously multiple, and each can be primarily theoretical, primarily practical, or equally both. For example: the table is revealed

---

[7] Although I do not pursue the point here, it is also possible, within this conception, to see the overall hermeneutic structures of intelligibility as plural and historically variable, and thus as capturing what the later Heidegger understands as the succession of historical "epochs" or regimes of the intelligibility of being that collectively define, for him, the history of metaphysics.

as crooked, in the context of our practical activity of dining on it; Fermat's theorem is revealed – in Wiles' proof – as holding, in the theoretical context of contemporary mathematics; the Higgs boson is revealed as existing and having the properties it does, in the theoretical and practical surrounding of contemporary particle physics, as well as – simultaneously – the much less specialized and less formalized context of our broadest and deepest collective understanding of nature as a whole.

Because it is holistically conditioned in this way, one can speak of the unconcealment of any individual entity as dependent, among its various structural conditions, on the "prior" unconcealment or "disclosure" of (a) world as such: the "prior" and often implicit availability of (at least) a *relatively* total structure of entities and ways for them to be, or an overall "hermeneutic" *interpretation* (in the sense of the German *Auslegung*) of them in their possible ways of being. Thus, Heidegger will speak of world-disclosure as the prior "openness" of world for Dasein, the "projection" for Dasein of a domain of significance or sense. But this projection of sense, in the way it is to be thought of here, is not a matter of the external application of the terms or concepts independently produced by the activity of a subject, or by the imposition of the prior structure of a language or conceptual scheme onto an otherwise shapeless reality in itself. Rather, since it is plausibly a requirement for realism about disclosive sense that it *be able* to present entities just as they are, the prior projection of any domain must itself make available, in its holistic structure, ways that the entities in that domain are, or can be. And *if* this (relatively) total structure is indeed conceived as *maximally* total (though we will return to this question later), it will be such as to make available, as a precondition for the presentation of any individual entity, the prior structure of ways that entities, *as such and as a whole*, can be. Then the overall characterization of the sense of any entity as given – the explication of the entity in its being – is, in each case, ultimately a matter of the ontic-ontological difference: the difference between being, on the one hand, and whatever is, as such and as a whole, on the other.

On Heidegger's own account, the maximally general formal characterization of the structure of givenness, and hence of presentational sense, is that of a (so-called) "existential-hermeneutical" "as"-structure: the basic structure whereby something is presented *as* something.[8] In this structure, in general, something is revealed as something, or as being some way: the entity is revealed, or "unveiled," and, further, is unveiled *as* being some way or other. This structure of the "existential-hermeneutical" "as" is not, in general, linguistic: it precedes

---

[8] See *Being and Time*, pp. 148–150, 158–59.

and grounds, phenomenologically and ontologically, the explicit "as" of linguistic predication, or of the "copula." Thus, in the predicative sentence, proposition, or judgment, "S is (a) P," S is unveiled or unconcealed as (as being (a)) P. But this explicit, linguistic unconcealment has a prior basis in the "existential-hermeneutical" "as," which need not be explicit or linguistic at all, but rather is, in its structure, the most basic condition for the meaningful availability of entities overall.

The "existential-hermeneutical" as-structure is thus very widely applicable, across different modalities of presentation or availability of entities, and examples can be multiplied. The picture on the wall is unveiled as "askew" in my visual perception of it. The hammer appears as "too heavy" in the course of my unthematic, "circumspect" practice of building, without any explicit assertion or even any conscious thematization of it as such.[9] As I enter the café, Pierre is uncovered as "not here": this time, I do thematize, albeit in a privative mode, but still without any necessity of explicit judgment or assertion. Or again, I assert or affirm linguistically that "the cat is on the mat": then, the explicit and thematizing judgment is itself a mode of the disclosure or presentation of the relevant entities (the cat and the mat) and is thus grounded in the ways in which they, themselves, are thereby presented, as well as the relevant ways they can be.

In each case, the "prior" existential-hermeneutic structure captures, with maximal generality, the way in which the entities themselves are initially presented or given, such that they can intelligibly be thought at all. It is then, as Heidegger argues, reasonable to take the structure of this presentation as the structure underlying explicit predication in the sentence, as the underlying phenomenological/ontological basis for the (only apparently synthetic) structure that shows up, in the linguistic assertion, in the bridging of subject and predicate with the copula or the "is" of predication. And furthermore, since we can understand the structure of predication, relative to its possibilities of truth, as a matter of the way the truth-possibilities of a sentence are determined by the senses of its constitutive terms, so too can we understand the presentational possibilities of the entities themselves, their "ontological" senses, as presentations of what is thinkable in their being. As I shall argue in the next section, to do so is to maintain a global realism about presentational sense; and, correlatively, in a way that can be shown by its formal schematism, to maintain a certain positional figure of the thought-being relationship, or the place of the empty indexical positionality of thought insofar as it bears, in its structure, some relationship to whatever is.

---

9 *Being and Time*, p. 157.

2

The realism about sense contemplated in the last section is, essentially, an attitude of realism about the relationship of thought to the being of *whatever is*. As such, its appropriate overall formulation must be *neutral*, in the sense that that formulation cannot make it depend upon the existence, or the properties, of any specified class or type of entities. The formulation of overall realism cannot depend, that is, on any sub-region taking in just some (but not all) of *what there is*, or on any specified relation to some (but not all) of *those entities which there are*. For this reason, it is not adequately formulated as a realism about entities characterized according to any specific feature they are thereby supposed, universally, to have. Thus it is neither a naturalism nor an "empirical" realism: that is, it is not (for example) adequately formulated as a realism about entities that belong to nature, or those that are accessible to empirical investigation as opposed (say) to "empty" speculation.[10] But, for the same reason, it cannot be formulated in such a way as to identify any specific domain of entities, restricted as to their essential characteristics or properties, to which it eminently or primarily applies: the "really real" ones as opposed to those that are (by contrast) secondary, derived or constructed. It is thus not appropriately formulated as any kind of reductionist position, or any "metaphysical" realism that operates by identifying some class of entities – for example the referents of "primitive" terms – that are semantically or metaphysically atomic with respect to others built from them.[11] Nor, again, can it be appropriately formulated in terms of a theory of truth that requires the correlation or correspondence of some class of entities (for instance linguistic sentences) with another (for example "extra-linguistic" states of affairs): for any such theory does, after all, turn on some non-neutral distinctions within *what is*, even if it simply be the overall "distinction" between language and world. And finally, for the same reason, it is not appropriately formulated as a matter of the relationship of "mind" and "world," or indeed of any sort of "relationship" between subject and object at all. For any such relationship is, logically and grammatically, one between two entities or classes of entities, metaphysically distinguished as to type, and, as such, does not capture the requisite, global and neutral, realism about the being of what is, as such.

---

10 This does not mean, however, that it is *incompatible* with these positions: since it is appropriately formulated, as we shall see, in terms of the semantic requirement of bivalence for ontological statements overall, it simply remains neutral on questions such as the question whether all entities are material, or governed by natural laws, or accessible to empirical investigation.
11 As, for instance, in Wittgenstein's *Tractatus*.

It might seem that such a broadly neutral realism cannot be formulated at all: if it is not grounded on any characterization of how things are with entities, or on any specifiable relationships among them, how can the structural provision of sense be characterized, without any such formulation being completely empty? However, even if it cannot thus be specified in terms of the determinate properties or features of anything that is, it may be possible to specify the requisite realism, rather, in terms of the constitutive links among sense, being and truth which are displayed – as we have seen – both by Frege's own theory (albeit there in a way that restricts them to the consideration of *linguistic* sense) and, plausibly, any overall account of sense that is structurally realist at all. In particular, if presentational sense is (as argued in the last section) primarily a matter of the *disclosive* truth of entities across ontological difference, the appropriate formulation of realism about it will be able to capture, in neutral terms, the essential mutual dependence of the structure of truth on the structure of being. This dependence can then also be understood as the determination, across ontological difference, of the sense of entities, as such and in general.

Such an appropriate formulation can indeed be found in a generalization of Dummett's classical formulation of the logical structure of genuinely realist discourse about any domain. This formulation requires that statements within the relevant domain be seen, universally, as *bivalent:* that is, as determinately either true or false, quite independently of our knowledge of them as such or, more generally, our abilities to determine them as such. To adopt realism about a particular domain is thus, on Dummett's formulation, to apply the semantic analogue of the law of excluded middle universally across the domain, and accordingly to see the truth values of statements about its entities as determined, in principle, independently of any of our own epistemic capacities or procedures. Because realism is thus formulated as committing its adherent to such a view of the complete and bivalent determination of the truth values of sentences, it simultaneously commits the adherent to a similarly realist view of the determination of what we may term (along with Frege) their sense: that is, to a view on which the provision of sense for the relevant statements does not itself depend upon our own ways of providing sense for them, but rather on the ways the entities themselves are, or can be. As such, its formulation and maintenance, for a domain, will connect the sense of that domain's entities, in an appropriate way, to what Heidegger terms their "being."

If Dummett's schema is to be used to formulate a global realism about intentional sense of the sort contemplated in the last section, however, it must first be generalized in two ways. First, as we have seen, its appropriate formulation must be seen as schematizing the determination of sense, not only for some *particular* domain of entities or statements (such as, for instance, the domain of mathematical proofs, or statements about the past), but *globally*, that is, as bearing on the sense of *whatever is*, as such and in general, without restriction or limitation to any specific domain. And second, it must be extended, as we have seen, to take in not only the determination of the (linguistic) sense of terms and sentences of a natural language, but also, more basically, that of the presentational sense of entities as such, without regard to (linguistic or non-linguistic) modality. In the context of the discussion of the structure of a natural language – to which Dummett, like Frege, mainly restricts himself – the first extension naturally takes the form of the global bivalence of that language's *semantic* discourse: discourse, that is, *about* language, meaning, and (linguistic) truth. This includes, for example, sentences about the nature or structure of truth (in that language), as well as sentences quoting or referring to the meaning of other sentence; it also plausibly includes sentences involving intensional verbs applied to propositional constructions, such as those reporting or involving attributions of "propositional attitudes."

In each of these cases, the requisite extension, in the linguistic context, requires that the relevant semantic statements be seen as themselves determinately true or false, quite independently of our means of verifying or confirming them: what this reflects is that the sense of the language's terms and sentences is seen as determined in such a way as to track their relation to what there is or can be, rather than just the ways *we* represent things as being. But if, then, the second extension is made, so that bivalence is applied not only to semantic discourse about sentences, but rather globally to the broader structure of presentational sense as the disclosive truth of entities, we thereby gain an appropriate formulation of global realism about presentational sense, as grounded in realism about (what we may term) the being of those entities themselves.[12] Switching again to Heidegger's idiom, we can then understand the requisite realism also, and equally, as what we may term an "ontological" realism: realism, that is,

---

[12] In fact, as Dummett himself points out, (Dummett 1981, pp. 229–32), it is plausible that any conception of what is involved in knowing the sense of a singular term will require some account of the presentation of entities, couched on a more general and basic level than that of narrowly linguistic reference itself. Since, for example, to know or understand the (linguistic) sense of a proper name, for Frege, is to have an ability to recognize, as such, the object so named, we can pose the question of what is involved in this recognition; and this account will necessarily involve at least in part, in each case, the question of how the requisite entity is *itself* given or presented, such that this ability can be actualized. It is trivial, and thus empty, to say only that knowledge of the sense of "the morning star" requires the ability to recognize the morning star as the morning star; what is needed for a significant theory of sense is some account of how the recognition can be grounded in the presentation of a specific entity, or of the ways in which *precisely this* entity can show up or appear.

about (what Heidegger terms) "being," and about its difference from entities. This realism will then be naturally formulated as requiring, among other things, bivalence with respect to "ontological" discourse: discourse, that is (such as, but not limited to, Heidegger's own), about "being itself," about entities as such and as a whole, and about the relationship (of difference) between the two.

Of course, it is a main part of Dummett's own aim in introducing the connection of realism to bivalence to argue, in a variety of specific domains, rather for *anti-realism* about those domains. Thus, for example, in the case of mathematical number theory, statements about the past, and statements about sensations and putatively "private" contents of experience, among others, Dummett maintains or at least suggests jointly epistemologically- and semantically-motivated arguments leading to the conclusion that discourse about the relevant entities *cannot* be conceived as subject to the uniform requirement of bivalence, for meaningful discourse must be rather seen (on Dummett's individual arguments) as essentially constrained by the extent of our knowledge or epistemic procedures. Often, Dummett's reasoning for this involves an appeal to the consideration (which he supposes to be Wittgenstein's) that "meaning is determined by use": that is, that sense in the relevant domain can only be determined by means of our capacities and practices of linguistic usage, and therefore can go no further, in point of overall determinacy, than these capacities and practices do. The route from (what is supposed to be) a use-account of meaning to anti-realism about the provision of sense goes by way of a consideration of what is involved in our learning determinate practices of linguistic usage, or what can be manifest in intersubjective communication, within such practices, about the regularities governing this use. In either case, the decisive thought in motivating anti-realism is that the practices with respect to a domain, as themselves specified and determined in finite or otherwise restricted terms, cannot reasonably be seen as sustaining a globally realist (and hence globally bivalent) conception of the determination of truth-values in the domain.

However, this suggestion is in fact sufficiently overcome when we recall that our disclosive practices are *as* such (i.e., as genuinely *disclosive* practices) able to show entities in ways that are not simply determined by or contained within those practices, but are rather intelligibly grounded in their (i.e. the relevant entities') ways of being themselves. As such, they are grounded not only in our contingent practices but also, more basically and primarily, in the ontological difference between entities and their being. In particular, if our disclosive practices are not seen simply as various practical comportments, but rather, in the way suggested above, as further grounded in ontological difference itself, their results can readily be seen, in realist terms, as outstripping those practices themselves, in the sense that they are responsive to realities not simply constituted by, or within, them. Contrary to Dummett's anti-realist suggestion, there is, in other words, something "there," external to our practices themselves, which is such as to determine the truth or falsity of the claims that we make in the course of those practices. This is not to deny that the possibility of our comprehension of the senses of things is, typically and essentially, provided to us only through and in our acquisition of, and participation in, our practices of engaging those things. But it is to uphold the suggestion that, however finitely they are specified or specifiable, our disclosive practices themselves are (*qua* disclosive) typically "on to" realities that essentially outstrip them. These realities characterize the ways they really are or can be, and thus the practical disclosure of entities is itself amenable to a realist reading, as involving essentially these practices' (veridical or non-veridical) presentation of those entities themselves in the ways they, in fact and as a matter of their own sense, can be.

3

The realist picture that I have discussed so far has, at its core, a conception of what senses are: ways in which *whatever is* can be presented to thought. But for that reason, it also embodies a realist conception of this presentation itself: if (as their realist conception requires) senses themselves *are*, they, themselves, must belong, along with the thinking that presents beings by means of them, to *whatever is*. But then the thinking of *whatever is*, as such and in general, always takes place from some position, which is *itself* located within *it*, i.e., within *whatever is*. As this formulation suggests, though, realism about sense then implies a basic structure of formal-positional paradox, which must subsequently be seen as structurally characteristic, in general, of the thinking-being relationship itself. This paradoxical structure of the place of thinking, or of the reality of sense, formally determines the place at which or from which something like a presentation of the world can occur, the place at which the traditional concept of subjectivity is then, retrospectively, recognizable as inserting its figure.[13]

---

[13] To invoke such a formal position, along with its constitutive antinomy, is not to assume, however, the existence of a thinking subjectivity, or its necessity as a prior condition for anything whatsoever. This is because, as I argue in *The Logic of Being*, the relevant formal-positional antinomy is already sufficiently implied, quite independently of any assumptions about the existence of a subject or an actually thinking being, simply by a position of overall realism about the fact of temporal becoming; and this temporal realism, along with its formal structure, can be formulated quite independently of any requirement for an existent being, capable of thought.

This structural paradoxicality of the thinking-being relationship is, at bottom, the result of the unlimited generality of this relationship.[14] If being is, just as such, able to be thought, and conversely thought is, as such, the thought of what is, then there is no place left over, *outside* the being of whatever is, for an exterior position of something capable of thinking it. It follows from this that, if there is a position from which *whatever is* can be thought, this position must be located within *what is*; if there is sense, as the presentation of what is, this presentation must take place somewhere within, and not outside, what is. But then the being of thinking within what is, must be marked, both by an inherent formal indexicality which shows up in its having – and being able to present to itself – its "here," and a corresponding formal reflexivity which enjoins it to think it, itself, among the totality of whatever is. In this way, presentation must locate itself, simultaneously, both within the world it presents, and also, if it is able to present beings as such and in general, outside that world; the sense of things, or their being, will both have, and lack, being as something that is.

It follows that, if the senses of things *are* at all (but *that* they are is just the content of realism about them), then the position of thought with respect to whatever is, is from the start and irredeemably, contradictory.

This formal contradictoriness has a variety of more specific manifestations. For example, in the context of the characterization of (formal or natural) languages that include their own truth-predicate, it shows up as the semantic paradoxes, perhaps most characteristically, the Liar. As Tarski showed, for any language with sufficiently complete expressive resources and the ability to refer, in general, to its own sentences, the inclusion of a truth-predicate that functions in accordance with the disquotational T-schema will result in contradiction.[15] But since, as we saw above, one form of the requirement of realism about sense, for a natural language, is just the general maintenance of bivalence with respect to semantic discourse in that language (including, of course, discourse about truth) this recognition of the structural paradoxicality of such a language's own semantic discourse is evidently a direct consequence of just this realist attitude itself. The structural paradoxicality of sense is not, though, limited to language: in the phenomenological tradition, for instance, it shows up in the formal structure of the position of a reflexive intentionality which is

---

14 This is the generality characteristic of Parmenides' inaugural declaration of the "sameness" of thinking and being, and it is also evidently involved in the motivating idea of Aristotle's conception, at *Metaphysics* 1003a21, of metaphysics as a possible science (and hence thinking) of whatever is, as such, in its being (compare the argument of Sebastian Rödl's "The Metaphysical Project," this volume). Of course, neither Parmenides nor Aristotle notes the paradox explicitly.
15 Tarski (1933) and (1944).

conceived, already in Husserl, as allowing the reflective bracketing of the entirety of the natural world, and which receives fittingly antinomical formulation in Sartre's problematic discussions of the "detotalized totality" of the (officially impossible) overall relationship of the for-itself with the in-itself. Here, the constituting position of consciousness from which it is possible to gain reflective access to the totality, in principle, of presentational sense is at the same time both included in, and excluded from, the field of its reference, pointing to the paradox of its positioning in a way that is quite independent of Husserl's setting of it in the context of transcendental idealism. Once again, the formal situation remains the same with respect to the set-theoretical paradoxes, most notably Russell's paradox, which confirm the inconsistency of a principle of universal comprehension, or of the universal determination of extension by intension, whenever impredicativity and predicates designating the totality of extensions are permitted. Here again, the formal issues are not limited to the specific domain in which they show up – here, set theory – for they plausibly bear on the underlying structure of the relationship, in general, between a concept and what is comprehended by it, or on what it means for anything to "have" some property, to be some way, at all.[16]

As we have seen, if a realist theory of sense, as mode of presentation, is phenomenologically broadened beyond the narrowly linguistic context, this realism can take the form of the maintenance of bivalence with respect to *ontological* discourse: discourse, that is, about being, about what is as such and as a whole, and about the relation – the difference – between these two. In this case, however, each of the manifestations of its structural paradoxicality noted above can also be seen as grounded in the structural features of ontological difference and, most decisively, in the fact of its *own* contradictoriness.

The most direct way of showing this is by way of the defining articulation of ontological difference. This is the claim that "being (itself) is not an entity:" there is a difference between being, on one hand, and *whatever is*, as such and as a whole, on the other.[17] This claim attempts to articulate ontological difference as such, by indicating the distinction of being from entities as such and in general. But to maintain a realist attitude toward *it* is to assume that this claim has a determinate truth value: it is either true or false. However, as Dummett's framework shows, to maintain this assumption just is to assume that its truth value

---

[16] This will be explicit, in particular, if we understand the set-theoretical '$\in$' as capturing the general structure of predicative comprehension (whether linguistic or non-), or indeed of "being-as" something-or-other.

[17] For recent presentations of the structure of this paradox, see Priest (2002), chapter 15, and Casati (2017).

(whether true or false) is determined by *how things are* with the real referents of its (grammatically) referential terms; and one of these terms is "being" (itself). In other words, to treat a sentence which articulates the ontological difference as having bivalent sense is to treat "being" as a referential term, and thus as referring to *something that is*, i.e. something which is (in Heidegger's jargon) an entity. So to affirm the truth of the claim of difference is also to imply its falsity. Furthermore, if we take the claim of ontological difference simply to be false (while still construing it as meaningful), then we conclude that there is *no* difference between being and entities as a whole: that is, "being" just refers to the totality of entities, or the totality of whatever is.[18] Then, though, *this totality* both is and is not something within its own field, both (as we may put it) one among *those which are*, and not.

It follows that any realist discourse about the underlying basis or form of the sense of entities *as a whole* will be a contradictory one. Both being and ontological difference are locatable within that which is, and are not; they are entities, and are not; they exist, and they do not. As we have seen, moreover, the contradictoriness of such a discourse is just the result of the application of realism and bivalence, reflexively, to the statements that attempt to articulate, globally, that realism. In this way, the contradictoriness of the realist discourse follows, both semantically and ontologically, from the inherent positional contradiction involved in there being a real reflexive position, within what is, from which sense, as such, can be determined.

As a variety of realism, this might seem directly self-undermining. Does not the claim, about any domain, that an adequate conception of it requires inherent and unavoidable contradictions, indeed fly in the face of any possible attitude of realism about that domain? However, here it is essential to remember that realism, as Dummett formulates it, requires only that discourse about a particular domain be seen as (at least) bivalent: that is, that every statement about entities in the domain be seen as provided with a (i.e., *at least* one) determinate truth value (T or F), determined by the ways those entities are, or that the semantic analogue of the *law of excluded middle* be maintained for those statements. It is no part of this requirement, and neither is it in any evident way necessary for semantic realism as thus understood and formulated, further to require that none of these statements can be determined by their referents as *both* true *and* false, or that the semantic analogue of the *law of non-contradiction*

---

[18] In this case, the position is that of Parmenides' "One-All" and its essential paradoxes are those that Plato documents in rigorous detail in the deductions affirming the being of the One in the *Parmenides*.

be univocally maintained. Thus, it appears possible to suppose that referents in a particular domain are supplied in such a way as to fix truth-values independently of us, and *also* to suppose that this fixing allows for some statements about these referents to be *both* true *and* false. This kind of contradiction will then plausibly characterize, for example, any statements concerning the totality of facts, or truths: for instance, that "The world is all that is the case" will both *be* the case, and not. And given an underlying attitude of realism about the sense of the totality of whatever is, this supposition appears, with respect to ontological, phenomenological, and semantic discourse about senses in general, not only possible, but actually necessary.

4

What options remain open for the overall characterization of the constitution of sense, once the formal-positional paradox discussed in the last section is seen and appreciated? In each of its determinate forms as well as its underlying configuration, the formal-positional paradox evidently poses a dilemma on the level of overall theory between *completeness* and *consistency*. The contradiction is produced, with respect to the overall provision of sense, by way of the assumption that this provision must be *total* with respect to the domain of *all* referents, or of (in the Heideggerian jargon) "beings as such and as a whole." If, on the other hand, it is maintained that the provision of sense is *not* such as to bear on the totality of entities from a position wholly within it, there is no general reason to suppose that the position must be a contradictory one.

Formally speaking, there are, then, exactly two ways to maintain that it is, indeed, not such as to bear on the totality of entities. The first is to hold that the provision of sense does not bear on the totality of what there is, since it bears only on what is, within that totality, a limited or constrained range. The position from which sense is determined can then be seen as non-contradictory, but since it is, itself, exempted from the range for which sense is thereby determined, it cannot be realist about sense in an overall way: indeed, for the position of the provision of sense, the question of the sense of *its* (purported) being remains open, and indeed, cannot be formulated in any terms available to this conception itself. But the second option is to maintain that the provision of sense does not bear on the totality of what there is, not because it bears, rather, on some sub-totality within it, but rather because there is, or can be, no such totality at all: no such thing as the field, or whole, of whatever there is. This option, by precluding the overall positional paradox from arising, allows for the overall consistency of the provision of sense to be maintained even in its face.

When conjoined with a more specified account of the actual process of the provision of sense in each specific domain thereby constituted, it will require some variety of anti-realism about each such domain. But nevertheless, there is no evident reason why this consistency cannot be conjoined with *overall* bivalence – and hence, realism – about sense in general, as well as the formal position from which sense is itself supplied.

More broadly, the formally available options can be presented by means of a tabular schematism of "orientations of thought." These are figures of the relationship of finitely constituted thought to the infinity of whatever is, or of thinking-being relationship as such. Each of the orientations schematizes this relationship differently according to the ways it specifically understands and combines the overarching "meta-formal" ideas of reflexivity, completeness (or totality), and consistency.[19]

I here present the orientations, along with their formally defining features, and the indicative names of some representative figures of each; the implications of each with respect to possible realism about sense are summarized in italic text.

	Critical Orientations	*"Dogmatic" Orientations*
Post-Cantorian Orientations	Paradoxico-Critical:	Generic:
	Completeness, inconsistency	Consistency, incompleteness
	global immanent-ist realism	*global transcendental realism; local anti-realism*
	[Derrida, Deleuze, Lacan, Late Wittgenstein]	[Badiou, Gödel]
Pre-Cantorian Orientations	Constructivist:	Onto-Theological:
	global transcendental idealism; local (empirical) realism	*global transcendent-ist realism*
	[Kant, Carnap, Early Wittgenstein]	[Aristotle, Aquinas]

In the schema, the bottom two orientations – the "pre-Cantorian" or "sovereign" ones – have in common that they fail to problematize the combination, which

---

19 The terminology of "orientations of thought" is adapted from Badiou (2006), who effectively discerns three of the four discussed here, but does not recognize what I term the "paradoxico-critical" orientation. The possibility of understanding the space of possible orientations of thought – and especially those available today, after the Cantorian event – in terms of a centrally organizing "metalogical" duality of completeness and consistency was suggested to me by John Bova in discussions we had in 2008 and 2009. For related but different developments, see Bova (2016) and (2018).

they instead presuppose in different ways, of *completeness* and *consistency* with respect to the sense (or the thinkable being) of whatever is. Within the Onto-Theological orientation, this assumption of the conjunction of consistency and completeness takes the form of the combination of the assumption of a possible knowing of the being of whatever is with the enunciation of its "most firm" logical-metaphysical principle, that of the impossibility of contradiction. This means that the totality of the thinkable is here seen as both complete and consistent in itself, though necessarily beyond the grasp of finite cognition, which can only, at best, imperfectly approach it. Here, insofar as the question of sense is treated at all, it is seen as provided from the assumed position of a transcendency situated above or beyond this totality, but nevertheless capable of maintaining it as exhaustively determined and self-consistent, though necessarily obscure to situated and discursive thought. This is the orientation, then, of a "view from nowhere": a global realism that is maintained only at the (significant) cost of situating its source forever offstage, locating it instead as a theological one, beyond being, that necessarily exempts itself, for just that reason, from any possibility of description or discursive illumination.

By contrast with this, the constructivist (or criteriological) orientation, original with Kant, characteristically understands the provision of sense as taking place from a stable position *outside* the total field of (maximally determinate) sense thereby provided. Thus the field of maximally determined sense is seen as constituted, by thought, from an existent, stable, and thinkable (even if unknowable) position outside of it, whereas this position is still understood as one which *is* (and which is thereby governed by the principle of non-contradiction). Sense is thus seen as constituted *from* an essentially finite position – typically, that of a thinking subjectivity – while, owing to the exclusion of this position itself from the domain (or domains) of sense thus constituted, it is held immune from the effects of the reflexive-positional paradox. The result is that bivalence, and realism about sense, cannot be maintained globally with respect to the (larger) whole of *what is* in general and as such; it is, rather, only within the more restricted domain in which sense is maximally or completely determined that it is possible to maintain that truth values are (thereby) fully determinate. Thus, the position of the constructivist orientation combines a global or overall anti-realism (in Kant's terms, transcendental idealism) with a local (in Kant's terms, "empirical") realism.

Again, by marked contrast with both of these, both of the top two orientations – the paradoxico-critical and the generic – crucially acknowledge, and figure in a basic way in their motivation, the structure of reflexive paradox which (as Cantor was perhaps the first to see, despite his desperate attempts to deny it under the heading of a mysticism of the "unincreasable" or unthinkable absolute-infinite) henceforth disrupts any attempt to conjoin completeness and consistency with respect to the thought of whatever is.

The paradoxico-critical orientation does so by maintaining completeness on the level of its consideration of the *total* structure of sense while, at the same time, witnessing the irreducible contradictoriness of this structure, and the consequently paradoxical relationship that must then characterize, at a formal level, the thought-being relationship and the provision of overall sense. Here are to be located, then, the significant critical resources of a conception of the sense of words and things, in close relationship to the constitutive problems of temporality, as a "paradoxical entity" (Deleuze), as structured *essentially* by the paradoxical-temporal trace of an irreducibly deferring-differing *différance* (Derrida), or as always already inscribed in the essential undecidability of the relationship of a finitely comprehensible rule to the infinitude of the instances of its application (late Wittgenstein). What is crucial here, in each case, is that sense is always structured, just as such and at its "deepest" level, by the positional paradox of its provision and availability, one ultimately demanded by the paradoxical structure of temporality itself. The relationship between thinking and being involved in the provision of sense is, then, inconsistent overall, and the law of non-contradiction must be accordingly be denied. But it is then also entirely coherent, as we have seen, to maintain a global and thoroughgoing realism, affirming (that is) the law of the excluded middle, globally and throughout the whole of whatever is.

The generic orientation, on the other hand, maintains the formal consistency of the thought-being relationship overall while rejecting the idea of completeness or totality: there just is no such thing as the totality of thinkable beings, or the whole of all that can be thought, at all. In this way, consistency can be saved on the level of the determination of sense, even in the face of paradox: specifically, the reflexive paradox that results from the assumption of a position, within the field of what is, from which sense is provided for the whole of this field, is avoided simply by denying that there is any such total field. There is thus no such thing as providing sense, once and for all, across the whole of the totality of beings or of entities, and there is, for that reason, in general no reflexive problem with its (always-partial) provision for locally delimited domains, fields, or worlds. *Within* these local or delimited domains – or for the *entities* seen as appearing within them – bivalence and hence realism will be denied: the truth value, for instance, of a statement about an entity, involving a predicate whose sense is determined only in a particular field, will not be determined outside that field. But it is nevertheless possible to maintain an *overall* realism about sense: this is marked in the formal maintenance of bivalence, and hence full determinacy, on the *overall* level of the position from which sense is related to being, or the level on which the various more local fields are themselves structured and determined.

The commitments of the generic orientation appear, in contemporary thought, in a clearly defined way in the ontological projects of Alain Badiou – especially in the analyses of the (now) three volumes of *Being and Event* – as well as (with different inflections) Markus Gabriel, in his recent *Fields of Sense*. Both projects have in common that they begin with an inaugural declaration of the impossibility or incoherence of the world, universe, or totality of what is as such. In both cases, as well, the key arguments for this denial of the totality are premised directly on the paradoxes of reflexive totality. Thus (Badiou) the assumption of the existence of a universal set, or a set of all sets, leads directly to the contradiction of Russell's paradox and thus demands that there can be no such set; or (Gabriel) the idea of a list capable of referring to all entities undermines itself, owing to the existence of that very list: again, this shows that there can be no such list.[20] Furthermore, in both cases, the demonstrated contradictoriness of the assumption of such a totality – or of the unitary provision, at one stroke, of a sense for the whole of entities that are – is seen as decisively supporting, instead, the intuition of an irreducible *plurality* of fields or domains of sense, each understood as a relatively *local* field or domain of the presentation of entities, constraining the ways these entities can, within them, be or appear. At the same time, though, for both, this does not preclude an overall realist position about sense, itself: even as they are irreducibly structured by, and fully determinate only relative to, their specific fields, senses remain ways of presenting entities as they are, or can be; and the fields or worlds of appearance – of their determination – are themselves objective domains, thereby capable of defining (in Badiou's terms) an "objective phenomenology" that owes nothing to the constitutive being of a thinking or presentational subject.

Given, then, the apparent meta-formal availability of both the paradoxico-critical and the generic orientations, what, in general, can be said to decide between them? For the generic orientation, as we have seen, sense is related to being in an overall realist way, so that the sense of entities can always, and globally, reflect ways they actually are, or can be. As a consequence of this orientation's way of handling reflexive paradox, this global reflection is never able to be fully captured from any local position. But it is nevertheless essential for the orientation to be able to formulate it, at least in broad or overall terms, and thereby to clarify how it is that the senses of things are determined ultimately by the

---

[20] See, in particular, Badiou (1988), Meditations 1 and 3; Badiou (2006), pp. 109–111, and Gabriel (2015), pp. 17–18.

ways they are, or can be, even as these senses can show up always only partially, relative to specific domains. It is for this reason that, despite its inaugural and essential denial of the being of the "one-all," the generic orientation nevertheless necessarily invokes, on the level of the being-thinking relationship, something like a background structure which itself functions, in relation to the determination of sense, as a kind of metaphysical absolute, by contrast with (always-local) appearing itself. This is the significance, in Badiou's project, of the guiding and always-essential theorization of being, insofar as it *can* be presented by means of ZFC set theory, itself situated within a classical-logical framework. Similarly, in Gabriel's project, despite the relativization of determinate appearance to fields, it is nevertheless affirmed that an object can be ontologically identified with the totality of truths about it, across the different fields in which it can occur; and hence, with its being, in radical traversal of any of the various domains in which it may appear. This means that the idea of such a totality of truths or descriptions, characteristic of each entity on the level of what Gabriel calls its "governing" sense, must be able to be invoked, at least abstractly and generically, in order for the identity of a thing itself to be understood: this totality, even if it is not specifiable or knowable as such, must in some way be "there," borne by the entity itself, wherever, and in whatever fields or relations, it may appear.

For the generic orientation, then, being and appearance are never wholly on the same level: ontological difference is here maintained as neither global nor local inconsistency, but rather as the mobile or "functional" difference between fields and the entities appearing within them. Even when – as in Badiou – the level of localized appearance is seen as capable of producing, through the dynamism of its own paradoxical structure, a kind of transformative "retroaction" on the structure of being itself, still the formalism itself requires that the levels of being and appearance – ontology and phenomenology – remain essentially separate, both formally and logically. Thus, the generic orientation remains committed, after all, to some variety of that dualism of the existent and its appearances which Sartre declared, on the first page of *Being and Nothingness*, no longer to be "entitled to any legal status" within philosophy, ever since the "considerable progress" attained by phenomenological thought in reducing the one to the other.[21]

By contrast with this, as we have seen, for the paradoxico-critical orientation there is, in general, no distinction to be drawn, either globally or locally, between the ways an entity can intelligibly appear and the ways it is, or can be. This is the

---

21 Sartre, *Being and Nothingness*, pp. 3–4.

source of the neutrality of the kind of realism about sense which it is thereby able to propound: the sense of a thing is, here, not to be understood as relative to specified fields or domains, but is rather just characteristic of the entity itself, as it is or can be. There is thus no need for the orientation to differentiate between levels, as the generic orientation does, or to modulate being and appearance according to any overall differentiation at all.

To this it will be objected, from the generic side, that on the level of the structure of sense, the paradoxico-critical orientation, avoiding such an overall dualism, nevertheless invokes what is an even more problematic "metaphysical" absolute – namely, that of the presumed unitary totality of entities, universe, or world – which the generic orientation, by contrast, denies at a basic level. This unity is at least reminiscent of the Onto-Theological one, that is, of the assumed unity of a jointly total and consistent domain of "beings as such and as a whole" that characterizes theological thought of the absolute since Parmenides, and is more broadly, according to Heidegger, characteristic of the history of metaphysics and the obscurity of the ontological difference as such.

But as we have in fact already seen, the neutrality of the paradoxico-critical orientation's realism about sense already suffices to establish its radical formal distinction from metaphysics, either in its Onto-Theological or constructivist forms. By maintaining such a neutral but paradoxical realism, not only about sense as such but also about the position of its constitution or availability, it is radically distinguished from the Eleatic assumption of the unity of being and thinking in the figure of the presumption of the *consistent* whole; as well as, equally, from the neo-Platonic attempt to solve the constitutive paradoxes of this unity (to the documentation of which, without attempted resolution, Plato rather devoted the strenuous exercises of the *Parmenides*) by means of the essentially theological invocation of a mystical, transcendent One. Because of this radical and formally required distinction, the interest of the paradoxico-critic can never lie in anything like the positive projects of metaphysics: never, that is, in verifying, maintaining, or articulating the *consistency* of the (assumed) unity of thinking and being, but rather, in adumbrating the consequences of their formal mutual incompatibility, or of the real incommensurability with themselves that must then radically characterize the overall structures of sense, truth, and the being of whatever is. It is thus that paradoxico-criticism can venture terms of critique which go all the way to the very sense of what is involved in the thinking of being at all, and thus bear radically not only on metaphysics but, more basically, on the sense of truth, meaning, and being as these enter into the ordinary pursuit of our lives and practices. And it is only by posing such terms that it can then offer a formally radical basis for the critique of any picture of the world – including, decisively, that which forms the ideological, material, and real basis for contemporary capitalist life and practice – that fundamentally operates by propounding the self-consistent decidability of such a whole, and holding it concretely in force.

Bibliography

Badiou, Alain (2005 [1988]): *Being and Event*. Transl. by Oliver Feltham. London: Continuum.
Badiou, Alain (2009 [2006a]): *Logics of Worlds: Being and Event II*. Translated by Alberto Toscano. London: Continuum.
Badiou, Alain (2006b): *Briefings on Existence: A Short Treatise on Transitory Ontology*. Translated by Norman Madarasz. Albany: State University of New York Press.
Bova, John (2016): *A Metalogical Approach to Platonic Dialectic*. Ph.D. Dissertation, Villanova University.
Brentano, Franz (1995 [1874]): *Psychology From an Empirical Standpoint*. Translated by Antos C. Rancurello, D. B. Terrell, and Linda L. McAlister. London: Routledge.
Casati, Filippo (2017): *Being: A Dialetheic Interpretation of the Late Heidegger*. Ph.D. Dissertation, University of St. Andrews School of Philosophical, Anthropological, and Film Studies.
Dummett, Michael (1978 [1963]): *Truth and Other Enigmas*. London: Duckworth.
Dummett, Michael (1981): *Frege: Philosophy of Language*. 2nd ed. Cambridge, MA: Harvard University Press.
Dummett, Michael (1993 [1982]): "Realism." In *The Seas of Language*. Oxford: Clarendon.
Evans, Gareth (1981): "Understanding demonstratives." In: Herman Parret (Ed.): *Meaning and Understanding*. Oxford: Clarendon, pp. 280–304.
Evans, Gareth (1982): *The Varieties of Reference*. Oxford: Clarendon.
Føllesdal, Dagfinn (1969): "Husserl's notion of noema." *Journal of Philosophy* 66 (20): 680–687.
Gabriel, Markus (2015): *Fields of Sense: A New Realist Ontology*. Edinburgh: Edinburgh University Press.
Heidegger, Martin (2006 [1929]): *Sein und Zeit*, 19th Auflage. Tübingen: Max Niemeyer Verlag. Translated by John Macquarrie and Edward Robinson as *Being and Time* (San Francisco: Harper San Francisco, 1962).
Livingston, Paul (2017): *The Logic of Being: Realism, Truth, and Time*. Evanston, IL: Northwestern University Press.
Sartre, Jean-Paul (1984 [1943]): *Being and Nothingness: A Phenomenological Essay on Ontology*. Translated by Hazel E. Barnes. New York: Washington Square Press.
Smith, David W. (2016): "Truth and Époché: The Semantic Conception of Truth in Phenomenology." In Jeffrey A. Bell, Andrew Cutrofello, and Paul M. Livingston (Eds.): *Beyond the Analytic-Continental Divide: Pluralist Philosophy in the Twenty-First Century*. New York: Routledge, 111–128.

Graham Harman
Realism without Hobbes and Schmitt: Assessing the Latourian Option

Abstract: The essay contrasts "realism" in the usual sense (of referring to the existence of a reality outside the human mind) with Harman's own Object-Oriented Ontology, which broadens the meaning of the term to refer to the existence of a reality outside any relation, including inanimate causal relations. The idea here is that the real is a surplus that is never quite reflected in any actual state of the world. In political theory, "realism" generally refers to a "hardcore" actualist theory of politics, represented prominently by Thomas Hobbes and the later Carl Schmitt, that tries to get rid of hypocritical high-minded ideals, instead looking at political power in the way it actually works. Again by contrast with this, Harman defends a different sense of political realism, consistent with Object-Oriented Ontology and represented by recent works of Bruno Latour, according to which our understanding of politics must acknowledge both the inherent fallibility of our understanding of the world and the relevance of non-human actors and agencies to political problems and actions.

1 Two Senses of Realism

This article will argue for political realism in a sense very different from the usual one of cold, hard *Realpolitik*. To do so, I will argue that Bruno Latour's recent writings on climate politics resonate in important ways with the concerns of Object-Oriented Ontology (OOO) (Harman 2018). "Realism," of course, is one of many important theoretical terms that can mean different things depending on the field in which it is used. Yet it is one of the few such terms that can also mean *opposite* things in different contexts; thus, it goes beyond the common scenario of the incalculable polysemia of a word. For there are in fact just two basic meanings of "real," depending on what we take to be its most important contrary term.

In a first sense, "real" means the opposite of "imaginary." When we tell someone to wake up and get back to reality, shaking them out of "unrealistic" thinking, we are trying to alert them to unpleasant brute facts that they need to take into account. They are thirty-nine years old and still living with their parents; their alcohol or gambling problem is out of control; they are working a dead-end job, still hoping pathetically that their rock band strikes it rich.

Such warnings, of course, also occur on the geopolitical rather than the personal level, as when anti-Brexit citizens of the United Kingdom argue that there will no longer be a reliable insulin supply after their departure from the European Union; or when someone floats the unpleasant prospect that India, with its billion citizens, might be uninhabitable within decades due to global warming. Admittedly, it is not always obvious who has the best handle on reality in any given case. To give one recent example, most educated Americans thought it impossible that the documented lifelong con artist Donald Trump could possibly be nominated by the Republican Party for President, and once he was we were sure that he would take that Party down in flames in ludicrous defeat. In that instance, of course, the joke was on us: a painful jest from which the United States has not yet recovered. In any case, we know the type of political realism that emerges from this sense of the term. It belittles naively idealistic motivations in global affairs in favor of a cool calculation of stability and national interest. Like nearly any political standpoint, this one has its golden moments, though at times it can seem alarmist in retrospect. Consider the following passage by the thoughtful conservative philosopher Eric Voegelin concerning the aftermath of the Second World War:

> If a war has a purpose at all, it is the restoration of a balance of forces and not the aggravation of disturbance; it is the reduction of the unbalancing excess of force, not the destruction of force to the point of creating a new unbalancing power vacuum. Instead the [liberal] politicians have put the Soviet army on the Elbe, surrendered China to the Communists, at the same time demilitarized Germany and Japan, and in addition demobilized our own [American] army... [I]t is perhaps not sufficiently realized that never before in the history of mankind has a world power used a victory deliberately for the purpose of creating a power vacuum to its own disadvantage. (Voegelin 1987, p. 172)

The same has often been said of the more recent American wars in Afghanistan and Iraq, which created two separate power vacuums on the borders of Iran, despite many American military theorists viewing the latter country as the real long-term threat.

From this type of realist standpoint, since the world is filled with frail humans rather than angels, we should not expect the earth to be a paradise, but must steel ourselves against the grim unchanging truths of human nature. As Voegelin laments further: "practically every great political thinker who recognized the structure of reality, from Machiavelli to the present, has been branded as an immoralist by [liberal] intellectuals..." (Voegelin 1987, p. 170). We might call this attitude Cold Shower Realism, since it is always deployed in an effort to scold someone's daydreaming failure to be in contact with the way the world really is rather than how they wish it to be. Its usual political target is the naïve idealist who too quickly assumes that ours could be a world of peace and justice if everyone would just put aside their petty differences and dethrone the corrupt corporate and military interests that manufacture conflict for their own benefit. Against these purportedly sweet but gullible Pollyannas, the Cold Shower Realist insists on recognizing the way things really are.

Yet there is a second and opposite sense of "realism." It is one that does not take facts on the ground to be the ultimate reality, but merely a superficial and transient appearance, or even an immoral or untruthful one. Here the target of criticism is not the gullible dreamer, but the one who is *too* focused on mere present-day realities. The critic driven by this second sense of realism calls our attention to deeper underlying realities, beyond the sphere of contemporary fact, that the Cold Shower Realist fails to take into account. One example occurs when some on the Israeli Left argue that demographic realities require a different national security approach than the continued deployment of crushing military superiority, which is likely to prove less feasible under demographic conditions several decades from now. Here again, this sort of realist is not always right: we recall the grim but inaccurate predictions about the Y2K computer bug causing global chaos on the first day of the year 2000, and similar if lesser worries about the introduction of the Euro in 2002. In any case, this is a second and different form of realism, one that looks beyond appearances toward the supposedly deeper factors in a situation not currently registered in its balance of forces, either because they have not yet emerged or because by nature they can never fully emerge. We thus call this version the Realism of Depth, since it is fixed on something deeper than the actual, whether it be optimistic or pessimistic in spirit.

Cold Shower Realism is the sort we generally find proclaimed in artistic movements and manifestoes. Literary realism wants to replace romantic and heroic narratives with detailed, sometimes disgusting portraits of the way things supposedly really are. Émile Zola does this so comprehensively that Nietzsche famously describes his writing as a "delight in stinking" (Nietzsche 1997, p. 51). Upton Sinclair's *The Jungle* gave such a repellent portrait of the American meat-packing industry that new regulations were demanded and finally imposed (Sinclair 1906). Realist painters did something similar, giving us de-idealized portraits of lower-class suffering and the undistinguished grind of peasant life; Michael Fried's book *Courbet's Realism* shows us some of the technical aspects that this shift entailed (Fried 1990). By contrast, the Realism of Depth turns its back on what seems to be the reality of present experience and digs for something beyond what meets the eye. Plato seeks the otherworldly perfect forms of which the imperfect entities of everyday life are pale copies or gloomy shadows. Likewise, Platonist mathematicians – who make up a majority in their field –

consider mathematical objects to have a real existence over and above their instantiation in practical life or in our minds. Among current realist philosophies, OOO is distinguished by its insistence that objects are real not only "outside the mind," but outside any relation with other objects whatsoever. In this way, OOO finds reality in a place that no fact on the ground can ever possibly express (Harman 2011).

When it comes to politics, we have already had a glance at Voegelin's balance-of-power version of realism. More generally, when speaking of realism in international relations theory, we are speaking of a Cold Shower Realism stripped of all rosy delusions, as in the work of Hans Morgenthau (1950), academic mentor of Henry Kissinger. Political realists are seen as hard-headed strategists who focus on what is genuinely possible rather than on ideal conditions and optimistic scenarios. This is why political realism is so frequently found in the company of geographical determinism: "England has no eternal allies or enemies, but only eternal interests," as Palmerston's words are often simplified to say, since England is a relatively safe island nation historically focused on obstructing whichever continental power – usually France or Germany, but sometimes Russia – has had the upper hand at any given time (Palmerston 1848). The United States is essentially an island naval power like England, due to the comparative weakness of its land neighbors Canada and Mexico throughout American history. Under conditions of rising Canadian or Mexican militancy, American strategy would probably veer more towards a continental European balance of power policy rather than its familiar long-term swings between isolation and intervention, both of which are tinged with a specific form of moralism known as "American exceptionalism." Strategic and geographic conditions are seen to change slowly when contrasted with the ongoing human pageant of shifting political incident and changing individual leaders. American governments of whatever political party will likely continue to support Israel, South Korea, and the United Kingdom, and will usually oppose both Russia and whichever East Asian country is strongest: currently China, though recently enough it was Japan.

Obviously, a great deal of modern political theory has not been realist at all, even in those cases when it calls itself "materialist." Although modern political discussions tend to revolve around the polarity between Left and Right that arose during the French Revolution, I have argued elsewhere that there is a more important distinction cutting across these two: namely, that between what I have called Truth Politics and Power Politics (Harman 2014). The former group thinks itself to be already aware of the ideal political form, which is prevented from coming into existence only by one or more unfortunate factors: usually class conflict or more general corruption in government or society. The most obvious examples of this attitude in the modern period are found on the Left, with Rousseau and Marx coming immediately to mind (Rousseau 1992, Marx 1992). But we find Truth Politicians on the Right as well, as when the late Straussian philosopher Stanley Rosen writes that for Nietzsche (though more for Rosen himself), "there cannot be a radically unique creation... The fundamental task is one of rank-ordering [human] types that have always occurred and will always exist" (Rosen 2004, p. 5). We also find countless Truth Politicians in the pre-modern era, with Plato and al-Farabi being among the most prominent modellers of ideal cities, however literally or not they may have been intended. By contrast, Power Politics amounts to the claim that there is no transcendent truth governing the political sphere, so that the only political truth is the immanent struggle for power itself, and to the victor go the spoils. Prominent in this group are such figures as Machiavelli (1992), Hobbes (1996), and Schmitt (1996). But we will see that there is an important difference between Hobbes and Schmitt, and that neither figure gives us the sort of political realism we need.

Finally, I would also mention two authors who have an interesting relation to these Power Politicians without quite belonging to their group. The first is the aforementioned Voegelin, a Christian thinker who is more deeply committed to transcendence than any of the Machiavelli/Hobbes/Schmitt trio (including Schmitt, also a Christian), but who adds that transcendence should be restricted to spiritual and intellectual life, given the danger of all attempts to "immanentize the eschaton" in the political sphere (Voegelin 1987, p. 121).

The second exceptional author, not often read as a political philosopher, is Bruno Latour. His ontology, widely implemented in the social sciences as Actor-Network Theory (ANT), is committed to the sheer immanence of actors entering and exiting from networks, consisting in nothing more than the sum total of their actions, with no unexpressed surplus in things beyond what they actually do (Latour 2005). For this reason, it should come as no surprise that the young Latour sings the praises of such remorseless political theorists of immanence as Machiavelli and Hobbes (Callon & Latour 1981). In *We Have Never Been Modern*, Latour describes the Hobbesian stance nicely:

> Civil wars will rage as long as there exist supernatural entities that citizens feel they have a right to petition when they are persecuted by the authorities of this lower world. The loyalty of the old medieval society – to God and King – is no longer possible if all people can petition God directly, or designate their own King. Hobbes wanted to wipe the slate clean of all appeals to entities higher than civil authority. (Latour 1993, p. 19)

Yet his previous approval of this immanent standpoint is abandoned in the very same work: for here Latour finds his mature voice in a surprising *attack* on Hobbes, with the claim that immanent political force is no less subject to deconstruction than scientific truth (Latour 1993). Less than a decade later, Latour already insists – against the Hobbesian doctrine he once adored – on the need for the *polis* to detect those entities that transcend it (Latour 2004). This includes both the work of scientists in discovering new entities, and that of the moralists in championing those who have previously been excluded: two classes of humans feared by Hobbes as disturbers of civil peace. Latour eventually comes to agree with John Dewey (2012) that, far from being a purely immanent affair, politics involves coming to temporary consensus about issues that are never fully clear to anyone: a liberal attitude toward compromise combined with a metaphysical doubt about the very possibility of transparent political knowledge (Latour 2013). This residual lack of clarity in issues of political dispute opens a window beyond immanence like nothing else in Latour's philosophy, and puts him somewhere beyond the reach of Power Politics, while also separating him from Truth Politicians who think they can grasp the very essence of political matters. Yet Latour also belongs outside the usual Left-Right polarity, in which both sides are largely defined by their view of human nature as either inherently good or evil, respectively. Evidence for this can be found in the uniquely pivotal role Latour grants in his political theory to non-human objects, which act as important stabilizers in the political realm (Strum & Latour 1987). This is another issue to be considered below.

In any case, the meaning of this article's title is as follows. There is something to be said for the differing Cold Shower Realisms of Hobbes and Schmitt, which help to dispel the excessive idealism found in many forms of contemporary political theory. Yet the excessive immanence of their realism gives it too much the aspect of a mere struggle for survival *hic et nunc*, and makes a poor fit with the metaphysical realism advocated by OOO. In what follows, a first section will be devoted to Hobbes and Schmitt, as well as an important contrast drawn between their positions by the conservative political philosopher Leo Strauss on behalf of knowledge or truth. A second section will consider the benefits of Latour's own unorthodox realism in politics, laying stress on his recent work *Down to Earth*, in which climate politics is plausibly defined as our new collective horizon (Latour 2018).

2 Schmitt and Hobbes

Latour once stated for the record, in London, that it "is a common thing in political philosophy, that reactionary thinkers are more interesting than the progressive ones… in that you learn more about politics from people like Machiavelli and Schmitt than from Rousseau" (Latour, Harman, & Erdélyi 2011, p. 96). Although Latour does not specify the source of this maxim, it seems probable that it was the apparently sinister Nazi-supporter Schmitt. Though it is common for Leftists to admire Schmitt's conception of politics as existential struggle – against the "bourgeois" liberal preference for individual economic and intellectual freedom within a relatively de-politicized sphere – Latour is the rare liberal who frequently looks to Schmitt as a political North Star. While this passing salute to "reactionaries" may seem to mark a reversion by Latour to the Hobbesian stance of his early career, there is a crucial difference between Schmitt and Hobbes, one that colors Latour's own recent political writings. Let's begin with Schmitt, even though he is later than Hobbes chronologically.

Schmitt opens Section 7 of his 1932 work *The Concept of the Political* with a statement that sounds a great deal like Latour's London formula. There we read as follows: "One could test all theories of state and political ideas according to their anthropology and thereby classify these as to whether they consciously or unconsciously presuppose man to be by nature evil or by nature good... [by their] answer to the question whether man is a dangerous being or not, a risky or a harmless creature" (Schmitt 1996, p. 58). There are at least three separate things going on in this brief statement. First, Schmitt declares himself to be one of what Latour calls the "reactionaries," in opposition to liberals who think that mutual economic interest, abstract humane principles, and theoretical debate should ultimately be enough to bring humanity together. There is little surprise here, and no one familiar with the spirit of Schmitt's writings would expect otherwise. Second, Schmitt does not divide the world into morally good and evil individuals, but rather sees every *people* as potentially dangerous to every other: as a possible existential threat to a people's own way of life. Here again, liberals are Schmitt's target, given their tendency to wage war only in the name of abstract causes such as human rights: as in the case of the Allied Powers in World War I, who saw it as a war for democracy and the right of self-determination, as a "war to end all wars." Schmitt objects that this sort of war on principle tends to dehumanize one's enemies, depicting them as monsters and justifying their outright annihilation rather than mere defeat. Third – and here is Schmitt's Cold Shower Realist moment – there is his famous principle that "the specific political distinction to which political actions and motives can be reduced is that between friend and enemy" (Schmitt 1996, p. 26).

Only the sovereign – defined here as the state – can determine the enemy, who is understood in an existential sense as one who seeks to destroy our way of life. No moral principle can surmount this fundamental distinction between friend and enemy, and therefore the political marks the summit of human existence, given that physical death at the hands of the enemy is the ultimate concrete possibility for each of us. As for the Christian injunction to love one's enemies, Schmitt flatly denies its relevance to the political sphere: "Never in the thousand-year struggle between Christians and Moslems did it occur to a Christian to surrender rather than defend Europe out of love toward the Saracens or Turks" (Schmitt 1996, p. 29). Even the tolerance defended by Locke (1983) is not liberal enough to include Muslims, and though liberal tolerance today is far broader in scope than Locke's early modern version, no Western liberal of our time would accept living under the self-described Caliphate of ISIS or the Kim regime in North Korea. Liberals would immediately embrace death-struggle with these entities if they were to threaten us directly, and would simply moralize the struggle into one of good versus evil. On the same note, it is well known that the United States has difficulty waging conflict without demonizing the leaders of its enemies, even while insisting to the world that it does not hate the German, Japanese, Russian, Vietnamese, Afghani, or Iraqi people per se.

Though Schmitt cannot receive the full treatment he deserves here, a few additional words are in order. He is well aware that existential struggle with the enemy can also occur *within* a given polity rather than between two separate states, as in cases of civil war, and even considers the possibility of a global class war of the sort envisaged by Marx. For this reason, Slavoj Žižek is unfair with his Marxist complaint that Schmitt "already displaces the *inherent* antagonism constitutive of the political on to the *external* relationship between Us and Them," (Žižek 1999, p. 27) rather than focusing as one should on the class struggle. Schmitt's formula tying politics above all to the threat of death is not aimed – as with Hobbes – at the death of distinct individuals, but at that of the group. Thus, "[i]n case of need, the political entity must demand the sacrifice of life. Such a demand is in no way justified by the individualism of liberal thought… For the individual as such there is no enemy with whom he must enter into a life-and-death struggle if he personally does not want to do so" (Schmitt 1996, p. 71). Finally, the formula of existential threat is a "realist" one in the sense that it points to what lies radically outside one's polity or faction, in a thoroughly "non-immanent" sense. The sort of realism that impresses Schmitt is the kind found in those clear-headed thinkers who have been able to recognize the enemy concretely. He cites examples: "the fanatical hatred of Napoleon felt by the German barons Stein and Kleist… Lenin's annihilating sentences against bourgeois and western capitalism. All these are surpassed by Cromwell's enmity towards papist Spain" (Schmitt 1996, p. 67). At the opposite pole of such clarity, "the incapacity or unwillingness to make this distinction [between friend and enemy] is a symptom of the political end," as with the naïve French and Russian aristocracies who romanticized the very social classes who were about to destroy them (Schmitt 1996, p. 68). In Schmitt's eyes, such struggle for survival is the sole place where the political can be found; any fantasies about a future benevolent world government have nothing to do with our present concrete existence.

In his staunch opposition to liberal idealism, Schmitt certainly qualifies as a Cold Shower Realist. The question is whether he remains in this position, or whether he also attempts a further step into what I have called a Realism of Depth, a position from which – we will see – Strauss criticizes his work. Schmitt tends to view struggle between peoples as a matter of survival rather than principles, the latter serving mostly to provide hypocritically idealistic cover for an existential death match with the enemy beyond good and evil. If Thrasymachus in Plato's *Republic* views justice cynically as "the advantage of the stronger," Schmitt sees justice as beside the point, and treats struggle as the attempt to ensure the survival of one's own people as a whole (Plato 1992, 338c). Yet it is not difficult to imagine a situation in which citizens of one nation decide that justice is on the side of their enemy in a particular conflict, on the basis of transcendent principles of the sort that Schmitt excludes through his doctrine of war as existential struggle; widespread American opposition to the war in Vietnam is one obvious example. Is Schmitt's immanent focus on the survival of a people enough to count as political realism in more than the unapologetic Cold Shower sense? Whether or not one is persuaded by the essentials of Schmitt's doctrine, it seems clear that he cannot pass the realist test, since the enemy counts as nothing more than a traumatic Other that must be repulsed at all costs. It is somewhat reminiscent of "the Real" in the psychoanalysis of Jacques Lacan, which does not have an autonomous existence outside the symbolic and imaginary orders, but functions only as an immanent impasse or breakdown in these orders (Lacan 2005). Although the trauma for Schmitt comes from the outside rather than from within one's own national or social group, he strips us of the ability to come to terms with what lies beyond except through defeating it; he also silently consolidates the human realm as an immanent sphere constituted by the darkness of human nature and closed off to non-human entities. Lacan – much like the German idealist philosopher J.G. Fichte (1982) – is a "traumatist" without being a realist, and I would say the same about Schmitt.

Let's turn briefly to another of Latour's reactionaries, Thomas Hobbes, who seems at first glance to have much in common with Schmitt. The possibility of violent death is the foundation of Hobbes's political philosophy as well. It is not only the weak who must fear death, since "as to the strength of body, the weakest has strength enough to kill the strongest, either by secret machination, or by confederacy with others, that are in the same danger with himself" (Hobbes 1996, p. 82). He identifies three causes of war among humans: the love of gain, the fear of loss, and the desire for reputation. All are sufficiently intense that "during the time men live without a common power to keep them all in awe, they are in that condition which is called war; and such a war, as is of every man, against every man" (Hobbes 1996, p. 84). War leaves no room for cultivation of the earth, for commerce and industry, or for arts and letters, leading to a situation of "continual fear, and danger of violent death; and the life of man [is] solitary, poor, nasty, brutish, and short" (Hobbes 1996, p. 84). There can be no relevant conception of justice in this bellicose state of nature, given that "[f]orce, and fraud, are in war the two cardinal virtues" (Hobbes 1996, p. 85).

Justice exists only on the interior of a society already established, and to attain such a peaceful condition requires that certain sacrifices be made. For "as long as the natural right of every man to every thing endureth, there can be no security to any man (how strong or wise however he be) of living out the time which nature ordinarily alloweth every man to live" (Hobbes 1996, p. 87). And thus it is required "that a man be willing, when others are too… to lay down [the] right to all things; and be contented with so much liberty against other men, as he would allow other men against himself" (Hobbes 1996, p. 87; emphasis removed). Hence "there must be some coercive power, to compel men equally to the performance of their covenants, by the terror of some punishment, greater than the benefit they expect by the breach of their covenant…" (Hobbes 1996, pp. 95–96). This power, the commonwealth or "great Leviathan," emerges when everyone renounces their natural right to self-rule, so that the sovereign "hath the use of so much power and strength conferred on him, that by terror thereof, he is enabled to conform to the wills of them all, to peace at home, and mutual aid to their enemies abroad" (Hobbes 1996, p. 114). The natural right of individuals to preserve themselves from harm is retained as long as no else is harmed, but any appeal to a transcendent outside is excluded. Note that what Hobbes finds threatening is not only religious transcendence, but the transcendence claimed by scientific truth as well, as recounted in an important book by Steven Shapin and Simon Schaffer (2011) on the rivalry between Hobbes and the chemist Robert Boyle.

This quick summary of the respective standpoints of Schmitt and Hobbes has already revealed important similarities between the two. Above all, both have a pessimistic assessment of human nature. Both are preoccupied with the danger of sudden death, and end up defending authoritarian systems of government as a bulwark against this danger. Beyond this, Schmitt and Hobbes alike want peace at home while permitting the most rampant violence in conflicts between nations, as if the state of nature were still in force when it comes to foreign affairs. Yet there are crucial differences as well. Despite his negative view of human nature, Hobbes can plausibly be called the founder of liberalism due to his exclusive delegation of politics to the sovereign and the creation of an internal space of peace (Strauss 1996). By contrast, Schmitt is an explicit anti-liberal, someone who apparently *wants* humans to face up seriously to the existential danger at the root of human life, rather than remaining safely engaged in a peaceful zone of cultural and economic development. There is also the important detail of Hobbes's liberal stress on the individual right to self-preservation and the *voluntary* character of military service, whereas Schmitt's group-oriented stance emphasizes the sovereign right to demand the sacrifice of individual life.

But where do Schmitt and Hobbes stand on the realist question, the topic of the present article? We know, at the very least, that realism in politics as in philosophy requires dealing with an outside rather than remaining enclosed within one's own immanent sphere. And here Strauss finds both thinkers the same in their lack of focus on *truth*, the ultimate access to what lies beyond immanence. As Strauss puts it:

> whereas the liberal respects and tolerates all '*honest*' convictions, so long as they merely acknowledge the legal order, *peace*, as sacrosanct, he who affirms the political as such respects and tolerates all '*serious*' convictions, that is, all decisions oriented to the real possibility of *war*. Thus [Schmitt's] affirmation of the political as such proves to be a liberalism with the opposite polarity. (Strauss 1996, p. 120)

The way out of this dilemma, for Strauss, is to seek the outside in the form of political *knowledge:* "the life-and-death quarrel: the political – the grouping into friends and enemies – owes its legitimation to the seriousness of the question of what is right" (Strauss 1996, p. 118). In other words, Schmitt remains a kind of Thrasymachus as long as he makes no search for truth beyond the arbitrariness of the sovereign decision. This is why Schmitt is often called a "decisionist," and a link could easily be established with Heidegger's principle of resoluteness, in which firm commitment to any life decision is more important than the specific content of any such decision (Heidegger 1962, p. 278).

We now have what looks like a continuum running from least to most realist positions among the authors we have mentioned, as follows:

Less Realist
- Liberal idealism. Too optimistic about human nature and wrongly committed to the idea of humans as indefinitely improvable.
- Hobbesian liberalism. Walls off the citizenry from direct contact with the perilous state of nature, but at least (unlike liberal idealism) is clear-headed about the dire character of human nature.
- Lacan and Fichte. More open to our direct contact with the Real than Hobbes, but only in the form of an immanent breakdown or resistance of

the Real to our efforts. This is "traumatism," not realism, since here the real is known only as that which obstructs or contests us.
- Schmitt. Open to direct contact with a reality that is not just immanent, but transcends us in the shape of a dangerous foreign element that might cost us our lives: namely, the enemy.
- Voegelin. Transcendent truth may be attainable in spiritual and intellectual matters, but not in the political sphere.
- Strauss. It is possible to make direct contact with a reality that can in principle be known, in the form of true political content.

More Realist

Nonetheless, it seems to me that Strauss is not a political realist in the best sense of the term any more than are Hobbes or Schmitt. It is true that philosophical realism often implies not only that something exists "outside the mind," but also that this outside can be known. This is the sort of realism defended, for instance, by my New Realist friends Maurizio Ferraris (2014) and Markus Gabriel (2015), who are opposed, above all else, to relativism. Yet the idea that one can have knowledge of the real implies the non-Socratic claim that beyond *philosophia* (or love of wisdom) we can directly attain *sophia* (or wisdom itself). Reality is what it is, and to translate it into knowable terms will always require a good degree of distortion or simplification; the form of a thing cannot be neatly extracted from the matter in which it inheres and transported into our brains without alteration. A form cannot be moved from one place to another without transformation, whether we are speaking of knowledge or mere causal interaction between mindless things. For this reason I would be inclined to move Strauss somewhat further back on our realist list, perhaps even midway between the liberal idealist and Hobbes. Any attempt to make contact with reality will have to find some way to acknowledge not only that it is autonomous from us, but also that we cannot know exactly what it is. A realist politics, one that does justice to reality, rather than simply indulging in theoretical fantasies about reality, must somehow incorporate our ultimate uncertainty as to the nature of things. On this note I turn to that paradoxical and misunderstood thinker, Latour.

3 Latour's Object-Oriented Politics

As mentioned, Latour has built a philosophy that might look as immanent as Hobbes's own. His ANT strips the world of transcendence to the point that an actor (meaning any entity at all) is defined solely in terms of what it does. There are no properties in things that remain currently unexpressed; an actor exhausts its being in every instant, and becomes something different in succeeding instants when it does something new (Harman 2009). This in itself already sounds anti-realist, since it grants nothing outside the sum total of actions *hic et nunc*. Latour has the additional anti-realist tendency – occasionally but not often avoided – of behaving as if any network of actors needs to be registered ultimately by a human observer. In his most extreme moments, this leads him to make openly shocking claims, as in his argument that the Egyptian Pharaoh Ramses II cannot have died of tuberculosis since that disease had not yet been discovered in ancient Egypt (Latour 2000). There is also his somewhat ironic use of the term "realism" in the opening pages of *Pandora's Hope* (Latour 1999), which he does in the same tone often employed by anti-realists to deflate the challenge posed by the term "realism" altogether.

Nonetheless, there are at least two places in Latour's philosophy where he opens himself to a form of transcendence so robust that Hobbes could only have scowled in response. The first comes in his important but neglected rejection of materialism on the grounds that materialists always assume that they know what "matter" is, thereby reducing it to a limited number of abstract properties (Latour 2007). Here Latour is actually more Socratic than Socrates's admirer Strauss, given Latour's awareness that the nature of matter must remain to some extent a mystery in view of our inability to reach a "right" definition of it. The second comes in Latour's political theory, where knowledge and technocratic expertise are downplayed to the point of irrelevance, and we are led to something like Dewey's model of a deliberative provisional consensus between various stakeholders.

Yet an even more important realist moment in Latour comes from his awareness of the role of inanimate objects, in politics as elsewhere. It is not a question of granting political rights to rocks, shadows, and pipelines, but of recognizing the way in which debates over the goodness or badness of human nature are somehow beside the point. After all, what separates human from baboon society is primarily the great number of objects we humans deploy to differentiate our identities and roles: contracts, proper names, titles, money, wedding rings, identification cards, brick walls, eyeglasses, trains, and so forth (Strum & Latour 1987). Failed states are often the result of material rather than human failure, as Peer Schouten has demonstrated in the case of present-day Congo (Schouten 2013). While this commitment to non-human agents has always been a hallmark of Latour's political philosophy, it has attained new urgency in connection with global warming: a problem that Hobbes, Schmitt, and Strauss alike would have difficulty handling from their existing standpoints, oriented as they are by what they take to be the specific features of human nature.

In his Edinburgh Gifford Lectures, eventually published in book form as *Facing Gaia* (Latour 2017, pp. 220–254), Latour seems to make a Schmittian gesture, proposing that global warming deniers be treated as the "enemy" in a manner no longer worthy of rational debate. Yet his recently published booklet *Down to Earth* (Latour 2018) shows more of a turn from Schmitt back to Dewey, as interpreted by Noortje Marres (2005). The Deweyan element of Latour's realism, one that is missing from Hobbes, Schmitt, and Strauss alike, is his ongoing search for a form of transcendence-without-knowledge that would properly characterize the political sphere. Modernization, Latour's career-long enemy, is marked by the attempt to *purify* two taxonomically distinct realms from one another: the human and the non-human, the cultural and the natural, the humanities/social sciences and the hard sciences, truth and politics. His alternative is to point to the proliferation in our world of hybrids that cannot always be neatly classified as belonging to one of these two zones alone: the ozone hole is both an artifact of human behavior and a portion of the earth itself (Latour 2003). As we saw when Latour denied the existence of tuberculosis prior to its registration by human science, he often tarnishes this insight by claiming that *every* actor in the world is a mixture of human and non-human associations, a claim that fails as soon as we consider entities in distant galaxies or pre-human eras of the earth; to deny their existence apart from humans would be a form of rank idealism, as Meillassoux (2008) argues with his concept of the "ancestral."

Nonetheless, Latour provides us with two powerful tools for moving beyond the political immanence and political humanness of moderns like Hobbes and Schmitt, without laying claim to a political knowledge that Socratic *philosophia* is always prepared to debunk. The first tool is his insistence that politics always remains shrouded in our ultimate ignorance, which is precisely why technocrats cannot save us. Our inability to make *direct* proofs of global warming in the manner of modern science is a powerful index of this fact, and is the main reason that Latour had recourse to Schmitt when lecturing on Gaia. Donald Trump's escapist effort to deny the existence of global warming and the closely associated migration time bomb is parasitical on our inability to *know* global warming in the same way we can know the mass of an electron. While it may seem easy to deny the political element of subatomic physics, it is much more difficult to produce knowledge about the climate without a political assembling of the scientists and governments who can design (or "engender," as Latour prefers) a world in which humans are fruitfully interwoven with their environment rather than merely modernizing it beyond any plausible resource base. We can no longer be modernizing globalists, but Trumpian escapist anti-realism shows us –by way of contrast– the sort of realists we need to be: *terrestrials*, meaning those who must find a way to live in common with fish, birds, ice, CO_2, methane, and our former Schmittian national enemies. In Latour's own words, "[a] territory... is not limited to a single type of agent. It encompasses the entire set of animate beings – far away or nearby – whose presence has been determined – by investigation, by experience, by habit, by culture – to be indispensable to the survival of the terrestrial" (Latour 2018, pp. 95–96). If the enemy is no longer a foreign people, but a Gaia that may heat up by 7 degrees Celsius in the next century, political immanence is a luxury we can no longer afford. The outside environment will need to be woven into the polis as it has never been before, whether in political practice or the books of political theorists.

But this immediately brings us to the second new tool provided by Latour: the need to construct a political theory that takes into account not just "the entire set of animate beings," but numerous inanimate ones as well. In this sense Latour has to push even further than James Lovelock, who was primarily interested in Gaia as an environment produced and maintained by living things rather than just a stable backdrop for them (Lovelock 1995; Latour 2018, p. 76). If modern philosophy always foundered on the problem of animals, not knowing whether to place them closer to *res cogitans* or *res extensa* and unable to develop a plausible alternative, modern thinkers have failed as well to describe the inanimate world. They have simply abandoned it to the natural sciences. Yet a successful climate politics will have to embrace the inanimate as a political actor intimately intertwined with human politics, rather than as dead matter invested with accurately measurable properties. When Latour insists on the need for all things to be made terrestrial rather than global, it is not only Trump who provides the negative impetus, but Hobbes, Schmitt, and Strauss as well.

Bibliography

Callon, Michel and Bruno Latour (1981): "Unscrewing the Big Leviathan: How Actors Macro-Structure Reality and How Sociologists Help Them to Do So." In: Karin Knorr-Cetina and A.V. Cicourel (Eds.): *Advances in Social Theory and Methodology: Toward an Integration of Micro- and Macro-Sociologies.* London: Routledge & Kegan Paul, pp. 277–303.

Dewey, John (2012): *The Public and its Problems: An Essay in Political Inquiry.* University Park, PA: Pennsylvania State University Press.

Ferraris, Maurizio (2014): *Manifesto of New Realism.* Translated by S. De Sanctis. Albany, NY: State University of New York Press.

Fichte, Johann G. (1982): *The Science of Knowledge: With the First and Second Introductions.* Translated by J. Lachs and P. Heath. Cambridge: Cambridge University Press.
Fried, Michael (1990): *Courbet's Realism.* Chicago: The University of Chicago Press.
Gabriel, Markus (2015): *Fields of Sense: A New Realist Ontology.* Edinburgh: Edinburgh University Press.
Harman, Graham (2009): *Prince of Networks: Bruno Latour and Metaphysics.* Melbourne: re.press.
Harman, Graham (2011): *The Quadruple Object.* Winchester: Zero Books.
Harman, Graham (2014): *Bruno Latour: Reassembling the Political.* London: Pluto.
Harman, Graham (2018): *Object-Oriented Ontology: A New Theory of Everything.* London: Pelican.
Heidegger, Martin (1962): *Being and Time.* Translated by J. Macquarrie and E. Robinson. New York: Harper.
Hobbes, Thomas (1996): *Leviathan.* Oxford: Oxford University Press.
Lacan, Jacques (2005): *Ecrits: The First Complete Edition in English.* Translated by B. Fink. New York: Norton.
Latour, Bruno (1993): *We Have Never Been Modern.* Translated by C. Porter. Cambridge, MA: Harvard University Press.
Latour, Bruno (1999): *Pandora's Hope: Essays on the Reality of Science Studies.* Cambridge, MA: Harvard University Press.
Latour, Bruno (2000): "On the Partial Existence of Existing *and* Non-Existing Objects." In: Lorrain Daston (Ed.): *Biographies of Scientific Objects.* Chicago: The University of Chicago Press, pp. 247–269.
Latour, Bruno (2004): *Politics of Nature, or How to Bring the Sciences Into Democracy.* Translated by C. Porter. Cambridge, MA: Harvard University Press.
Latour, Bruno (2005): *Reassembling the Social: An Introduction to Actor-Network Theory.* Oxford: Oxford University Press.
Latour, Bruno (2007): "Can We Get Our Materialism Back, Please?" In: *Isis* 98, pp. 138–142.
Latour, Bruno (2013): *An Inquiry Into Modes of Existence: An Anthropology of the Moderns.* Translated by C. Porter. Cambridge, MA: Harvard University Press.
Latour, Bruno (2017): *Facing Gaia: Eight Lectures on the New Climactic Regime.* Cambridge: Polity.
Latour, Bruno (2018): *Down to Earth: Politics in the New Climactic Regime.* Cambridge: Polity.
Latour, Bruno, Graham Harman, and Peter Erdélyi (2011): *The Prince and the Wolf: Latour and Harman at the LSE.* Winchester: Zero Books.
Locke, John (1983): *A Letter Concerning Toleration.* Indianapolis: Hackett.
Lovelock, James (1995): *The Ages of Gaia: A Biography of Our Living Earth.* New York: Norton.
Machiavelli, Niccolò (1992): *The Prince*, Second Edition. Translated by R. Adams. New York: Norton.
Marres, Noortje (2005): "No Issue, No Public: Democratic Deficits After the Displacement of Politics." Ph.D. Dissertation, University of Amsterdam, The Netherlands. http://dare.uva.nl/record/165542.
Marx, Karl (1992): *Capital, Volume One: A Critique of Political Economy.* London: Penguin.
Meillassoux, Quentin (2008): *After Finitude: Essay on the Necessity of Contingency.* Translated by R. Brassier. London: Continuum.

Morgenthau, Hans (1950): *Politics Among Nations: The Struggle for Power and Peace.* New York: Knopf.

Nietzsche, Friedrich (1997): *Twilight of the Idols.* Translated by R. Polt. Indianapolis: Hackett.

Palmerston, Henry Temple 3rd Viscount of (1848): "Treaty of Adrianople–Charges Against Viscount Palmerston." https://api.parliament.uk/historic-hansard/commons/1848/mar/01/treaty-of-adrianople-charges-against.

Plato (1992): *Republic.* Translated by G.M.A. Grube. Indianapolis: Hackett.

Rosen, Stanley (2004): *The Mask of Enlightenment: Nietzsche's Zarathustra, Second Edition.* New Haven: Yale University Press.

Rousseau, Jean-Jacques (1992): *Discourse on the Origin of Inequality.* Translated by D. Cress. Indianapolis: Hackett.

Schmitt, Carl (1996): *The Concept of the Political.* Translated by G. Schwab. Chicago: The University of Chicago Press.

Schouten, Peer (2013): "The Materiality of State Failure: Social Contract Theory, Infrastructure, and Governmental Power in Congo." In: *Millennium: Journal of International Studies* 41, No. 3, pp. 553–574.

Shapin, Steven and Simon Schaffer (2011): *Leviathan and the Air-Pump: Hobbes, Boyle, and the Experimental Life.* Princeton: Princeton University Press.

Sinclair, Upton (1906): *The Jungle.* New York: Doubleday, Jabber & Co.

Strauss, Leo (1996): "Notes on Carl Schmitt, *The Concept of the Political.*" In: *Carl Schmitt: The Concept of the Political.* Translated by G. Schwab. Chicago: The University of Chicago Press, pp. 99–122.

Strum, Shirley and Bruno Latour (1987): "Redefining the Social Link: From Baboons to Humans." In: *Social Science Information* 26, No. 4, pp. 783–802.

Voegelin, Eric (1987): *The New Science of Politics: An Introduction.* Chicago: The University of Chicago Press.

Žižek, Slavoj (1999): "Carl Schmitt in the Age of Post-Politics." In: Chantal Mouffe (Ed.): *The Challenge of Carl Schmitt.* London: Verso.

Paul Redding
The Objectivity of the *Actual:* Hegelianism as a Metaphysics of Modal Actualism

Abstract: This paper focuses on the notion of objectivity from a modal point of view. It maintains that what is found desirable about objectivity can be better obtained from the notion of *actuality*, but only when the latter is understood in a modally rich way as somehow containing possible alternatives to it *within* itself. This approach contrasts, for example, with David Lewis's conception of possible worlds, which locates the actual within a broader conception of reality in which it is not essentially privileged. Robert Stalnaker counts, for Redding, as a major representative of this "actualist" alternative to Lewis. He argues that the roots of such an approach to metaphysics are to be found in the idealist tradition and, in particular, in Hegel.

Objectivity, it could be said (in somewhat Hegelian fashion), only became a problem for *modern* philosophy with the rise of its contrasting dual, *subjectivity*. This systematic opposition first seems to have caught on in the context of an aesthetic dispute between the "ancients and the moderns," with the objectivity attributed to ancient Greek culture coming to be contrasted with the subjectivity of the modern. Thus it was said that works of art typical of the Greeks and described as "naïve" (Schiller) or "classical" (Friedrich Schlegel) gave expression to an unproblematically experienced, common *objective* world, while opposing and more distinctly modern "sentimental" or "romantic" forms expressed the often idiosyncratic worlds of particular individuals. Within the more specific realms of epistemological and metaphysical concern, the modern mode would come to be represented by Descartes, the arch "subjectivist" for whom knowledge was understood as first and foremost *self-knowledge*, and such subjectivism would be the framework of much subsequent philosophy in the 17th and 18th centuries.

Schiller's "naive," applied to Greek poetry, was meant to capture a type of unselfconscious or ingenuous style meant to be characteristic of it, and Aristotle's objectivism might be said to be naïve in a similar sense, in not being self-consciously and systematically held against any subjectivist contrary – indeed, such an attitude in philosophy is often referred to as "naïve realism." We might appreciate this in relation to Aristotle's account of the relations of word, thought, and perceived substance in *De Interpretatione*. Words can contingently represent actual substances because they express perceptually based "affections in the soul," which are likenesses to those things (Aristotle 1984 vol. 1,

p. 25). But how exactly *is* this more fundamental mental representation to be conceived? Aristotle seems to have little to say. Later, Kant, in a letter to Marcus Herz in 1772 (Kant 1999, pp. 132–134), would remark on the centrality of the need to address this hitherto unposed question. The answer he would eventually offer in his critical philosophy would portray a mind's capacity to represent an external object as dependent upon its capacity to achieve a unity *among* its representations. Inasmuch as each representation could be grasped as a representation by a single unifying mind, they could be grasped collectively as representing a unified *world*. Objectivity could now be understood as that which results from the elimination of idiosyncratic features of an individual's subjectivity by the adoption of a universalized subjectivism – captured with the notion of a "transcendental unity of apperception" linked to a universalizable thinking subject.

This has profound consequences, however. Integrating one's beliefs into a centerless social web for which there is a type of universal suffrage means that this universalized knowledge can be no longer conceived as akin to knowledge of the universe as a type of knowable *object* writ large. *This* goal Kant criticises as the consequence of reason's use of ideas to "unite the manifold of concepts … by positing a certain collective unity as the goal of the understanding's actions" (Kant 1998, A644/B672). In contrast to this "collective unity" – a unified totality as if "viewed" by a transcendent subject – the "understanding" is properly concerned with only a "distributive" unity, an idea gesturing toward a modern conception of the contents of an individual's theoretical commitments, *qua* commitments to some centerless theoretical framework or ensemble of frameworks into which the givens of perception feed in a somewhat mediated and indirect way.

The picture of the world that results resembles that found in modern naturalistic accounts, the Sellarsian "scientific image of the world" that provides no apparent place within it for human subjects as beings with freedom and rationality (Sellars 1963). Kant was, of course, no naturalist, and so distinguished such a theoretical attitude from an agent's practical attitude. One must *treat* others as having properties such as freedom that can, however, not be represented from a theoretical point of view. This means that the theoretical point of view cannot be comprehensive: it can only give objective knowledge *qua* knowledge of objective *appearances*, not knowledge of "things in themselves." For the German idealists who followed Kant, this *ersatz* sense of "objectivity" was unacceptable, and they demanded a more robust one like that found in classical philosophy. And at the same time, they demanded that the non-naturalistic capacities Kant attributed to humans *qua* objects of *practical* intentions be somehow accommodated in this broader objectivity.

Clearly Hegel belonged to this camp, but exactly how to understand his attempts to integrate the modern Kantian perspective with the classical realist one remains one of the most contested issues in contemporary Hegel scholarship. Here I suggest that core features of Hegel's resolution come into focus when his position is related to one within contemporary metaphysics as shaped by the revival of modal concerns since the second half of the twentieth century, one that has been characterized as "modal actualism" and that emerged as an alternative to the metaphysics of "possible worlds" as advocated by David Lewis. In Hegel's case, actualism was offered as an alternative to the possibilism of Leibniz and Kant. Moreover, Hegel's version of actualism, I suggest, is best understood on a *meta*-metaphysical level in the sense of constituting a *re*-definition of the object of metaphysical inquiry. Metaphysics thus becomes an inquiry into the *actual world*, but understood in a modally enriched way of *containing* possibilities, a conception that, in turn, allows the actual world to be conceived as *containing subjects*. In this sense, Hegel's actualism has features similar to those found in Robert Stalnaker, a contemporary actualist critic of the possibilism of David Lewis. In the section that follows I first bring out structural features of the underlying *possibilism* involved in Leibniz's and Kant's versions of objectivity, and then turn to how *modal* features of Hegel's logic suggest an "actualist" alternative.

1 From Leibnizian and Kantian forms of possibilism to Hegelian actualism

In *Discourse on Method* Leibniz had employed the imagery of perspective or "point of view" to capture the role of subjectivity in experience and knowledge, thereby opening up a type of "objective" correlate of the subjective to which it could be linked. While a finite substance (later called a *monad*) neither exists "in" space nor has extension, it nevertheless represents the universe *as if* from a point of view "rather as the same town is differently represented according to the different situations of the person who looks at it" (Leibniz 1989, pp. 41–42). In the model we conceive of a viewer observing a town *from* a particular point of view, and conjoin the subjective features of the experience *enjoyed* from that point of view to a *more objective* conception of *that point of view itself*, gained from a broader, more inclusive one. When we substitute the universe itself for the town, and a plurality of monadic knowers located at specific points, such that each "expresses the universe in its own fashion," we start to get a sense of Leibniz's interlocking epistemological and metaphysical ideas, but we must go beyond the simple *spatiality* of the model. To this end Leibniz brought forward a range of distinctively *modern* logical innovations (Letzen 2004) so as to transform existing accounts of the differences between "obscure," "confused," and "distinct" ideas.

Influenced by medieval nominalist logicians, Leibniz took *general* cognitions to be "confused" because they "fused" within them distinct *singular* representations. When one thinks of "Greek philosophers," for example, the *real* objects of one's thoughts are *individuals* – Socrates, Plato, Aristotle, and so on – the symbols for whom are "fused" in a general symbol such as "Greek philosopher." Analogously, a mixture of fine blue and yellow grains might produce a powder that looks to the naked eye *green*, this perception being similarly "fused." Utilizing his idea of a "universal characteristic" as an algebraically tractable language into which everyday judgements shaped by general terms could be translated (Leibniz 1989, pp. 5–18), he conceived the method of "analysis" as meant to take the rational thinker from some initial "confused" perception or conception to one that showed its underlying *reasons* or *grounds* by demonstrating the relations among its distinct components.

Presupposing the ancient Platonic imagery of the pursuit of objectivity as ascending a type of ladder,[1] Leibniz treats each step as involving the analytic correction to the subjective features implicit in the prior step. Thus, one moves from conceptions that are "clear" but "*confused*" to ones that are "clear and *distinct*." With the application of algebra to logic Leibniz could conceive of propositions as akin to *equations*, and could construe the goal of such a series as "an equation that is an identity," representing a type of *sui generis* truth. In such a proposition/equation, *all* the implicit singular contents originally fused in the subject term would be now laid out explicitly in the predicate (Leibniz 1989, p. 96). In the case of *analytic* propositions, analysis could be thought of as systematically unpacking the parts of the subject concept in the way that geometric truths can be deduced from initial axioms. Such logical necessities are independent of the will of God and must be distinguished from the necessities "ex hypothesi" that, by contrast, *do* depend on the will of God – these are the necessities that hold together the world that God has chosen to actualize, and that would now be called *natural* necessities (Leibniz 1989, pp. 44–46).

We finite subjects with our initially fused/confused conceptions will require something other than a type of conceptual factoring to grasp these latter truths. Located at any one moment on some particular step of the Platonic ladder, one

---

[1] Leibniz had apparently taken this idea from his teacher Jacob Thomasius. See Mercer 2002, p. 36.

can grasp a truth informed by confused concepts by seeking an *explanation* or *reason* for that truth, thus rendering the confused idea *distinct* – a move legitimated by the *principle of sufficient reason*. Moreover, each step can be then repeated, the inquirer thus seeking a *reason* for that reason, making movement up the ladder a matter of "giving reasons for reasons" (Leibniz 1989, p. 28).

Thus, logically driven analysis takes us towards objectivity, but we should not think of the knowledge attained at this summit as simply a knowledge of the world as it *actually* is. The divine knowledge at the *telos* is a knowledge of *possibles* – *scientia simplicis intelligentiae* (Leibniz 1989, p. 74). Moreover, this realm of possibilities is itself organized as an infinite plurality of "universes," each one of which coincides with the totality itself as grasped confusedly from the point of view of each of the monads within it (Leibniz 1989, p. 42). These possibilities are objective, with God needing to select the actual world *from among* them.

In his *pre-critical* writings, Kant had followed something like Leibniz's "analytic method," and the proximity that he maintains to Leibniz after the critical philosophy is manifest in his own version of this Platonic ladder in the Transcendental Deduction of the *Critique of Pure Reason*, with the idea of a "prosyllogistic chain" which a thinker can ascend towards objectivity. Of course, the *telos* of this ascent must now fall short of divine knowledge (Kant 1998, A330–332/B386–389), and the inquirer must settle for a goal of *knowledge of objective appearances* – effectively the truths of the natural sciences – rather than a knowledge of "things in themselves," but many of the features of Leibniz's analytic ladder remain.

The idea of a step-like ascent from an empirical judgment to a more abstract judgment meant to *explain it* seems to have found its way into German philosophy of this period from an atypical version of Aristotle's logic developed by the renaissance Italian philosopher Jacobo Zabarella.[2] Here one ascends from a known "mere fact" to some more general principle in terms of which that fact can come to be understood by being conceived as the conclusion of a syllogism, and so as explained by the syllogism's premises. Thus Kant notes that in each component syllogism of his prosyllogistic chain, the rule expressed in the major premise "says something universal under a certain condition" (Kant 1998, A330/B386–387), while the minor premise tells us that in the case before us (the actual judgment represented by the *conclusion* of the syllogism) the rule obtains. For example, a major premise such as "all men are mortal" effectively asserts that *something* will be mortal given a certain condition, the condition

---

[2] For a synoptic account, see Redding 2007, ch. 5.

of that thing's being *a man*, while the minor premise that, say, "Socrates is a man," asserts that that condition holds of Socrates. It thus gives the explanation of Socrates' mortality. But the major premise, according to Kant, will *itself* have a "condition" under which it stands, let's say, "all men are *animals*," which in turn explains why *they* are mortal. This is precisely Leibniz's "reason for the reason" structure, and hence suggests a series of syllogisms ascending to a "supreme condition." While this goal is beyond our epistemic reach, we must still hold to it as, Kant says, "a demand of reason" (Kant 1998, A332/B389).

Such talk of a chaining of reasons is reflected in Kant's use of the notion of "exponent," a term used in eighteenth-century mathematics for an iterable ratio with which a numerical series can be generated (Longuenesse 1998, pp. 97–99). Like Leibniz, I suggest, Kant had drawn together two different ideas from Aristotle's logic, attempting to wed the idea of the type of explanatory loop, invoked by Zabarella, with the more traditional "tree of Porphyry" idea that had been based upon Aristotle's "Analytics." But another way in which Leibnizian features of the *telos* persist in Kant is that each step of the Kantian ascent is similarly possibilistic. What such steps provide in Kant's case are *hypotheses* – epistemically conceived possibilities as to how the empirical world might turn out to be upon guided observation, a feature like that of the modern "hypothetico-deductive" approach to science. A hypothesis must be tested, and this relies on the existence of something extraconceptual that is not given by logical relations, the input of empirical intuition. While in Leibniz, an actual state of affairs had been "chosen" from among an array of possible ones, for Kant this choice is now made on empiricist grounds, Kant's possibilities being understood as conditions of *possible experience*.

Hegel, I have suggested, opposes to this possibilism a form of *actualism*, and evidence for a *prima facie* case for such an actualist reading of Hegel's metaphysics is not difficult to find. Thus early in the *Encyclopedia Logic* Hegel straightforwardly declares that "the content of philosophy is *actuality* [*Wirklichkeit*]," and in the development of the categories in the Objective Logic of both *The Science of Logic*, and the *Encyclopaedia Logic*, "Actuality" is the concluding category of a developmental series that had commenced with Being. There, his treatment of Actuality is clearly meant to contest Leibnizian *possibilist* as well as Spinoza's *necessitarian* alternatives. Specifically, in relation to the former he notes in the *Encyclopaedia Logic* that "the notion of possibility appears initially to be the richer and more comprehensive determination, and actuality, in contrast, as the poorer and more restricted one. But, in fact, i.e., in thought, actuality is what is more comprehensive, because, being the concrete thought, it contains possibility within itself as an abstract moment" (Hegel 1991, § 143, addition). This idea of actuality as "contain[ing] possibility within itself" can be likened to the position of Robert Stalnaker, who has sought to employ possible-world semantics without accepting David Lewis's *realism* of a plurality of possible worlds. For Stalnaker, talk of possible worlds is shorthand for talking of possible states of the *one* world, and thus he treats alternate possibilities as unrealized *properties* of the actual world considered as a whole (Stalnaker 2012, ch. 1.2). While the notion of property is not itself metaphysically uncontentious, many nevertheless accept the idea of a property as something that is exemplifiable (see, for example, Orilia and Swoyer 2017, section 1.1), and Stalnaker's analogy effectively extends the range of property bearers from individual objects to the universe itself. From a semantic point of view, part of the strategy Stalnaker employs against Lewis is to regard the semantics for our talk about non-actual possibilities as *deriving* from our talk about the actual world, an approach also found in the earlier actualist position of Arthur Prior. A similar suggestion can also be found in Hegel's approach to the logic of judgments.

2 Hegel and 20th Century Logic

The story of Hegel's philosophical excommunication from the emerging analytic philosophy at the start of the twentieth century is well known,[3] but the way that the subsequent history of logic may have shaped the conditions for his return is less so. Early in the analytic tradition, Bertrand Russell dismissed Hegel for having a metaphysics based on an outdated logic: the type of quantified predicate logic originating with Frege in the late 19th century allowed for judgments with *many-placed* predicates, and replaced the traditional subject-predicate conception of judgment to which Hegel had been uncritically attached. But even in these early years, a counter-movement to Russell's interpretation of the new logic was emerging from a broadly idealist direction. C. I. Lewis criticized Russell's approach to implication that, he argued, failed to capture the *necessity* implicit in implication itself (Lewis 1912), and went on to develop various systems of the modal logic of necessary and possible propositions to accommodate the *necessity* needed for the notion of implication (Lewis & Langford 1934). This logic had an idealist provenance, Lewis insisting that his *intensional* approach to logic was continuous with the logic of the earlier idealists (Lewis 1930).

---

3 See, for example, my sketch in Redding 2007, Introduction.

Lewis himself had been a student of the American idealist Josiah Royce, and influenced especially by his teacher's approach to logic.[4]

Later, in the 1950s and 60s, modal logic underwent extensive development when Saul Kripke introduced the idea of quantification by extending the range of universal and existential quantifiers to "possible worlds." Taken strictly, Kripke's innovation concerned only the mathematical modelling of meaningful talk about possibility: it did not necessarily imply, nor did Kripke take it to imply, any realistic attitude to possibilia. Nevertheless, Kripke's approach did raise the question of making sense of the notion of possible worlds, thereby raising metaphysical issues that dated back to Leibniz. In relation to classical *non*-modal logic, the "domain" of objects to which the quantifiers were applied was relatively straightforward – they were existing, i.e., *actual*, objects. But what sense could be made of talking of quantifying over merely *possible* objects? Here David Lewis accepted the ontological consequences of this move, treating thoughts about non-actual possible objects as made true or false by things in *possible worlds* regarded as equally real as the actual world. To think of the actual world as somehow metaphysically privileged, he argued, is like thinking of one's *temporal* location, one's "now," as a metaphysically privileged *time. Other possible worlds* and their occupants are no less real than *other times and their occupants.* [D. Lewis 1973, p. 86.] A version of seventeenth-century Leibnizianism had seemingly reappeared, *sans* Leibniz's God.

In drawing on an analogy between existence at one time rather than others and existence in one *possible world* rather than others, Lewis was drawing on work on *tense logic*, a modal logic developed early in the mid-century revival by Arthur Prior (Prior 1957, 1967). But Prior objected to the "platonic" metaphysics implicit in Lewis's treatment of both possibility and time (Prior & Fine 1977, pp. 92–93), asserting the irreducible and primary sense of *the present* for tense logic and *the actual* for alethic modal logic. In this Prior had been influenced by the views on tense of his teacher John N. Findlay (Prior 1967, p. 1; Findlay 1941), who had strong Hegelian leanings and who, in the 1950s, had endeavoured to reintroduce Hegel back into the analytically dominated Anglophone philosophical scene (Findlay 1958). In those endeavours, Findlay read Hegel in an atypical way. Hegel was *not*, he claimed, the extravagant metaphysician of tradition: "there never has been a philosopher by whom the *Jenseitige*, the merely tran-

---

[4] Lewis acknowledged the influence of Royce in *A Survey of Symbolic Logic*, adding "much that is best in this book is due to him" (1918, p. vi). Royce had become interested in the relations of logic and metaphysics, especially after having attended a lecture series by C. S. Peirce in the late 1890s, and had increasingly engaged with issues in mathematical logic from then. See in particular the essays in Royce 1951.

scendent, has been more thoroughly 'done away with,' more thoroughly shown to exist only *as revealed* in human experience" (Findlay 1958, p. 19). For Findlay, in his thorough-going rejection of any beyond of human experience, Hegel was a this-worldly thinker, what would later be called an "actualist," but one for whom actuality was modally enriched, a "modal actualist,"[5] and just as modern modal actualists can be understood in contrast to the possibilists they opposed, so too Hegel might be understood in his opposition to the possibilism of Leibniz and Kant.

I have suggested that Hegel shares the ontology of actualists like Prior and Stalnaker who make judgments about the actual world semantically more basic than ones about alternative possible worlds, but other aspects of the modern modal problematic need to be presented in order to understand the link to Hegel's idealism. Crucially, modern modal logics cover a range of different logics beyond the "alethic" modal logic of necessary and possible truths. We have already noted *tense* logic, and others include the logic of belief (doxastic logic) and the logic of action intention (deontic logic). All such modal logics are concerned with contents that are in some sense *context*-dependent. For example, the truth values of *tensed* sentences are relative to the time at which they are said, while those of doxastic logic are relevant to the *particular believer* whose beliefs are at issue. In a similar way, even the "alethic" modal logic of necessity and possibility is to be understood as relative to a context, in this case the context being the *actual* world. Such context-dependence is now taken as the defining feature of modal logic *per se* (Blackburn et. al. 2001), and this in turn brings in the issue of mind-relatedness.

Most obviously, the "objects" of doxastic and deontic logics are *mind-related* in ways that the objects of classical logic (propositions) are not, but this really only makes explicit the way in which modal logics *more generally* build subject-relatedness into their logical structures. Take, for example, a *tensed* assertion such as "it is raining (*now*)" in which the "now" to which the assertion is contextualized is, surely, *somebody*'s now. *Standardly* such "ego-reflexive" features had been treated by classical logicians as the target for elimination: Russell, for example, had treated such subjective time references as reducible to objective ones (Russell 1915). Moreover, for most practitioners of analytic modal metaphysics, all modal judgments are to be so reduced.

---

[5] The term "modal actualism" was first applied to the work of Prior by Kit Fine (Prior & Fine 1977, p. 116). For Findlay's way of reading Hegel in the context of such modal issues, see Redding 2017.

This is apparent in David Lewis's approach to alethic modal judgments in which a judgment as to what may possibly be the case in *this* world is analysed in terms of what *is* the case in some set of alternate possible worlds. Let's say an individual in the actual world, *Ripov*, is a cheat, but we nevertheless believe that he *could have been honest*. For the modal realist, this modal judgment is made true by their existing possible worlds in which Ripov (or technically, his "counterparts") *is* honest, but note that the facts that hold in these alternate realities are not themselves *modal* facts.[6] Lewis's possibilism thus reduces modal judgments to non-modal ones, thus avoiding the "problem" of mind-dependence.

Actualists such as Prior and Stalnaker, however, resist the reduction of the modal to the non-modal (hence the designation "*modal* actualism"), being thereby left with mind-dependence as an ineliminable aspect of judgment and thus *mind* as an ineliminable part of the world. But any such "idealism" implicit here would seem non-toxic when one reflects that the idea of the presence of mind in the actual world – a fact many would surely be happy to accept – need not be understood as implying the *necessary* presence of mind in the actual world. Mind need only be present in *some* possible world, the actual one – ours.

Something like this, I suggest, was behind Findlay's implicitly modal actualist version of Hegel's idealism, an approach effectively *re-*defining the object of metaphysical inquiry, making metaphysics an inquiry into the *actual world*, understood as *containing* alternate possibilities, rather than an inquiry into what is *necessarily the case* in virtue of holding in *all* possible worlds. And as we have seen, *this* can be linked to Hegel's idealism in that it can be thereby conceived as *containing subjects*, although not necessarily so.

With this background, we might now examine the way Hegel's treatment of modal issues in his logic challenges the remnants in Kant of Leibniz's platonic ladder.

3 Modality in Hegel's logic

Towards the end of the *Science of Logic* Hegel describes scientific method as a circle or cycle (*Kreis*) that "winds around itself" – a "cycle of cycles," such that for any component cycle, an initial item will return in a more logical complex form at its conclusion, and so commence a new cycle (Hegel 2010, p. 751). Earlier, Hegel had referred to such "cycles of determination" that constitute the

---

[6] This is obscured by the misleading common designation "modal realist," which is strictly *reductionist* rather than realist about modal facts.

logical development at the heart of logic as a science, the "progress of the concept in the exposition of itself" (Hegel 2010, p. 95), and such a cyclical pattern involving the logical complexification of the terms involved can be observed within his account of the development of the various *judgment types* in the Subjective Logic.

Here such cycles are typically characterized by a pattern in which the cycle starts with some distinctly *de re* judgment about a concrete substance which, in the cycle's "ascending" phase, becomes transformed into a more abstract and so less determinate *de dicto* form (call this the phase of *de-determination*), and then a "descending" phase in which these abstract judgments are transformed back into further *de-re* judgments with logically more complex subjects (the phase of *re*-determination). Thus, in the very first cycle, judgments made about individual concrete items become transformed in such a way that the cycle ends with a judgment, similar in general shape, but now about the *kinds* instantiated by those items. For example, an initiating judgment might be about an individual rose, judged to be *red*, while the equivalent terminating judgment will be about the *kind* rose, which is, say, judged to be a *plant*. This looks like the type of step to be taken up Kant's pro-syllogistic chain, such that a *new*, more general and encompassing standpoint has been reached, from which the *reason* for initial judgment is made explicit. Thus, understanding the rose as a plant may help explain the individual rose's properties: a rose as the *type of thing* that *can be* coloured red or have a particular scent. But *whatever* Hegel's image of a "circle of circles" is meant to convey, it does not lend itself to the idea of the type of ascent driven by "reasons for reasons."

Thus, Hegel's first cycle starts with the *judgment of existence* (Hegel 2010, pp. 557–568) in which some *existing* thing, an individual rose for example, is judged as bearing some perceivable quality, it might be *fragrant* or *red* (Hegel 2010, pp. 558–559). It is a judgment of *existence* [*Dasein*] because the concrete object in question is immediately perceived to *exist* (*sein*), *there* (*da*), and so is directly available for sensuous experience. And as one of Hegel's other examples shows ("It is daytime now," Hegel 2010, p. 562; c.f. Hegel 1975, § 95), such judgments are clearly "modal" or contextually sensitive *qua* tensed. The fragrant or red rose exists in the perceiving judge's *now*.

Such a positive judgment barely counts as a judgment at all, as Hegel had earlier made it clear that an uttered sentence or "*Satz*" only counts as a genuine judgment when it exists in some contestative dialectical context (Hegel 2010, p. 553) within which it can be *argued for*. Thus this "positive" judgment must be conceived as facing challenges or "negations," of which there will be two, and the dialectic that plays out in these contexts will have the overall result of *redetermining* the logical structure of the subject and predicate terms of that original positive judgment, rendering them more abstract or less *immediately* determinate.

A first negation will concern simple assertions to the contrary: that the rose is *red*, for example, can be met with the denial that "it is *not* red," implying that it is *some other colour* (Hegel 2010, p. 565), this corresponding to the "term negation" of the traditional Aristotelian conception of judgment. Hegel points out that the opposing *negated* judgment will be *less determinate* than the original,[7] because what is no longer expressed is the particular *way* in which the rose is *not red*, its implied contrary colour not being specified. Such a denial still counts as a type of positive judgment because it still asserts something *of* the rose (its indeterminate non-red *colour*) and so *it* must, therefore, still face a further, now *stronger*, negation – the type of negation typically conceived as "external" or "propositional," as in "*it is not the case that* the rose is red." What is now included in the scope of the negation is the *kind of predicate* that had been retained in the first negation, the stronger negation thus eliminating the assumption that the rose is coloured. Moreover, the scope of this negation extends as well to the *kind of subject*, thus stripping both subject *and* predicate of their kind determinations.

The effects of this second negation are apparent in the examples Hegel gives of those "infinite" (or *indefinite*) judgments that result – they are the sorts of claims that would be offered in response to assertions expressing "category mistakes" ("the rose is not an elephant, the understanding is not a table," Hegel 2010, p. 567). Moreover, these negations have deprived the original judgments of existence of their existential status, because, within Aristotelian logic, while positive judgments carry existential claims about their subjects, *negative* judgments do *not*.

Hegel's "infinite judgments" should be familiar to the modern reader: they express the "propositions" that are standardly taken as the abstract contents of judgments in contemporary logic – abstract entities *qua* bearers of truth and falsity and objects of "propositional attitudes." Later, Hegel will identify this pseudo-judgment structure as the structure of those "analysed" judgments of Leibniz's universal characteristic (Hegel 2010, pp. 602–603), this fitting with what Leibniz says about the "eternal" truths of geometry for which a "contrary implies a contradiction" (Leibniz 1989, p. 45). But this is also how Kant conceives of the decentred logically consistent set of judgments constituting the

---

[7] The "negative of a concept" is to be taken as "the mere *indeterminate* extent of the *other* of the positive concept" (Hegel 2010, p. 564). Hegel thus describes the predicate of this judgment as *particular* (Hegel 2010, p. 563), whereas that of the original positive judgment was *singular* (p. 560).

"distributed" unity of a subject's knowledge. Hegel, however, denies that infinite judgments are judgments at all because they have a logical structure in which both subject and predicate express *universals*. For genuine judgments, the conceptual determinations of subject and predicate terms need to be different because this distinction is necessary to allow *reasons* to be given to justify judgments.[8]

In criticising abstract propositions as proper contents *for* judgments, Hegel can also be read as adopting an actualist position within contemporary debates about the relation of modal to classical logic. Hegel's initial judgment of existence can be likened to the judgments of Prior's "tense logic" for which Prior had resisted the attempt to treat as "incomplete" any proposition in need of being made complete by the *objective* specification of the time at which the judgment took place. On Russell's analysis, a judgment such as "the rose is fragrant now," in not expressing a stable truth value, is more like a "propositional function" that produces a proposition only when applied to a further argument term referring to the time at which the judgment was made. But Prior, following Findlay (1941), thought of the tensed judgment as irreducible, with the "objective" judgment a type of artificial construction based upon the more basic "tensed" form and so unable to replace it. Similarly for Hegel, these abstract "propositional" forms can only represent a type of *transitional* proto-judgment which must be subject to *further* redetermination to become a proper judgment.

In the first cycle, the outcome of this redetermination is the "judgment of reflection" (Hegel 2010, pp. 568–575), and once again, two further *re*-determining negations result in the "judgment of necessity" terminating the circuit. The subject term of this judgment form is no longer about things like individual roses but about the *species* they instantiate, and as the name of this judgment implies, this is another modal judgment in that the predicates of its subject term represent *necessary* properties of the instances of this kind.

Importantly, the reflective judgment had inherited features that resulted from the doubly negated immediate judgment of existence, the *indeterminate* (because kind-less) conception of the range of things that the judgment is meant to be about, and this in turn allowed a richer conception of the properties of those things than those recorded in simple perceptual judgments. Thus the reflective judgment instantiates a different type of predication to the judgment of existence: while in the earlier judgment the predicate (quality) was conceived as

---

8 In more modern terms, we might describe Hegel's "infinite judgments" as higher-order judgments about *the concepts* otherwise involved in first order judgments. In saying "the rose is not an elephant" one is saying something about the concepts "rose" and "elephant" and not *about* roses and elephants.

"inhering" in the subject (the substance), the subject is now conceived as "subsumed" by an abstractly universal predicate (Hegel 2010, p. 555). As such, the objects these judgments are about can no longer be conceived straightforwardly as bearers of inherent phenomenal qualities such as colour or smell. Rather they are conceived as bearers of *relational* properties revealed only when put "in *relationship* and *connectedness*" with other things in the external world (Hegel 1991, § 174). Were a plant, say, to be fed to sick animals, subsequent observation of *them* may reveal a property of the *plant* – its being "curative" – and "to say, 'this plant is curative' implies that it is not merely this single plant that is curative, but that some or many plants are, and this gives us the *particular* judgment ('Some plants are curative…')" (Hegel 1991, § 175 add). This in turn raises the question of universal judgments of this type that suggest *modal* judgments about *kinds:* "The advance from the allness-type of the judgment of reflection to the judgment of necessity can already be found in our ordinary consciousness when we say that what pertains to all pertains to the kind and is therefore necessary" (Hegel 1991, § 176 add). In the first instance, in this judgment of necessity, the subject names a species, and the predicate its *genus*, as in "Gold is a metal" and "The rose is a plant."

This new judgment form provides the starting point for a *further* cycle of determination, within which the initial judgment type will be transformed into the "judgment of the concept," which is essentially an *evaluative* judgment about a human action or product, Hegel's examples being a house or a human action judged *good* or *bad* (Hegel 2010, pp. 583–584). That contestation is a necessary context for the status of judgment here becomes explicit as the *assertoric* judgment becomes *problematic*, in response to which it becomes expanded so as to include its justification – what it is about the house or action that makes it good or bad (Hegel 2010, pp. 584–586). Such a complex judgment can effectively be parsed as a syllogism, and this provides the first syllogistic form of a series of cycles analogous to those that have played out in the judgment (Hegel 2010, pp. 588–624).

In short, what we have observed through Hegel's account of judgment is a series of redeterminations of the nature of *substances*, and of the relations such substances bear to their properties, to other substances as well as *to subjects*. A substance was thus initially thought of as a simple thing with sensuous qualities, but came to be understood as an instance of some kind. We might think of this stage as broadly coinciding with the qualitatively determined substances of an Aristotelian world, but both the perceivable individual substances and the conceivable kinds to which they belong are to be understood in relation to subjects who can grasp them in that way. Moreover, passage through the mediating "subsumptive" abstract judgment forms has linked such kinds, in a more modern way, to empirically discoverable universal laws holding of their instances, able to be grasped by more "reflective" subjects.

The next cycle, however, leading to the judgment of concept, has in turn replaced the kind itself as subject by concrete individual items, now explicitly conceived as human actions or products that are subject to contestable *normative* evaluations. This is a type of content that calls for *another* type of modal logic, "deontic" logic, and this brings out a further dimension of the irreducible role of modal notions in these cycles. The universe, understood from the point of view of the applicability of these judgment forms, we might say, is one that includes an *irreducible place* for human agents, who not only act but evaluate their own and others' actions, including *their actions of judging and inferring*. Each cycle thus results in a broader context within which elements of earlier judgments can be considered and redetermined, and while alternative possibilities are generated within the cycles by the negations faced by opposing judgments, there is no sense of the thinker as being thereby taken to some transcendental position *beyond* the actual world from which an *a priori knowledge of its structuring possibilities* can be grasped.

Hegel had aimed at an *objective* conception of the objective world and this meant finding a place for minds within it, and had accepted the consequences of this in that such minds must thereby be conceived as always "located" *somewhere* within the world. Being brought into dialectical communication with the contents of other *differently located* minds provides a way beyond the immediate conditioning features of such location, but this does not offer a ladder *out of* the actual world to some place beyond, from where that world can be grasped free from all worldly conditioning.

4 Conclusion: The metaphysics of Hegel's modal logic

Hegel's logic, it is commonly said, is, unlike *other* logics, *really* a metaphysics – a claim that carries the questionable assumption that *other logics* are somehow free of metaphysical commitments. It might rather be better to think that what distinguishes Hegel's logic from others is *the type* of metaphysical, and *meta*-metaphysical assumptions, with which it is compatible. The actual *content* of Hegel's metaphysics will only be spelled out in those parts of his system that follow the *Logic* – his philosophy of nature and philosophy of spirit. Thus, it is only there that we should expect to find details of how an otherwise *natural* actual world (one with natural kinds, the instances of which behave in lawlike ways), might nevertheless include within it a place for minds or "spirit" (*Geist*). On this latter issue, one might expect to find evidence for how *living entities* exhibit mind-like capacities, as well as for a role for intersubjective "recognition" (*Anerkennung*) in linking the living and spiritual realms, together with a role for language, the linking of these last two items seemingly implicit in the "contestative" pragmatics suggested by Hegel's account of judgments and syllogisms.

One must of course avoid interpreting Hegel's *Logic* in ways that *presuppose* such metaphysical results, but I contend that appeals to the modal aspects of Hegel's account of judgments and syllogisms briefly surveyed above can suggest a place *for minds* in the logical fabric of the actual world without leaving the field of logic itself. Thus, while pointing to the way irreducibly modal logical judgments encode a place for "judging subjects" in their structure will surely signal *something* about Hegel's later treatment of these metaphysical issues, this "something" will be as yet restricted to an abstractly conceptual level awaiting further determination. Nevertheless, the metaphysical hints found within this logic are specific enough to indicate a conception of metaphysics that runs counter to common alternatives. Specifically, it suggests a metaphysics along the lines of those that have been called forms of "modal actualism."[9]

Bibliography

Aristotle (1984): *The Complete Works of Aristotle: The Revised Oxford Translation*. Edited by Jonathan Barnes. Princeton: Princeton University Press.
Blackburn, Patrick, Maarten di Rijke, and Yde Venema (2001): *Modal Logic*. Cambridge: Cambridge University Press.
Findlay, John N. (1941): "Time: A Treatment of Some Puzzles." In: *Australasian Journal of Psychology and Philosophy* 19, pp. 216–235.
Findlay, John N. (1958): *Hegel: A Re-examination*. London: Allen & Unwin.
Hegel, Georg W. F. (1977): *Phenomenology of Spirit*. Translated by A. V. Miller with Analysis of the Text and Foreword by J. N. Findlay. Oxford: Clarendon Press.
Hegel, Georg W. F. (1991): *The Encyclopaedia Logic*. Translated by T. F. Geraets, W. A. Suchting, and H. S. Harris. Indianapolis: Hackett.
Hegel, Georg W. F. (2010): *The Science of Logic*. Translated and edited by George di Giovanni. Cambridge: Cambridge University Press.
Hegel, Georg W. F. (1968): *Gesammelte Werke*. Hamburg: Felix Meiner.
Kant, Immanuel (1999): *Correspondence*. Translated and edited by Arnulf Zweig. Cambridge: Cambridge University Press.

---

[9] I am most grateful to Dominik Finkelde and Paul Livingston for very helpful comments on an earlier draft.

Kant, Immanuel (1998): *Critique of Pure Reason.* Translated and edited by Paul Guyer and Allen W. Wood. Cambridge: Cambridge University Press.
Leibniz, Gottfried W. (1989): *Philosophical Essays.* Translated and edited by Roger Ariew and Daniel Garber. Indianapolis: Hackett.
Lenzen, Wolfgang (2004): "Leibniz's Logic." In: Dov M. Gabbay and John Woods (Eds.): *Handbook of the History of Logic, Volume 3, The Rise of Modern Logic: From Leibniz to Frege.* Amsterdam: Elsevier, pp. 5–92.
Lewis, Clarence I. (1912): "Implication and the Algebra of Logic." In: *Mind* 21, pp. 522–531.
Lewis, Clarence I. (1918): *A Survey of Symbolic Logic.* Berkeley: University of California Press.
Lewis, Clarence I. (1930): "Logic and Pragmatism." In: George P. Adams and William P. Montague (Eds.): *Contemporary American Philosophy* 2. New York: Macmillan, pp. 31–51.
Lewis, Clarence I., and C. H. Langford (1931): *Symbolic Logic.* New York: Century.
Lewis, David K. (1973): *Counterfactuals.* Oxford: Blackwell.
Longuenesse, Beatrice (1998): *Kant and the Capacity to Judge: Sensibility and Discursivity in the Transcendental Analytic of the Critique of Pure Reason.* Princeton: Princeton University Press.
Mercer, Christia (2002): *Leibniz's Metaphysics: Its Origins and Development.* Cambridge: Cambridge University Press.
Orilia, Francesco and Chris Swoyer: "Properties." In Edward N. Zalta (Ed.): *The Stanford Encyclopedia of Philosophy* (Winter 2017 Edition).
<https://plato.stanford.edu/archives/win2017/entries/properties/>.
Prior, Arthur (1957): *Time and Modality.* Oxford: Clarendon Press.
Prior, Arthur (1967): *Past, Present and Future.* Oxford: Clarendon Press.
Prior, Arthur and Kit Fine (1977): *Worlds, Times and Selves.* Amherst: University of Massachusetts Press.
Redding, Paul (2007): *Analytic Philosophy and the Return of Hegelian Thought.* Cambridge: Cambridge University Press.
Redding, Paul (2017): "Findlay's Hegel: Idealism as Modal Actualism." In: *Critical Horizons* 18, pp. 359–377.
Royce, Josiah (1951): *Royce's Logical Essays: Collected Logical Essays of Josiah Royce.* Edited by Daniel S. Robinson. Dubuque, IA: Wm C. Brown Co.
Russell, Bertrand (1915): "On the Experience of Time." In *The Monist* 25, pp. 212–233.
Sellars, Wilfrid (1963): "Philosophy and the Scientific Image of Man." In: *Science, Perception and Reality.* London: Routledge and Kegan Paul, pp. 1–40.
Stalnaker, Robert (2012): *Mere Possibilities.* Princeton: Princeton University Press.

Dieter Sturma
Nomological Realism

Abstract: This paper considers several debates within theoretical and practical philosophy in which certain forms of naturalism are in conflict with anti-naturalistic interpretations of morality, especially within the field of ethics. An important reaction to this conflict is Wilfrid Sellars' integrative worldview that includes both the "manifest image" and the "scientific image" of man. On the basis of Sellars' worldview and with the help of an analysis of linguistic behavior, the framework of a nomological realism is developed which combines an extended naturalism with a Kantian conception of normative constraints. This integrative approach can avoid both eliminativism and the fallacies of traditional realism, especially its reification of values.

1 Scientific Realism and Moral Realism

It is commonly assumed that the relationship between realism and anti-realism is characterized by strong opposition – an impression reinforced by the numerous metaethical attempts to defend realism against anti-realism and vice versa.[1] Recently, realist positions have emerged which – unlike traditional realism – are increasingly concerned with perspectives of ontology, epistemology, and the philosophy of language. They also take anti-realist concerns highly seriously.[2] Scientific realism plays an important role in these developments, as both realists and anti-realists refer to it when answering questions regarding the reality of morality.

The disagreement between realism and anti-realism comes down to the question of who knows more about what there is. The natural sciences are regarded as a reliable source in answering this question. Even though the limits of scientific methods and models are undeniably narrow, they stand out in comparison with claims based on mere opinion or ideological positions as being open to procedures of examination and verification. According to the version of realism defended here, our ontological commitment is based on the develop-

---

[1] Cf. Harman/Thomson (1996); cf. Sayre-McCord (1988) and Rachels (1998).
[2] Cf. Darwall/Gibbard/Railton (1992), p. 187: "Moral realists, constructivists, and quasi-realists alike look to the responses and reasons of persons, rather than some self-subsistent realm, to ground moral practice."

https://doi.org/10.1515/9783110670349-016

ment of the human life-form and its interaction with the environment. The natural sciences are, among other institutions, an important element in this process.

The ontological core of philosophical naturalism is scientific realism. In general, naturalists tend to suggest that they are equipped with forms of justification that meet the methodological standards of the natural sciences. From a naturalist standpoint, questions on what is can only be answered with reference to the state of the art in the natural sciences. How this orientation has to be spelled out in detail is – in contrast to the assumptions of mainstream naturalistic positions – not obvious from the outset. Furthermore, the ontological question cannot be answered by the natural sciences alone.

There are many properties and capacities of the human life-form that the framework of the natural sciences does not cover. This applies above all to morality and normative constraints. Eliminativist positions take this as a pretext for excluding morality as such from descriptions of the world.[3] The assumption of the ontological primacy of the natural sciences causes tension between the ontology of scientific realism on the one hand and the ontological requirements of practical philosophy on the other.[4]

Irrespective of its compatibility with scientific realism, moral realism is confronted with much more comprehensive criticism from eliminative naturalism, which extrapolates a radical program of naturalization and elimination from the presupposed ontological primacy of scientific realism. Logical Empiricism is an early paradigm for this position. The success of the natural sciences in the twentieth century, and of modern physics in particular, has been crucial to the calls of eliminative naturalism for the naturalization of all sciences.

For Logical Empiricism, physics is the universal language of science. This conviction is grounded in the realist belief that physics is occupied with nomol-

---

3 Cf. Blackburn (1998), pp. 48–49: "The natural world is the world revealed by the senses, and described by the natural sciences: physics, chemistry, and notably biology, including evolutionary theory. However we think of it, ethics seems to fit badly into that world. Neither the senses nor the sciences seem to be good detectors of obligations, duties, or the order of value of things. [...] But we nearly all want to be naturalists and we all want a theory of ethics. So the problem is one of finding room for ethics, or of placing ethics within the disenchanted, non-ethical order which we inhabit, and of which we are a part."

4 This contradiction has been used by much of analytic ethics as an opportunity to depart from realist ethical positions. John L. Mackie's *Ethics: Inventing Right and Wrong* begins with the statement: "There are no objective values" (Mackie 1977, p. 15). Judith Jarvis Thomson answered this anti-realistic and relativistic slogan years later with a cautious realist thought: "It is often said to be a deep and difficult question whether there is value in the world. I am [...] tempted to say, displaying two good umbrellas: Here is one good umbrella and here is another. Therefore there is value in the world" (Thomson 2008, p. 36, note).

ogies, observable states, objects, and events which are taken to be the essential elements of universality, intersubjectivity, and objectivity. Logical Empiricism identifies in physics the potential for a systematic language of all sciences which allows for a unifying project in the form of a general translatability of non-physicalist assertions into physicalist sentences. This assumption does not require every scientific discipline to reform its terminology. The requirement of a general translatability is ultimately a reduction claim according to which all methodologically justified sentences must refer directly or indirectly to sentences of physics. Although the disciplinary spectrum of scientific realism is in no way restricted to the natural sciences, eliminativist programs of naturalization draw one-sided conclusions from their methodological standards.

As morality does not appear in the worldview of the natural sciences, the translatability of moral statements into a physicalist vocabulary is not possible without loss of meaning. From an eliminativist standpoint, subjects of morality, i.e. human persons, dissolve entirely into the elements and mechanisms of the scientific realm of causes. The universe of physical objects and events is taken to consist of local elements that function in specific domains and behave according to universal laws. It is further assumed that the elements of the various local domains stand in no relation to elements outside their immediate vicinity. In the view of narrow or scientistic naturalism, this has the immediate eliminative consequence that the behavior of persons is understood as consistently determined – like every other process in the world – by locally effective micro-mechanisms, and that the corresponding human activities can in principle be fully described by the mechanisms of the natural micro-world.[5]

The elimination of phenomena and world descriptions that are not captured by the natural sciences is commonly carried out by naturalizations. They focus on the methodological assimilation of answers to the question of what a scientific concept of nature consists of. In analytical philosophy, naturalization is generally understood to be a fundamental methodological reduction of descriptions regarding manifestations of the human life-form to models of the natural sciences. In the understanding of eliminativists, morality and moral philosophy are intentional objects and not active part of naturalization or scientific practice in general.

Naturalization is not the only way to deal with persons and manifestations of the human life-form from a scientific perspective. In the history of philosophy, we find classical positions integrating human expression into a comprehensive

---

5 Exemplary versions of this kind of argument can be found in French Materialism and in many versions of the identity theory and the eliminative materialism of the twentieth century.

concept of nature. Unlike eliminativist projects, they follow the path of what can be called an extended or integrative naturalism.⁶ Versions of an extended naturalism can be found in the works of Aristotle, Spinoza, Rousseau, and Schelling. These approaches have been further developed in the twentieth century, in particular in the context of analytic philosophy – this is the case, for example, for Peter F. Strawson, Stuart Hampshire, and John McDowell. They allow conceptual and ontological room for the human life-form and treat persons as psychophysical subjects and normative actors. According to this view, the beliefs that accompany the consciousness of our activities are not necessarily derivative phenomena.⁷ When it comes to beliefs, experiences, and self-awareness, the fallibility of human consciousness does not justify *as such* any sort of global scenario of self-deception. The attitudes and behavior of persons are anchored in a shared lifeworld. This fact sets a high bar for scientific eliminations or revisions. It is also questionable whether the ontologies inspired by the natural sciences have sufficient phenomenological and descriptive content to overcome these difficulties.⁸

Our notions of reality are to a large extent based upon perceptual and experiential access to what is. Therefore, the explanatory division of labor of justified appropriations of reality cannot be carried out in an abstract way, but must be negotiated case by case on the basis of an evaluation of the relevant phenomena and facts. It is obvious to scientific realism due to its methodology that, if it can be adequately applied to what is the case in the world, it can claim priority over other conceptions of reality.

Moral realism appears in a variety of forms throughout the history of philosophy – from Plato and Aristotle via Kant⁹ to Thomas Nagel. Rules for the manifestation of virtues and for the development of morally justified ends are decisive for virtue ethics (see Lovibond 1995). Classical intuitionism draws from our practice of moral evaluation the conclusion that there have to be entities with intrinsic normative qualities, while moral-sense-views and value-ethics imply

---

6 On the concept of extended or integrative naturalism, see Sturma (2005), pp. 26–44; cf. Sturma (2008), (2012), (2015), and (2018).
7 In his rejection of the eliminative approaches of French Materialism, Jean-Jacques Rousseau concluded that the models of the natural sciences can make no claim to methodological primacy regarding the explanation of life in general and the human life-form in particular; see Rousseau (1969), p. 575, note: "J'ai fait tous mes efforts pour concevoir une molécule vivante, sans pouvoir en venir à bout. L'idée de la matière sentant sans avoir des sens me paroit inintelligible et contradictoire; pour adopter ou rejetter cette idée il faudroit commencer par la comprendre, et j'avoüe que je n'ai pas ce bonheur-là."
8 See section 2.
9 Kant's ethics is not usually considered to be moral realism. His understanding of moral objectivity is, nevertheless, illustrative of the realist position developed below; see section 4.

the reality of intentional correlates of a moral sense. For some forms of consequentialism, moral facts result from rational interpretations of individual and societal utility or well-being. Finally, deontology and the ethics of autonomy work with a system of concepts and ethical rules that limit our scope of action.

The concept of reality in moral realism consists of the presupposition of moral facts or rules whose normative potential is not exclusively dependent on our normative constructions. According to this concept, ethical propositions always contain reference to moral facts. Whoever presupposes the reality of morality also requires either implicitly or explicitly that persons act and can behave normatively in a strict sense.

Overall, moral realism follows three goals in particular. It seeks (1) to refute ethical relativism, (2) to justify moral objectivity, and (3) to prove that non-cognitive and some cognitive positions fail to explain moral behavior adequately. In general, moral realism begins with the idea that there are moral facts or morality as such and that distinctions between true and false, better and worse, or justified and unjustified can be applied to moral statements.

2 Extended Naturalism

Early modern philosophy did not remain unaffected by the new explanations and worldviews of the emerging natural sciences. In its main systematic areas, early modern philosophy sought from the seventeenth century onwards to adjust its ontological framework to the natural sciences – as can be seen in Hobbes, Descartes, Spinoza, Leibniz, and Kant. This approach is to a great extent responsible for the rise of the naturalistic approach in contemporary philosophy.

We must neither underestimate nor overrate the significance and impact of the natural sciences for and on conceptions of reality. Natural sciences provide the most reliable models of reality for its various fields of competence. But they are at best approaches which are, by and by, replaced in the course of advancing scientific practice.[10]

---

[10] Cf. Nicholas Rescher (1987), p. xii: "While the theoretical entities envisioned by natural science do not actually exist in the way current science claims them to be, science does (increasingly) have 'the right general idea'. Something roughly like those putative theoretical entities does exist – something which our scientific conception only enables us to 'see' inaccurately and roughly. Our scientific conceptions aim at what exists in the world but only hit it imperfectly and 'well off the mark'. The fit between our scientific ideas and reality itself is loose and well short of accurate representation. But there indeed is some sort of rough consonance."

With the orientation towards the natural sciences, naturalism in any case faces the task of systematically identifying, at least approximately, the ontological area *not* included in the naturalized models. There are obviously many qualities and capabilities of the human life-form not addressed within the framework set by the natural sciences. This limitation makes it epistemologically very difficult to exclude normativity and morality from a scientific account of what is – just because something is not addressed does not mean that it is not there.

Within the system of scientific realism, the methods of the natural sciences play a prominent role. However, scientific realism is not the expression *of a single* disciplinary approach. All disciplines that achieve methodological justification within and beyond their disciplinary fields contribute to the scientific concept of reality. Musical notes and melodies are equally justifiable answers to the question of what is, as are genes or laws of nature. It must also be borne in mind that scientific realism is not an invariant structure. It changes constantly and represents the latest developments in various disciplines.

Even advocates of a narrow naturalism must concede that this approach is just as unable to appropriately capture epistemic or moral attitudes, institutions, conventions, social rules, and normative laws as it is to capture works of art, music, or numbers, and they will not go so far as to deny these phenomena – especially since they constantly encounter and react to them. The narrow naturalism is neither able to ward off questions about the reality of normativity, nor to answer them on the basis of its methodological approach. In contrast to a narrow naturalism with its eliminations and naturalizations, an extended or integrative naturalism works with empirical, methodological, and semantic improvements.

The perspectives of the manifest image and the scientific image are both incomplete in their perceptions of the world (see Sellars 1963, pp. 18–32). However, they are by no means unrelated. They are interdependent – both in an epistemological and ontological sense. In both perspectives, questions have to be answered as to which objects or facts are actually accessible within their conceptual frameworks. Extended naturalism has to address the requirements of the life of persons, such as actions, as something which can only be related to the scientific image by means of *additional* methodological investments.[11]

---

[11] Wilfrid Sellars has insistently emphasized that the methodical process of the scientific image goes along with a necessity of descriptive and conceptual extensions. The conceptual framework of persons is a reason for extending the scientific image – not a pretext for elimination. In this way, we connect the scientific view with the human life-form; see Sellars 1963, pp. 38, 40: "Even if the constructive suggestion of the preceding section were capable of being elaborated into an adequate account of the way in which the scientific image could recreate in its own terms the

Extended naturalism is an epistemologically enlightened realism which in no way believes methodological reductions and models to include ontological determinations. The relationship between facts and explanations or theories is one of mutual underdetermination. The assessment of facts is based on theoretical assumptions that do not follow directly from them. Because each theory must have a certain perspective on reality for constructive reasons, it cannot grasp the world in its entirety for simple syntactical or formal reasons.[12] There is no general model or conceptual framework for the world as such. Each scientific approach remains restricted to its field of investigation in terms of description and explanation. Extensions can only be carried out in additional and justifiable steps.

Extended naturalism differs from the naturalistic mainstream in *not* pursuing any elimination scenarios which try to dissolve the space of reasons into the realm of causes. Like all versions of naturalism, it takes a strictly monistic approach and recognizes the primacy of scientific realism in answering the question of what is. The answers presuppose epistemological as well as semantic clarifications and interdisciplinary collaboration in the form of a division of labor. It is in the broad realm of extended naturalism that scientific and moral realism meet.

---

sensations, images, and feelings of the manifest image, the thesis of the primacy of the scientific image would scarcely be off the ground. There would remain the task of showing that categories pertaining to man as a *person* who finds himself confronted by standards (ethical logical, etc.) which often conflict with his desires and impulses, and to which he may or may not conform, can be reconciled with the idea that man is what science says he is. [...] Thus the conceptual framework of persons is the framework in which we think of one another as sharing the community intentions which provide the ambience of principles and standards (above all, those which make meaningful discourse and rationality itself possible) within which we live our own individual lives. A person can almost be defined as a being that has intentions. Thus the conceptual framework of persons is not something that needs to be *reconciled with* the scientific image, but rather something to be *joined* to it. Thus, to complete the scientific image we need to enrich it *not* with more ways of saying what is the case, but with the language of community and individual intentions, so that by construing the actions we intend to do and the circumstances in which we intend to do them in scientific terms, we *directly* relate the world as conceived by scientific theory to our purposes, and make it *our* world and no longer an alien appendage to the world in which we do our living."

12 See Rescher (1985), pp. 57–73. Chapter I: "Die Unvollständigkeit der Wissenschaft – ein Missverständnis" is missing in Rescher (1984).

3 The Relativistic Challenge

Apart from naturalistic challenges, moral realism is confronted with criticism that questions moral objectivity and ethical validity in their entirety. According to this approach, morality in the sense of shared normative codes can be granted while at the same time validity over and above its local scope is contested. This position is often called ethical relativism.[13]

An influential connection between the ontological and relativistic critiques of traditional moral positions has been elaborated by John Mackie. He connects naturalistic doubts regarding the validity of normativity with relativistic objections. Mackie argues that moral realists have strange ontological ideas about independently existing values: "If there were objective values, then they would be entities or qualities or relations of a very strange sort, utterly different from anything else in the universe" (Mackie, 1977, p. 38). He enriches ontological skepticism with the epistemological critique that this kind of moral knowledge presupposes strange moral entities which are not found among ways of perceiving and experiencing the world.

Mackie's idea of the "fabric of the world" (Mackie, 1977, p. 15) is obviously determined by a narrow reading of scientific realism. He consequently blocks the path to ethical objectivity by referring to the fact of various moral codes, between which he does not see any overlapping agreement.[14] Mackie follows the classical relativistic strategy of removing moral claims or normative evaluations from the realm of justifiable propositions. He admits that there are various moral codes in different social domains but denies that they have any normative authority outside their local use. Many objections have been raised against ethical relativism, especially with regard to its methodology. This applies above all to its self-referential inconsistency in failing to consider how global skepticism undermines the foundations of its own position as well as concealing abstract generalizations behind supposed empirical statements.

Relativistic positions aim to exploit cultural pluralism. However, nothing can be inferred from the fact that normative attitudes and beliefs operate in specific

---

[13] On the defense of ethical relativism, see Gilbert Harman (1975), (1977). A debate on the problem of moral objectivity between Gilbert Harman and Judith Jarvis Thomson from the point of view of both anti-realism and realism can be found in Harman/Thomson (1996).

[14] See Mackie (1977), p. 36: "The argument from relativity has as its premise the well-known variation in moral codes from one society to another and from one period to another, and also the differences in moral beliefs between different groups and classes within a complex community. Such variation is in itself merely a truth of descriptive morality, a fact of anthropology which entails neither first nor second order ethical views."

cultural contexts. Diverse manifestations of normativity allow for different interpretations: (1) The *skeptical* version maintains that there are only local ethical beliefs that cannot be universalized; there is no ethical system that is valid outside the local code. (2) The *evaluative* reading concedes that ethical beliefs are, regardless of their specific social contexts, open to evaluations of justifiability. (3) According to the *constructivist* version, all ethical codes can contribute to ethical innovation as long as they allow for justifiable generalizations. This fact can be deduced from the history of human rights, throughout which normative concepts have been developed and expanded.

The diversity of normative and moral codes is exceedingly complex. It conceals historical and geographical asynchronicities as well as normative innovations and improvements. Differing moral codes are not hermetic entities – they interact with one another and change. Diversity does not contradict the possibility of comprehensive universalization. The violation of human rights is to a great extent sanctioned by all known moral codes – even those that deviate in important respects from the modern concept of human rights.[15] The fact of normative diversity shows that questions of justification must be decided on a case-by-case basis. The normative discourse of giving and taking moral reasons is a serious obstacle for positions that aim to cast doubt on the reality of morality and moral objectivity. Criticism of the anti-realist strategies of eliminativism and relativism creates room for considerations of the reality of morality. Nevertheless, anti-realist objections have to be taken seriously. The rejection of extreme forms of naturalism and relativism alone does not exempt us from determining the ontological and metaethical boundaries of practical philosophy and developing a positive account of the reality of morality.

4 Nature and Normativity

The lesson we can learn from eliminativist and relativistic challenges is that moral realism can only be developed justifiably if it is anchored in the world described at least partly by the natural sciences. Moral realism does not escape the methodological requirements of scientific realism simply by rejecting eliminativist claims. Naturalism rightly points to the fact that the standpoint of scientific

---

15 Normative development is nevertheless confronted with devastating violations of human rights. These violations are disputed by the perpetrators or declared acts of self-defense. No one, however, defends himself by saying that it is morally good to violate human rights. Jean-Jacques Rousseau defended universalized ethics by pointing out that there is no country in the world where perfidy is honored. See Rousseau (1969), p. 599.

realism and its fundamental concept of the realm of causes has an ontological primacy (see Sellars 1963, pp. 32–37).

The systematic starting point of moral realism is the conceptual convergence of the realm of causes and the space of reasons.[16] The space of reasons is the epistemic and logical condition for statements about reality. It also constitutes the realm of causes,[17] and in this respect the realm of causes and the space of reasons are always interrelated in an epistemological and ontological division of labor.

The space of reasons opens up ways to introduce morality into the world of actions and events. John McDowell – guided by the Aristotelian concept of second nature and Sellars's inferential system of the space of reasons – argues that reasons are integral components of the constitution of the human life-form and therefore always operate within the world of events, i.e. the realm of causes. In this regard, McDowell rejects both a narrow naturalism and a return to the dualism of mind and world. He subscribes to a version of naturalism that can integrate the specific properties of the human life-form as second nature with a comprehensive ontological concept of nature. A naturalistic integration of the space of reasons should make it possible to keep the human life-form in the ontological domain, as it is conceived by scientific naturalism, without having to eliminate human properties and capabilities. In this respect, McDowell's position is well suited to introduce naturalistic realism into the field of ethics.[18]

The ontological integration of moral realism is made possible by an extended naturalism[19] which does not assume that the program of naturalization can describe experiences and events in every respect. An extended naturalism concedes that scientific realism and the natural sciences are the best candidates to answer the question of what is. In contrast to eliminative programs of naturali-

---

16 On the concept of the space of reasons, see Sellars (1997), p. 76: "The essential point is that in characterizing an episode or a state as that of knowing, we are not giving an empirical description of that episode or state; we are placing it in the logical space of reasons, of justifying and being able to justify what one says."

17 Relations in the realm of causes are reducible to mechanisms of the micro-, meso- and macro-world and their respective nomologies.

18 See McDowell (1994), p. 84: "[H]uman beings are intelligently initiated into this stretch of the space of reasons by ethical upbringing, which instils the appropriate shape into their lives. The resulting habits of thought and action are second nature. This should defuse the fear of supernaturalism. Second nature could not float free of potentialities that belong to a normal human organism. This gives human reason enough of a foothold in the realm of law to satisfy any proper respect for modern natural science."

19 Cf. note 6.

zation, it retains the phenomenological and explanatory competence of non-physicalist disciplines.

In dealing with the attitudes, dispositions, and behavior of persons, an extended naturalism operates within a psychophysical world. It organizes its ontological requirements with the help of a wide disciplinary spectrum. It adheres to both the unity of reality and the unity of science without maintaining the ontological primacy of one discipline. The unity of the sciences does not mean homogeneity of the disciplinary landscape, but rather rules out disciplines' ontological self-legitimization.

Extended naturalism widens its monistic ontology with an epistemological framework and works with the realm of causes *and* the space of reasons. This approach avoids dualist dichotomies with the help of an epistemological analysis of the scope of application of the respective scientific vocabularies. In particular, the analysis concentrates on the reconstruction of a phenomenologically and semantically adequate description of specific capabilities, dispositions, and events. An important result of this extension is that the mental and the physical become aspects of one and the same worldview.[20] The space of reasons proves to be a further development of the system of representation which we know from other life-forms. Representations generally express specific forms of independent orders within physical or natural processes.

The inferential relations in the space of reasons follow specific rules but remain at any rate indirectly dependent on processes that can be addressed at least partially within nomologies of the realm of causes. The intentions of a person do not float, as it were, in a vacuum. Rather, they evolve out of an understanding of past events. The planning and acting person associates them with specific expe-

---

[20] See Spinoza's original insight: "The human mind perceives not only the affections of the Body, but also the ideas of these affections" (Spinoza 1985, II, p. 22). Cf. Hampshire (1971), p. 226: "My self-conscious materialist [Spinoza] argues that the relation between a man's thought and sentiment, and the physical state that embodies it, is in these ways too close to be counted as a causal relation, or as analogous to the relation between two physical states, one of which adequately explains the other. It is precisely the point of materialism to assert a much closer relation between processes of thought and physical processes than is implied in most of the idioms of ordinary speech. My philosopher is a genuine materialist in the narrow sense that he asserts that every change in the state of the organism, which is a change in thought, is also a change in some bodily state, and usually in the principal instrument of thought, the brain. From the standpoint of an observer, a person's bodily and mental processes are each reflections of the other, with neither of them privileged as substance to shadow. According to one possible criterion of identity, the same process in the organism, which for the subject is his thought or sequence of thoughts, may also be observed and described, by an observer, as a physical state or sequence of physical states."

riences that she has had in the formation and realization of intentions and goals. These experiences determine the identification of the scope of actions.

Actions result from the interactions of a person with her natural and social environment, which are initiated in the form of active or reactive behavior.[21] The action of a person is thus a multidimensional process in which reasons and causes are equally involved. Contrary to eliminative assumptions, the constraints of the realm of causes do not determine what the individual person does. In their deliberations and intentions, they move within the framework of the rules of the space of reasons and related social conditions.[22]

The life of a person is the result of the internal connection of her self-consciousness, linguistic behavior, and action. Persons are only exonerated from their responsibilities when they have no influence at all. As soon as a person determines specific causal dependencies in her behavior, she is in principle able to analyze them and divert their effects. In the space of reasons, persons will not be able to change hard facts, but they decide how they should relate to them and what importance they are prepared to accord them.

5 Nomological Realism

A major obstacle for moral realism is the problem of representation, for which traditional versions have found no solution. The problem of representation consists in the assumption that moral expressions stand for something. Moral statements are true when what they refer to is the case. The moral realist appears to be determined by strong metaphysical requirements that amount to a connection between true moral statements and the intrinsic characteristics of moral facts, objects, or values. The truth of moral claims is justified by the appropriate representation of independent facts or objects. Moral realism – whether in the form of Platonism, classical intuitionism, or value ethics – has been unable to avoid working with reifications of representations or quasi-objects. The simple model of representation of moral knowledge and independent facts results in an ontological position which is left wide open to naturalistic and relativistic criticism.

A moral realist who wants to meet the naturalistic challenge has to avoid reifications and accept that moral facts appear in a world to which natural sciences can refer. The moral realist, therefore, has to show that moral facts are not *entirely* dependent on non-moral elements. If a person behaves in accordance

---

[21] See Strawson 1974, pp. 6–13; and Hacker 2007, pp. 144–160.
[22] See Brandom 1994, pp. 89–94; Hacker 2007, pp. 199–232.

with moral reason and acts correspondingly, then she moves both in the space of reasons and in the realm of causes. Her behavior is not fully determined by the realm of causes, although she cannot under any circumstances escape its physical restrictions.

An essential characteristic of an epistemologically clarified realism is that it identifies normative constraints and determinations *as such*. The naturalist challenge makes it impossible to introduce these constraints by way of a simple representational model. In looking for ontologically less straightforward approaches, an analysis of linguistic behavior in the development of the human life-form due to the internal connection between language and the space of reasons appears as a plausible starting point.

The linguistic behavior of persons belongs to the natural history of the human life-form and therefore to natural history in general. Humans have altered their personal conduct and environments via linguistically constituted activities since the dawn of man. Linguistic behavior takes place in the world of events and expresses facts of the realm of causes in the space of reasons in such a reliable way that it even allows for predictions. Due to their sophisticated linguistic behavior, persons are responsive to normative demands and constraints. To the extent that they have conceptual capacities, they have solutions for epistemic, moral, and aesthetic problems at their disposal.[23]

Even the use of specific expressions for psychic conditions such as pain, happiness, or fear comes about as a result of attitudes and modes of behavior with which persons react to external conditions.[24] The reality of the human life-form is extremely complex. It consists of a variety of connected domains to which the physical dimension belongs just as much as the moral and the aesthetic dimensions. We are permanently confronted with acts, events, objects, and states of affairs that are practically resistant and in this respect ontologically independent from us.

---

23 Cf. McDowell (1994), p. 82: "The ethical is a domain of rational requirements, which are there in any case, whether or not we are responsive to them. We are alerted to these demands by acquiring appropriate conceptual capacities. When a decent upbringing initiates us into the relevant way of thinking, our eyes are opened to the very existence of this tract of the space of reasons. Thereafter our appreciation of its detailed layout is indefinitely subject to refinement, in reflective scrutiny of our ethical thinking."
24 See Wittgenstein (1960), p. 390 (§ 244); cf. Lovibond (1983), p. 149: "The possibility of the language-game with the word 'pain' is conditioned by certain uniformities in the way human beings react to the impact of external conditions on their bodies, or to events and processes inside their bodies."

In propositional attitudes, linguistic behavior manifests a form of objectivity that cannot be understood as consisting in simple referential relations. Such propositional attitudes create semantic situations in which persons seem to have no choice but to react in predictable and limited ways.[25] Willard V. O. Quine spoke of a "pull toward objectivity" or an "objective pull" (Quine 1960, pp. 7, 8)[26] that drives us away from subjective associations. The *pull toward objectivity* is an element of our interaction with the world. It orders and stabilizes our linguistic behavior and social practice through a variety of epistemic and normative corrections.

Moral facts belong to the reality of the human life-form just as much as do events in space and time. Persons refer to moral facts differently than to events in space and time. They apprehend the observable behavior of other persons when they make decisions and act. It would be an oversimplification to say that the perception of events is a hard fact of our world, while moral attitudes only express relative states. In fact, moral attitudes are determined by rule-governed behavior and follow "a kind of grammar of conduct" (Hampshire 1983, p. 92). In the moral space of reasons, rule-governed behavior allows for situationally determined normative differences between true and false statements, or between better and worse options.[27] These differences rarely take the shape of moral certainties, but they represent normative constraints in the process of giving and taking moral reasons.

In principle, moral conflicts can be solved in the space of reasons – even if it is not always practically possible. Accordingly, *one* goal of the project of moral realism is achieved: the limitation of ethical relativism, as normative differences are in form and content independent of the respective motivations of persons and the cultural coloring of the various moral language games. This form of realism is furthermore in a position to refute the exaggerated ontological claims of

---

25 Cf. Wittgenstein on the hardness of the logical must; see Wittgenstein (1974), pp. 352–353, 430–431.

26 Cf. Lovibond, (1983), pp. 58–68.

27 Crispin Wright pointed out that there is a harmless way to introduce representational correspondence in ethics. These correspondence relations come under consideration when the truth of statements is being determined; see Wright, Crispin (1995), pp. 219–220: "Reverting to the issue of realism, there may seem to be a tension between the suggestion that the hallmark of a realist conception of truth is its implication of the notion of representation, or fit, and the inclusion, among the set of basic platitudes constitutive of any truth predicate, of one to the effect that to be true is to correspond to the facts. It is crucial to see that this is not really a difficulty. It is indeed a platitude that a statement is true if and only if it corresponds to the facts. [...] Correspondence phraseology – and all the paraphrases of it that we are likely to think of – are co-licensed, as it were, with talk of truth."

narrow naturalism. The appropriate view of the reality of the human life-form shows that the natural sciences do not grasp everything that exists. This, however, in no way requires moral realists to maintain that the natural-scientific account *as such* is incomplete – it is just what it is: a reliable answer to specific questions about what is.

For moral realism, objectivity relates to forms of normative commitment and to moral constraints on possible actions.[28] The classification of moral objectivity as a justifiable normative limitation shares formal characteristics with the Kantian concept of moral laws. Kant responds to the semantic and normative constraints of our moral consciousness in the *Critique of Practical Reason* with the expression "order of concepts in us."[29] The form of the moral law is the source of normative constraints. In this respect, it can be said that the rules or maxims supported by the categorical imperative have the potential to affect the attitudes and behavior of persons.[30] The realism of normative constraints subsists without reifications – to this extent, we are dealing with a *nomological* realism. Its source of objectivity is law-governed behavior – not a mysterious relation to reified values. In the case of moral actions, the formal qualities of the moral law determine the attitudes and behavior of the acting person. She follows formal standards with regard to what one may or may not do under the conditions of ethical justifiability.

Nomological realism is a *framework in action,* not an invariant system. From the perspective of nomological realism, the normative aspects of reality unfold as the outcome of a rule-governed practice.[31] Whoever addresses moral facts and raises normative demands must have consistent rules and a corresponding vocabulary at her disposal in order to conform to semantic standards and master the practice of giving and taking moral reasons. She must not resort to the intrinsic qualities of a metaphysical domain. It is entirely sufficient that she be in possession of assertoric contents under the conditions of normative constraints (see Wright 1995, pp. 213–216).

---

[28] In this regard, Stuart Hampshire speaks of how morality functions as a barrier in carrying out our actions. See Hampshire (1983), pp. 87–92.
[29] Kant (2003), p. 40: "Ordnung der Begriffe in uns".
[30] Christine Korsgaard interprets a good maxim as an "intrinsically normative entity." Only because a moral statement has the form of a law it is intrinsically suited to answering normative claims. See Korsgaard, (1996), p. 108.
[31] The "pull towards objectivity" lies in the formal qualities of the moral law. In his defense of Neo-Kantian constructivism, John Rawls points out that the categorical imperative carries formal requirements that in procedural terms can be compared to arithmetic sequences. See Rawls (1993), pp. 102–110.

Nomological Realism invents, construes, and discovers.[32] Its elements are (1) ethical objectivity in the form of normative constraints, (2) the rejection of reifications and discoveries of independent values, (3) an inferential system of rules and maxims, and (4) rules and standards for reasonable disagreements and conflicts. Nomological realism shares elements with Neo-Kantian constructivism[33] that allow for strong cognitive requirements[34] and with Neo-Spinozist anti-dualism in the form of a framework for the joint workings of nature, mind, and normativity. With its normative constraints, nomological realism is in the privileged position of introducing moral objectivity into the conceptual and ontological realm of naturalism.

Bibliography

Blackburn, Simon (1998): *Ruling Passions*. Oxford: Clarendon Press.
Brandom, Robert (1994): *Making it Explicit*. Cambridge, Mass.: Harvard University Press.
Darwall, Stephen, Allan Gibbard, and Peter Railton (1992): "Toward *Fin de Siècle* Ethics: Some Trends." In: *The Philosophical Review* 101, pp. 115–189.
Hacker, Peter (2007): *Human Nature. The Categorial Framework*. Oxford: Blackwell.
Hampshire, Stuart (1971): "A Kind of Materialism." In: *Freedom of Mind and Other Essays*. Princeton: Princeton University Press, pp. 210–231
Hampshire, Stuart (1983): *Morality and Conflict*. Cambridge, Mass.: Harvard University Press.
Harman, Gilbert (1975): "Moral Relativism Defended." In: *Philosophical Review* Vol. 84, pp. 3–22.
Harman, Gilbert/Thomson, Judith J. (1996): *Moral Relativism and Moral Objectivity*. Oxford: Blackwell.
Kant, Immanuel (2003): *Kritik der praktischen Vernunft*. Hamburg: Meiner.
Korsgaard, Christine (1996): *The Sources of Normativity*. Cambridge, Mass.: Cambridge University Press.
Korsgaard, Christine (2003): "Realism and Constructivism in Twentieth-Century Moral Philosophy." In: *Journal of Philosophical Research* Vol. 28, pp. 99–122.
Lovibond, Sabina (1983): *Realism and Imagination in Ethics*. Minneapolis: University of Minnesota Press.

---

[32] David Wiggins paraphrased this in the following way: "In as much as invention and discovery are distinguishable, and in so far as either of these ideas properly belongs here, life's having a point may depend as much upon something contributed by the person whose life it is as it depends upon something discovered" (Wiggins (1987), p. 132.).

[33] Cf. Korsgaard (1996), p. 34 ff. Korsgaard describes a procedural moral realism that is identifiable through its claim that there are right and wrong answers to moral questions. On the difference between Kantian constructivism and moral realism, cf. Korsgaard (2003).

[34] Cf. Wright (1992), pp. 33–75.

Lovibond, Sabina (1995): "Aristotelian ethics and 'enlargement of thought.'" In: Robert Heinaman (Ed.): *Aristotle and Moral Realism.* Boulder: Westview, pp. 99–120.
Mackie, John (1977): *Ethics: Inventing Right and Wrong.* New York: Penguin.
McDowell, John (1994): *Mind and World.* Cambridge, Mass.: Harvard University Press.
Quine, Willard V. O. (1960): *Word and Object.* Cambridge, Mass.: MIT Press.
Rachels, James (Ed.) (1998): *Ethical Theory 1: The Question of Objectivity.* Oxford: Oxford University Press.
Rawls, John (1993): *Political Liberalism.* New York: Columbia University Press.
Rescher, Nicholas (1984): *The Limits of Science.* Berkeley: University of California Press.
Rescher, Nicholas (1985): *Die Grenzen der Wissenschaft.* Stuttgart: Reclam.
Rescher, Nicholas (1987): *Scientific Realism.* Dordrecht: Reidel.
Rousseau, Jean-Jacques (1969): *Émile ou de l'éducation.* In: *Œuvres complètes IV.* Paris: Gallimard, pp. 241–877.
Sayre-McCord, Geoffrey (Ed.) (1988): *Essays on Moral Realism.* Ithaca: Cornell University Press.
Sellars, Wilfried (1997): *Empiricism and the Philosophy of Mind.* Cambridge, Mass.: Harvard University Press.
Sellars, Wilfrid (1963): *Science, Perception and Reality.* Atascadero: Ridgeview.
Spinoza, Benedictus de (1985): *Ethics.* In: *The Collected Works of Spinoza, Vol. 1.* Princeton: Princeton University Press.
Strawson, Peter F. (1974): *Freedom and Resentment and Other Essays.* London: Methuen.
Sturma, Dieter (2005): *Philosophie des Geistes.* Leipzig: Reclam.
Sturma, Dieter (2008): "Die Natur der Freiheit: Integrativer Naturalismus in der theoretischen und praktischen Philosophie." In: *Philosophisches Jahrbuch* 115, pp. 385–396.
Sturma, Dieter (2012): "Freiheit und Selbstbewusstsein im Raum der Gründe." In: Dieter Sturma (Ed.), *Vernunft und Freiheit: Zur praktischen Philosophie von Julian Nida-Rümelin.* Berlin: de Gruyter, pp. 157–177.
Sturma, Dieter (2015): "Handeln: Freiheit im Raum der Ursachen und im Raum der Gründe." In: Sebastian Muders, Bettina Schöne-Seifert, Markus Rüther (Eds.): *Willensfreiheit im Kontext: Interdisziplinäre Perspektiven auf das Handeln.* Münster: mentis, pp. 19–42.
Sturma, Dieter (2018): "Persons: A Thick Description of the Human Life Form." In: Jörg Noller (Ed.): *Was sind und wie existieren Personen? Tendenzen der aktuellen Forschung.* Münster: mentis, pp. 147–166.
Thomson, Judith J. (2008): *Normativity.* Chicago: Open Court.
Wiggins, David (1987): "Truth, Invention, and the Meaning of Life." In: David Wiggins: *Needs, Values, Truth: Essays in the Philosophy of Value.* Oxford: Blackwell, pp. 87–137.
Wittgenstein, Ludwig (1960): *Philosophische Untersuchungen* (Schriften 1, pp. 279–544). Frankfurt/M.: Suhrkamp.
Wittgenstein, Ludwig (1974): *Bemerkungen über die Grundlagen der Mathematik* (Schriften 6). Frankfurt am Main: Suhrkamp.
Wright, Crispin (1992): *Truth and Objectivity.* Cambridge, Mass.: Harvard University Press.
Wright, Crispin (1995): "Truth in Ethics." In: *Ratio* 8, pp. 209–226.

Jocelyn Benoist
Realism Without Entities

To my friend Thierry Paul

Abstract: The true realist is not the philosopher who endorses, in the name (for example) of a Russellian project of analysis, the task of displaying the furniture of the world in some kind of idealized "list of entities." Instead, within realist projects, full weight should be given to reality in the way it is actually talked or thought about in the context of our actual concerns and practical lives. The claim here is not that our talk or thought determines reality, but rather that this thought and talk nevertheless essentially leaves its imprint, in some way, on any coherent conception of what this reality is like. To address reality, therefore, is not just to list entities, but rather, to consider and focus on actual uses that come to grips with reality in diverse ways.

1

One common mistake about realism in general is to think that adopting it would consist in overpopulating the world – even more so if this world itself 'does not exist' – with entities. The more things or non-things you take there to be, the more of a realist you would be.

There is certainly some truth in this. Realism does not come down to reductionism; quite the contrary. To be a realist requires an open mind: i.e., a mind open to the multiplicity of senses of what exists. The problem, however, might reside in this very notion of 'sense.' For the fact that there are diverse senses of reality does not amount to the pure and simple *reality of these senses* – as if, in introducing senses, you had introduced some more things, besides what they are senses of. Of course, some realities are required in order to bear senses and, so to speak, let them work. However, senses precisely *work*, and are not just given things to be added to an ontological collection.

To reify senses and to deal with them as some kind of (super-)natural entities, and thus to forget that there is no sense but a sense that is *made*, is, as a position, usually called 'Platonism' in contemporary philosophy. This designation, as such, stems from the philosophy of mathematics and logic. However, its meaning is essentially metaphysical, starting with a metaphysical interpretation of mathematics and logic themselves, which is paradigmatic of what metaphysics does in general: to interpret metaphysically what is not per se metaphysical.

In order to reach an *unshadowed realism*[1] – i.e. a kind of realism able to make sense of *the difference between reality and the sense(s) of reality* instead of treating those senses as some shadowy pieces of reality – the debate with Platonism seems therefore to be a priority. By dispersing the mirages[2] of realism allegedly to be found outside the Cave, we may hope to become more able to see that there are no walls to this Cave and to make sense of what there is inside (which is outside): reality.

2

In order to tackle this issue, let us return to the field in which the notion originates. By focusing on this field, we might expect to clarify the presuppositions of such a view. So far, Platonism has been quite a central issue in the philosophy of mathematics, to the extent that it sometimes seems to be its *unique* issue. The philosopher keeps asking whether mathematical objects exist or not, and she does this in such an abstract way that it is often very difficult to see whether the question makes any sense: as if the ontological decision about mathematics lay *beyond mathematics*, in some purely metaphysical discussion.

On the other side, Platonism, very likely with a different meaning, seems to be *the belief by default* of the working mathematician. It certainly makes sense: how can one work on entities without taking them to exist?

However, first, maybe it is not so clear that mathematics always consists in working on *entities*. One should ask: what are the particular conditions under which the mathematical practice can be thus described? It may be the case that some parts of mathematics absolutely call for that kind of description, others not. 'Mathematical objects' as such may be just *some part* of what mathematical activity is about. Of course, then, they are still a part of it, and the philosopher should take into account that aspect, as well, of the picture that the mathematician has of her own activity.

Second, if Platonism comes down to taking some particular entities to exist, the question of what it means 'to exist' unavoidably arises. After all, if it is just about *positing* some entities and affirming that 'they are' – or, more exactly, that 'there is/are some entity/entities such that...' – as we constantly do in mathematics, for instance as the result of a proof of existence, it is really doubtful that in

---

[1] In the very sense in which Travis 2000 talks of 'unshadowed thought.' Look at his interesting considerations on 'Platonism' at the beginning of his book.
[2] For an ontology of mirages, see the beautiful passage on *fata morgana* in Gabriel 2016, p.196.

this any 'Platonism' should be entailed. 'Platonism' seems to call for a more substantial ontological commitment. One technical way to put this is precisely to say that Platonism consists in the belief that the so-called entities exist *beyond and independently of their proof of existence.*

Thus, we enter into the logical space of the traditional debate of which 'Platonism' is the title. It is common in that debate to draw a contrast between to *invent* on the one side and to *discover* on the other side: *erfinden* versus *entdecken*, as for instance Friedrich Waismann discusses in his *Introduction to Mathematical Thinking* (Waismann 1936). One *invents* what would not have been independent of this invention. On the other hand, one *discovers* what is *already there* to be discovered.

What makes the whole debate tricky is that there is something fishy in that very alternative. It seems that, so far, Platonism has won all its victories by using a guilt trip. Platonists usually try to convince us that if we do not buy their alleged transcendent entities, then we fall back into some kind of *fictionalism*: either the mathematical entities, whatever they might be, are transcendent *or* they are mere *fictions* – which gives them over to the arbitrariness of subjectivity. On the second horn of the alternative, it seems that these entities can just be *anything*, which we do not want; therefore we have to buy into Platonism. Probably there is indeed something mistaken in the idea of 'invention' applied to mathematical entities. It is as if we created them arbitrarily, independent of any structural constraint, as if *we made them up*. This full-fledged fictionalist interpretation of mathematics is certainly difficult to buy. It is at odds with the strong *sense of objectivity* experienced by the working mathematician.

However, I cannot see why the collapse of the purely constructionist model should compel us to buy the opposite model of the (so to speak) *naïve finding*. The complex shape of the leaves of a tree can certainly be described by using a mathematical object; however, mathematical objects do not grow on trees. I mean: they are not *'naturally given.'* Now, one way to formulate the question of Platonism would precisely be to ask whether what cannot be 'naturally given' might be '*given*' at all. This is not to say that some objects would be 'too good' for them to be given, and would stay beyond the scope of givenness, but rather that 'being given' *is* just 'being naturally given' (in one way or another, perceptual or not): that is to say, being encountered as something that is what it is *independently of what we do*. From this point of view, one might say that Platonism is a *naturalistic* model of mathematics – characterized by the fact that it deals with the mathematical realm as *a kind of nature.*

It seems that the discussion of Platonism has so far excessively – and almost exclusively – focused on the ontology of that 'nature.' The common sense view has issues with buying what it perceives as a hyper-nature – a nature that is not like the one that common sense is acquainted with. On the other side, mathematical Platonists insist that there is not only that familiar nature, but also that mathematicians are really acquainted with their non-physical objects, in a way more or less analogous to the way in which ordinary people are acquainted with their sensible objects. Of course, the whole point of the controversy is that this acquaintance should, at the same time, *be the same and not be the same* as the ordinary one. Mathematical objects are not to be perceived – as they commonly say: the mathematical circle is *not to be seen* – yet it is nevertheless *as if* the mathematician perceived these objects in their transcendent being. Mathematical Platonism feeds on this tacit parallel with ordinary perception, which at the same time it is supposed to transcend.

Now, in my view, the problem in this case might not be so much with the idea of a hyperphysical (non-physical) nature as with the very idea of *nature*. The metaphor of discovery that is linked up with it is actually misleading.

Of course, this is not to say that there are no *discoveries* in mathematics or that they cannot sometimes take on the specific form of the discovery of objects. Once more, philosophy should take into account that essential dimension of the mathematician's experience.

However, those discoveries that are made by the working mathematician make sense *only within a mathematical context*. If there is an ontology to be found in mathematics – that is to say: to be found *within the mathematical framework* – it is definitely not an ontology of gatherers roaming in the jungle, but of farmers who have staked out their fields. Is mathematics not all about 'harvest and sowing', in Grothendieck's[3] words? This is not to deny that sometimes one happens to find a rock in one's field, or that boundary quarrels ever break out. It just means that 'discoveries' are only possible *in an already mathematized universe*. They are no *mere encounters* with a naked exteriority.

Now, the problem with mathematical Platonism is probably that it tends to make mathematical objectivity so strong as to place it, so to speak, *beyond* mathematics; as if mathematical beings had a being on their own independently of *their life in mathematics*.

From this point of view, I think Jean-Yves Girard's sarcastic remark makes a lot of sense, when he derides our naïve picture of the set of the integers as an infinite showroom of hunting trophies (see Girard 2006, p. 4). If we are going

---

[3] Alexander Grothendieck was one of the greatest mathematicians of the twentieth century. He invented a new branch of mathematics, algebraic geometry, characterized by its capacity to integrate different domains. *Harvest and Sowing* (*Récoltes et semailles*, sometimes translated as *Reaping and Sowing*) is a long autobiographical text, which is also a meditation on the nature of mathematical activity.

to address mathematical objectivity, we want to look at it *where it works – and how it works* – not where it is stuffed and, so to speak, deprived of any life.

But my point is not about mathematical Platonism as such; that might turn out to be a local question, which keeps all its legitimacy within a mathematical framework, once its metaphysical basis has been destabilized. As a philosopher, I would rather like to address a definite interpretation of mathematical Platonism, which seems to provide *a general standard in philosophy*, to the extent that it is possible to talk of Platonism in very different areas – as Putnam, for instance, does in ethics, making it the target of his criticism (see Putnam 2005) – and maybe as characterizing a general posture of mind.

In order to make sense of this generalization, we should ask what is really characteristic of the attitude of which Girard makes fun in his picturesque description. According to that description, it seems that Platonism about integers for instance, simply comes down to *considering them independently of their (real) use*. As they stand, pinned to our mental wall, they are just *useless*.

Now, in such a state, they are precisely *not* what they are: that is to say, *numbers*. A number is something with which one can calculate. To take it independently of those calculations in which it can play some part is not only to *abstract* it, as some philosophers might be prone to say, but to *miss* its nature as a number, since, as a number, *it is meant for that*. Thus, the very nature of the number comes to the fore in the calculations we perform with it. A kind of number is defined by a way to calculate, and one might say that there are *as many various kinds of numbers as diverse ways to calculate with numbers*. It is a possible answer to the traditional question whether the notion of 'number' is univocal or not, already triggered by the invention of irrational numbers in antiquity: *just look at what you do with your numbers!*

In this sense, the meaning of a number is determined by *its (mathematical) use*. It cannot be described apart from this use. A number definitely belongs to a mathematical theory, but it belongs to a *mathematical practice* as well,[4] insofar as, at some level, one cannot separate mathematical theory and mathematical practice: in mathematics, as a rule, a theory defines a set of *possible operations* (or transformations).

This is not to say that numbers just 'do not exist,' but are the mere artefacts of use. There is no necessity in the inference that would take us from the desta-

---

[4] This is the general orientation of the philosophy of mathematics set out in Wittgenstein 1978.

bilization of the alleged Platonic picture to the endorsement of a reductionist, revisionist, intuitionist[5] attitude.

'Use' is not a thing that anything can be 'reduced to.' *If there is use, there is something to be used*. Thus, to put the emphasis on *the (mathematical) use of numbers* as something to which we should give the pride of place if we want to make sense of what numbers are, is not at all to get rid of numbers as legitimate citizens of the mathematical world nor even as 'objects.' It is, much more, to highlight the particular conditions of their objectivity – of their *diverse* objectivity. In contrast to this, Platonism is the stance that consists in *making the objects use-less*.

By saying that Platonism makes the objects whose existence it claims 'useless,' I do not mean that it deprives them of any *practical* utility, as if mathematical meaning were to depend essentially on the possibility of an extra-mathematical application – so, for instance, on the possibility of mathematized physics. Possibly, extra-mathematical application is far more important to mathematics than one usually takes it to be, to the extent that it is very often a part of mathematical meaning itself. However, in this case, one might suspect that, finally, the alleged 'extra-mathematical' indeed turns out to be mathematical, and that we should revise our initial view about what was mathematical – as opposed to 'non-mathematical' – in the story we tell.[6]

Nonetheless, if any kind of 'utility' is of concern here, it is *the utility in the context of a mathematical practice*. Or maybe, more exactly, since utility inopportunely suggests some kind of transcendent end that it should help to reach, the mere fact of *being used in such a practice*. Platonism makes things etymologically 'use-less' in the sense that it just cuts them off from use, hanging them on the wall of trophies.

In other words, one might say that Platonism is the ontological counterpart of that attitude that philosophers usually adopt towards language, according to Wittgenstein: they are looking at language as it is when it "goes on holiday" (see

---

[5] In the sense of a metaphysical conception according to which we should countenance the mathematical existence only of what can be constructed – and, thus, in some sense, 'given in intuition.' My Wittgensteinian point is not metaphysical: I do not say 'exists only the kind of things that... .' My point is grammatical: I rather say 'if you want to make sense of the existence of anything, pay attention to its use(s)!' As a matter of fact, a great deal of metaphysics was involved is the position that was called 'intuitionism' – in the sense of Brouwer, for instance – in the history of the philosophy of mathematics.

[6] On this topic, see Benoist 2013. The concept of 'perturbations' as a physical phenomenon, for instance, may be introduced first as something external to mathematical structure and the limits to it, and, in a second step, become just part of it and acquire an intrinsic mathematical meaning.

Wittgenstein 1958, § 38, p. 19). In a quite analogous way – maybe exactly *the same way* – Platonism might turn out to be the *objectual* side of the essentialization of meaning: Platonism invites us to look at objects independently of any definite use in which our referring to those objects can be involved. Or at least, it is the mythology of *a super-Use that would go beyond uses.*

This point, of course, is not just about mathematics. One might even say that it is very incidentally about mathematics, since, in this story, *mathematical practice does not matter as such*. Thus, 'mathematical Platonism' is certainly the paradigm of a very general posture of mind: what we might call *'the metaphysical mind.'* Throughout the history of philosophy, from Pythagoras to Badiou, indeed, a fantasy of mathematical ontology has very often been used to set the tone of metaphysics in general.

Following the path set by our analysis of mathematical Platonism, we can give this characterization of the metaphysical view: *it claims to get at things as they are 'independently of any way to go about dealing with them.'* Thus, the prevalence of ontology in some (classical) sense of the term is characteristic of the metaphysical mind. To it, every question can and should be turned into an *ontological question*, as if ontology, precisely, could be independent of any more *specific* question.

To question the legitimacy of any such project is a top priority in the present philosophical situation. The return of metaphysics, understood as substantial ontology, independent of epistemology and semantics and to some extent prior to them, is a blatant fact in contemporary philosophy on both sides of the cracking wall which, to some extent, is still supposed to divide it into two different worlds: the so-called Analytic and Continental ones. Our time is thirsting for ontology, a need apparently to be satisfied by one means or another. Contrary to many philosophers who, on either side, nowadays are willing to satisfy it, I shall personally prefer the sobering therapeutic option.

What's wrong with ontology? Nothing, if it really did what it is supposed to do: *really* address the issue of *what there is*. However, that question has a cost and, in order to tackle the problem seriously, one should become aware of the conditions under which it might be formulated correctly. The problem with what is usually called 'ontology' is that it is an attempt at formulating the problem *unconditionally*. Ontology is essentially *de-contextualization*, the quest for an acontextual description of what there is. In contrast, the ordinary *local* question about what there is does not call for an answer to the question about what there is *in general*, but in particular, from some definite point of view and in a definite situation. Thus, it might not be a (purely) ontological question in the traditional sense of the term.[7]

Now, this is not to say that everything should be discarded in the present 'ontological turn.' Of course, this turn has its reasons that may be found, in particular, in the context of the history of analytic philosophy after the Second World War. The revival of 'metaphysics,' understood as 'ontology,' in analytic philosophy at the end of the twentieth century should be assessed against the backdrop of the domination of the semantic perspective in the previous era. From this point of view, the ontological turn might have been a real step forward. It expressed the craving for a more substantial conception of truth, the view that the world is not just what I am talking about, but has structures of its own, which are what is captured if I am talking about it adequately.

What does 'adequacy' mean? It means that thought exerts a real grip on the world, does not stop short of it, but gives it to us *as it is*, in its being that is independent of thought. That kind of 'realistic' constraint is certainly something that we want to retain from the 'ontological turn.' Our language and the thought that it expresses are not cut off from the world they refer to, but they are ploughing deep normative furrows in that very world, determining what should count as *this* or *that* – which certainly requires first that something *be* for it to count as this or that. On the other hand, what is thus captured is not just what is talked or thought about, but is *some being*, which usually has properties other than those of simply being talked or thought about. And to talk and to think, is, very commonly, to talk and to think of those 'other properties.' Thus, the overcoming of a mere 'semantic' perspective – one that deals with things as mere correlates of talk or thought[8] – does not mean that we should have to open any kind of back door in order to get to 'the things themselves' beyond language or thought. To some extent, it just comes down to *taking language and thought seriously* – in their actual commitment to reality.

Consequently, the issue of 'realism' correctly understood has just nothing to do with the so-called debate between 'correlationism' and 'anti-correlationism' characteristic of the last stage of what is called 'Continental thought.' What makes reality real is not – necessarily – that it is beyond or within our reach.

---

[7] In this regard, I agree with a good part of what Gabriel (2016) says, as far as it is an attempt to put forward a *contextualized ontology*. The only problem is that contextualizing ontology is something that ontology itself cannot do.

[8] For the sake of the argumentation, I pretend here that there is no difference (from this point of view), but in fact there is: it is not clear at all that it makes any sense to talk of *a 'correlate' to a thought*. To be exact, there is nothing like a *mental semantics*.

The question is rather, under which conditions our reach may be 'real' or not, i.e. may deal correctly with reality.

What would happen to the world if I disappeared, as I surely will? It would certainly remain the same, except for some details. However, as independent as it is from me, it would still be just what I imagine: 'the world without me.' Our being overwhelmed by the world is a possible take of ours on the world, as uncomfortable as that take might prove to be – which is a real *metaphysical* (but not an ontological) issue.[9]

So, the point is that to give full weight to the reality of what is talked or thought about is not to abstract from talking or thinking. On the contrary, in order to make sense of that 'reality' we should focus on how we talk and think about it, on *our real ways* of doing that.[10] Not that our talk or thought 'determines reality,' as is sometimes said, but it *makes it count in some way*. And reality is exactly *what might count, in one way or another.*

To address reality, therefore, is not just to list entities, as if we had some back door view of the museum of useless objects, to make *lists*, which are by definition *acontextual* (even when they are 'local'), but to consider *uses, real uses* that come to grips with reality.

The big mistake of modern relativism is to believe that, because reality is necessarily to be described by the standard of some use, it is so to speak *less real for that*. In such views we find a mistake about the nature of 'use' as well. It implies the assumption that uses did not take place in the world and were not many ways to facilitate orientation within reality, and thus, to be engaged in it.[11]

The alternative picture could be the following: thinking is essentially *something we do*. That does not mean that it should come down to any kind of background practices that would not themselves be *thinking*, but much more that it is itself a practice, *a conceptual practice*, and so a real way to proceed. There are, in the proper sense of the term, *ways to think.*

---

9 To make sense of the kind of difference between metaphysics and ontology that I am making now, see Benoist 2014. There is metaphysics as far as sense, and responsibility for sense, are involved.
10 Incidentally, it was exactly Plato's way, far from what has been called 'Platonism' in contemporary philosophy.
11 In a sense that might be not far from the one in which John McDowell uses the word in the title of McDowell 2009.

3

To give an example of the sense of 'reality' that thus emerges, we can focus on quantum mechanics. The blatant problem with quantum mechanics is that it seems to be at odds with our traditional familiar sense of objectivity. Usually, we take it that objects satisfy some definite conditions of individuation. As a matter of fact, identity is not a property that some objects happen to have, but objects are defined by *the kind of identity* they have. To some extent, one might say that they are just operators of identification: to be an 'object' is to remain the same in different circumstances.

Now, a part of that sense of *sameness* seems to be the fact that the object as such can be *kept track of*. One has just to give a thought to this: would the objects that we single out, point out, and name in our ordinary life still qualify as objects if it were not ever possible to keep track of them? To say it again, this does not seem to be a *property* of these objects, but much more a part of their definition, a *grammatical feature* of the talk of 'objects.'

The problem is, then, that it seems that there cannot be any 'object' in quantum mechanics, since it is impossible to know about the position and the speed of a 'particle' at the same time. Thus, I cannot 'keep track' of a particle in the ordinary sense of this phrase – the sense that is associated with the traditional notion of an 'object.'

The result of this point is that a lot of philosophers endorse an idealistic interpretation of quantum mechanics. Because what QM says about reality does not seem to be compatible with the traditional picture of reality as made out of objects, it is very tempting to conclude that QM just does not deal with reality. Thus, quantum objectivity, *which is not an object* – does not have the kind of individuation that is characteristic of objects –, would be a sort of construction, an ideal product.

Now, it might seem that there are two possible solutions. *First*, to take it that, beyond the ostensible *tensorial* structure of quantum objectivity, which *projects* but does not *factorize*, there are 'real objects' – i.e. entities which do satisfy the conditions of individuation constitutive of objects – but that we simply do not have access to them. Thus, to make them visible, we would have either to *interpret* our formalism, giving ourselves diverse ranges of objects or even diverse worlds – that is the 'multiple interpretation' strategy[12] – or to *complete* it by in-

---

[12] See DeWitt/Graham 1973. One tempting metaphysical appropriation of Everett's interpretation of QM – such as DeWitt reformulated it – would be to translate it into a story about (actual) 'multiple worlds,' by using a metaphysical framework as exposed in Lewis 1986.

troducing objects into the formalism where at first sight they were not to be seen – that is, the 'hidden variables' strategy.[13] A good deal of the philosophical discussion about QM nowadays focuses on one or another of those perspectives, although they do not seem to make any real difference from the physical point of view. However, the issue is metaphysical: how difficult it seems to be to renounce the claim to objects, wherever objectivity matters.

The second option seems to follow this path: to jettison 'realism' as the cult of objects and to endorse an anti-realistic understanding of quantum mechanics. This is to acknowledge that quantum entities are mere *constructions* and that, here, there are no apples to be picked. (Apple picking could be a quite good paradigm for the classical sense of objectivity.) On such a view, quantum mechanics just *comes down to* its formalism. I take both pictures to be mistaken.

To stick to the classical model of objectivity and to try and find anything like traditional 'objects' beyond and behind the quantum formalism, is precisely *not to take QM seriously*. That is to say: not to follow it in its own referential purpose. As if there were no other way to make reference than the mere *denotation of objects*.

However, conversely, to reduce QM to its formalism, to the effect of some 'anti-realistic' interpretation, is *not to take that formalism seriously*, i.e. to ignore it as *a way to think*, thus to exert an identifying grip on reality.

What is 'reality' in QM? It is precisely what is captured by the tensorial formalism of which QM makes use. There is no need to translate this formalism[14] into something else that would simply lack the teeth of formalism – those teeth that allow it to bite into reality in such a way that there is no substitute for it. To substitute anything else for this formalism is to lose sight of the *specific dimension of reality* it allows us to capture.

Now, is it the case, as my friend Thierry Paul hypothesized in a conversation, that against both classical objectivism and anti-realistic anti-objectivism as well, according to my view, I would like to 'place reality in a Hilbert space' (of which QM makes use)? As if it made any sense to say: 'I have *discovered* that Reality (with a big R) is in a Hilbert space.'[15] Of course, I would not endorse such *metaphysical* position. This is because it is very difficult to see what it would mean for

---

13 See Bohm/Hiley 1993. Bohm's interpretation of QM may seem to be rather peripherical. The reason why it remains an important pole in the discussion among philosophers interested in QM is that it testifies to how it is difficult to give up the classical concept of objectivity.
14 See Poinat 2014 as a good critique of any attempt to translate the formalism of QM.
15 That is, in the function space in which the wave functions that are the basic "building-blocks" of reality, according to Quantum Mechanics, are defined (it is worth noting that these wave functions are not necessarily factorable or decomposable uniquely).

reality to be in such Hilbert space *in general*. However, the reality that the quantum physicist is talking about certainly is!

The point I want to focus on here is that reality is something about which we speak, or on which we operate *in definite ways*. Quantum mechanics is certainly one among those ways, and, as such, it captures something in reality. It even constitutes a very powerful insight into it. There are simply things that cannot be said, or rather made visible with more precision, in reality, but only through quantum formalism. The expression 'made visible' is better because it is not obvious that a *calculation* as such – and quantum mechanics is essentially calculation – *says* anything. Taking this into account, this does not diminish the fact that it *expresses* reality and allows us to see it from a definite point of view, in particular in its dynamics as a calculation, its capacity to combine and to recombine.

Thus, it is incorrect to deal always with 'formalism' as if it were '*mere* formalism,' as we ordinarily tend to do: as if on the one side there would be that which is (real) object, and on the other side that which is (merely) formal. In highly formalized theories, it is very commonly the case that formalism is not a 'simple (intermediate) calculation,' as they say, but sets up the cognitive take we are exercising on reality. To calculate is to think, and to break paths into reality.

Now, the point is not so much that there are no objects other than really bizarre entities – for instance, such as it is impossible to keep track of. My point is rather that *there are really diverse standards of objectivity* that essentially depend on what one does with that which one claims to be doing. *How one is operating with entities is not incidental to ontology.* The example of quantum mechanics, with the ontological import of the tensor product – thus of an operation that does not factorize in the sense in which classical operations do – shows that operation matters to ontology. However, what is true of QM is true of 'traditional' ontology as well. In fact, what sets up the standard of the traditional 'objects' but *certain ways of operating with their identity:* to treat them as stable or not in different circumstances and under different transformations? Thus, their so-called 'identity,' which is definitional of them, is essentially operational.

Thus, the question whether Reality (in general) is made out of objects or primarily out of something else (any other kind of entities), is – *as a general question* (or what they call an 'ontological question') – sheer nonsense. 'Objects' or 'operators' (like those in QM) are different ways to exert a cognitive grip on reality, and as such they respectively define different takes on that reality. Now, in each of these takes, we grasp reality itself. They are not different optional views, as if reality remained beyond our contemplation and, so to speak, untouched by it, but *different concrete ways to proceed* in our knowledge of reality, and by these different proceedings, to make sense of as many *dimensions* of it. The meaning of 'reality' is not impervious to our calculations.

Of course, one is always free to break off the calculation and to try to consider the entities as being – figuratively speaking – 'naked,' as they are allegedly 'by themselves' – an *isolation* which is a prerequisite for the 'in themselves' of metaphysics understood as ontology. This is a very traditional philosophical move. But what should we think of those use-less entities with which it provides us? To abstract them from use is to deprive them of their meaning, thus to posit a being of which it is unclear *in which sense* it should be.

To place reality beyond use *and* to try to make sense of it as that which our thinking and knowing is about (which might be the two conflicting claims of 'realism'), is to fall prey to that delusion that Frege derides, according to which one could 'wash the fur without wetting it' (*den Pelz waschen, ohne ihn nass zu machen*) (Frege 1974, § 26).[16]

If you want to make sense of 'reality,' keep it real! Get your fur soaked! Do not be afraid of calculations.

Bibliography

Benoist, Jocelyn (2013): "Appliquer." In: Jocelyn Benoist and Thierry Paul (Eds.): *Le formalisme en action. Aspects mathématiques et philosophiques*. Paris: Editions Hermann, pp. 87–110.

Benoist, Jocelyn (2014): "Apologie de la métaphysique." In: Danielle Cohen-Levinas and Alexander Schnell (Eds.): *Etudes sur Totalité et Infini*. Paris: Vrin, pp. 45–59.

Bohm, David and Hiley, Basil (1993): *The Undivided Universe: an ontological interpretation of quantum theory*, London and New York: Routledge.

Bouveresse, Jacques (1999): "Sur le sens du mot 'platonisme' dans l'expression 'platonisme mathématique.'" In: *Revue de Théologie et de Philosophie* 131, No. 4, pp. 353–370.

DeWitt, Bryce Seligman and Neill Graham (Eds.) (1973): *The Many-Worlds Interpretation of Quantum Mechanics*, Princeton: Princeton University Press.

Frege, Gottlob (1974): *The Foundations of Arithmetic*. 2nd revised edition. Translated by J. L. Austin. New York: Harper & Brothers.

Gabriel, Markus (2016): *Sinn und Existenz*. Berlin: Suhrkamp.

Girard, Jean-Yves (2006): *Le Point Aveugle*. No. 1: *Vers la perfection*. Paris: Editions Hermann.

Lewis, David (1986): *On the Plurality of Worlds*, Oxford: Blackwell Publishers.

McDowell, John (2009): *The Engaged Intellect. Philosophical Essays*. Cambridge, MA: Harvard University Press.

---

[16] Of course, it is significant that this German idiom is used in order to designate an *unrealistic* claim, like *avoir le beurre et l'argent du beurre* in French, 'have your cake and eat it' in English, *avere la botta piena e la moglie ubriaca* in Italian.

Poinat, Sébastien (2014): *Mécanique quantique: du formalisme mathématique au concept philosophique*, Paris: Ed. Hermann.
Putnam, Hilary (2005): *Ethics Without Ontology.* Cambridge, MA: Harvard University Press.
Waismann, Friedrich (1936): *Einführung in das mathematische Denken*. Vienna: Gerold. Reprint: Darmstadt: Wissenschaftliche Buchgesellschaft, 1996.
Wittgenstein, Ludwig (1958): *Philosophical Investigations.* 2nd edition. Translated by G.E.M. Anscombe. Oxford: Basil Blackwell.
Wittgenstein, Ludwig (1978): *Remarks on the Foundations of Mathematics.* 3rd edition. Oxford: Basil Blackwell.

Notes on the contributors

Jocelyn Benoist is Professor of Philosophy at Pantheon-Sorbonne University, Paris 1, and used to be the Director of the Husserl Archive of Paris. He has published numerous articles on Husserl, Kant, Frege, Bolzano, et al. His research concerns analytic philosophy, phenomenology, philosophy of mind, and metaphysics. His recent books include *Concepts: Introduction à l'analyse* (Champs, 2013) and *Elements de philosophie réaliste* (Vrin, 2011), *L'adresse du réel* (Vrin, 2017).

Ray Brassier is Professor of Philosophy at the American University of Beirut, Lebanon. He has published on Badiou, Deleuze, Hegel, Marx, Meillassoux, Kant, and Sellars. He is the author of *Nihil Unbound: Enlightenment and Extinction* (Palgrave MacMillan, 2007). Recent publications include "Correlation, Speculation and the Modal Kant-Sellars Thesis," in *The Legacy of Kant in Sellars and Meillassoux: Analytic and Continental Kantianism*, Fabio Gironi (ed.) (Routledge, 2017) and "Strange Sameness: Hegel, Marx and the Logic of Estrangement" in *Angelaki: Journal of the Theoretical Humanities* (24: 1, 2019), pp. 98–105.

G. Anthony Bruno is Lecturer in Philosophy at Royal Holloway University of London. He has published articles on freedom, mortality, pantheism, and idealism in *History of Philosophy Quarterly, Idealistic Studies, Dialogue: Canadian Philosophical Review*, and other journals. His current research concerns the development of logic in post-Kantian philosophy and its relation to systematicity, contingency, and subjectivity. He is co-editor of *Skepticism: Historical and Contemporary Inquiries* (Routledge, 2018) and editor of *Schelling's Philosophy: Freedom, Nature, and Systematicity* (Oxford University Press, forthcoming). Recent article: "Schelling on the Possibility of Evil: Rendering Pantheism, Freedom, and Time Consistent", *Northern European Journal of Philosophy* (18: 1, 2017), pp. 1–18.

Dominik Finkelde is Professor of Epistemology and Contemporary Philosophy at the Munich School of Philosophy. He has published on contemporary philosophy and German Idealism, especially on Hegel, Kant, Frege, Wittgenstein, and Badiou. Recent publications: *Logiken der Inexistenz. Figurationen des Realen im Zeitalter der Immanenz* (Passagen Verlag, 2019), *Excessive Subjectivity. Kant, Hegel, Lacan, and the Foundations of Ethics* (Columbia UP, 2017), "Lack and Excess / Zero and One. On Concrete Universality in Dialectical Materialism," *Philosophy Today* (63:4, forthcoming 2020), and "Logics of Scission. The Subject as 'Limit of the World' in Badiou and Wittgenstein," *Philosophy Today* (61: 3, 2017), pp. 595–618.

Markus Gabriel is Chair for Epistemology, Modern and Contemporary Philosophy at the University of Bonn and the Director of the International Centre for Philosophy. He has also held positions at the New School for Social Research and the University of California, Berkeley. His research interests include German Idealism, ancient and contemporary analytic philosophy. He has published extensively on a wide variety of philosophical topics both historical and systematic. His noted publications on realism, in particular, are: *Fields of Sense. A New Realist Ontology* (Edinburgh, 2015), *An den Grenzen der Erkenntnistheorie: Die Notwendige Endlichkeit des Wissens als Lektion des Skeptizismus* (Alber, 2008), and *Transcendental Ontology: Essays in German Idealism* (Bloomsbury, 2013).

Deborah Goldgaber is Assistant Professor of Philosophy and Women's and Gender Studies at Louisiana State University. She has research interests in feminist and contemporary continental metaphysics and epistemology. In terms of philosophical traditions, she works in 20th century French philosophy, especially, deconstruction; phenomenology; and critical theory. She is the author of *Speculative Grammatology: Deconstruction and the New Materialism* (Edinburgh UP, 2020 forthcoming) and her research appears in multiple edited volumes and journals including the Routledge *Handbook of Translation and Philosophy*, the Journal of *Speculative Philosophy, Philosophy Today* and *Parallax*.

Iain Hamilton Grant is Senior Lecturer at the University of the West of England in Bristol, United Kingdom. His research interests include ontology, European philosophy, German Idealism and the philosophy of nature. Publications include: *Philosophies of Nature After Schelling* (Continuum, 2006), *Idealism: The History of Philosophy* (together with Dunham and Watson) (Acumen, 2010), *Die Natur der Natur* (Merve, 2018), "Everything," *The Monist* (98:2, 2015), pp. 156–167; "Everything is primal germ or nothing," *Symposium. Canadian Journal of Continental Philosophy* (19:1, 2015), pp. 106–124.

Graham Harman is Distinguished Professor of Philosophy at the Southern California Institute of Architecture. He has published on the metaphysics of objects and developed an object-oriented ontology. He is a leading proponent of Speculative Realism and the Series editor of *Speculative Realism* published by Edinburgh UP. Recent books: with DeLanda *The Rise of Realism* (Polity, 2017), *Immaterialism: Objects and Social Theory* (Polity, 2016), *Object-Oriented Ontology: A New Theory of Everything* (Penguin 2018).

Johannes Hübner is Professor of Theoretical Philosophy at the University of Halle. His fields of research are ontology and metaphysics and ancient philosophy. Publications: *Der Begriff des eidos choriston bei Aristoteles* (Meiner, 2000), *Komplexe Substanzen* (DeGruyter, 2007), *Einführung in die theoretische Philosophie* (Metzler, 2015), "Existenz und Ontologie. Anmerkungen zu Markus Gabriels ontologischen Thesen", *Philosophisches Jahrbuch* (2015), pp. 522–536.

Andrea Kern is Professor for the History of Philosophy at the University of Leipzig. She has been a guest professor at the University of Chicago, the Université d'Amiens, the University of Vienna and the University of Frankfurt. Her main research interests are epistemology, the philosophy of perception, skepticism, philosophical anthropology and aesthetics. She has authored *Schöne Lust: Eine Theorie der ästhetischen Erfahrung* (Suhrkamp, 2000) and *Quellen des Wissens: Zum Begriff vernünftiger Erkenntnisfähigkeiten* (Suhrkamp, 2006; in English: *Sources of Knowledge*, Harvard UP, 2017), and has edited several volumes, including (with Ruth Sonderegger) *Falsche Gegensätze: Zeitgenössische Positionen zur philosophischen Ästhetik* (Suhrkamp, 2002) and (with James Conant) *Varieties of Skepticism: Essays after Kant, Cavell and Wittgenstein* (De Gruyter, 2014). Recent articles: "Does Knowledge Rest Upon a Form of Life?," *International Journal for the Study of Skepticism* (5:1, 2015), pp. 13–28. "On the Transformative Character of Collective Intentionality and the Uniqueness of the Human" (with Henrike Moll), *Philosophical Psychology* (30:3, 2017), pp. 315–333. "Human Life and Self-consciousness. The Idea of 'Our' Form of Life in Hegel and Wittgenstein", Christian Martin (Ed.), *Language, Form(s) of Life, and Logic* (De Gruyter 2018), pp. 93–112.

Anton Friedrich Koch is Professor of Philosophy at the University of Heidelberg. He held visiting professorships at Emory University (Atlanta, USA), and at the University of Chicago. His field of research is epistemology and ontology, drawing from Plato, Aristotle, Kant, Hegel, Heidegger, and analytic philosophy. Recent books: *Die Evolution des logischen Raumes* (Mohr Siebeck, 2014), and *Hermeneutischer Realismus* (Mohr Siebeck, 2016). Recent articles: "Die Mittelstellung des Wesens zwischen Sein und Begriff," Andreas Arndt / Günter Kruck (Ed.), *Hegels "Lehre vom Wesen"*. *Hegel-Jahrbuch Sonderband* (De Gruyter, 2016), pp. 9–20. "Neutraler oder hermeneutischer Realismus?", *Philosophisches Jahrbuch* (2015), pp. 163–172.

Martin Kusch is Professor of Philosophy of Science and Epistemology at the University of Vienna. He has published extensively on epistemology, philosophy of science, and philosophy of language. Between 2014 and 2019 he was Principal Investigator of an ERC Advanced Grant Project entitled "The Emergence of Relativism" (2014–2019). He is the author of *Psychologism: A Case Study in the Sociology of Philosophical Knowledge* (Routledge, 1995), *Psychological Knowledge* (Routledge, 1999), *Knowledge by Agreement* (Oxford UP, 2002), and *A Sceptical Guide to Meaning and Rules: Defending Kripke's Wittgenstein* (Acumen, 2006).

Paul Livingston is Professor of Philosophy at the University of New Mexico. His work focuses on the philosophy of mind, philosophy of language, phenomenology, and political philosophy. He has published widely on twentieth-century and contemporary philosophy, especially on Badiou, Wittgenstein, Heidegger, and Dummett. His recent publications include the monographs *The Logic of Being: Realism, Truth, and Time* (Northwestern, 2017) and *The Problems of Contemporary Philosophy* (co-authored with Andrew Cutrofello) (Polity, 2015). Recent article: "The Sense of Finitude and the Finitude of Sense," In *Semantics and Beyond: Philosophical and Linguistic Investigations* (Ontos Verlag, 2014).

Paul Redding is Professor Emeritus of Philosophy, University of Sydney. He is known for his research on Kantian philosophy and the tradition of German Idealism and its relation to analytic philosophy and pragmatism. He is a fellow of the Australian Academy of the Humanities. His publications include: *Continental Idealism: Leibniz to Nietzsche* (Routledge imprint of Taylor & Francis, 2009), *Analytic Philosophy and the Return of Hegelian Thought* (Cambridge UP, 2007), "Hegel's Lectures on the History of Ancient and Medieval Philosophy," Dean Moyar (Ed.), *The Oxford Handbook of Hegel* (Oxford UP, 2017), pp. 603–622, "Hegel and Sellars's 'Myth of Jones': Can Sellars have more in common with Hegel than Rorty and Brandom suggest?" in Patrick Reider (Ed.), *Wilfrid Sellars. Idealism and Realism* (Bloomsbury, 2017), pp. 41–58.

Sebastian Rödl is Chair in Practical Philosophy at the University of Leipzig. He has held positions at the University of Pittsburgh, the University of Chicago, the New School for Social Research, and the University of Basel. His systematic interests lie in philosophy of mind and language, epistemology, moral philosophy and philosophy of action. Historically, he is primarily concerned with Aristotle, Aquinas, Kant, Hegel, Frege, and Wittgenstein. He is the author of *Self-Consciousness* (Harvard UP, 2007), *Categories of the Temporal* (Harvard UP, 2012) and *Self-Consciousness and Objectivity* (Harvard UP 2018). He has published a number of articles on epistemology and the philosophy of mind.

Dieter Sturma is Professor of Philosophy at the University of Bonn. He is also director of the Institute of Science and Ethics and the German Reference Centre for Ethics in the Life Sciences, both in Bonn, and of the Institute of Ethics in the Neurosciences at the Research Centre Juelich. His research focusses on philosophical anthropology, philosophy of mind, philosophy of neurosciences, ethics and applied ethics. His publications include *Philosophie der Person. Die Selbstverhältnisse von Subjektivität und Moralität* (Mentis, 1997/2008), *Robotik* (Springer, 2001), and *Philosophie des Geistes* (Reclam, 2005). He is the editor of numerous books, including *Philosophie und Neurowissenschaften* (Suhrkamp, 2006), *Kants Ethik* (with Karl Ameriks) (Mentis, 2004), and he is also the editor of the *Yearbook for Science and Ethics*.

Index of Names

Adorno, Theodor W.   7f., 81–83, 86, 88f., 92–94
Ameriks, Karl   51
Anscombe, Elizabeth   63
Aristotle   6, 8, 17–19, 81, 89–92, 220, 245, 249, 275f., 278–280, 296
Austin, John L.   63, 203

Badiou, Alain   155–159, 161–163, 165, 249, 252f., 317
Barad, Karen   10, 193–195, 197, 200–202, 205–207
Barnes, Barry   145f.
Behar, Katherine   3
Bennett, Karen   115, 202
Benoist, Jocelyn   10–12, 226–228, 311, 316, 319
Benveniste, Émile   168
Bergson, Henri   227
Bloor, David   9, 143–148
Boghossian, Paul   2, 117, 146–152, 164f.
Bohm, David   321
Brandom, Robert   304
Brassier, Ray   2, 4, 6, 9, 175
Brentano, Franz   236
Bruno, G. Anthony   6f., 47f., 51f.
Butler, Judith   10, 195f., 198, 202–207

Callon, Michel   261
Cavell, Stanley   52
Churchland, Patricia   3, 211
Conant, James   51
Crane, Tim   5

de Beauvoir, Simone   198–200, 203
Deleuze, Gilles   181, 249, 251
Dennett, Daniel   168
Devitt, Michael   116
Dewey, John   262, 269f.
Dummett, Michael   5, 10, 233–235, 241–244, 246f.

Evans, Gareth   236

Ferraris, Maurizio   2, 4, 108, 268
Feuerbach, Ludwig   176f., 183, 185
Fichte, Johann G.   36, 42f., 48, 265, 267
Field, Hartry   137f.
Findlay, John N.   282–284, 287
Fine, Kit   282f.
Finkelde, Dominik   6, 9, 152, 155, 165
Føllesdal, Dagfinn   236
Frank, Philip   144
Frege, Gottlob   5, 10, 81, 87, 93, 98, 160, 167, 225, 233, 235–237, 241f., 281, 323
Fried, Michael   259

Gabriel, Markus   2, 4f., 10, 83, 156, 217f., 222–227, 229f., 252f., 268, 312, 318
Gadamer, Hans-Georg   86, 89
Garcia, Tristan   5
Gardner, Sebastian   48
Girard, Jean-Yves   314f.
Grant, Iain Hamilton   2, 4, 8, 97, 152
Grosz, Elizabeth   193f., 200
Guattari, Felix   181

Hacking, Ian   196–198, 201f., 209–211
Hampshire, Stuart   296, 303, 306f.
Harman, Gilbert   293, 300
Harman, Graham   2, 4f., 10f., 159–161, 257, 260, 262, 269
Harris, Sam   168
Haslanger, Sally   196–198, 200, 209
Hegel, Georg W.F.   4, 8f., 11, 36, 47–49, 81f., 88f., 92, 155–168, 171, 176, 183, 189, 275, 277, 280–290
Heidegger, Martin   4f., 7f., 10, 81–84, 86f., 89–92, 222f., 233, 235, 237–239, 241–243, 247, 254, 267
Hirsch, Eli   8f., 115f., 118–123, 125–129
Hobbes, Thomas   11, 257, 261–271, 297
Hogrebe, Wolfram   107
Hübner, Johannes   4, 8, 115

https://doi.org/10.1515/9783110670349-019

Index of Names

Jacobi, Friedrich H.   7, 35–43, 45–47, 49–52, 54, 170
James, William   134

Kant, Immanuel   5, 7–9, 27, 35–37, 39–53, 61, 69–73, 81, 88, 91, 100, 110, 155–157, 160 f., 163, 165, 170, 176, 249 f., 276 f., 279 f., 283–286, 296 f., 307
Kern, Andrea   4, 6 f., 57, 63, 77, 164
Kimhi, Irad   8, 81, 91–94
Kinzel, Katharina   149
Kirby, Vicki   193, 200, 202, 204
Koch, Anton Friedrich   2, 4, 7 f., 81, 83, 227, 229 f.
Kolozova, Katerina   3
Korsgaard, Christine   307 f.
Kreis, Guido   229
Kuhn, Thomas S.   134, 139 f., 143, 164
Kusch, Martin   9, 131, 147, 149, 165

Lacan, Jacques   9, 155, 157 f., 160–170, 249, 265, 267
Ladyman, James   3, 160
Langford, C.H.   281
Latour, Bruno   11, 257, 261–263, 265, 268–271
Leibniz, Gottfried W.   277–280, 282–284, 286, 297
Lewis, Clarence I.   281
Lewis, David K.   11, 131 f., 275, 277, 281 f., 284, 320
Lipton, Peter   137, 139 f.
Livingston, Paul   4 f., 10 f., 233
Locke, John   264
Longuenesse, Beatrice   280
Lovelock, James   271
Lovibond, Sabina   296, 305 f.

Machiavelli, Niccolò   258, 261 f.
Mackie, John   294, 300
Marion, Jean-Luc   222
Marx, Karl   8 f., 81, 94, 175–186, 189–191, 261, 264
McDowell, John   7, 35–37, 43–50, 57, 59–64, 69, 71 f., 78, 84, 100 f., 170, 296, 302, 305, 319

Meillassoux, Quentin   4 f., 7, 35–37, 50–53, 229 f., 270
Melikh, Yulia   227, 229 f.
Miller, Jacques-Alain   169
Minelli, Alessandro   106–108

Nagel, Thomas   103, 296
Nietzsche, Friedrich   176, 259, 261

Peirce, Charles S.   282
Pippin, Robert   47
Plato   87, 100, 156, 220, 247, 254, 259, 261, 265, 278, 296, 304, 319
Poinat, Sébastien   321
Priest, Graham   10, 138–140, 217, 222, 224, 229, 246
Prior, Arthur   140, 281–284, 287
Putnam, Hilary   3, 101, 115, 119, 162, 164 f., 315

Quine, Willard Van Orman   2, 81, 161, 220 f., 306

Rawls, John   307
Redding, Paul   6, 11, 275, 279, 281, 283
Rescher, Nicholas   297, 299
Rödl, Sebastian   4, 6 f., 17, 48 f., 245
Ross, Don   160
Rousseau, Jean-Jacques   261 f., 296, 301
Russell, Bertrand   87, 141, 167, 220 f., 246, 252, 281, 283, 287

Sartre, Jean-Paul   246, 253
Schelling, Friedrich W.J.   4, 8, 97, 100–103, 107–109, 296
Schmitt, Carl   11, 257, 261–271
Searle, John   4
Sellars, Wilfrid   4, 9, 11, 81, 84, 87, 90, 276, 293, 298, 302
Sinclair, Upton   259
Sohn-Rethel, Alfred   184
Sosa, Ernest   118
Spinoza, Benedictus de   38, 40 f., 167, 181, 280, 296 f., 303
Spivak, Gayatri Chakravorty   205
Stalnaker, Robert   6, 11, 275, 277, 281, 283 f.

Strauss, Leo   262, 265–271
Strawson, Peter F.   7, 39, 45f., 48f., 81, 296, 304
Stroud, Barry   6f., 17, 19–25, 27–34, 63–72, 78
Strum, Shirley   262, 269
Sturma, Dieter   11, 293, 296

Teller, Paul   136f.
Thomasson, Amy L.   115
Travis, Charles   63, 312

Unger, Peter   2

van Fraassen, Bas   9, 131–146, 148, 150–152, 164
Voegelin, Eric   258, 260f., 268

Wilson, Elizabeth A.   193–195, 200, 208
Wittgenstein, Ludwig   3, 5, 10, 52, 81f., 84, 87, 222f., 233, 240, 243, 249, 251, 305f., 315–317
Wittig, Monique   198–200, 202f.
Wright, Crispin   117, 120, 306–308

Young, Iris Marion   199–203

Zahavi, Dan   52
Žižek, Slavoj   155, 159–161, 264

Index of Subjects

Actualism   277, 280
– modal actualism   11, 275, 277, 283 f., 290

Consciousness   6 f., 36, 57 f., 60 – 63, 66 – 69, 73, 76, 155, 162, 167 f., 175 – 179, 181 – 184, 226, 246, 288, 296, 304, 307
– reified consciousness   181
Correlationism   5, 37, 50 f., 318

Deflationism   118
– metaontological deflationism   8, 115 f., 118, 121, 129
– ontological deflationism   8, 115
Dialectical Materialism   7 f., 81 – 83, 92, 94
Dialectics   9, 82 f., 86, 88, 155, 162, 229
– negative dialectics   82, 89

Empiricism   43, 63, 131 – 133, 137, 143 f., 146 f., 156, 177, 294 f.
Epistemic voluntarism (see Voluntarism)

Feminist theory   3, 9, 193 – 195, 197, 204
Fields of sense   4 f., 10, 156, 217, 224, 252

Gender   8 f., 93, 194 – 207
– gender and sex   205
– gendered bodies   194, 197 f., 201 – 203, 208

Hermeneutic Realism   7 f., 81, 86 – 89, 92, 94

Idealism   1 – 3, 6 f., 35 – 37, 41 – 43, 48 – 52, 58, 82 f., 155, 183, 262, 265, 267, 270, 283 f.
– transcendental idealism   1, 27, 35 – 37, 40 f., 49, 51 f., 246, 249 f.

Judgment   7, 25, 27, 29 f., 32, 43 f., 48, 50, 53 f., 57, 59, 62 – 76, 78, 88 – 91, 99, 136, 139, 161, 236, 239, 279, 281, 283 – 290

Knowledge   4, 6 – 9, 17, 21 f., 24 – 26, 31, 35 f., 38 f., 50 – 52, 57 – 60, 62 f., 67 – 69, 71 – 78, 143 – 146, 156, 161 – 166, 170, 226, 234, 241 – 243, 262, 267 – 270, 275 – 277, 279, 287, 300, 304, 322
– a priori knowledge   23, 289
– inferential knowledge   64, 71, 75
sources of knowledge   6, 77

Materialism   1 – 4, 83, 94, 133, 144, 175 – 178, 180, 183, 269, 295 f., 303
– eliminative materialism   170, 295
Mathematics   18, 238, 280, 311 – 317
– mathematical objects   260, 312 – 314
– mathematical Platonism   314 f., 317
metaphysical dissatisfaction   6, 17
Metaphysics   3, 6 f., 11, 17 – 22, 24, 28, 30, 32 – 34, 41, 50, 90 f., 115, 131 – 133, 137 f., 142 f., 146 f., 162, 176, 180, 185 f., 200 f., 220, 222 – 224, 229, 231, 237, 245, 254, 275, 277, 280 – 284, 289 f., 311, 316 – 319, 323
Modality   11, 52 f., 86, 233 f., 236, 242, 284

Naturalism   11, 98, 110, 144, 162, 170, 176, 240, 293 – 299, 301 – 303, 307 f.
negative judgment   20, 25, 30, 91, 286
– synthetic judgment   7, 53
– warranted judgment   43
new realism   1 f., 4, 158
– speculative realism   1 f., 4, 158

Objectivity   1 – 3, 6 – 8, 10 f., 35 – 37, 40, 42, 45, 49 – 51, 54, 66, 139, 162, 165, 168, 179, 185, 188, 217 f., 233, 275 – 279, 295 – 297, 300 f., 306 – 308, 313 – 316, 320 – 322
– conditions of objectivity   53 f.
Object-oriented Ontology   159, 161
Ontological difference   10, 233, 235, 238, 241, 243, 246 f., 253 f.
Ontology   1 – 3, 8 – 11, 50, 87, 94, 97, 101, 107, 109 f., 115, 121, 128, 155 f., 158 f.,

189, 217, 220, 222–224, 230, 253, 257, 261, 283, 293f., 303, 312–314, 317–319, 322f.

Perception   7, 42f., 57–73, 75–78, 84, 87, 144, 157, 163, 233f., 236f., 239, 276, 278, 298, 306, 314
– perceptual knowledge   7, 57, 59, 61–69, 71–73, 75–78
– self-knowledge   42, 50, 275
Phenomenology   2, 48, 159, 163, 166, 171, 236, 252f.

Quantifier variance   8, 115f., 118f., 123

Realism   1–6, 8–11, 35, 37–40, 49, 52, 57–59, 68, 78, 81, 83, 92, 108, 115–118, 128f., 160, 164, 193, 201, 204f., 233–235, 238–251, 254, 257–262, 264f., 267–270, 275, 281, 293–302, 304–308, 311f., 318, 321, 323
Relativism   1, 3f., 8f., 115–118, 120f., 129, 131, 136, 138, 140f., 143–152, 164, 268, 297, 300f., 306, 319

Self-consciousness (see Consciousness)

Skepticism   39, 54, 300
Stances   9, 131, 133–137, 139–144, 147–151, 164
– stance relativism   147
Subjectivity   6, 8f., 46, 83f., 86, 94, 155, 157, 159f., 162, 165, 168, 170f., 198, 234, 244, 250, 275–277, 313
– excessive subjectivity   6

Truth   1–5, 10, 19, 24, 29, 31, 37f., 47, 59, 62, 66, 76, 78, 83–88, 90f., 93, 116f., 119, 121f., 125–127, 129, 134, 138, 144f., 147, 156, 161, 163–165, 169f., 176, 178, 181, 183, 188, 204, 220, 225, 229, 233–235, 237, 239–248, 250f., 253f., 258, 260–262, 266–268, 270, 278f., 283, 286f., 300, 304, 306, 311, 318
– threefold structure of truth   84

Unconcealment   5, 8, 10, 81, 84–87, 90, 233, 235, 237–239

Voluntarism   9, 131, 139f., 143
– epistemic voluntarism 9, 131, 134f., 137–139, 141–143, 145, 148–152

www.ingramcontent.com/pod-product-compliance
Lightning Source LLC
Chambersburg PA
CBHW030521230426
43665CB00010B/708